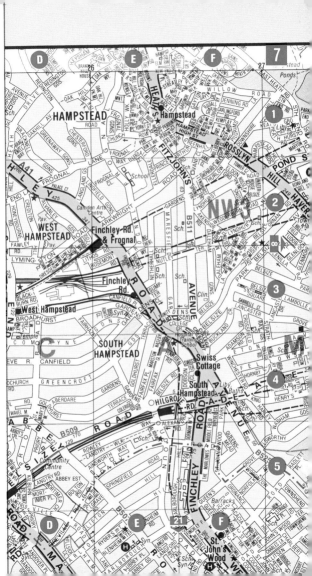

CONTENTS

Key to Map Pages	2-3	Index to Streets	88-192
Map Pages	4-87	Underground Map	back cover

REFERENCE

Motorway	▬▬▬	Post Town & London Postal Boundaries	▬▬▬
Dual Carriageway	▬▬	Disabled Toilet	♿
'A' Road	A2	Fire Station	■
'B' Road	B2036	Hospital	⊞
One Way Street One way traffic flow is indicated on 'A' roads by a heavy line on the drivers left	→	House Numbers 'A' and 'B' roads only	4 ▬ 43
Map Continuation	89	Information Centre	ℹ
British Rail Station	▬■▬	National Grid Reference	540
Underground Station	●	Places of Worship	✛
Docklands Light Railway Station	▬DLR▬	Police Station	▲
District & Borough Boundaries	▬ · ▬ ·	Post Office	★

SCALE

approx. 3 inches to 1 mile or 1:21.477

```
0        ¼          ½          ¾          1 mile
├────────┼──────────┼──────────┼──────────┤
0    250    500    750 m    1 Kilometre
```

Geographers' A-Z Map Co. Ltd.

Head Office : Fairfield Road,
Borough Green, Sevenoaks, Kent TN15 8PP
Telephone 0732- 781000

Showrooms :
44 Gray's Inn Road, London, WC1X 8LR
Telephone 071-242 9246

© Copyright of the Publishers
Edition 1 1991

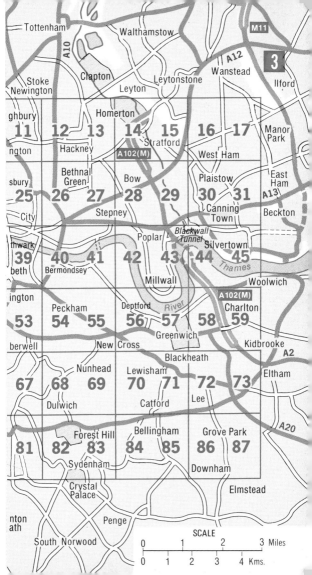

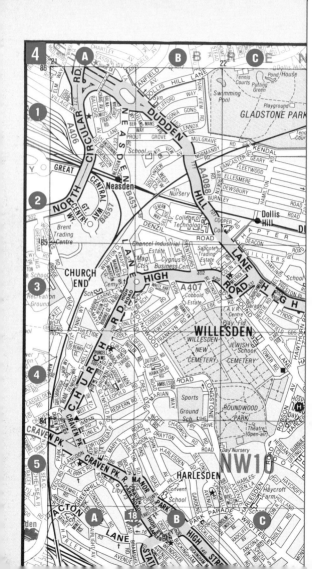

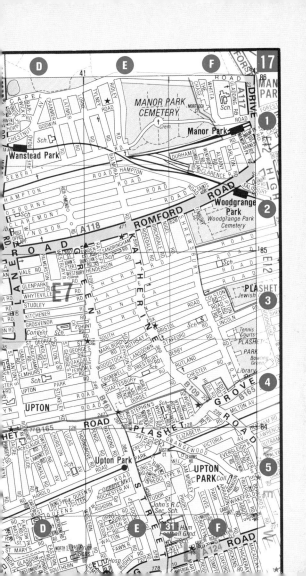

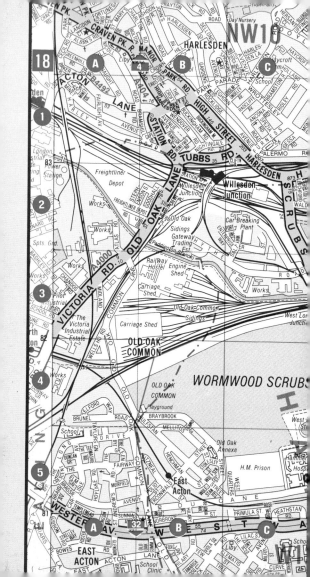

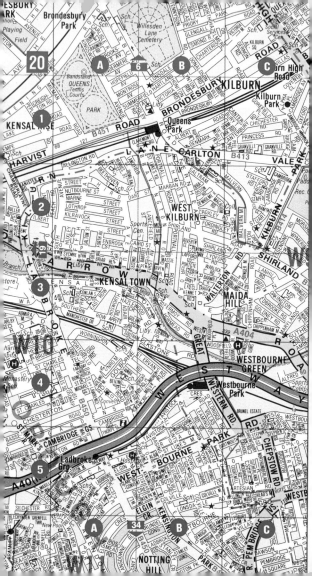

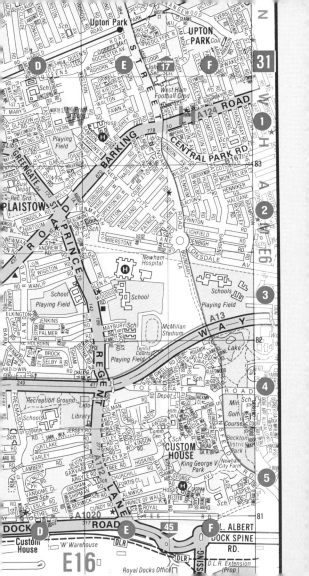

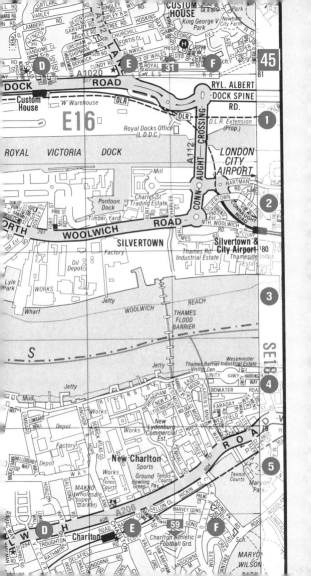

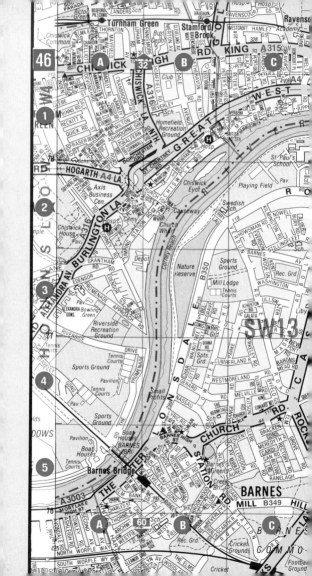

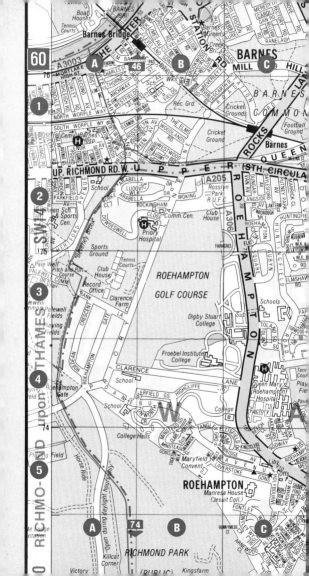

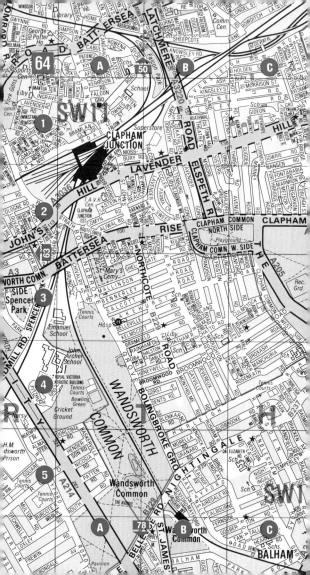

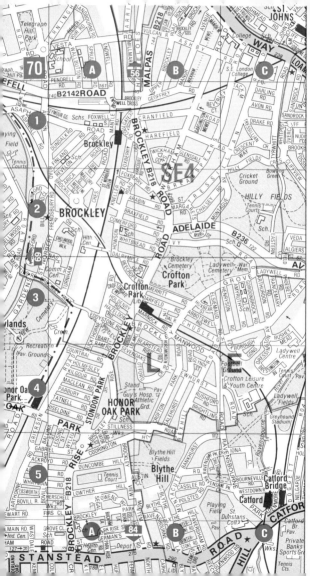

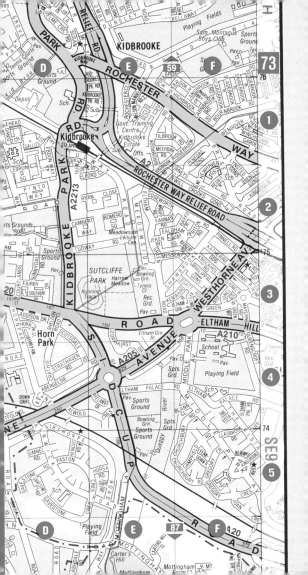

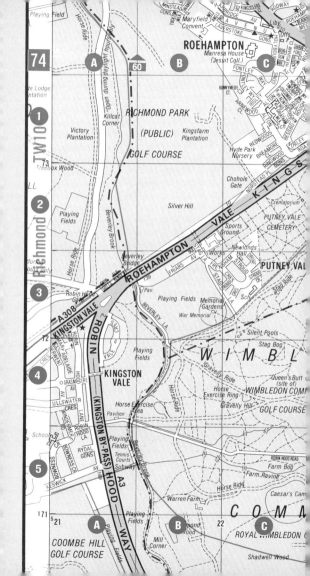

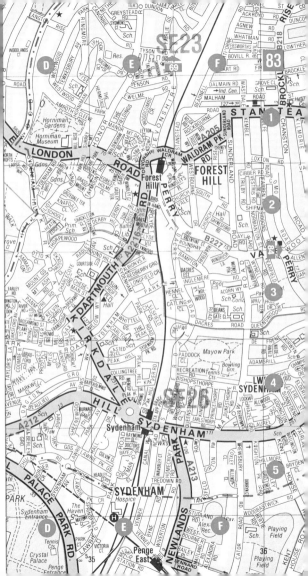

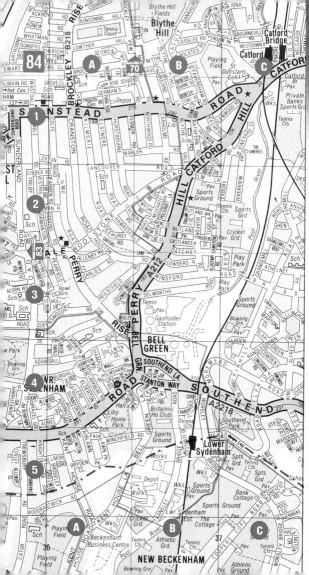

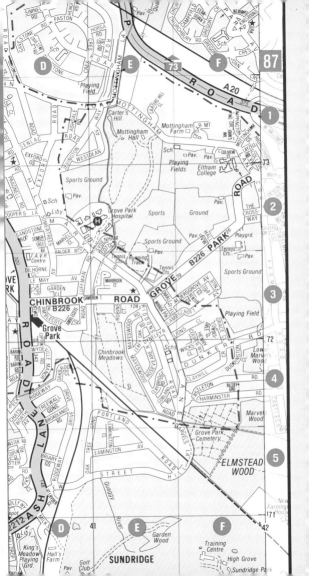

INDEX TO STREETS

HOW TO USE THIS INDEX

1. Each street name is followed by its Postal District (or, if outside the London Postal District, by its Post Town), and then by its map reference; e.g. Ashgrove Rd. Brom. 5F 85 is in the Bromley Post Town and is to be found in square 5F on page 85.

2. A strict alphabetical order is followed in which Av., Rd., St. etc. (though abbreviated) are read in full and as part of the street name; e.g. Abbots La. appears after Abbotshall Rd. but before Abbotsleigh Rd.

3. With the now general usage of Postal Coding, it is not recommended that this index be used as a means of addressing mail.

GENERAL ABBREVIATIONS

All : Alley
App : Approach
Arc : Arcade
Av : Avenue
Bk : Back
Boulevd : Boulevard
Bri : Bridge
B'way : Broadway
Bldgs : Buildings
Chu : Church
Chyd : Churchyard
Circ : Circle
Cir : Circus
Clo : Close
Comn : Common
Cotts : Cottages
Ct : Court
Cres : Crescent

Dri : Drive
E : East
Embkmt : Embankment
Est : Estate
Gdns : Gardens
Ga : Gate
Gt : Great
Grn : Green
Gro : Grove
Ho : House
Junct : Junction
La : Lane
Lit : Little
Lwr : Lower
Mnr : Manor
Mans : Mansion
Mkt : Market
M : Mews

Mt : Mount
N : North
Pal : Palace
Pde : Parade
Pk : Park
Pas : Passage
Pl : Place
Rd : Road
S : South
Sq : Square
Sta : Station
St : Street
Ter : Terrace
Up : Upper
Vs : Villas
Wlk : Walk
W : West
Yd : Yard

POST TOWN and PLACE NAME ABBREVIATIONS

Abb L : Abbots Langley
Amer : Amersham
Asc : Ascot
Ashf : Ashford
Asht : Ashtead
Bans : Banstead
Bark : Barking
Barn : Barnet
Bea : Beaconsfield
Beck : Beckenham
Belv : Belvedere
Bex : Bexley
Bexh : Bexleyheath
Borwd : Borehamwood

Bren : Brentford
Brtwd : Brentwood
Brom : Bromley
Buck H : Buckhurst Hill
Bush : Bushey
Cars : Carshalton
Cat : Caterham
Chal : Chalfont St Giles
Cher : Chertsey
Che : Chesham
Chess : Chessington
Chig : Chigwell
Chst : Chislehurst
Chob : Chobham

Cob : Cobham (Surrey)
Coul : Coulsdon
Croy : Croydon
Dag : Dagenham
Dart : Dartford
Dor : Dorking
E Mol : East Molesey
Edgw : Edgware
Egh : Egham
Enf : Enfield
Epp : Epping
Eps : Epsom
Eri : Erith
Esh : Esher

Eyns : Eynsford
F'ham : Farningham
Felt : Feltham
Ger X : Gerrards Cross
God : Godstone
Grav : Gravesend
Grays : Grays
Gnfd : Greenford
Grnh : Greenhithe
Guild : Guildford
Hmptn : Hampton
Harr : Harrow
Hat : Hatfield
Hav : Havering atte Bower
Hay : Hayes (Middlesex)
Hem : Hemel Hempstead
High W : High Wycombe
Horn : Hornchurch
Houn : Hounslow
Ilf : Ilford
Ing : Ingatestone
Iswth : Isleworth
Iver : Iver
Kenl : Kenley
Kes : Keston
K Lan : King's Langley
King : Kingston upon Thames
Lea : Leatherhead
Long : Longfield
Lou : Loughton
M'head : Maidenhead
Mitc : Mitcham
Mord : Morden

N Mald : New Malden
N'holt : Northolt
N'wd : Northwood
Ong : Ongar
Orp : Orpington
Oxt : Oxted
Pinn : Pinner
Pot B : Potters Bar
Purf : Purfleet
Purl : Purley
Rad : Radlett
Rain : Rainham
Red : Redhill
Reig : Reigate
Rich : Richmond upon Thames
Rick : Rickmansworth
Roch : Rochester
Romf : Romford
Ruis : Ruislip
St Alb : St Albans
Sev : Sevenoaks
Shen : Shenley
Shep : Shepperton
Sidc : Sidcup
Slou : Slough
S'hall : Southall
S Croy : South Croydon
S Dar : South Darenth
S Ock : South Ockendon
Stai : Staines
Stanf : Stanford-le-Hope
Stan : Stanmore
Stap T : Stapleford Tawney

Sun : Sunbury-on-Thames
Surb : Surbiton
Sutt : Sutton
S at H : Sutton at Hone
Swan : Swanley
Swans : Swanscombe
Tad : Tadworth
Tedd : Teddington
Th Dit : Thames Ditton
T Hth : Thornton Heath
Twic : Twickenham
Upm : Upminster
Uxb : Uxbridge
Vir W : Virginia Water
Wall : Wallington
Wal A : Waltham Abbey
Wal X : Waltham Cross
W on T : Walton-on-Thames
Warl : Warlingham
Wat : Watford
Well : Welling
Wemb : Wembley
W Dray : West Drayton
West : Westerham
W Wick : West Wickham
Wey : Weybridge
Whyt : Whyteleafe
Wind : Windsor
Wok : Woking
Wfd G : Woodford Green
Wor Pk : Worcester Park
Wray : Wraysbury

INDEX TO STREETS

Abbess Clo. SW2—1D 81
Abbeville Rd. SW4—4E 65
Abbey Business Centre. SW8
—4D 51
Abbey Dri. SW17—5C 78
Abbey Est. NW8—5D 7
Abbeyfield Est. SE16—5E 41
Abbeyfield Rd. SE16—5E 41
(in two parts)
Abbey Gdns. NW8—1E 21
Abbey Gdns. W6—2A 48
Abbey La. E15—1E 29
Abbey Orchard St. SW1—4F 37
Abbey Rd. E15—1F 29
Abbey Rd.—5D 7
NW8 1-117 & 2-98

NW6 remainder
Abbey St. E13—3C 30
Abbey St. SE1—4B 40
Abbotsbury Clo. E15—1E 29
Abbotsbury Clo. W14—3B 34
Abbotsbury Rd. W14—3A 34
Abbots Clo. N1—3E 11
Abbotshall Rd. SE6—1F 85
Abbots La. SE1—2A 40
Abbotsleigh Rd. SW16—4E 79
Abbot's Mnr. Est. SW1—1D 51
Abbots Pk. SW2—1C 80
Abbot's Pl. NW6—5D 7
Abbot's Rd. E6—5F 17
Abbotstone Rd. SW15—1E 61
Abbot St. E8—3B 12

Abbotswell Rd. SE4—3B 70
Abbotswood Rd. SW16—3F 79
Abbott Rd. E14—5E 29
(in two parts)
Abchurch La. EC4—1F 39
Abdale Rd. W12—2D 33
Aberavon Rd. E3—2A 28
Abercorn Clo. NW8—2E 21
Abercorn Pl. NW8—2E 21
Abercrombie St. SW11—5A 50
Aberdare Gdns. NW6—4D 7
Aberdeen La. N5—2E 11
Aberdeen Pk. N5—2E 11
Aberdeen Pl. NW8—3F 21
Aberdeen Rd. N5—1E 11
Aberdeen Rd. NW10—2B 4

Aberdeen Ter. SE3—5F 57
Aberdour St. SE1—5A 40
Aberfeldy St. E14—5E 29
 (in two parts)
Abergeldie Rd. SE12—4D 73
Abernethy Rd. SE13—2A 72
Abersham Rd. E8—2B 12
Abingdon Clo. NW1—3F 9
Abingdon Rd. W8—4C 34
Abingdon St. SW1—4A 38
Abingdon Vs. W8—4C 34
Abinger Gro. SE8—2B 56
Abinger M. W9—3C 20
Abinger Rd. W4—4A 32
Ablett St. SE16—1E 55
Aboyne Rd. SW17—3F 77
Abyssinia Clo. SW11—2A 64
Acacia Gdns. NW8—1F 21
Acacia Gro. SE21—2F 81
Acacia Pl. NW8—1F 21
Acacia Rd. NW8—1F 21
Acanthus Rd. SW11—1C 64
Acfold Rd. SW6—4D 49
Achilles Rd. NW6—2C 6
Achilles St. SE14—3B 56
Achilles Way. W1—2C 36
Acklam Rd. W10—4A 20
Ackmar Rd. SW6—4C 48
Ackroyd Dri. E3—4B 28
Ackroyd Rd. SE23—5F 69
Acland Cres. SE5—1F 67
Acland Rd. NW2—3D 5
Acol Rd. NW6—4D 7
Acorn La. NW10—1A 18
Acorn Pde. SE15—3D 55
Acorn Wlk. SE16—2A 42
Acorn Way. SE23—3F 83
Acre La. SW2—2A 66
Acre Rd. SW19—5F 77
Acris St. SW18—3E 63
Acton La. NW10—1A 18
Acton St. E8—5B 12
Acton St. WC1—2B 24
Acton Vale Industrial Pk. W3
      —2B 32
Acuba Rd. SW18—2D 77
Ada Gdns. E14—5F 29
Ada Gdns. E15—5B 16
Adair Rd. W10—3A 20
Adam & Eve M. W8—4C 34
Adams Ct. EC2—5A 26
Adams Gdns. Est. SE16—3E 41
Adamson Rd. E16—5C 30
Adamson Rd. NW3—4F 7
Adams Pl. N7—2B 10
Adamsrill Rd. SE26—4F 83
Adam's Row. W1—1C 36
Adam St. WC2—1A 38
Ada Pl. E2—5C 12

Adare Wlk. SW16—3B 80
Ada Rd. SE5—3A 54
Ada St. E8—5D 13
Adderley Gro. SW11—3C 64
Adderley St. E14—5E 29
Addington Gro. SE26—4A 84
Addington Rd. E3—2C 28
Addington Rd. E16—3A 30
Addington Sq. SE5—2F 53
Addington St. SE1—3B 38
Addison Av. W11—2A 34
Addison Bri. Pl. W14—5B 34
Addison Cres. W14—4A 34
Addison Dri. SE12—3D 73
Addison Gdns. W14—4F 33
Addison Gro. W4—4A 32
Addison Pl. W11—2A 34
Addison Rd. W14—3A 34
Addle Hill. EC4—5D 25
Addle St. EC2—5E 25
Adelaide Av. SE4—2B 70
Adelaide Gro. W12—2C 32
Adelaide Rd. NW3—4F 7
Adelaide St. WC2—1A 38
Adelaide Wlk. SW9—2C 66
Adela St. W10—3A 20
Adelina Gro. E1—4E 27
Adeline Pl. WC1—4F 23
Adelphi Ter. WC2—1A 38
Adeney Clo. W6—2F 47
Aden Gro. N16—1F 11
Adenmore Rd. SE6—5C 70
Aden Ter. N16—1F 11
Adie Rd. W6—4E 33
Adine Rd. E13—3D 31
Adler St. E1—5C 26
Adley St. E5—2A 14
Admiral Hyson Industrial Est.
      SE16—1D 55
Admiral M. W10—3F 19
Admiral Pl. SE16—2A 42
Admiral Sq. SW10—4E 49
Admiral St. SE8—4C 56
Admirals Way. E14—3C 42
Adolf St. SE6—4D 85
Adolphus St. SE8—3B 56
Adpar St. W2—4F 21
Adrian M. SW10—2D 49
Ady's Rd. SE15—1B 68
Affleck St. N1—1B 24
Afghan Rd. SW11—5A 50
Agamemnon Rd. NW6—2B 6
Agar Gro. NW1—4F 9
Agar Gro. Est. NW1—4F 9
Agar Pl. NW1—4E 9
Agar St. WC2—1A 38
Agate Clo. E16—5F 31

Agate Rd. W6—4E 33
Agatha Clo. E1—2D 41
Agave Rd. NW2—1E 5
Agdon St. EC1—3D 25
Agincourt Rd. NW3—1B 8
Agnes Rd. W3—2B 32
Agnes St. E14—5B 28
Agnew Rd. SE23—5F 69
Aileen Wlk. E15—4B 16
Ailsa St. E14—4E 29
Ainger M. NW3—4B 8
Ainsley St. E2—2D 27
Ainslie Wlk. SW12—5D 65
Ainsty Est. SE16—3F 41
Ainsty St. SE16—3E 41
Ainsworth Rd. E9—4E 13
Ainsworth Way. NW8—5E 7
Aintree St. SW6—3A 48
Airdrie Clo. N1—4B 10
Airedale Av. W4—5B 32
Airedale Av. S. W4—1B 46
Airedale Rd. SW12—5B 64
Airlie Gdns. W8—2C 34
Air St. W1—1E 37
Aisgill Av. W14—1B 48
Aislibie Rd. SE12—2A 72
Aitken Clo. E8—5C 12
Aitken Rd. SE6—2D 85
Ajax Rd. NW6—2C 6
Akehurst St. SW15—5C 60
Akenside Rd. NW3—2F 7
Akerman Rd. SW9—5D 53
Aland Ct. SE16—4A 42
Alan Rd. SW19—5A 76
Alanthus Clo. SE12—4C 72
Alaska St. SE1—2C 38
Albacore Cres. SE13—4D 71
Albany Pl. N7—1C 10
Albany Rd. E12—1F 17
Albany Rd. SE5—2F 53
Albany Rd. SW19—5D 77
Albany St. NW1—1D 23
Alba Pl. W11—5B 20
Albatross Way. SE16—3F 41
Albemarle St. W1—1E 37
Albemarle Way. EC1—3D 25
Alberta Est. SE17—1D 53
Alberta St. SE17—1D 53
Albert Av. SW8—3B 52
Albert Bri. SW3 & SW11—2A 50
Albert Bri. Rd. SW11—3A 50
Albert Carr Gdns. SW16—5A 80
Albert Clo. E2—5D 13
Albert Ct. SW7—3F 35
Albert Dri. SW19—2A 76
Albert Embkmt. SE1—1A 52
 (in two parts)

Albert Gdns. E1—5F 27
Albert Ga. SW1—3B 36
Albert Hall. Mans. SW7—3F 35
Albert M. W8—4E 35
Albert Pl. W8—4D 35
Albert Rd. NW6—1B 20
Albert Sq. E15—2A 16
Albert Sq. SW8—3B 52
Albert St. NW1—5D 9
Albert Studios. SW11—4B 50
Albert Ter. NW1—5C 8
Albert Ter. M. NW1—5C 8
Albion Av. SW8—5F 51
Albion Clo. W2—1A 36
Albion Dri. E8—4B 12
Albion Gdns. W6—5D 33
Albion Gro. N16—1A 12
Albion M. N1—4C 10
Albion M. NW6—4B 6
Albion M. W2—1A 36
Albion Pl. EC1—4F 25
Albion Pl. EC2—4D 25
Albion Rd. N16—1F 11
Albion Sq. E8—4B 12
Albion St. SE16—3E 41
Albion St. W2—5A 22
Albion Ter. E8—4B 12
Albion Vs. Rd. SE26—3E 83
Albion Way. SE13—2E 71
Albrighton Rd. SE22—1A 68
(in two parts)
Albury St. SE8—2C 56
Albyn Rd. SE8—4C 56
Aldbourne Rd. W12—2B 32
Aldbridge St. SE17—1A 54
Aldebert Ter. SW8—3B 52
Aldeburgh St. SE10—1C 58
Alden Av. E3—2B 30
Aldenham St. NW1—1F 23
Aldensley Rd. W6—4D 33
Alderbrook Rd. SW12—4D 65
Alderbury Rd. SW13—2C 46
Alder Clo. SE15—2B 54
Alderholt Way. SE15—3A 54
Alder Lodge. SW6—4F 47
Aldermanbury. EC2—5E 25
Aldermanbury Sq. EC2—4E 25
Alderman's Wlk. EC2—4A 26
Aldermaston St. W10—5F 19
Alderminster Rd. SE1—1C 54
Aldermoor Rd. SE6—3B 84
Alderney Rd. E1—3F 27
Alderney St. SW1—1D 51
Aldersford Clo. SE4—2F 69
Aldersgate St. EC1—4E 25
Aldersgrove Av. SE9—3F 87
Aldershot Rd. NW6—5B 6

Alderson St. W10—3A 20
Alderton Rd. SE24—1E 67
Alderville Rd. SW6—5B 48
Aldford St. W1—2C 36
Aldgate. EC3—5B 26
Aldgate Av. E1—5B 26
Aldgate High St. EC3—5B 26
Aldine Pl. W12—3E 33
Aldine St. W12—3E 33
Aldington Rd. SE18—4F 45
Aldis M. SW17—5A 78
Aldis St. SW17—5A 78
Aldred Rd. NW6—2C 6
Aldren Rd. SW17—3E 77
Aldrich Ter. SW18—2E 77
Aldridge Rd. Vs. W11—4B 20
Aldrington Rd. SW16—5E 79
Aldsworth Clo. W9—3D 21
Aldworth Gro. SE13—4E 71
Aldworth Rd. E15—4A 16
Aldwych. WC2—5B 24
Alestan Beck Rd. E16—5F 31
Alexa Ct. W8—5C 34
Alexander Av. NW10—4D 5
Alexander Ct. SE16—2B 42
Alexander M. W2—5D 21
Alexander Pl. SW7—5A 36
Alexander Sq. SW3—5A 36
Alexander St. W2—5D 21
Alexandra Av. SW11—4C 50
Alexandra Cotts. SE14—4B 56
Alexandra Cres. Brom—5B 86
Alexandra Dri. SE19—5A 82
Alexandra Gdns. W4—3A 46
Alexandra Mews. SW19—5B 76
Alexandra Pl. NW8—5E 7
Alexandra Rd. NW8—5E 7
Alexandra Rd. SW19—5B 76
Alexandra St. E16—4C 30
Alexandra St. SE14—3A 56
Alexis St. SE16—5C 40
Alfearn Rd. E5—1E 13
Alford Pl. N1—1E 25
Alford Rd. SW8—4F 51
Alfreda St. SW11—4D 51
Alfred M. W1—4F 23
Alfred Pl. WC1—4F 23
Alfred Rd. E15—2B 16
Alfred Rd. W2—4C 20
Alfred St. E3—2B 28
Alfreton Clo. SW19—3F 75
Alfriston Rd. SW11—3B 64
Algarve Rd. SW18—1D 77
Algernon Rd. NW6—5C 6
Algernon Rd. SE13—2D 71
Algiers Rd. SE13—2C 70
Alice St. SE1—4A 40

Alie St. E1—5B 26
Aliwal Rd. SW11—2A 64
Alkerden Rd. W4—1A 46
Allardyce St. SW4—2B 66
Allcroft Rd. NW5—2C 8
Allenby Rd. SE23—3A 84
Allendale Clo. SE5—5F 53
(in two parts)
Allendale Clo. SE26—5F 83
Allen Edwards Dri. SW8—4A 52
Allen Rd. E3—5B 14
Allen Rd. N16—1A 12
Allensbury Pl. NW1—4F 9
Allen St. W8—4C 34
Allerford Rd. SE6—3D 85
Allestree Rd. SW6—3A 48
Alleyn Cres. SE21—2F 81
Alleyn Pk. SE21—2F 81
Alleyn Rd. SE21—3F 81
Allfarthing La. SW18—4D 63
Allgood St. E2—1B 26
Allhallows La. EC4—1F 39
Alliance Rd. E13—4E 31
Allingham St. N1—1E 25
Allington Clo. SW19—5F 75
Allington Rd. W10—1A 20
Allington St. SW1—4D 37
Allison Clo. SE10—4E 57
Allison Gro. SE21—1A 82
Allitsen Rd. NW8—1A 22
Allnutt Way. SW4—3F 65
Alloa Rd. SE8—1A 56
Alloway Rd. E3—2A 28
All Saints Dri. SE3—5A 58
All Saints Pas. SW18—3C 62
All Saints Rd. W11—4B 20
All Saints St. N1—1B 24
Allsop Pl. NW1—3B 22
All Souls Av. NW10—1D 19
All Soul's Pl. W1—4D 23
Allwood Clo. SE26—4A 84
Almack Rd. E5—1E 13
Alma Gro. SE1—5B 40
Alma Pl. NW10—2D 19
Alma Rd. SW18—2E 63
Alma Sq. NW8—2F 21
Alma St. E15—3F 15
Alma St. NW5—3D 9
Alma Ter. SW18—5F 63
Almeida St. N1—5D 11
Almeric Rd. SW11—2B 64
Almond Clo. SE15—5C 54
Almond Rd. SE16—5D 41
Almorah Rd. N1—4F 11
Alnwick Rd. E16—5E 31
Alnwick Rd. SE12—5D 73
Alperton St. W10—3B 20

Alpha Clo. NW1—3A 22
Alpha Gro. E14—3C 42
Alpha Pl. NW6—1C 20
Alpha Pl. SW3—2A 50
Alpha Rd. SE14—4B 56
Alpha St. SE15—5C 54
Alpine Rd. SE16—5E 41
Alsace Rd. SE17—1A 54
Alscot Rd. SE1—5B 40
  (in two parts)
Alscot Way. SE1—5B 40
Alston Rd. SW17—4F 77
Altenburg Gdns. SW11—2B 64
Althea St. SW6—5D 49
Althorpe M. SW11—4F 49
  (in two parts)
Althorp Rd. SW17—1B 78
Alton Rd. SW15—1C 74
Alton St. E14—5D 29
Alvanley Gdns. NW6—2D 7
Alverstone Av. SW19—2C 76
Alverstone Rd. NW2—4E 5
Alverton St. SE8—1B 56
Alvey St. SE17—1A 54
Alvington Cres. E8—2B 12
Alwold Cres. SE12—4D 73
Alwyne La. N1—4D 11
Alwyne Pl. N1—3E 11
Alwyne Rd. N1—4E 11
Alwyne Rd. SW19—5B 76
Alwyne Sq. N1—3E 11
Alwyne Vs. N1—4D 11
Amazon St. E1—5C 26
Ambassador Sq. E14—5D 43
Ambergate St. SE17—1D 53
Amberley Gro. SE26—5D 83
Amberley Rd. W9—4C 20
Amber St. E15—3F 15
Amblecote Clo. SE12—3D 87
Amblecote Rd. SE12—3D 87
Ambleside. Brom—5F 85
Ambleside Av. SW16—4F 79
Ambleside Clo. E9—2E 13
Ambleside Gdns. SW16—5F 79
Ambleside Rd. NW10—4B 4
Ambrosden Av. SW1—4E 37
Ambrose M. SW11—5B 50
Ambrose St. SE16—5D 41
Ambrose Wlk. E3—1C 28
Amelia St. SE17—1E 53
Amen Corner. EC4—5D 25
Amen Corner. SW17—5B 78
Amen Ct. EC4—5D 25
America Sq. EC3—1B 40
America St. SE1—2E 39
Amerland Rd. SW18—4B 62
Amersham Gro. SE14—3B 56

Amersham Rd. SE14—4B 56
Amersham Vale. SE14—3B 56
Amery Gdns. NW10—5D 5
Amesbury Av. SW2—2A 80
Amethyst Rd. E15—1F 15
Amhen Way. SE22—3A 68
Amhurst Pas. E8—2C 12
Amhurst Rd.—1B 12
  E8 1-233 & 2-240
  N16 remainder
Amhurst Ter. E8—1C 12
Amiel St. E1—3E 27
Amies St. SW11—1B 64
Amina Way. SE16—4C 40
Amity Rd. E15—4B 16
Amner Rd. SW11—4C 64
Amor Rd. W6—4E 33
Amos Est. SE16—2F 41
Amott Rd. SE15—1C 68
Amoy Pl. E14—1C 42
Ampthill Est. NW1—1E 23
Ampton Pl. WC1—2B 24
Ampton St. WC1—2B 24
Amroth Clo. SE23—1D 83
Amsterdam Rd. E14—4E 43
Amwell St. EC1—2C 24
Amyruth Rd. SE4—3C 70
Anchorage Clo. SW19—5C 76
Anchor & Hope La. SE7—4D 45
Anchor M. SW12—4D 65
Anchor St. SE16—5D 41
Anchor Yd. EC1—3E 25
Ancill Clo. W6—2F 47
Ancona Rd. NW10—1C 18
Andalus Rd. SW9—1A 66
Anderson Rd. E9—3F 13
Anderson St. SW3—1B 50
Anderton Clo. SE5—1F 67
Andover Pl. NW6—1D 21
Andre St. E8—2C 12
Andrew Borde St. WC2—5F 23
Andrew Pl. SW8—3F 51
Andrew's Rd. E8—5D 13
Andrew St. E14—5E 29
Andrews Wlk. SE17—2D 53
Anerley Hill. SE19—5B 82
Anerley St. SW11—5B 50
Anfield Clo. SW12—5E 65
Angel All. E1—5B 26
Angel Centre, The. N1 & EC1
                       —1C 24
Angel Ct. EC2—5F 25
Angel Ct. SW1—2E 37
Angel La. E15—3F 15
Angell Pk. Gdns. SW9—1C 66
Angell Rd. SW9—1C 66
Angel M. N1—1C 24

Angel Pas. EC4—1F 39
Angel Pl. SE1—3F 39
Angel Sq. N1—1C 24
Angel St. EC1—5E 25
Angel Wlk. W6—5E 33
Angerstein La. SE3—4B 58
Angler's La. NW5—3D 9
Angles Rd. SW16—4A 80
Anglo Rd. E3—1B 28
Angus Rd. E13—2E 31
Angus St. SE14—3A 56
Anhalt Rd. SW11—3A 50
Anley Rd. W14—3F 33
Annabel Clo. E14—5D 29
Anna Clo. E8—5B 12
Annandale Rd. SE10—2B 58
Annandale Rd. W4—1A 46
Anna Neagle Clo. E7—1C 16
Annesley Rd. SE3—4D 59
Anne St. E13—3C 30
Annett's Cres. N1—4E 11
Annie Besant Clo. E3—5B 14
Anning St. EC2—3A 26
Annis Rd. E9—3A 14
Ann La. SW10—2F 49
Ansdell Rd. SE15—5E 55
Ansdell St. W8—4D 35
Ansdell Ter. W8—4D 35
Ansell Rd. SW17—3A 78
Anselm Rd. SW6—2C 48
Ansford Rd. Brom—5E 85
Anson Rd. N7—1F 9
Anson Rd. NW2—2D 5
Anstey Rd. SE15—1C 68
Anstice Clo. W4—3A 46
Anthony St. E1—5D 27
Antill Rd. E3—2A 28
Antill Ter. E1—5F 27
Anton St. E8—2C 12
Antrim Gro. NW3—3B 8
Antrim Rd. NW3—3B 8
Apollo Industrial Business
        Centre. SE8—2A 56
Apollo Pl. SW10—3F 49
Apothecary St. EC4—5D 25
Appach Rd. SW2—4C 66
Appleby Rd. E8—4C 12
Appleby Rd. E16—5B 30
Appleby St. E2—1B 26
Appledore Clo. SW17—2B 78
Appleford Rd. W10—3A 20
Applegarth Rd. W14—4F 33
Apple Tree Yd. SW1—1E 37
Appold St. EC2—4A 26
Apprentice Way. E5—1D 13
Approach Rd. E2—1E 27
April Glen. SE23—3F 83

April St. E8—1B 12
Apsley Way. W1—3C 36
Aquila St. NW8—1F 21
Aquinas St. SE1—2C 38
Arabella Dri. SW15—2A 60
Arabin Rd. SE4—2B 70
Arbery Rd. E3—2A 28
Arbour Sq. E1—5F 27
Arbuthnot Rd. SE14—5F 55
Arbutus St. E8—5B 12
Arcadia St. E14—5C 28
Archangel St. SE16—3F 41
Archbishop's Pl. SW2—5B 66
Archdale Rd. SE22—2B 68
Archel Rd. W14—2B 48
Archer St. W1—1F 37
Archery Clo. W2—5A 22
Archibald Cres. NW2—3D 5
Archibald M. W1—1C 36
Archibald Rd. N7—1F 9
Archibald St. E3—2C 28
Arch St. SE1—4E 39
Archway Clo. SW19—3D 77
Archway St. SW13—1A 60
Arcola St. E8—2B 12
Arctic St. NW5—2D 9
Arcus Rd. Brom—5A 86
Ardbeg Rd. SE24—3F 67
Arden Cres. E14—5C 42
Arden Est. N1—1A 26
Ardfillan Rd. SE6—1F 85
Ardgowan Rd. SE6—5A 72
Ardilaun Rd. N5—1E 11
Ardleigh Rd. N1—3A 12
Ardley Clo. SE6—3A 84
Ardlui Rd. SE27—2E 81
Ardmere Rd. SE13—4F 71
Ardoch Rd. SE6—2F 85
Ardshiel Clo. SW15—1F 61
Ardwell Rd. SW2—2A 80
Ardwick Rd. NW2—1C 6
Argon M. SW6—3C 48
Argon Rd. SW6—3C 48
Argyle Pl. W6—5D 33
Argyle Rd. E1—3F 27
Argyle Rd. E15—1A 16
Argyle Rd. E16—5E 31
Argyle Sq. WC1—2A 24
Argyle St. WC1—2A 24
Argyle Wlk. WC1—2A 24
Argyll Clo. SW9—1B 66
Argyll Rd. W8—3C 34
Argyll St. W1—5E 23
Arica Rd. SE4—2A 70
Ariel Rd. NW6—3C 6
Ariel Way. W12—2E 33
Aristotle Rd. SW4—1F 65
Arkindale Rd. SE6—3E 85

Arklow Rd. SE14—2B 56
Arkwright Rd. NW3—2F 7
Arlesey Clo. SW15—3A 62
Arlesford Rd. SW9—1A 66
Arlingford Rd. SW2—3B 66
Arlington Av. N1—5E 11
Arlington Rd. NW1—5D 9
Arlington Sq. N1—5E 11
Arlington St. SW1—2E 37
Arlington Way. EC1—2C 24
Armada Ct. SE8—2C 56
Armadale Rd. SW6—2C 48
Armagh Rd. E3—5B 14
Arminger Rd. W12—2D 33
Armitage Rd. SE10—1B 58
Armour Clo. N7—3B 10
Armoury Way. SW18—3C 62
Armstrong Rd. SW7—4F 35
Armstrong Rd. W3—2B 32
Arnal Cres. SW18—5A 62
Arndale Centre. SW18—4D 63
Arndale Wlk. SW18—3D 63
Arne St. WC2—5A 24
Arne Wlk. SE3—2B 72
Arneway St. SW1—4F 37
Arnewood Clo. SW15—1C 74
Arngask Rd. SE6—5F 71
Arnhem Wharf Development. E14
—4C 42
Arnold Cir. E2—2B 26
Arnold Est. SE1—3B 40
Arnold Rd. E3—2C 28
Arnould Av. SE5—2F 67
Arnside St. SE17—2F 53
Arnulf St. SE6—4B 85
Arnulls Rd. SW16—5D 81
Arodene Rd. SW2—4B 66
Arragon Rd. E6—5F 17
Arran Rd. SE6—2D 85
Arran Wlk. N1—4E 11
Arrow Rd. E3—2D 29
Artesian Rd. W2—5C 20
Arthingworth St. E15—5A 16
Arthurdon Rd. SE4—3C 70
Arthur Rd. N7—1B 10
Arthur Rd. SW19—4B 76
Arthur St. EC4—1F 39
Artichoke Hill. E1—1D 41
Artichoke Pl. SE5—4F 53
Artillery La. E1—4A 26
Artillery Pl. SW1—4F 37
Artillery Row. SW1—4F 37
Arundel Clo. E15—1A 16
Arundel Clo. SW11—3A 64
Arundel Gdns. W11—1B 34
Arundel Gro. N16—2A 12
Arundel Pl. N1—3C 10

Arundel Sq. N7—3C 10
Arundel St. WC2—1B 38
Arundel Ter. SW13—2D 47
Arvon Rd. N5—2C 10
Ascalon St. SW8—3E 51
Ascham St. NW5—2E 9
Ascot Rd. SW7—5C 78
Ashbourne Gro. SE22—2B 68
Ashbourne Gro. W4—1A 46
Ashbridge St. NW8—3A 22
Ashburn Gdns. SW7—5E 35
Ashburnham Gro. SE10—3D 57
Ashburnham Pl. SE10—3D 57
Ashburnham Retreat. SE10
—3D 57
Ashburnham Rd. NW10—2E 19
Ashburnham Rd. SW10—3E 49
Ashburn M. SW7—5E 35
Ashburn Pl. SW7—5E 35
Ashburton Gro. N7—1C 10
Ashburton Rd. E16—5C 30
Ashburton Ter. E13—1C 30
Ashbury Rd. SW11—1B 64
Ashby Gro. N1—4E 11
Ashby Rd. SE4—5B 56
Ashby St. EC1—2D 25
Ashchurch Gro. W12—4C 32
Ashchurch Pk. Vs. W12—4C 32
Ashchurch Ter. W12—4C 32
Ashcombe Rd. SW19—5C 76
Ashcombe St. SW6—5D 49
Ashcroft Rd. E3—2A 28
Ashcroft Sq. W6—5E 33
Ashdale Rd. SE12—1D 87
Ashdon Rd. NW10—5B 4
Ashdown Cres. NW5—2C 8
Ashdown Est. E11—1F 15
Ashdown Way. SW17—2C 78
Ashenden Rd. E5—2A 14
Ashen Gro. SW19—3C 76
Asher Way. E1—1C 40
Ashfield Rd. W3—2B 32
Ashfield St. E1—4D 27
Ashford Pas. NW2—1F 5
Ashford Rd. NW2—1F 5
Ashford St. N1—2A 26
Ash Gro. E8—5D 13
(in two parts)
Ash Gro. NW2—1F 5
Ashgrove Rd. Brom—5F 85
Ashington Rd. SW6—5B 48
Ashlake Rd. SW16—4A 80
Ashland Pl. W1—4C 22
Ashleigh Rd. SW14—1A 60
Ashley Cres. SW11—1C 64
Ashley Gdns. SW1—4E 37
Ashley Pl. SW1—4E 37

Ashley Rd. E7—4E 17
Ashley Rd. SW19—5D 77
Ashlin Rd. E15—1F 15
Ashlone Rd. SW15—1F 61
Ashmead Rd. SE8—5C 56
Ashmere Gro. SW2—2A 66
Ashmill St. NW1—4A 22
Ashmole Pl. SW8—2B 52
Ashmole St. SW8—2B 52
Ashmore Rd. W9—2B 20
Ashness Rd. SW11—3B 64
Ash Rd. E15—2A 16
Ashton Rd. E15—2F 15
Ashton St. E14—1E 43
Ashvale Rd. SW17—5B 78
Ashwater Rd. SE12—1C 86
Ashwin St. E8—3B 12
Ashworth Clo. SE5—5F 53
Ashworth Rd. W9—2D 21
Aske St. N1—2A 26
Askew Cres. W12—3B 32
Askew Rd. W12—3B 32
Askham Ct. W12—2C 32
Askham Rd. W12—2C 32
Askill Dri. SW15—3A 62
Asland Rd. E15—5A 16
Aslett St. SW18—5D 63
Asmara Rd. NW2—2A 6
Aspen Gdns. W6—1D 47
Aspenlea Rd. W6—2F 47
Aspen Way. E14—1D 43
Aspern Gro. NW3—2A 8
Aspinall Rd. SE4—1F 69
Aspinden Rd. SE16—5D 41
Aspley Rd. SW18—3D 63
Assam St. E1—5C 26
Assembly Pas. E1—4E 27
Astbury Rd. SE15—4E 55
Astell St. SW3—1A 50
Aste St. E14—3E 43
Astey's Row. N1—4E 11
Astle St. SW11—5C 50
Aston St. E14—4A 28
Astonville St. SW18—1C 76
Astoria Wlk. SW9—1C 66
Astrop M. W6—4E 33
Astrop Ter. W6—3E 33
Astwood M. SW7—5E 35
Asylum Rd. SE15—3D 55
Atalanta St. SW6—3F 47
Atheldene Rd. SW18—1E 77
Athelney St. SE6—3C 84
Athelstane Gro. E3—1B 28
Athenlay Rd. SE15—3F 69
Athens Gdns. W9—3C 20
Atherden Rd. E5—1E 13

Atherfold Rd. SW9—1A 66
Atherstone M. SW7—5E 35
Atherton Dri. SW19—4F 75
Atherton M. E7—3B 16
Atherton Rd. E7—3B 16
Atherton Rd. SW13—3C 46
Atherton St. SW11—5A 50
Athlone Clo. E5—2D 13
Athlone Rd. SW2—5B 66
Athlone St. NW5—3C 8
Athol Sq. E14—5E 29
Atkinson Rd. E16—4E 31
Atkins Rd. SW12—5E 65
Atlantic Rd. SW9—2C 66
Atlas Gdns. SE7—5E 45
Atlas M. N7—3B 10
Atlas Rd. E13—1C 30
Atlas Rd. NW10—2A 18
Atley Rd. E3—5C 14
Atney Rd. SW15—2A 62
Atterbury St. SW1—5A 38
Attneave St. WC1—2C 24
Atwater Clo. SW2—1C 80
Atwell Rd. SE15—5C 54
Atwood Rd. W6—5D 33
Aubert Ct. N5—1D 11
Aubert Pk. N5—1D 11
Aubert Rd. N5—1D 11
Aubrey Pl. NW8—1E 21
Aubrey Rd. W8—2B 34
Aubrey Wlk. W8—2B 34
Aubyn Hill. SE27—4E 81
Aubyn Sq. SW15—3C 60
Auckland Hill. SE27—4E 81
Auckland Rd. SW11—2A 64
Auckland St. SE11—1B 52
Auden Pl. NW1—5C 8
Audley Clo. SW11—1C 64
Audley Sq. W1—2C 36
Audrey St. E2—1C 26
Augurs La. E13—2D 31
Augusta St. E14—5D 29
Augustine Rd. W14—4F 33
Augustus Ct. SW16—2F 79
Augustus Rd. SW19—1A 76
Augustus St. NW1—1D 23
Aulton Pl. SE11—1C 52
Auriga M. N1—2F 11
Auriol Rd. W14—5A 34
Austin Clo. SE23—5B 70
Austin Ct. E6—5C 17
Austin Friars. EC2—5F 25
Austin Rd. SW11—4C 50
Austin St. E2—2B 26
Australia Rd. W12—1D 33
Austral St. SE11—5D 39
Autumn St. E3—5C 14

Avalon Rd. SW6—4D 49
Avarn Rd. SW17—5B 78
Avebury St. N1—5F 11
Aveline St. SE11—1C 52
Ave Maria La. EC4—5D 25
Avenell Rd. N5—1D 11
Avening Rd. SW18—5C 62
Avening Ter. SW18—5C 62
Avenons Rd. E13—3C 30
Avenue Clo. NW8—5A 8
Avenue Gdns. SW14—1A 60
Avenue Pk. Rd. SE27—2D 81
Avenue Rd. E7—1D 17
Avenue Rd.—4F 7
  NW8 1-95 & 2-86
  NW3 remainder
Avenue Rd. NW10—1B 18
Avenue, The. NW6—5A 6
Avenue, The. SE7—3E 59
Avenue, The. SE10—3F 57
Avenue, The. SW4—3D 65
Avenue, The. SW18 & SW11—5A 64
Avenue, The. W4—4A 32
Averill St. W6—2F 47
Avery Farm Row. SW1—5D 37
Avery Row. W1—1D 37
Aviary Clo. E16—4B 30
Avignon Rd. SE4—1F 69
Avington Way. SE15—3B 54
Avis Sq. E1—5F 27
Avoca Rd. SW17—4C 78
Avondale Ct. E16—4A 30
Avondale Pk. Gdns. W11—1A 34
Avondale Pk. Rd. W11—1A 34
Avondale Rise. SE15—1B 68
Avondale Rd. E16—4A 30
Avondale Rd. NW11—5D 7
Avondale Rd. Brom—5B 86
Avondale Sq. SE1—1C 54
Avonley Rd. SE14—3E 55
Avonmore Rd. W14—5B 34
Avonmouth St. SE1—4E 39
Avon Pl. SE1—3E 39
Avon Rd. SE4—1C 70
Axis Business Centre. W4
  —2A 46
Aybrook St. W1—4C 22
Aycliffe Rd. W12—2C 32
Aylesbury Clo. E7—3B 16
Aylesbury Rd. SE17—1F 53
Aylesbury St. EC1—3D 25
Aylesford St. SW1—1F 51
Aylestone Av. NW6—4F 5
Aylmer Rd. W12—3B 32
Aylsham Centre, The. SE15
  —4C 54
Aylward Rd. SE23—2F 83

Aylward St. E1—5F 27
Aylward St. E1
Aylwin Est. SE1—4A 40
Aynhoe Rd. W14—5F 33
Ayres Clo. E13—2C 30
Ayres St. SE1—3E 39
Ayrton Rd. SW7—4F 35
Aysgarth Rd. SE21—5A 68
Aytoun Pl. SW9—5B 52
Aytoun Rd. SW9—5B 52
Azenby Rd. SE15—5B 54
Azof St. SE10—5A 44

Baalbec Rd. N5—2D 11
Babington Rd. SW16—5F 79
Babmaes St. SW1—1F 37
Bache's Rd. N1—2F 25
Bk. Church La. E1—5C 26
Back Hill. EC1—3C 24
Back La. E15—1F 29
Back La. NW3—1E 7
Bacon Gro. SE1—4B 40
Bacon St.—3B 26
    E1 1-21 & 2-22
    E2 remainder
Bacton St. E2—2E 27
Baden Pl. SE1—3F 39
Badminton Rd. SW12—4C 64
Badsworth Rd. SE5—4E 53
Bagford St. N1—5F 11
Bagley's La. SW6—4D 49
Bagshot St. SE17—1A 54
Baildon St. SE8—3B 56
Bailey Pl. SE26—5F 83
Bainbridge St. WC1—5F 23
Baird Gdns. SE19—4A 82
Baird St. EC1—3E 25
Baizdon Rd. SE3—5A 58
Baker Rd. NW10—5A 4
Baker's Field. N7—1F 9
Bakers Hall Ct. EC3—1A 40
Baker's M. W1—5C 22
Baker's Rents. E2—2B 26
Baker's Row. E15—1A 30
Baker's Row. EC1—3C 24
Baker St.—3B 22
    W1 1-133 & 2-136
    NW1 remainder
Balaam St. E13—3C 30
Balaclava Rd. SE1—5B 40
Balben Path. E9—4E 13
Balchen Rd. SE3—5F 59
Balchier Rd. SE22—4D 69
Balcombe St. NW1—3B 22
Balcorne St. E9—4E 13
Balder Rise. SE3—2D 87

Balderton St. W1—5C 22
Baldock St. E3—1D 29
Baldry Gdns. SW16—5A 80
Baldwin Cres. SE5—4E 53
Baldwin's Gdns. EC1—4C 24
Baldwin St. EC1—2F 25
Baldwin Ter. N1—1E 25
Balfern Gro. W4—1A 46
Balfern St. SW11—5A 50
Balfe St. N1—1A 24
Balfour M. W1—2C 36
Balfour Pl. SW15—2D 61
Balfour Pl. W1—1C 36
Balfour Rd. N5—1E 11
Balfour St. SE17—5F 39
Balham Gro. SW12—5C 64
Balham High Rd.—3C 78
    SW12 1-197 & 2-222
    SW17 remainder
Balham Hill. SW12—5D 65
Balham New Rd. SW12—5D 65
Balham Pk. Rd. SW12—1B 78
Balham Sta. Rd. SW12—1D 79
Balkan Wlk. E1—1D 41
Ballamore Rd. Brom—3C 86
Ballance Rd. E9—3F 13
Ballantine St. SW18—2E 63
Ballast Quay. SE10—1F 57
Ballater Rd. SW2—2A 66
Ballina St. SE23—5F 69
Ballingdon Rd. SW11—4C 64
Balliol Rd. W10—5E 19
Balloch Rd. SE6—1F 85
Ballogie Av. NW10—1A 4
Ballow Clo. SE5—3A 54
Balls Pond Rd. N1—3F 11
Balmer Rd. E3—1B 28
Balmes Rd. N1—5F 11
Balmoral Clo. SW15—4F 61
Balmoral Gro. N7—3B 10
Balmoral M. W12—4B 32
Balmoral Rd. E7—5E 17
Balmoral Rd. NW2—3D 5
Balmuir Gdns. SW15—2E 61
Balnacraig Av. NW10—1A 4
Balniel Ga. SW1—1F 51
Baltic Ct. SE16—3F 41
Baltic St. EC1—3E 25
Balvaird Pl. SW1—1F 51
Balvernie Gro. SW18—5B 62
Bamborough Gdns. W12—3E 33
Bamford Rd. Brom—5E 85
Bampton Rd. SE23—3F 83
Banbury Rd. E9—4F 13
Banbury St. SW11—5A 50
Banchory Rd. SE3—3D 59
Bancroft Rd. E1—2F 27

Bangalore St. SW15—1F 61
Banim St. W6—5D 33
Banister Rd. W10—2F 19
Bank End. SE1—2E 39
Bankfoot Rd. Brom—4A 86
Bankhurst Rd. SE6—5B 70
Bank La. SW15—3A 60
Bankside. SE1—1E 39
Bankside Way. SE19—5A 82
Bankton Rd. SW2—2C 66
Bankwell Rd. SE13—2A 72
Banner St. EC1—3E 25
Banning St. SE10—1A 58
Bannister Rd. SW2—1C 80
Banstead St. SE15—1E 69
Bantry St. SE5—3F 53
Banyard Rd. SE16—4D 41
Baptist Gdns. NW5—3C 8
Barandon Wlk. W11—1F 33
Barbara Brosnan Ct. NW8
                    —1F 21
Barbers All. E13—2D 31
Barbers Rd. E15—1D 29
Barbican. EC2—4E 25
Barb M. W6—4E 33
Barbon Clo. WC1—4B 24
Barchard St. SW18—3D 63
Barchester St. E14—4D 29
Barclay Clo. SW6—3C 48
Barclay Rd. E13—3E 31
Barclay Rd. SW6—3C 48
Barclay Way. SE22—1C 82
Barcombe Av. SW2—2A 80
Bardolph Rd. N7—1A 10
Bard Rd. W10—1F 33
Bardsey Pl. E1—3E 27
Bardsey Wlk. N1—3E 11
Bardsley La. SE10—2E 57
Barfett St. W10—3B 20
Barford St. N1—5C 10
Barforth Rd. SE15—1D 69
Barge Ho. St. SE1—2C 38
Bargery Rd. SE6—1D 85
Bargrove Cres. SE6—2B 84
Baring Clo. SE12—2C 86
Baring Rd. SE12—5C 72
Baring St. N1—5F 11
Barker Dri. NW1—4E 9
Barker St. SW10—2E 49
Barker Wlk. SW16—3F 79
Barker Way. SW22—5C 68
Barking Rd.—4B 30
    E16 1-233 & 2-242
    E13 remainder
Barkis Way. SE16—1D 55
Bark Pl. W2—1D 35
Barkston Gdns. SW5—5D 35

Barkworth Rd. SE16—1E 55
Barlborough St. SE14—3F 55
Barlby Gdns. W10—3F 19
Barlby Rd. W10—4E 19
Barleycorn Way. E14—1B 42
Barlow Rd. NW6—3B 6
Barlow St. SE17—5F 39
Barmeston Rd. SE6—2D 85
Barmouth Rd. SW18—4E 63
Barnabas Rd. E9—2F 13
Barnard Gro. E15—4B 16
Barnard M. SW11—2A 64
Barnardo St. E1—5F 27
Barnard Rd. SW11—2A 64
Barnby Sq. E15—5A 16
Barnby St. E15—5A 16
Barnby St. NW1—1E 23
Barn Elms Pk. SW15—1E 61
Barnes Av. SW13—3C 46
Barnes Clo. E12—1F 17
Barnes Ct. E16—4E 31
Barnes High St. SW13—5B 46
Barnes St. E14—5A 28
Barnet Gro. E2—2C 26
Barnett St. E1—5D 27
Barney Clo. SE7—1E 59
Barnfield Pl. E14—5C 42
Barnham St. SE1—3A 40
Barnsbury Gro. N7—4B 10
Barnsbury M. N1—4C 10
Barnsbury Pk. N1—4C 10
Barnsbury Rd. N1—5C 10
Barnsbury Sq. N1—4C 10
Barnsbury St. N1—4C 10
Barnsbury Ter. N1—4B 10
Barnsdale Av. E14—5D 43
Barnsdale Rd. W9—3B 20
Barnsley St. E1—3D 27
Barnwell Rd. SW2—3C 66
Barnwood Clo. W9—3D 21
Barnwood Ct. E16—2D 45
Baron Clo. N1—1C 24
Baroness Rd. E2—2B 26
Baron's Ct. Rd. W14—1A 48
Barons Keep. W14—1A 48
Baronsmead Rd. SW13—4C 46
Baron's Pl. SE1—3C 38
Baron St. N1—1C 24
Baron Wlk. E16—4B 30
Barque M. SE8—2C 56
Barrett's Gro. N16—2A 12
Barrett St. W1—5C 22
Barrhill Rd. SW2—2A 80
Barriedale. SE14—5A 56
Barrie Est. W2—1F 35
Barrier App. SE7—4F 45
Barringer Sq. SW17—4C 78

Barrington Clo. NW5—2C 8
Barrington St. SW9—1D 67
Barrow Hill Rd. NW8—1A 22
Barrow Rd. SW16—5F 79
Barry Rd. SE22—4C 68
Barset Rd. SE15—1E 69
(in three parts)
Barston Rd. SE27—3E 81
Barstow Cres. SW2—1B 80
Barter St. WC1—4A 24
Bartholomew Clo. EC1—4E 25
Bartholomew Clo. SW18—2E 63
Bartholomew La. EC2—5F 25
Bartholomew Rd. NW5—3E 9
Bartholomew Sq. E1—3D 27
Bartholomew Sq. EC1—3E 25
Bartholomew St. SE1—4F 39
Bartholomew Vs. NW5—3E 9
Bartle Rd. W11—5A 20
Bartlett Clo. E14—5C 28
Bartlett Ct. EC4—5C 24
Barton Clo. E9—2C 13
Barton Clo. SE15—1D 69
Barton St. W14—1A 48
Barton Rd. W14—1A 48
Barton St. SW1—4A 38
Bartram Rd. SE4—3A 70
Barwick Rd. E7—1D 17
Basil St. SW3—4B 36
Basing Ct. SE15—4B 54
Basingdon Way. SE5—2F 67
Basinghall Av. EC2—5F 25
Basinghall St. EC2—5F 25
Basing Ho. Yd. E2—2A 26
Basing Pl. E2—2A 26
Basing St. W11—5B 20
Basire St. N1—5E 11
Baskerville Rd. SW18—5A 64
Baslow Wlk. E5—1F 13
Basnett Rd. SW11—1C 64
Bassano St. SE22—3B 68
Bassein Pk. Rd. W12—3B 32
Bassett Rd. W10—5F 19
Bassett St. NW5—3C 8
Bassingham Rd. SW18—5E 63
Basswood Clo. SE15—1D 69
Bastwick St. EC1—3E 25
Basuto Rd. SW6—4C 48
Batavia M. SE14—3A 56
Batavia Rd. SE14—3A 56
Batchelor St. N1—5C 10
Bateman's Row. EC2—3A 26
Bateman St. W1—5F 23
Bate St. E14—1B 42
Bathgate Rd. SW19—3F 75
Bath Pl. EC1—2A 26

Bath Rd. E7—3F 17
Bath Rd. W4—5A 32
Bath St. EC1—2E 25
Bath Ter. SE1—4E 39
Bathurst Gdns. NW10—1D 19
Bathurst M. W2—1F 35
Bathurst St. W2—1F 35
Batman Clo. W12—2D 33
Batoum Gdns. W6—4E 33
Batson St. W12—3C 32
Batten St. SW11—1A 64
Battersby Rd. SE6—2F 85
Battersea Bri. SW3 & SW11
—3F 49
Battersea Bri. Rd. SW11—3A 50
Battersea Chu. Rd. SW11
—4F 49
Battersea High St. SW11
—4F 49
Battersea Pk. Rd.—5A 50
SW8 1-179 & 2-18
SW11 remainder
Battersea Rise. SW11—3A 64
Battishill St. N1—4D 11
Battle Bri. La. SE1—2A 40
Battle Bri. Rd. NW1—1A 24
Battledean Rd. N5—2D 11
Batty St. E1—5C 26
Baudwin Rd. SE6—2A 86
Baulk, The. SW18—5C 62
Bavent Rd. SE5—5E 53
Bawdale Rd. SE22—3B 68
Bawtree Rd. SE14—3A 56
Baxendale St. E2—2C 26
Baxter Rd. E16—5E 31
Baxter Rd. N1—3F 11
Bayes Clo. SE26—5E 83
Bayfield Rd. SE9—2F 73
Bayford Rd. NW10—2F 19
Bayford St. E8—4D 13
Bayham Pl. NW1—1E 23
Bayham St. NW1—5E 9
Bayley St. WC1—4F 23
Baylin Rd. SW18—4D 63
Baylis Rd. SE1—3C 38
Baynes M. NW3—3F 7
Baynes St. NW1—4E 9
Bayonne Rd. SW6—2A 48
Bayswater Rd. W2—1D 35
Baythorne St. E3—4B 28
(in two parts)
Baytree Rd. SW2—2B 66
Bazely St. E14—1E 43
Beacham Clo. SE7—2F 59
Beachborough Rd. Brom—4E 85
Beachy Rd. E3—4C 14
Beacon Hill. N7—2A 10

Beacon Rd. SE13—4F 71
Beaconsfield Clo. SE3—2C 58
Beaconsfield Rd. E16—3B 30
Beaconsfield Rd. NW10—3B 4
Beaconsfield Rd. SE3—3B 58
Beaconsfield Rd. SE17—1A 54
Beaconsfield Ter. Rd. W14
—4A 34
Beaconsfield Wlk. SW6—4C 48
Beadman St. SE27—4D 81
Beadnell Rd. SE23—1F 83
Beadon Rd. W6—5E 33
Beak St. W1—1E 37
Beale Pl. E3—1B 28
Beale Rd. E3—5B 14
Beamish Ga. NW1—4F 9
Beanacre Clo. E9—3B 14
Bear All. EC4—5D 25
Beardsfield E13—1C 30
Bear Gdns. SE1—2E 39
Bear La. SE1—2D 39
Bearstead Rise. SE4—3B 70
Bear St. WC2—1F 37
Beatrice Clo. E13—3C 30
Beatrice Rd. SE1—5C 40
Beaton Wlk. SE16—2A 42
Beatty Rd. N16—1A 12
Beatty St. NW1—1E 23
Beauchamp Pl. SW3—4A 36
Beauchamp Rd. E7—4D 17
Beauchamp Rd. SW11—2A 64
Beauchamp St. EC1—4C 24
Beauchamp Ter. SW15—1D 61
Beauclerc Rd. W6—4E 33
Beaufort Clo. SW15—5D 61
Beaufort Gdns. SW3—4A 36
Beaufort St. SW3—2F 49
Beaufoy Wlk. SE11—5B 38
Beaulieu Av. SE26—4D 83
Beaulieu Clo. SE5—1F 67
Beaumont Av. W14—1B 48
Beaumont Cres. W14—1B 48
Beaumont Gro. E1—3F 27
Beaumont M. W1—4C 22
Beaumont Pl. W1—3E 23
Beaumont Rd. E13—2D 31
Beaumont Rd. SW19—5A 62
Beaumont Sq. E1—4F 27
Beaumont St. W1—4C 22
Beaumont Wlk. NW3—4B 8
Beauval Rd. SE22—4B 68
Beavor La. W6—5C 32
Beccles St. E14—1B 42
Beck Clo. SE13—4D 57
Beckenham Business Centre.
Beck—5A 84
Beckenham Hill Est. Beck
—5D 85

Beckenham Hill Rd.—5D 85
SE6 1-95 & 2-62
Beck remainder
Becket St. SE1—4F 39
Beckett Clo. NW10—3A 4
Beckett Clo. SW16—2F 79
Beckford Pl. SE17—1E 53
Becklands Rd. SW17—5C 78
Becklow Rd. W12—3B 32
Beck Rd. E8—5D 13
Beckton Rd. E16—4B 30
Beckway St. SE17—5A 40
(in two parts)
Beckwith Rd. SE24—3F 67
Becmead Av. SW16—4F 79
Becondale Rd. SE19—5A 82
Bective Pl. SW15—2B 62
Bective Rd. E7—1C 16
Bective Rd. SW15—2B 62
Bedale St. SE1—2B 40
Bedford Av. WC1—4F 23
Bedfordbury. WC2—1A 38
Bedford Ct. WC2—1A 38
Bedford Gdns. W8—2C 34
Bedford Hill—1D 79
SW12 1-203 & 2-210
SW16 remainder
Bedford Pk. Corner. W4—5A 32
Bedford Pas. W1—4E 23
Bedford Pl. WC1—4A 24
Bedford Rd. SW4—2A 66
Bedford Rd. W4—4A 32
Bedford Row. WC1—4B 24
Bedford Sq. WC1—4A 24
Bedford St. WC2—1A 38
Bedford Way. WC1—3F 23
Bedgebury Gdns. SW19—2A 76
Bedgebury Rd. SE9—2F 73
Bedivere Rd. Brom—3C 86
Bedwin Way. SE16—1D 55
Beeby Rd. E16—4D 31
Beech Av. W3—2A 32
Beech Clo. SE8—2C 56
Beech Clo. SW15—5C 60
Beech Clo. SW19—5E 75
Beechcroft Clo. SW16—5B 80
Beech Croft Ct. N5—1D 11
Beechcroft Rd. SW17—2A 78
Beechdale Rd. SW2—4B 66
Beechen Pl. SE23—2F 83
Beeches Rd. SW17—3A 78
Beechfield Rd. SE6—1B 84
Beechmont Clo. Brom—5A 86
Beechmore Rd. SW11—4B 50
Beech St. EC2—4E 25
Beechwood Gro. W3—1A 32
Beechwood Rd. E8—3B 12
Beecroft Rd. SE4—3A 70

Beehive Pl. SW9—1C 66
Beeston Clo. E8—2C 12
Beeston Pl. SW1—4D 37
Beethoven St. W10—2A 20
Begbie Rd. SE3—4E 59
Begonia Wlk. W12—5B 18
Beira St. SW12—5D 65
Bekesbourne St. E14—5A 28
Belasis Av. SW2—2A 80
Belfast Gdns. SE3—2B 58
Belfont Wlk. N7—1A 10
Belfort Rd. SE15—5E 55
Belgrade Rd. N16—1A 12
Belgrave Gdns. NW8—5D 7
Belgrave M. N. SW1—3C 36
Belgrave M. S. SW1—4C 36
Belgrave M. W. SW1—4C 36
Belgrave Pl. SW1—4C 36
Belgrave Rd. E13—3E 31
Belgrave Rd. SW1—5D 37
Belgrave Rd. SW13—3B 46
Belgrave Sq. SW1—4C 36
Belgrave St. E1—5F 27
Belgrove St. WC1—2A 24
Belinda Rd. SW9—1D 67
Belitha Vs. N1—4B 10
Bellamy Clo. W14—1B 48
Bellamy St. SW12—5D 65
Bell Dri. SW18—5A 62
Bellefields Rd. SW9—1B 66
Bellenden Rd. SE15—5B 54
Belleville Rd. SW11—3A 64
Bellevue Pl. E1—3E 27
Bellevue Rd. SW13—5C 46
Bellevue Rd. SW17—1A 78
Bellew St. SW17—3E 77
Bellgate M. NW5—1D 9
Bell Grn. SE26—4B 84
Bell Grn. La. SE26—5B 84
Bellingham Grn. SE6—3C 84
Bellingham Rd. SE6—3D 85
Bell Inn Yd. EC3—5F 25
Bell La. E1—4B 26
Bell La. E16—2C 44
Bell Meadow. SE19—5A 82
Bellot St. SE10—1A 58
Bells All. SW6—5C 48
Bell St. NW1—4A 22
Bell Trees Gro. SW16—5B 80
Bell Wharf La. EC4—1E 39
Bellwood Rd. SE15—2F 69
Bell Yd. WC2—5C 24
Belmont Clo. SW4—1E 65
Belmont Gro. SE13—1F 71
Belmont Hill. SE13—1F 71
Belmont Pk. SE13—2F 71
Belmont Pk. Clo. SE13—2A 72

Belmont Rd. SW4—1E 65
Belmont St. NW1—4C 8
Belmore La. N7—2F 9
Belmore St. SW8—4F 51
Beloe Clo. SW13—1C 60
Belsham St. E9—3E 13
Belsize Av. NW3—3F 7
Belsize Ct. NW3—2F 7
Belsize Cres. NW3—2F 7
Belsize Gro. NW3—3A 8
Belsize La. NW3—3F 7
Belsize M. NW3—3F 7
Belsize Pk. NW3—3F 7
Belsize Pk. Gdns. NW3—3A 8
Belsize Pk. Gdns. NW3
Belsize Pk. M. NW3—3F 7
Belsize Pl. NW3—2F 7
Belsize Rd. NW6—5D 7
Belsize Sq. NW3—3F 7
Belsize Ter. NW3—3F 7
Beltane Dri. SW19—3F 75
Beltham Wlk. SE5—4F 53
Belthorn Cres. SW12—5E 65
Belton Rd. E7—4D 17
Belton Rd. E11—1A 16
Belton Rd. NW2—3C 4
Belton Way. E3—4C 28
Beltran Rd. SW6—5D 49
Belvedere Av. SW19—5A 76
Belvedere Bldgs. SE1—3D 39
Belvedere Dri. SW19—5A 76
Belvedere Gro. SW19—5A 76
Belvedere Pl. SE1—3D 39
Belvedere Rd. SE1—3B 38
Belvedere Sq. SW19—5A 76
Belvoir Rd. SE22—5C 68
Bembridge Clo. NW6—4A 6
Bemerton Est. N1—4A 10
Bemerton St. N1—5B 10
Bemish Rd. SW15—1F 61
Benbow Rd. W6—4D 33
Benbow St. SE8—2C 56
Benbury Clo. Brom—5E 85
Bendemeer Rd. SW15—1F 61
Bendon Valley. SW18—5D 63
Benedict Rd. SW9—1B 66
Bengeworth Rd. SE5—1E 67
Benham Clo. SW11—1F 63
Benhill Rd. SE5—3F 53
Benhurst Ct. SW16—5C 80
Benhurst La. SW16—5C 80
Benin St. SE13—5F 71
Benjamin Clo. E8—5C 12
Benjamin St. EC1—4D 25
Ben Jonson Rd. E1—4A 28
Benledi St. E14—5F 29
Bennerley Rd. SW11—3A 64

Bennet's Hill. EC4—1E 39
Bennet St. SW1—2E 37
Bennett Gro. SE13—4D 57
Bennett Pk. SE3—1B 72
Bennett Rd. E13—3E 31
Bennetts St. N16—1A 12
Bennett St. W4—2A 46
Bennett's Yd. SW1—4F 37
Benn St. E9—3A 14
Bensbury Clo. SW15—5D 61
Bensham's Pl. NW3—1E 7
Ben Smith Way. SE16—4C 40
Benson Av. E6—1F 31
Benson Quay. E1—1E 41
Benson Rd. SE23—1E 83
Bentfield Gdns. SE9—3F 87
Bentham Rd. E9—3F 13
Bentinck M. W1—5C 22
Bentinck St. W1—5C 22
Bentley Rd. N1—3A 12
Bentons La. SE27—4E 81
Bentons Rise. SE27—5F 81
Bentworth Rd. W12—5D 19
Benwell Rd. N7—2C 10
Benwick Clo. SE16—5D 41
Benworth St. E3—2B 28
Berber Rd. SW11—3B 64
Berens Rd. NW10—2F 19
Beresford Rd. N5—2F 11
Beresford Ter. N5—2E 11
Berestede Rd. W6—1B 46
Bere St. E1—1F 41
Berger Rd. E9—3F 13
Bergholt M. NW1—4E 9
Bering Wlk. E16—5F 31
Berkeley Gdns. W8—2C 34
Berkeley M. W1—5B 22
Berkeley Rd. SW13—4C 46
Berkeley Sq. W1—1D 37
Berkeley St. W1—1D 37
Berkley Gro. NW1—4C 8
Berkley Rd. NW1—4B 8
Berkshire Rd. E9—3B 14
Bermans Way. NW10—1A 4
Bermondsey Sq. SE1—4A 40
Bermondsey St. SE1—3A 40
Bermondsey Wall E. SE16
                      —3D 41
Bermondsey Wall W. SE16
                      —3C 40
Bernard Cassidy St. E16—4B 30
Bernard Gdns. SW19—5B 76
Bernard St. WC1—3A 24
Bernay's Gro. SW9—2B 66
Berners M. W1—4E 23
Berners Pl. W1—5E 23
Berners Rd. N1—5D 11

Berners St. W1—4E 23
Berridge Rd. SE19—5F 81
Berry Clo. NW10—4A 4
Berryfield Rd. SE17—1D 53
Berry La. SE21—4F 81
Berryman's La. SE26—4F 83
Berry Pl. EC1—2D 25
Berry St. EC1—3D 25
Bertal Rd. SW17—4F 77
Berthon St. SE8—3C 56
Bertie Rd. NW10—3C 4
Bertie Rd. SE26—5F 83
Bertrand St. SE13—1D 71
Berwick Rd. E16—5D 31
Berwick St. W1—5E 23
Berwyn Rd. SE24—1D 81
Beryl Rd. W6—1F 47
Besant Rd. NW2—1A 6
Bessborough Gdns. SW1—1F 51
Bessborough Pl. SW1—1F 51
Bessborough Rd. SW15—1C 74
Bessborough St. SW1—1F 51
Bessemer Rd. SE5—5E 53
Besson St. SE14—4F 55
Bessy St. E2—2E 27
Bestwood St. SE8—5F 41
Beswick M. NW6—2D 7
Bethell Av. E16—3B 30
Bethnal Grn. Rd.—3B 26
  E1 1-99 & 2-94
  E2 remainder
Bethwin Rd. SE5—3D 53
Betterton St. WC2—5A 24
Bettons Pk. E15—5A 16
Bettridge Rd. SW6—5B 48
Betts Rd. E16—1D 45
Betts St. E1—1D 41
Beulah Hill. SE19—5D 81
Bevan St. N1—5E 11
Bevenden St. N1—2F 25
Beveridge Rd. NW10—4A 4
Beverley Clo. SW11—2F 63
Beverley Clo. SW13—5C 46
Beverley Ct. SE4—1B 70
Beverley Gdns. SW13—1B 60
Beverley La. SW15—3B 74
Beverley Path. SW13—5B 46
Beverley Rd. E6—2F 31
Beverley Rd. SW13—1B 60
Beverley Rd. W4—1B 46
Beverstone Rd. SW2—3B 66
Bevill Allen Clo. SW17—5B 78
Bevin Clo. SE16—2A 42
Bevington Rd. W10—4A 20
Bevington St. SE16—3C 40
Bevin Way. WC1—1C 24
Bevis Marks. EC3—5A 26

Bewdley St. N1—4C 10
Bewick St. SW8—5D 51
Bewley St. E1—1E 41
Bewlys Rd. SE27—5D 81
Bexhill Rd. SE4—4B 70
Bexhill Wlk. E15—5A 16
Bianca Rd. SE15—2C 54
Bibury Clo. SE15—2A 54
Bickenhall St. W1—4B 22
Bickersteth Rd. SW17—5B 78
Bickley St. SW17—5A 78
Bicknell Rd. SE5—1E 67
Bidborough St. WC1—2A 24
Bidder St. E16—4A 30
(in two parts)
Biddestone Rd. N7—1B 10
Biddulph Rd. W9—2D 21
Bideford Rd. Brom—3B 86
Bidwell St. SE15—4D 55
Biggerstaff Rd. E15—5E 15
Biggs Row. SW15—1F 61
Bigland Est. E1—5D 27
Bigland St. E1—5D 27
Bignold Rd. E7—1C 16
Billingford Clo. SE4—2F 69
Billing Pl. SW10—3D 49
Billing Rd. SW10—3D 49
Billingsgate. E14—1C 42
Billing St. SW10—3D 49
Billington Rd. SE14—3F 55
Billiter St. EC3—5A 26
Billson St. E14—5E 43
Bilsby Gro. SE9—4F 87
Bina Gdns. SW5—5E 35
Binden Rd. W12—4B 32
Binfield Rd. SW4—4A 52
Bingfield St. N1—5A 10
(in two parts)
Bingham Pl. W1—4C 22
Bingham St. N1—3F 11
Bingley Rd. E16—5E 31
Binney St. W1—5C 22
Binns Rd. W4—1A 46
Birch Clo. E16—4A 30
Birch Clo. SE15—5C 54
Birchdale Rd. E7—2E 17
Birches, The. SE7—2D 59
Birchfield St. E14—1C 42
Birch Gro. SE12—5B 72
Birchington Rd. NW6—5C 6
Birchin La. EC3—5C 25
Birchlands Av. SW12—5B 64
Birchmere Row. SE3—5B 58
Birchwood Rd. SW17—5D 79
Birdbrook Rd. SE3—1E 73
Birdcage Wlk. SW1—3E 37
Birdhurst Rd. SW18—3E 63

Bird-in-Bush Rd. SE15—3C 54
Bird-in-Hand Pas. SE23—2E 83
Birdlip Clo. SE15—2A 54
Bird St. W1—5C 22
Birkbeck Hill. SE21—1D 81
Birkbeck Pl. SE21—2E 81
Birkbeck Rd. E8—2B 12
Birkbeck Rd. SW19—5D 77
Birkbeck St. E2—2D 27
Birkenhead St. WC1—2A 24
Birkhall Rd. SE6—1F 85
Birkwood Clo. SW12—5F 65
Birley St. SW11—5C 50
Biscay Rd. W6—1F 47
Biscoe Way. SE13—1F 71
Bishop King's Rd. W14—5A 34
Bishop's Av. E13—5D 17
Bishop's Av. SW6—5F 47
Bishop's Bri. Rd. W2—5D 21
Bishopsgate. EC2—5A 26
Bishopsgate Chu. Yd. EC2
—5A 26
Bishop's Pk. Rd. SW6—5F 47
Bishop's Rd. SW6—4B 48
Bishop's Rd. SW11—3A 50
Bishop's Ter. SE11—5C 38
Bishopsthorpe Rd. SE26—4F 83
Bishop St. N1—5E 11
Bishop's Way. E2—1D 27
Bishops Way. NW10—4A 4
Bisson Rd. E15—1E 29
Bittern St. SE1—3E 39
Blackall St. EC2—3A 26
Blackburne's M. W1—1C 36
Blackburn Rd. NW6—3D 7
Blackett St. SW15—1F 61
Blackford's Path. SW15—5C 60
Blackfriars Bri. SE1 & EC4
—1D 39
Black Friars La. EC4—5D 25
Blackfriars Pas. EC4—1D 39
Blackfriars Rd. SE1—3D 39
Blackheath Av. SE10—3F 57
Blackheath Gro. SE3—5B 58
Blackheath Hill. SE10—4E 57
Blackheath Pk. SE3—1B 72
Blackheath Rise. SE13—5E 57
Blackheath Rd. SE10—4D 57
Blackheath Vale. SE3—5A 58
Blackheath Village. SE3—1B 72
Blackhorse Rd. SE8—2A 56
Blacklands Rd. SE6—4E 85
Blacklands Ter. SW3—5B 36
Black Lion La. W6—5C 32
Blackpool Rd. SE15—5D 55
Black Prince Rd. SE1 & SE11
—5B 38

Blackshaw Pl. N1—4A 12
Blackshaw Rd. SW17—4E 77
Blacks Rd. W6—5E 33
Blackstone Est. E8—4D 13
Blackstone Rd. NW2—2E 5
Black Swan Yd. SE1—3A 40
Blackthorn St. E3—3C 28
Blacktree M. SW9—1C 66
Blackwall La. SE10—1A 58
Blackwall Tunnel—2F 43
Blackwall Tunnel App. E14
—1E 43
Blackwall Tunnel Northern App.
E3 & E14—1D 29
Blackwall Tunnel Southern App.
SE10—4A 44
Blackwall Way. E14—1E 43
(in two parts)
Blackwater St. SE22—3B 68
Blackwell Clo. E5—1F 13
Blackwood St. SE17—1F 53
Blade M. SW15—2B 62
Blagdon Rd. SE13—4D 71
Blagrove Rd. W10—4A 20
Blair Clo. N1—3E 11
Blairderry Rd. SW2—2A 80
Blair St. E14—5E 29
Blake Gdns. SW6—4D 49
Blakeley Cotts. SE10—3F 43
Blakemore Rd. SW16—3A 80
Blakeney Clo. E8—2C 12
Blakeney Clo. NW1—4F 9
Blakenham Rd. SW17—4B 78
Blake Rd. E16—3B 30
Blaker Rd. E15—5E 15
Blake's Rd. SE15—3A 54
Blanchard Way. E8—3C 12
Blanch Clo. SE15—3E 55
Blanchedowne. SE5—2F 67
Blanche St. E16—3B 30
Blandfield Rd. SW12—5C 64
Blandford Rd. W4—4A 32
Blandford Sq. NW1—3A 22
Blandford St. W1—4C 22
Bland St. SE9—2F 73
Blann Clo. SE9—4F 73
Blantyre St. SW10—3F 49
Blashford St. SE13—5F 71
Blasker Wlk. E14—1D 57
Blechynden St. W10—1F 33
Blegborough Rd. SW16—5E 79
Blendworth Way. SE15—3A 54
Blenheim Cres. W11—1A 34
Blenheim Gdns. NW2—3E 5
Blenheim Gdns. SW2—4B 66
Blenheim Gro. SE15—5C 54
Blenheim Pas. NW8—1E 21

Blenheim Rd. E6—2F 31
Blenheim Rd. E15—1A 16
Blenheim Rd. NW8—1E 21
Blenheim Rd. W4—4A 32
Blenheim St. W1—5D 23
Blenheim Ter. NW8—1E 21
Blenkarne Rd. SW11—4B 64
Blessington Clo. SE13—1F 71
Blessington Rd. SE13—2F 71
Bletchley St. N1—1E 25
Bletsoe Wlk. N1—1E 25
Blincoe Clo. SW19—2F 75
Bliss Cres. SE13—5D 57
Blissett St. SE10—4E 57
Blithfield St. W8—4D 35
Bloemfontein Av. W12—2D 33
Bloemfontein Rd. W12—1D 33
Blomfield Rd. W9—4D 21
Blomfield St. EC2—4F 25
Blomfield Vs. W2—4D 21
Blondel St. SW11—5C 50
Blondin St. E3—1C 28
Bloomburg St. SW1—5F 37
Bloomfield Ter. SW1—1C 50
Bloom Gro. SE27—2D 81
Bloomhall Rd. SE19—5F 81
Bloom Pk. Rd. SW6—3B 48
Bloomsbury Pl. SW18—3E 63
Bloomsbury Pl. WC1—4A 24
Bloomsbury Sq. WC1—4A 24
Bloomsbury Sq. WC1—4F 23
Bloomsbury Way.WC1—4A 24
Biore Clo. SW8—4F 51
Blossom St. E1—3A 26
Blount St. E14—5A 28
Blucher Rd. SE5—3E 53
Blue Anchor La. SE16—5C 40
Blue Anchor Yd. E1—1C 40
Blue Ball Yd. SW1—2E 37
Bluebell Clo. SE26—4B 82
Blundell St. N7—4A 10
Blurton Rd. E5—1E 13
Blyth Clo. E14—5F 43
Blythe Clo. SE6—5B 70
Blythe Hill. SE6—5B 70
Blythe Hill La. SE6—5B 70
Blythe Rd. W14—4F 33
Blythe St. E2—2D 27
Blythe Vale. SE6—1B 84
Boade's M. NW3—1F 7
Boadicea St. N1—5B 10
Boathouse Wlk. SE15—3C 54
Bob Anker Clo. E13—2C 30
Bobbin Clo. SW4—1E 65
Bob Marley Way. SE24—2C 66
Bocking St. E8—5D 13
Boddicott Clo. SW19—2A 76

Bodley Mnr. Way. SW2—5C 66
Bodmin St. SW18—1C 76
Bodney Rd. E8—2D 13
Bohemia Pl. E8—3C 13
Boileau Rd. SW13—3C 46
Bolden St. SE8—5D 57
Boleyn Rd. E6—1F 31
Boleyn Rd. E7—4C 16
Boleyn Rd. N16—2A 12
Bolina Rd. SE16—1E 55
Bolingbroke Gro. SW11—3A 64
Bolingbroke Rd. W14—4F 33
Bolingbroke Wlk.SW11—4A 50
Bolney Ga. SW7—3A 36
Bolney St. SW8—3B 52
Bolsover St. W1—3D 23
Bolt Ct. EC4—5C 24
Bolton Cres. SE5—3D 53
Bolton Gdns. NW10—1F 19
Bolton Gdns. SW5—1D 49
Bolton Gdns. M. SW10—1E 49
Bolton Rd. E15—3B 16
Bolton Rd. NW8—5D 7
Bolton Rd. NW10—5A 4
Boltons, The. SW10—1E 49
Bolton St. W1—2D 37
Bombay St. SE16—5D 41
Bomore Rd. W11—1A 34
Bonar Rd. SE15—3C 54
Bonchurch Rd. W10—4A 20
Bonding Yd. Wlk. SE16—4A 42
Bond St. E15—2A 16
Bond St. (New) W1—5D 23
Bond St. (Old) W1
Bond W4—5A 32
Bond Way. SW8—2A 52
Bonfield Rd. SE13—2E 71
Bonham Rd. SW2—3B 66
Bonhill St. EC2—3F 25
Bon Marche Ter. SE27—4A 82
Bonner Rd. E2—1E 27
Bonner St. E2—1F 27
Bonneville Gdns. SW4—4E 65
Bonnington Sq. SW8—2B 52
Bonny St. NW1—4E 9
Bonsor St. SE5—3A 54
Bonville Rd. Brom—5B 86
Booker Clo. E14—4B 28
Boones Rd. SE13—2A 72
Boone St. SE13—2A 72
Boord St. SE10—4A 44
Booth's Pl. W1—4E 23
Boot St. N1—2A 26
Border Cres. SE26—5D 83
Border Rd. SE26—5D 83
Bordon Wlk. SW15—5C 60
Boreham Av. E16—5C 30

Borland Rd. SE15—2E 69
Borneo St. SW15—1E 61
Borough High St. SE1—3E 39
Borough Rd. SE1—4D 39
Borrett Clo. SE17—1E 53
Borrodaile Rd. SW18—4D 63
Borthwick M. E15—1A 16
Borthwick Rd. E15—1A 16
Borthwick St. SE8—1C 56
Bosbury Rd. SE6—3E 85
Boscobel Pl. SW1—5C 36
Boscobel St. NW8—3F 21
Boscombe Clo. E5—2A 14
Boscombe Rd. W12—3C 32
Boss St. SE1—3B 40
Boston Gdns. W4—2A 46
Boston Pl. NW1—3B 22
Boston St. E2—1C 26
Boswell Ct. WC1—4A 24
Boswell St. WC1—4A 24
Bosworth Rd. W10—3A 20
Botha Rd. E13—4D 31
Bothwell Clo. E16—4B 30
Bothwell St. W6—2F 47
Botolph La. EC3—1A 40
Botts M. W2—5C 20
Boulcott St. E1—5F 27
Boulevard, The. SW17—2C 78
Boundaries Rd. SW12—2B 78
Boundary La. E13—3F 31
Boundary La. SE17—2E 53
Boundary Pas. E2—3B 26
Boundary Rd. E13—1E 31
Boundary Rd. NW8—5E 7
Boundary Rd. SW19—5F 77
Boundary Row. SE1—3D 39
Boundary St. E2—2B 26
(in two parts)
Boundfield Rd. SE6—3A 86
Bourbon Ho. SE6—4E 85
Bourchier St. W1—1F 37
Bourdon St. W1—1D 37
Bourke Clo. NW10—3A 4
Bourke Clo. SW4—4A 66
Bourlet Clo. W1—4E 23
Bournbrook Rd. SE3—1F 73
Bourne Est. EC1—4C 24
Bournemouth Rd. SE15—5C 54
Bourneside Gdns. SE6—5E 85
Bourne St. SW1—5C 36
Bourne Ter. W2—4D 21
Bournevale Rd. SW16—4A 80
Bourneville Rd. SE6—5C 70
Bousefield Rd. SE14—5F 55
Boutflower Rd. SW11—2A 64
Bouverie Pl. W2—5F 21
Bouverie St. EC4—5C 24

Boveney Rd. SE23—5F 69
Bovill Rd. SE23—5F 69
Bovingdon Rd. SW6—4D 49
Bowater Clo. SW2—4A 66
Bowater Pl. SE3—3D 59
Bowater Rd. SE18—4F 45
Bow Bri. Est. E3—2D 29
Bow Comn. La. E3—3A 28
Bowden St. SE11—1C 52
Bowditch. SE8—1B 56
Bowen Dri. SE21—3A 82
Bowen St. E14—5D 29
Bower Av. SE10—4A 58
Bowerdean St. SW6—4D 49
Bowerman Av. SE14—2A 56
Bower St. E1—5F 27
Bowes Rd. W3—1A 32
Bowfell Rd. W6—2E 47
Bowie Clo. SW4—5F 65
Bow Industrial Pk. E15—3C 16
Bowland Rd. SW4—2F 65
Bow La. EC4—5E 25
Bowl Ct. EC2—3A 26
Bowles Rd. SE1—2C 54
Bowley La. SE19—5B 82
Bowley St. E14—1B 42
Bowling Grn. Clo. SW15—5D 61
Bowling Grn. La. EC1—3C 24
Bowling Grn. Pl. SE1—3F 39
Bowling Grn. St. SE11—2C 52
Bowling Grn. Wlk. N1—2A 26
Bowman Av. E16—1B 44
Bowman M. SW18—1B 76
Bowmans Lea. SE23—5E 69
Bowness Cres. SW15—5A 74
Bowness Rd. SE6—5D 71
Bowood Rd. SW11—3C 64
Bow Rd. E3—2B 28
Bow St. E15—2A 16
Bow St. WC2—5A 24
Bowyer Pl. SE5—3E 53
Bowyer St. SE5—3E 53
Boxall Rd. SE21—4A 68
Boxley St. E16—2D 45
Boxworth Gro. N1—5B 10
Boyce Way. E13—3C 30
Boydel Ct. NW8—4F 7
Boyd Rd. SW19—5F 77
Boyd St. E1—5C 26
Boyfield St. SE1—3D 39
Boyland Rd. Brom—5B 86
Boyle St. W1—1E 37
Boyne Rd. SE13—1E 71
Boyne Ter. M. W11—2B 34
Boyson Rd. SE17—2E 53
Boythorn Rd. SE16—1D 55

Boythorn Way. SE16—1D 55
Boyton Clo. E1—3E 27
Brabazon St. E14—4D 29
Brabourne Clo. SE19—5A 82
Brabourn Gro. SE15—5E 55
Bracewell Rd. W10—4E 19
Bracken Av. SW12—5C 64
Brackenbury Gdns. W6—4D 33
Brackenbury Rd. W6—4D 33
Bracken Gdns. SW13—5C 46
Brackley Rd. W4—1A 46
Brackley St. EC1—3E 25
Brackley Ter. W4—1A 46
Bracklyn St. N1—1F 25
Bracknell Gdns. NW3—1D 7
Bracknell Way. NW3—1D 7
Bradbourne St. SW6—5C 48
Bradbury St. N16—2A 12
Braddyll St. SE10—1A 58
Braden St. W9—3D 21
Bradfield Rd. E16—3C 44
Bradford Clo. SE26—4D 83
Bradford Rd. W3—3A 32
Bradgate Rd. SE6—4D 71
Brading Rd. SW2—5B 66
Bradiston Rd. W9—2B 20
Bradley Clo. N7—3A 10
Bradley M. SW17—1B 78
Bradley Rd. SE19—5E 81
Bradley's Clo. N1—1C 24
Bradmead. SW8—3D 51
Bradmore Pk. Rd. W6—5D 33
Bradstock Rd. E9—3F 13
Brad St. SE1—2C 38
Brady St. E1—3D 27
Braemar Av. SW19—2C 76
Braemar Rd. E13—3B 30
Braeside. Beck—5C 84
Braes St. N1—4D 11
Braganza St. SE17—1D 53
Braham St. E1—5B 26
Braid Av. W3—5A 18
Braidwood Rd. SE6—1F 85
Braidwood St. SE1—2A 40
Brailsford Rd. SW2—4C 66
Braintree St. E2—2E 27
Bramah Grn. SW9—4C 52
Bramall Clo. E15—2B 16
Bramber Rd. W14—2B 48
Bramble Gdns. W12—1B 32
Bramcote Gro. SE16—1E 55
Bramcote Rd. SW15—2D 61
Bramdean Cres. SE12—1C 86
Bramdean Gdns. SE12—1C 86
Bramerton St. SW3—2A 50
Bramfield Rd. SW11—4A 64
Bramford Rd. SW18—2E 63

Bramham Gdns. SW5—1D 49
Bramhope La. SE7—2D 59
Bramlands Clo. SW11—1A 64
Bramley Rd. W10—1F 33
Bramley St. W10—5F 19
Brampton Rd. E6—2F 31
Bramshaw Rd. E9—3F 13
Bramshill Rd. NW10—1A 18
Bramshot Av. SE7—2C 58
Bramston Rd. NW10—1C 18
Brancaster Rd. SE16—3A 80
Branch Pl. N1—5F 11
Branch Rd. E14—1A 42
Brandlehow Rd. SW15—2B 62
Brandon Est. SE17—2D 53
Brandon Rd. N7—4A 10
Brandon St. SE17—5E 39
(in two parts)
Brandram Rd. SE13—1A 72
Brandreth Rd. SW17—2C 78
Brand St. SE10—3E 57
Brangbourne Rd. Brom—5E 85
Brangton Rd. SE11—1B 52
Branksea St. SW6—3A 48
Branksome Rd. SW2—3A 66
Branscombe St. SE13—1D 71
Bransdale Clo. NW6—5C 6
Brantwood Rd. SE24—3E 67
Brassey Rd. NW6—3B 6
Brassey Sq. SW11—1C 64
Brassie Av. W3—5A 18
Brasted Clo. SE26—4E 83
Brathway Rd. SW18—5C 62
Bratley St. E1—3C 26
Bravington Pl. W9—3B 20
Bravington Rd. W9—2B 20
Braxfield Rd. SE4—2A 70
Brayards Rd. SE15—5D 55
Braybrook St. W12—4B 18
Brayburne Av. SW4—5E 51
Bray Cres. SE16—3F 41
Bray Dri. E16—1B 44
Brayfield Ter. N1—4C 10
Brayford Sq. E1—5E 27
Bray Pas. E16—1C 44
Bray Pl. SW3—5B 36
Bread St. EC4—5E 25
Breakspears Rd. SE4—2B 70
Breamore Clo. SW15—1C 74
Bream's Bldgs. EC4—5B 24
Bream St. E3—4C 14
Breasley Clo. SW15—2D 61
Brechin Pl. SW7—5E 35
Brecknock Rd.—1E 9
N7 1-113 & 2-142
N19 remainder

Brecknock Rd. Est. N7—1F 9
Brecon Rd. W6—2A 48
Bredhurst Clo. SE20—5E 83
Bredon Rd. SE5—1E 67
Breer St. SW6—1D 63
Breezer's Hill. E1—1C 40
Bremner Rd. SW7—4E 35
Brenchley Gdns. SE23—4E 69
Brenda Rd. SW17—2B 78
Brendon Av. NW10—2A 4
Brendon St. W1—5A 22
Brenley Gdns. SE9—2F 73
Brenthouse Rd. E9—3E 13
Brenthurst Rd. NW10—3B 4
Brenton St. E14—5A 28
Brent Rd. E16—5C 30
Brent Trading Centre. NW10
—2A 4
Bressenden Pl. SW1—4E 37
Brettell St. SE17—1F 53
Brett Ho. Clo. SW15—5F 61
Brett Rd. E8—2D 13
Brewer St. W1—1E 37
Brewery Rd. N7—4A 10
Brewhouse La. E1—2D 41
Brewhouse St. SW15—1A 62
Brewhouse Wlk. SE16—2A 42
Brewhouse Yd. EC1—3D 25
Brewster Gdns. W10—4E 19
Briant St. SE14—4F 55
Briar Rd. NW2—1E 5
Briar Wlk. SW15—2D 61
Briar Wlk. W10—3A 20
Briarwood Rd. SW4—3F 65
Briary Clo. NW3—4A 8
Briary Gdns. Brom—5D 87
Brick Ct. EC4—5C 24
Brickfield Rd. E3—3D 29
Brickfield Rd. SW19—4D 77
Brick La.—3B 26
  E1 1-165 & 2-226
  E2 remainder
Brick St. W1—2D 37
Brickwood Clo. SE26—3D 83
Bride La. EC4—5D 25
Bride St. N7—3B 10
Bridewell Pl. E1—2D 41
Bridewell Pl. EC4—5D 25
Bridford M. W1—4D 23
Bridge App. NW1—4C 8
Bridge Av. W6—5E 33
Bridge Foot. SE1—1A 52
Bridgeford St. SW18—3E 77
Bridge Ho. Quay. E14—2E 43
Bridgeland Rd. E16—5C 30
Bridge La. SW11—4A 50
Bridgeman Rd. N1—4B 10

Bridgeman St. NW8—1A 22
Bridgend Rd. SW18—2E 63
Bridge Pk. SW18—3C 62
Bridgeport Pl. E1—2C 40
Bridge Rd. E15—5F 15
Bridge Rd. NW10—3A 4
Bridge Rd. SW11—1F 63
Bridges Pl. SW6—4B 48
Bridge St. SW1—3A 38
Bridge Ter. E15—4F 15
Bridgetown Clo. SE19—5A 82
Bridge View. W6—1E 47
Bridgewater Rd. E15—5E 15
Bridgewater Sq. EC2—4E 25
Bridgewater St. EC2—4E 25
Bridgeway St. NW1—1F 23
Bridge Yd. SE1—2F 39
Bridle La. W1—1E 37
Bridport Pl. N1—5F 11
  (in two parts)
Bridport Ter. SW8—4F 51
Bridstow Pl. W2—5C 20
Brief St. SE5—4D 53
Brierley Rd. E11—1F 15
Brierley Rd. SW12—2E 79
Brigade St. SE3—5B 58
Brightfield Rd. SE13—3A 72
Brightling Rd. SE4—4B 70
Brightlingsea Pl. E14—1B 42
Brightman Rd. SW18—1F 77
Brighton Gro. SE14—4A 56
Brighton Rd. N16—1A 12
Brighton Ter. SW9—2B 66
Brightside Rd. SE13—4F 71
Bright St. E14—5D 29
Brightwell Cres. SW17—5B 78
Brig M. SE8—2C 56
Brill Pl. NW1—1F 23
Brindley St. SE14—4B 56
Brindley Way. Brom—5C 86
Brinkworth Way. E9—3B 14
Brinsley St. E1—5D 27
Brion Pl. E14—4E 29
Brisbane St. SE5—3F 53
Briscoe Rd. SW19—5F 77
Briset Rd. SE9—1F 73
Briset St. EC1—4D 25
Bristol Gdns. SW15—5E 61
Bristol Gdns. W9—3D 21
Bristol M. W9—3D 21
Bristol Rd. E7—3E 17
Bristow Rd. SE19—5A 82
Britannia Clo. SW4—2F 65
Britannia Rd. SW6—3D 49
Britannia Row. N1—5D 11
Britannia St. WC1—2B 24

Britannia Wlk. N1—2F 25
  (in two parts)
British Gro. W4—1B 46
British Gro. Pas. W6—1B 46
British Gro. S. W6—1B 46
British St. E3—2B 28
Britten's Ct. E1—1C 40
Britten St. SW3—1A 50
Britton St. EC1—3D 25
Brixton Hill. SW2—5A 66
Brixton Hill Pl. SW2—5A 66
Brixton Rd. SW9—1C 66
Brixton Sta. Rd. SW9—1C 66
Brixton Water La. SW2—3B 66
Broadbent St. W1—1D 37
Broadbridge Clo. SE3—3C 58
Broad Ct. WC2—5A 24
Broadfield La. NW1—4F 9
Broadfield Rd. SE6—5A 72
Broadgate. EC2—4A 26
Broadgate Circle. EC2—4A 26
Broadgate Rd. SE16—5F 31
Broadgates Rd. SW18—1F 77
Broadhinton Rd. SW4—1D 65
Broadhurst Clo. NW6—3E 7
Broadhurst Gdns. NW6—3D 7
Broadlands Av. SW16—2A 80
Broadlands Clo. SW16—2A 80
Broadlands Rd. Brom—4D 87
Broadley St. NW8—4F 21
Broadley Ter. NW1—3A 22
Broadmead. SE6—3C 84
Broad Sanctuary. SW1—3F 37
Broadstone Pl. W1—4C 22
Broad St. Av. EC2—4A 26
Broad Wlk. NW1—1C 22
Broad Wlk. SE3—5E 59
Broad Wlk., The. W8—2D 35
Broadwall. SE1—2C 38
Broadwater Rd. SW17—4A 78
Broadway. E13—1D 31
Broadway. E15—4F 15
Broadway. SW1—4F 37
Broadway Mkt. E8—5D 13
Broadwick St. W1—1E 37
Broad Yd. EC1—3D 25
Brocas Clo. NW3—4A 8
Brockham Clo. SW19—5B 76
Brockham Dri. SW2—5B 66
Brockham St. SE1—4E 39
Brockill Cres. SE4—2A 70
Brocklebank Rd. SE7—5D 45
Brocklebank Rd. SW18—5E 63
Brocklebank Rd. Industrial Est.
  SE7—5D 45
Brocklehurst St. SE14—3F 55
Brockley Cross. SE4—1A 70

Brockley Footpath. SE4—3A 70
Brockley Footpath. SE15
—2E 69
Brockley Gdns. SE4—5B 56
Brockley Gro. SE4—3B 70
Brockley Hall Rd. SE4—3A 70
Brockley Pk. SE23—5A 70
Brockley Rise. SE23—1A 84
Brockley Rd. SE4—3A 70
Brockley View. SE23—5A 70
Brockley Way. SE4—3A 70
Brockman Rise. Brom—4F 85
Brock Pl. E3—3D 29
Brock Rd. E13—4D 31
Brock St. SE15—1E 69
Brockwell Pk. Gdns. SE24
—5D 67
Brockworth Clo. SE15—2A 54
Brodie St. SE1—1B 54
Brodlove La. E1—1F 41
Brodrick Rd. SW17—2A 78
Brokesley St. E3—2B 28
Broke Wlk. E8—5C 12
Bromar Rd. SE5—1A 68
Bromells Rd. SW4—2E 65
Bromfelde Rd. SW4—1F 65
Bromfelde Wlk. SW4—5A 52
Bromfield St. N1—1C 24
Bromley Hall Rd. E14—4E 29
Bromley High St. E3—2D 29
Bromley Hill. Brom—5A 86
Bromley Pl. W1—4E 23
Bromley Rd.—1D 85
 SE6 1-427 & 2-394
 Brom remainder
Bromley St. E1—5F 27
Brompton Pk. Cres. SW6
—2D 49
Brompton Pl. SW3—4B 36
Brompton Rd. SW3 & SW1
—5A 36
Brompton Sq. SW3—4A 36
Bromyard Av. W3—1A 32
Brondesbury M. NW6—4C 6
Brondesbury Pk. NW6—4E 5
 NW6 1-97 & 2-64
 NW2 remainder
Brondesbury Rd. NW6—1B 20
Brondesbury Vs. NW6—1B 20
Bronsart Rd. SW6—3A 48
Bronte Clo. E7—1C 16
Bronti Clo. SE17—1E 53
Bronze St. SE8—3C 56
Brookbank Rd. SE13—1C 70
Brookdale Rd. SE6—5D 71
Brook Dri. SE11—4C 38

Brookehowse Rd. SE6—2C 84
Brooke's Ct. EC1—4C 24
Brooke St. EC1—4C 24
Brookfield Rd. E9—3A 14
Brook Gdns. SW13—1B 60
Brook Ga. W1—1B 36
Brook Grn. W6—4F 33
Brooking Rd. E7—2C 16
Brooklands. SW19—2D 77
Brooklands Pk. SE3—1C 72
Brooklands St. SW8—4F 51
Brook La. SE3—5D 59
Brook La. Brom—5C 86
Brooklands Rd. SE8—4C 56
Brook Pas. SW6—3C 48
Brooksbank St. E9—3E 13
Brooksby M. N1—4C 10
Brooksby St. N1—4C 10
Brooksby's Wlk. E9—2F 13
Brook's M. W1—1D 37
Brooks Rd. E13—5C 16
Brook St. W1—1D 37
Brook St. W2—1F 35
Brooksville Av. NW6—5A 6
Brookview Rd. SW16—5E 79
Brookville Rd. SW6—3B 48
Brookway. SE3—1C 72
Brookwood Av. SW13—5B 46
Brookwood Rd. SW18—1B 76
Broome Way. SE5—3F 53
Broomfield St. E14—4D 29
Broomgrove Rd. SW9—5B 52
Broomhill Rd. SW18—3C 62
Broomhouse La. SW6—5C 48
Broomhouse Rd. SW6—5C 48
Broomsleigh St. NW6—2B 6
Broomwood Rd. SW11—4B 64
Broseley Gro. SE26—5A 84
Brougham Rd. E8—5C 12
Brough Clo. SW8—3A 52
Brough St. SW8—3A 52
Broughton Dri. SW9—2D 67
Broughton Rd. SW6—5D 49
Broughton St. SW8—5D 51
Brownfield St. E14—5E 29
Drown Hart Gdns W1—1C 36
Brownhill Rd. SE6—5D 71
Browning Clo. W9—3E 21
Browning M. W1—4C 22
Browning St. SE17—1E 53
Brownlow M. WC1—3B 24
Brownlow Rd. E7—1C 16
Brownlow Rd. E8—5C 12
Brownlow Rd. NW10—4A 4
Brownlow St. WC1—4B 24
Brown's Bldgs. EC3—5A 26

Browns La. NW5—2D 9
Brown St. W1—5B 22
Broxash Rd. SW11—4C 64
Broxholm Rd. SE27—3C 80
Broxted St. SE6—2B 84
Broxwood Way. NW8—5A 8
Bruce Clo. W10—4F 19
Bruce Hall M. SW17—4C 78
Bruce Rd. E3—2D 29
Brudenell Rd. SW17—3B 78
Bruges Pl. NW1—4E 9
Brunel Est. W2—4C 20
Brunel Rd. SE16—3E 41
Brunel Rd. W3—4A 18
Brunel St. E16—5B 30
Brune St. E1—4B 26
Brunner Ho. SE6—4E 85
Brunswick Centre. WC1—3A 24
Brunswick Ct. SE1—3A 40
Brunswick Gdns. W8—2C 34
Brunswick M. W1—5B 22
Brunswick Pk. SE5—4A 54
Brunswick Pl. N1—2F 25
Brunswick Quay. SE16—4F 41
Brunswick Rd. E14—5E 29
Brunswick Sq. WC1—3A 24
Brunswick Vs. SE5—4A 54
Brunton Pl. E14—5A 28
Brushfield St. E1—4A 26
Brussels Rd. SW11—2F 63
Bruton La. W1—1D 37
Bruton Pl. W1—1D 37
Bruton St. W1—1D 37
Bryan Av. NW10—4D 5
Bryan Rd. SE16—3B 42
Bryanston M. E. W1—4B 22
Bryanston M. W. W1—5B 22
Bryanston Pl. W1—4B 22
Bryanston Sq. W1—5B 22
Bryanston St. W1—5B 22
Bryant St. E15—4F 15
Bryantwood Rd. N7—2C 10
Bryden Clo. SE26—5A 84
Brydges Pl. WC2—1A 38
Brydges Rd. E15—2F 15
Brydon Wlk. N1—5A 10
Brymay Clo. E3—1C 28
Brynmaer Rd. SW11—4B 60
Bryony Rd. W12—1C 32
Buchanan Gdns. NW10—1D 19
Buchan Rd. SE15—1E 69
Bucharest Rd. SW18—5E 63
Buckden Clo. SE12—4C 72
Buckfast St. E2—2C 26
Buck Hill Wlk. W2—1F 35
Buckhold Rd. SW18—4C 62
Buckhurst St. E1—3D 27

Buckingham Ga. SW1—3E 37
Buckingham La. SE23—5A 70
Buckingham M. NW10—1B 18
Buckingham Pal. Rd. SW1
　　　　　　　　—5D 37
Buckingham Pl. SW1—4E 37
Buckingham Rd. E15—2B 16
Buckingham Rd. N1—3A 12
Buckingham Rd. NW10—1B 18
Buckingham St. WC2—1A 38
Buckland Cres. NW3—3F 7
Buckland St. N1—1F 25
Bucklers All. SW6—2B 48
Bucklersbury. EC4—5F 25
Buckle St. E1—5B 26
Buckley Rd. NW6—4B 6
Buckmaster Rd. SW11—3A 64
Bucknall St. WC2—5A 24
Bucknall Clo. SW2—2B 66
Buckner Rd. SW2—2B 66
Buckstone Clo. SE23—4E 69
Buck St. NW1—4D 9
Buckters Rents. SE16—2A 42
Buckthorne Rd. SE4—3A 70
Budge Row. EC4—1F 39
Buer Rd. SW6—5A 48
Bugsby's Way. SE10 & SE7
　　　　　　　　—5B 44
Bulinga St. SW1—5A 38
Bull All. SE1—1C 38
Bullard's Pl. E2—2F 27
Bullen St. SW11—5A 50
Buller Rd. NW10—2F 19
Bullivant St. E14—1E 43
Bull Rd. E15—1B 30
Bull's Gdns. SW3—5A 36
Bull Wharf La. EC4—1E 39
Bull Yd. SE15—4C 54
Bulmer M. W11—2C 34
Bulmer Pl. W11—2C 34
Bulstrode Pl. W1—4C 22
Bulstrode St. W1—5C 22
Bulwer St. W12—2E 33
Bunhill Row. EC1—3F 25
Bunhouse Pl. SW1—1C 50
Bunsen St. E3—1A 28
Burbage Clo. SE1—4F 39
Burbage Rd.—4E 67
　SE24 1-105 & 2-118
　SE21 remainder
Burcham St. E14—5E 29
Burchell Rd. SE15—4D 55
Burcote Rd. SW18—5F 63
Burder Clo. N1—3A 12
Burder Rd. N1—3A 12
Burdett M. NW3—3F 7

Burdett M. W2—5D 21
Burdett Rd.—3A 28
　E3 1-207 & 2-230
　E14 remainder
Burdett St. SE1—4C 38
Burfield Clo. SW17—4F 77
Burford Rd. E15—5F 15
Burford Rd. SE6—2B 84
Burford Wlk. SW6—3E 49
Burgess Hill. NW2—1C 6
Burgess Pk. Industrial Est. SE5
　　　　　　　　—3F 53
Burgess Rd. E15—1A 16
Burgess St. E14—4C 28
Burge St. SE1—4F 39
Burghill Rd. SE26—4A 84
Burghley Rd. NW5—1D 9
Burghley Rd. SW19—4A 76
Burgh St. N1—1D 25
Burgos Gro. SE10—4D 57
Burgoyne Rd. SW9—1B 66
Burke Rd. SE15—2A 60
Burke St. E16—4B 30
Burland Rd. SW11—3B 64
Burleigh Pl. SW15—3F 61
Burleigh St. WC2—1B 38
Burley Rd. E16—5D 31
Burlington Arc. W1—1E 37
Burlington Clo. W9—3C 20
Burlington Gdns. W1—1E 37
Burlington Pl. SW6—5A 48
Burlington Rd. SW6—5A 48
Burma M. N16—1F 11
Burma Rd. N16—1F 11
Burma Ter. SE19—5A 82
Burmester Rd. SW17—3E 77
Burnaby St. SW10—3E 49
Burnage Ct. SW19—4E 83
Bunbury Rd. SW12—1E 79
Burness Clo. N7—3B 10
Burne St. NW1—4A 22
Burnett Clo. E9—2E 13
Burney St. SE10—3E 57
Burnfoot Av. SW6—4A 48
Burnham St. E2—2E 27
Burnley Rd. NW10—2B 4
Burnley Rd. SW9—5B 52
Burnsall St. SW3—1A 50
Burns Rd. NW10—5B 4
Burns Rd. SW11—5B 50
Burnt Ash Hill. SE12—4B 72
Burnt Ash La. Brom—5C 86
Burnt Ash Rd. SE12—3B 72
Burnthwaite Rd. SW6—3B 48
Burntwood Clo. SW18—1A 78
Burntwood Grange Rd. SW18
　　　　　　　　—1A 78

Burntwood La. SW17—3E 77
Buross St. E1—5D 26
Burrard Rd. E16—5D 31
Burrard Rd. NW6—1C 6
Burr Clo. E1—2C 40
Burrell St. SE1—2D 39
Burrell's Wharf Development.
　　　　　　　　E14—1D 57
Burrows M. SE1—3D 39
Burrows Rd. NW10—2E 19
Burrow Wlk. SE21—5E 67
Burr Rd. SW18—1C 76
Burslem St. E1—5C 26
Burstock Rd. SW15—2A 62
Burston Rd. SW15—3F 61
Burton Gro. SE17—1F 53
Burton La. SW9—5C 52
Burton M. SW1—5C 36
Burton Pl. WC1—3F 23
Burton Rd. NW6—4B 6
Burton Rd. SW9—5D 53
　(in two parts)
Burtons Ct. E15—4F 15
Burton St. WC1—2F 23
Burt Rd. E16—2E 45
Burtwell La. SE27—4F 81
Burwell Clo. E1—5D 27
Burwell Wlk. E3—3C 28
Burwood Pl. W2—5A 22
Bury Ct. EC3—5A 26
Bury Pl. WC1—4A 24
Bury St. EC3—5A 26
Bury St. SW1—2E 37
Bury Wlk. SW3—5A 36
Busby M. NW5—3F 9
Busby Pl. NW5—3F 9
Busby St. E2—3B 26
Bushberry Rd. E9—3A 14
Bush Cotts. SW18—3C 62
Bushell Clo. SW2—2B 80
Bushell St. E1—2C 40
Bushey Hill Rd. SE5—4A 54
Bushey Rd. E13—1E 31
Bush La. EC4—1F 39
Bushnell Rd. SW17—3D 79
Bush Rd. E8—5D 13
Bush Rd. SE8—5F 41
Bushy Down. SW12—2D 79
Butcher Row—1F 41
　E1 4-12
　E14 remainder
Butchers Rd. E16—5C 30
Bute Gdns. W6—5F 33
Bute St. SW7—5F 35
Bute Wlk. N1—3F 11
Butler Rd. NW10—4A 4
Butler St. E2—2E 27

Buttermere Dri. SW15—3A 62
Buttermere Wlk. E8—3B 12
Butterwick. W6—5F 33
Buttesland St. N1—2F 25
Butts Rd. Brom—5A 86
Buxted Clo. E8—4B 12
Buxton Rd. E15—2A 16
Buxton Rd. NW2—3D 5
Buxton Rd. SW14—1A 60
Buxton St. E1—3B 26
Byam St. SW6—5E 49
Bye, The. W3—5A 18
Byfeld Gdns. SW13—4C 46
Byford Clo. E15—4A 16
Bygrove St. E14—5D 29
Byne Rd. SE26—5E 83
Byng Pl. WC1—3F 23
Byng St. E14—3C 42
Byrne Rd. SW12—1D 79
Byron Clo. E8—5C 12
Byron St. E14—5E 29
Bythorn St. SW9—1B 66
Byton Rd. SW17—5B 78
Byward St. EC3—1A 40
Bywater Pl. SE16—2A 42
Bywater St. SW3—1B 50

Cabbell St. NW1—4A 22
Cable Pl. SE10—4E 57
Cable St. E1—1C 40
Cabot Way. E6—5F 17
Cabul Rd. SW11—5A 50
Cactus Wlk. W12—5B 18
Cadbury Wlk. SE16—5B 40
Cadbury Way. SE16—5C 40
Cadell Clo. E2—1B 26
Cade Rd. SE10—4F 57
Cader Rd. SW18—4E 63
Cadet Pl. SE10—1A 58
Cadiz St. SE17—1E 53
Cadley Ter. SE23—2E 83
Cadogan Clo. E9—4B 14
Cadogan Gdns. SW3—5B 36
Cadogan Ga. SW1—5B 36
Cadogan La. SW1—4C 36
Cadogan Pl. SW1—4B 36
Cadogan Sq. SW1—4B 36
Cadogan St. SW3—5B 36
Cadogan Ter. E9—3B 14
Caedmon Rd. N7—1B 10
Cahill St. EC1—3E 25
Cahir St. E14—5D 43
Cairns Rd. SW11—3A 64
Caister M. SW12—5D 65
Caistor Pk. Rd. E15—5B 16

Caistor Rd. SW12—5D 65
Caithness Rd. W14—4F 33
Calabria Rd. N5—3D 11
Calais Ga. SE15—4D 53
Calais St. SE5—4D 53
Calbourne Rd. SW12—5B 64
Caldecot Rd. SE5—5E 53
Calderon Pl. W10—4E 19
Calderon Rd. E11—1E 15
Caldervale Rd. SW4—3F 65
Caldew St. SE5—2F 53
Caldwell St. SW9—3B 52
Caldwell Yd. EC4—1E 39
Caldy Wlk. N1—3E 11
Caleb St. SE1—3E 39
Caledonia M. SW11—1E 63
Caledonia St. N1—1A 24
Cale St. SW3—1A 50
Caletock Way. SE10—1B 58
Calico Row. SW11—1E 63
Callaghan Clo. SE13—2A 72
Callander Rd. SE6—2D 85
Callcott Rd. NW6—4B 6
Callcott St. W8—2C 34
Callender Rd. SW7—4F 35
Callingham Clo. E14—4B 28
Callow St. SW3—2F 49
Calmington Rd. SE5—2A 54
Calonne Rd. SW19—4F 75
Calshot St. N1—1B 24
Calthorpe St. WC1—3B 24
Calton Av. SE21—4A 68
Calverley Clo. BR3—5C 86
Calvert Av. E2—2B 26
Calvert Rd. SE10—1B 58
Calvert St. NW1—5C 8
Calvin St. E1—3B 26
Calydon Rd. SE7—1D 59
Calypso Way. SE16—5B 42
Cambalt Rd. SW15—3F 61
Cambert Way. SE3—2D 73
Camberwell Chu. St. SE5—4F 53
Camberwell Glebe. SE5—4A 54
Camberwell Grn. SE5—4F 53
Camberwell Gro. SE5—4F 53
Camberwell New Rd. SE5
—3C 52
Camberwell Pas. SE5—4E 53
Camberwell Rd. SE5—2E 53
Camberwell Sta. Rd. SE5
—4E 53
Camborne Rd. SW18—5C 62
Cambourne M. W11—5A 20
Cambray Rd. SW12—1E 79
Cambrian Clo. SE27—3D 81

Cambria Rd. SE5—1E 67
Cambria St. SW6—3D 49
Cambridge Av. NW6—1C 20
Cambridge Cir. WC2—5F 23
Cambridge Cres. E2—1D 27
Cambridge Dri. SE12—3C 72
Cambridge Gdns. NW6—1C 20
Cambridge Gdns. W10—5F 19
Cambridge Ga. NW1—3D 23
Cambridge Ga. M. NW1—3D 23
Cambridge Gro. W6—5D 33
Cambridge Heath Rd.—3D 27
 E1 1-183 & 2-154a
 E2 remainder
Cambridge Lodge Vs. E8—5D 13
Cambridge Pl. W8—3D 35
Cambridge Pl. NW6—2C 20
Cambridge Pl. W8—3D 35
Cambridge Rd. NW6—2C 20
 (in two parts)
Cambridge Rd. SW11—4B 50
Cambridge Rd. SW13—5B 46
Cambridge Sq. W2—5A 22
Cambridge St. SW1—5D 37
Cambridge Ter. NW1—2D 23
Cambridge Ter. M. NW1—2D 23
Cambus Rd. E16—4C 30
Camden Est. SE15—4B 54
Camden Gdns. NW1—4D 9
Camden High St. NW1—5D 9
Camden Hill. SE19—5A 82
Camdenhurst St. E14—5A 28
Camden La. N7—2F 9
Camden Lock Pl. NW1—4D 9
Camden M. NW1—3F 9
Camden Pk. Rd. NW1—3F 9
Camden Pas. N1—5D 11
Camden Rd.—4E 9
 NW1 1-227 & 2a-282
 N7 remainder
Camden Row. SE3—5A 58
Camden Sq. NW1—3F 9
Camden Sq. SE15—4B 54
Camden St. NW1—4E 9
Camden Ter. NW1—3F 9
Camden Wlk. N1—5D 11
Camelford Ct. W11—5A 20
Camelford Wlk. W11—5A 20
Camellia St. SW8—3A 52
Camelot Clo. SW19—4C 76
Camera Pl. SW10—2F 49
Cameron Pl. E1—5D 27
Cameron Rd. SE6—2B 84
Cameron Ter. SE12—3D 87
Camerton Clo. E8—3B 12
Camilla Rd. SE16—5D 41
Camlan Rd. Brom—4B 86
Camlet St. E2—3B 26

Camley St. NW1—4F 9
Camomile St. EC3—5A 26
Campana Rd. SW6—4C 48
Campbell Clo. SW16—4F 79
Campbell Rd. E3—2C 28
Campbell Rd. E15—1B 16
Campden Clo. SW19—2A 76
Campden Gro. W8—3C 34
Campden Hill. W8—3C 34
Campden Hill Gdns. W8—2C 34
Campden Hill Pl. W11—2B 34
Campden Hill Rd. W8—2C 34
Campden Hill Sq. W8—2B 34
Campden St. W8—2C 34
Camperdown St. E1—5B 26
Campfield Rd. SE9—5F 73
Campion Cres. SE26—4A 84
Campion Rd. SW15—3E 61
Camplin St. SE14—3F 55
Camp Rd. SW19—5E 75
(in two parts)
Campshill Pl. SE13—3E 71
Campshill Rd. SE13—3E 71
Camp View. SW19—5D 75
Cam Rd. E15—5F 15
Canada Est. SE16—4E 41
Canada Gdns. SE13—3E 71
Canada St. SE16—3F 41
Canada Way. W12—1D 33
Canadian Av. SE6—1D 85
Canal App. SE8—2A 56
Canal Clo. E1—3A 28
Canal Gro. SE15—2C 54
Canal Head. SE15—4C 54
Canal Rd. E3—3A 28
Canal St. SE5—2F 53
Canal Wlk. N1—5F 11
Canal Wlk. SE26—5E 83
Canal Way. W10—3F 19
Canary Wharf Development. E14
—2D 43
Canberra Rd. SE7—2E 59
Canbury M. SE26—3C 82
Cancell Rd. SW9—4C 52
Candahar Rd. SW11—5A 50
Candover St. W1—4E 23
Candy St. E3—5B 14
Canfield Gdns. NW6—4D 7
Canfield Pl. NW6—3E 7
Canford Rd. SW11—3C 64
Canham Rd. W3—3A 32
Cann Hall Rd. E11—1A 16
Canning Cross. SE5—5A 54
Canning Pas. W8—4E 35
Canning Pl. W8—4E 35
Canning Rd. E15—1F 29
Cannizaro Rd. SW19—5E 75

Cannon Dri. E14—2C 42
Cannon Hill. NW6—2C 6
Cannon Row. SW1—3A 38
Cannon St. EC4—5E 25
Cannon St. Rd. E1—5D 27
Canon Beck Rd. SE16—3E 41
Canonbie Rd. SE23—5E 69
Canonbury Gro. N1—4E 11
Canonbury La. N1—4D 11
Canonbury Pk. N. N1—3E 11
Canonbury Pk. S. N1—3E 11
Canonbury Pl. N1—3D 11
(in two parts)
Canonbury Rd. N1—3D 11
Canonbury Sq. N1—4D 11
Canonbury St. N1—4E 11
Canonbury Vs. N1—4D 11
Canon St. N1—5E 11
Canrobert St. E2—1D 27
Cantelowes Rd. NW1—3F 9
Canterbury Cres. SW9—1C 66
Canterbury Gro. SE27—4C 80
Canterbury Pl. SE17—5D 39
Canterbury Rd. NW6—1C 20
Canterbury Ter. NW6—1C 20
Canton St. E14—5C 28
Cantrell Rd. E3—3B 28
Canvey St. SE1—2E 39
Capel Rd.—1D 17
E7 1-165
E12 remainder
Capern Rd. SW18—1E 77
Cape Yd. E1—2C 40
Capland St. NW8—3F 21
Caple Rd. NW10—1B 18
Capper St. WC1—3E 23
Capstan Rd. SE8—5B 42
Capstan Sq. E14—3E 43
Capstan Way. SE16—2A 42
Capstone Rd. Brom—4B 86
Caradoc Clo. W2—5C 20
Caradoc St. SE10—1A 58
Caravel M. SE8—2C 56
Carbis Rd. E14—5B 28
Carburton St. W1—4D 23
Cardale St. E14—4E 43
Carden Rd. SE15—1D 69
Cardigan Rd. E3—1B 28
Cardigan Rd. SW13—5C 46
Cardigan St. SE11—1C 52
Cardinal Cap All. SE1—2E 39
Cardinal Pl. SW15—2F 61
Cardine M. SE15—3D 55
Cardington St. NW1—2E 23
Cardozo Rd. N7—2A 10
Cardross St. W6—4D 33
Cardwell Rd. N7—1A 10

Carew St. SE5—5E 53
Carey Gdns. SW8—4E 51
Carey La. EC2—5E 25
Carey St. WC2—5B 24
Carfax Pl. SW4—2F 65
Carfree Clo. N1—4C 10
Cargill Rd. SW18—1E 77
Carholme Rd. SE23—1B 84
Carisbrooke Gdns. SE15—3B 54
Carker's La. NW5—2D 9
Carleton Gdns. N19—2E 9
Carleton Rd. N7—2F 9
(in two parts)
Carlile Clo. E3—1B 28
Carlingford Rd. NW3—1F 7
Carlisle Av. EC3—5B 26
Carlisle Av. W3—5A 18
Carlisle La. SE1—4B 38
Carlisle M. NW8—4F 21
Carlisle Pl. SW1—4E 37
Carlisle Rd. NW6—5A 6
Carlisle St. W1—5F 23
Carlisle Wlk. E8—3B 12
Carlisle Way. SW17—5C 78
Carlos Pl. W1—1C 36
Carlow St. NW1—1E 23
Carlton Dri. SW15—3A 62
Carlton Gdns. SW1—2F 37
Carlton Grn. SW9—4D 53
Carlton Gro. SE15—4D 55
Carlton Hill. NW8—1D 21
Carlton Ho. Ter. SW1—2F 37
Carlton Rd. E12—1F 17
Carlton Sq. E1—3F 27
(in two parts)
Carlton St. SW1—1F 37
Carlton Ter. SE26—3E 83
Carlton Vale. NW6—1B 20
Carlwell St. SW17—5A 78
Carlyle Pl. SW15—2F 61
Carlyle Sq. SW3—1F 49
Carmalt Gdns. SW15—2E 61
Carmarthen Pl. SE1—3A 40
Carmelite St. EC4—1C 38
Carmen St. E14—5D 29
Carmichael Clo. SW11—1F 63
Carmichael M. SW18—4F 63
Carminia Rd. SW17—2D 79
Carnaby St. W1—5E 23
Carnac St. SE27—4F 81
Carnarvon Rd. E15—3B 16
Carnbrook Rd. SE3—1F 73
Carnegie Pl. SW19—3F 75
Carnegie St. N1—5B 10
Carnie Hall. SW17—3D 79
Carnoustie Dri. N1—4B 10
Carnwath Rd. SW6—1C 62

Caroline Clo. SW16—3B 80
Caroline Gdns. E2—2A 26
Caroline Pl. SW11—5C 50
Caroline Pl. M. W2—1D 35
Caroline St. E1—5F 27
Caroline Ter. SW1—5C 36
Caroline Wlk. W6—2A 48
Carol St. NW1—5E 9
Carpenters Pl. SW4—2F 65
Carpenter's Rd. E15—3C 14
Carpenter St. W1—1D 37
Carrara Wlk. SW9—2C 66
Carriage Dri. E. SW11—3C 50
Carriage Dri. N. SW11—3B 50
Carriage Dri. S. SW11—4B 50
Carriage Dri. W. SW11—3B 50
Carrick M. SE8—2C 56
Carrington Gdns. E7—1C 16
Carrington St. W1—2D 37
Carrol Clo. NW5—1D 9
Carroll Clo. E15—2B 16
Carroun Rd. SW8—3B 52
Carrow Clo. E14—5D 29
Carr St. E14—4A 28
(in two parts)
Carslake Rd. SW15—4E 61
Carson Rd. E16—3C 30
Carson Rd. SE21—2F 81
Carstairs Rd. SE6—3E 85
Carston Clo. SE12—3B 72
Carswell Rd. SE6—5E 71
Carteret St. SW1—3F 37
Carteret Way. SE8—5A 42
Cary Rd. E11—1A 16
Cascades Tower. E14—2C 42
Casella Rd. SE14—3F 55
Casewick Rd. SE27—5C 80
Casino Av. SE24—3F 67
Caspian St. SE5—3F 53
Caspian Wlk. E16—5F 31
Cassidy Rd. SW6—3C 48
(in two parts)

Cassland Rd. E9—4F 13
Casslee Rd. SE6—5B 70
Casson St. E1—4C 26
Castalia Sq. E14—3E 43
Castellain Rd. W9—3D 21
Castello Av. SW15—3E 61
Castelnau. SW13—4E 46
Castelnau Gdns. SW13—2D 47
Castelnau Pl. SW13—2D 47
Castelnau Row. SW13—2D 47
Casterbridge Rd. SE3—1C 72
Castillon Rd. SE6—2A 86
Castlands Rd. SE6—2B 84
Castle Baynard St. EC4—1D 39
Castle Clo. E9—2A 14
Castle Clo. SW19—3F 75
Castlecombe Dri. SW19—5F 61
Castlehaven Rd. NW1—4D 9
Castle Industrial Est. SE17
—5E 39
Castle La. SW1—4E 37
Castle M. NW1—3D 9
Castle Pl. W4—5A 32
Castlereagh St. W1—5B 22
Castle Rd. NW1—3D 9
Castle St. E6—1F 31
Castleton Rd. SE9—4F 87
Castletown Rd. W14—1A 48
Castle Way. SW19—3F 75
Castle Yd. SE1—2D 39
Castor La. E14—1D 43
Caterham Rd. SE13—1F 71
Catesby St. SE17—5F 39
Catford B'way. SE6—5D 71
Catford Hill. SE6—1B 84
Catford M. SE6—5D 71
Catford Rd. SE6—5C 70
Cathay St. SE16—3D 41
Cathcart Rd. SW10—2E 49
Cathcart St. NW5—3D 9
Cathedral Piazza. SW1—4E 37
Cathedral St. SE1—2F 39
Catherine Gro. SE10—4D 57
Catherine Pl. SW1—4E 37
Catherine St. WC2—1B 38
Catherine Wheel All. E1—4A 26
Cathles Rd. SW12—4D 65
Cathnor Hall Ct. W12—3D 33
Cathnor Rd. W12—3D 33
Catling Clo. SE23—3E 83
Catlin St. SE16—1C 54
Cato Rd. SW4—2F 65
Cator Rd. SE26—5F 83
Cator St. SE15—2B 54
(in two parts)
Cato St. W1—5A 22
Catton St. WC1—4B 24

Caudwell Ter. SW18—4F 63
Caulfield Rd. SE15—5D 55
Causeway, The. SW18—2D 63
Causeway, The. SW19—5E 75
Causton St. SW1—5F 37
Cautley Av. SW4—3E 65
Cavalry Gdns. SW15—3B 62
Cavaye Pl. SW10—1E 49
Cavell St. E1—4D 27
Cavendish Av. NW8—1F 21
Cavendish Clo. NW6—3B 6
Cavendish Clo. NW8—2F 21
Cavendish M. N. W1—4D 23
Cavendish M. S. W1—4D 23
Cavendish Pl. W1—5D 23
Cavendish Rd. NW6—4A 6
Cavendish Rd. SW12—4E 65
Cavendish Sq. W1—5D 23
Cavendish St. N1—1F 25
Cave Rd. E13—2D 31
Caversham M. SW3—2B 50
Caversham Rd. NW5—3E 9
Caversham St. SW3—2B 50
Caverswall St. W12—5E 19
Cawnpore St. SE19—5A 82
Caxton Gro. E3—2C 28
Caxton Rd. SW19—5E 77
Caxton Rd. W12—3F 33
Caxton St. SW1—4F 37
Caxton St. N. E16—5B 30
Caxton St. S. E16—1B 44
Caxton Wlk. WC2—5F 23
Cayton St. EC1—2F 25
Cearns Ho. E6—5F 17
Cecil Ct. WC2—1A 38
Cecilia Rd. E8—2B 12
Cecil Rd. E13—5C 16
Cecil Rd. NW10—5A 4
Cedar Clo. SE21—1E 81
Cedar Ct. N1—4E 11
Cedar Ct. SW19—2F 75
Cedarhurst Dri. SE9—3E 73
Cedar Mt. SE9—1F 87
Cedarne Rd. SW6—3D 49
Cedar Rd. NW2—1E 5
Cedars M. SW4—2D 65
Cedars Rd. E15—3A 16
Cedars Rd. SW4—1D 65
Cedars Rd. SW13—5C 46
Cedar Tree Gro. SE27—5D 81
Cedar Way. NW1—4F 9
Celandine Clo. E3—4C 28
Celandine Way. E15—2A 30
Celestial Gdns. SE13—2F 71
Celia Rd. N19—1E 9
Celtic St. E14—4D 29
Cemetery Rd. E7—1B 16

Centaur St. SE1—4B 38
Central Av. SW11—3B 50
Central Hill. SE19—5F 81
Central Pk. Rd. E6—1F 31
Central St. EC1—2E 25
Centre St. E2—1D 27
Centric Clo. NW1—5D 9
Centurion Clo. N7—4B 10
Cephas Av. E1—3E 27
Cephas St. E1—3E 27
Cerise Rd. SE15—5C 54
Cervantes Ct. W2—5D 21
Cester St. E2—5C 12
Ceylon Rd. W14—4F 33
Chadbourn St. E14—4D 29
Chad Grn. E13—5C 16
Chad St. E3—1B 28
Chadwell St. EC1—2C 24
Chadwick Rd. NW10—5B 4
Chadwick Rd. SE15—5B 54
Chadwick St. SW1—4F 37
Chadwin Rd. E13—4D 31
Chagford St. NW1—3B 22
Chalbury Wlk. N1—1B 24
Chalcot Cres. NW1—5B 8
Chalcot Gdns. NW3—3B 8
Chalcot Rd. NW1—4C 8
Chalcot Sq. NW1—4C 8
Chalcroft Rd. SE13—3A 72
Chaldon Rd. SW6—3A 48
Chale Rd. SW2—4A 66
Chalford Rd. SE21—4F 81
Chalgrove Rd. E9—3E 13
Chalk Farm Rd. NW1—4C 8
Chalkhill Rd. W6—5F 33
Chalk Rd. E13—4D 31
Challice Way. SW2—1B 80
Challoner Cres. W14—1B 48
Challoner St. W14—1B 48
Chalsey Rd. SE4—2B 70
Chalton St. NW1—1F 23
Chamberlain Cotts. SE5—4F 53
Chamberlain St. NW1—4B 8
Chamberlayne Rd. NW10—5E 5
Chambers La. NW10—4D 5
Chambers Rd. N7—1A 10
Chambers St. SE16—3C 40
Chamber St. E1—1B 40
Chambers Wharf. SE16—3C 40
Chambord St. E2—2B 26
Champion Gro. SE5—1F 67
Champion Hill. SE5—1F 67
Champion Hill Est. SE5—1A 68
Champion Pk. SE5—5F 53
Champion Rd. SE26—4A 84
Champness Clo. SE27—4F 81
Chancel Industrial Est. NW10
—3B 4

Chancellor Gro. SE21—3E 81
Chancellor's Rd. W6—1E 47
Chancellor's St. W6—1E 47
Chancel St. SE1—2D 39
Chancery La. WC2—5C 24
Chance St. E2 & E1—3B 26
Chandler Av. E16—4C 30
Chandler St. E1—2D 41
Chandlers Way. SW2—5C 66
Chandos Pl. WC2—1A 38
Chandos Rd. E15—2F 15
Chandos Rd. NW2—2E 5
Chandos Rd. NW10—3A 18
Chandos St. W1—4D 23
Change All. EC3—5F 25
Channelsea Rd. E15—5F 15
Chantrey Rd. SW9—1B 66
Chantry St. N1—5D 11
Chant Sq. E15—4F 15
Chant St. E15—4F 15
Chapel Ct. SE1—3F 39
Chapel Ho. St. E14—1D 57
Chapel Mkt. N1—1C 24
Chapel Pl. N1—1C 24
Chapel Pl. W1—5D 23
Chapel Rd. SE27—4D 81
Chapel Side. W2—1D 35
Chapel St. E15—4F 15
Chapel St. NW1—4A 22
Chapel St. SW1—4C 36
Chaplin Clo. SE1—3D 39
Chaplin Rd. E15—1B 30
Chaplin Rd. NW2—3C 4
Chapman Rd. E9—3B 14
Chapman St. E1—1D 41
Chapter Rd. NW2—2C 4
Chapter St. SE17—1D 53
Chapter St. SW1—5F 37
Chapter Ter. SE17—2D 53
Chardin Rd. W4—5A 32
Charecroft Way. W12—3F 33
Charford Rd. E16—4C 30
Chargeable La. E13—3B 30
Chargeable St. E16—3B 30
Chargrove Clo. SE16—3F 41
Charing Cross Rd. WC2—5F 23
Charlbert St. NW8—1A 22
Charlecote Gro. SE26—3D 83
Charles Barry Clo. SW4—1E 65
Charlesfield. SE9—3E 87
Charles La. NW8—1A 22
Charles Pl. NW1—2E 23
Charles Rd. E7—4E 17
Charles II St. SW1—2F 37
Charles Sq. N1—2F 25
Charles St. E16—2E 45
Charles St. SW13—5A 46

Charles St. W1—2D 37
Charles St. Trading Est. E16
—2E 45
Charleston St. SE17—5E 39
Charles Utton Ct. E8—1C 12
Charleville Cir. SE26—5C 82
Charleville Rd. W14—1A 48
Charlmont Rd. SW17—5A 78
Charlotte Despard Av. SW11
—4C 50
Charlotte M. W1—4E 23
Charlotte M. W14—5A 34
Charlotte Pl. SW1—5E 37
Charlotte Pl. W1—4E 23
Charlotte Rd. EC2—2A 26
Charlotte Rd. SW13—4B 46
Charlotte Row. SW4—1E 65
Charlotte St. W1—4E 23
Charlotte Ter. N1—5B 10
Charlton Chu. La. SE7—1E 59
Charlton Dene. SE7—3E 59
Charlton King's Rd. NW5—2F 9
Charlton La. SE7—5F 45
Charlton Pk. La. SE7—3F 59
Charlton Pk. Rd. SE7—2F 59
Charlton Pl. N1—1D 25
Charlton Rd. NW10—5A 4
Charlton Rd.—3C 58
   SE3 1-121 & 2-78
   SE7 remainder
Charlton Way. SE3—4A 58
Charlwood Pl. SW1—5E 37
Charlwood Rd. SW15—2F 61
Charlwood St. SW1—1E 51
Charlwood Ter. SW15—2F 61
Charminster Rd. SE9—4F 87
Charnwood Gdns. E14—5C 42
Charrington St. NW1—1F 23
Charsley Rd. SE6—2D 85
Charterhouse Bldgs. EC1—3E 25
Charterhouse M. EC1—4D 25
Charterhouse Sq. EC1—4D 25
Charterhouse St. EC1—4D 25
Charteris Rd. NW6—5B 6
Charters Clo. SE19—5A 82
Chartfield Av. SW15—3D 61
Chartfield Sq. SW15—3F 61
Chartham Gro. SE27—3D 81
Chart St. N1—2F 25
Charwood. SW16—4C 80
Chasefield Rd. SW17—4B 78
Chaseley St. E14—5A 28
Chase, The. E12—1F 17
Chase, The. SW4—2D 65
Chatfield Rd. SW11—1E 63
Chatham Pl. E9—3E 13
Chatham Rd. SW11—3B 64

Chatham St. SE17—5F 39
Chatsworth Av. Brom—4D 87
Chatsworth Rd. E5—1F 13
Chatsworth Rd. E15—2B 16
Chatsworth Rd. NW2—3F 5
Chatsworth Way. SE27—3D 81
Chatto Rd. SW11—3B 64
Chaucer Rd. E7—3C 16
Chaucer Rd. SE24—3C 66
Chaucer Way. SW19—5F 77
Cheam St. SE15—1D 69
Cheapside. EC2—5E 25
Chedworth Clo. E16—5B 30
Cheeseman's Ter. W14—1B 48
Chelford Rd. Brom—5F 85
Chelmer Rd. E9—2F 13
Chelmsford Clo. W6—2F 47
Chelmsford Sq. NW10—5E 5
Chelsea Bri. SW1 & SW8—2D 51
Chelsea Bri. Rd. SW1—1C 50
Chelsea Cres. SW10—4E 49
Chelsea Embkmt. SW3—2A 50
Chelsea Garden Mkt. SW10
—4E 49
Chelsea Harbour Dri. SW10
—4E 49
Chelsea Mnr. Gdns. SW3—1A 50
Chelsea Mnr. St. SW3—1A 50
Chelsea Pk. Gdns. SW3—2F 49
Chelsea Sq. SW3—1F 49
Chelsfield Gdns. SE26—3E 83
Chelsham Rd. SW4—1F 65
Cheltenham Rd. SE15—2E 69
Cheltenham Ter. SW3—1B 50
Chelverton Rd. SW15—2F 61
Chelwood Wlk. SE4—2A 70
Chenappa Clo. E13—2C 30
Cheney Ct. SE23—1F 83
Cheney Rd. NW1—1A 24
Cheltenham Gdns. W8—4D 35
Chepstow Clo. SW15—4A 62
Chepstow Cres. W11—1C 34
Chepstow Pl. W2—1C 34
Chepstow Rd. W2—5C 20
Chepstow Vs. W11—1B 34
Chepstow Way. SE15—4B 54
Chequer St. EC1—3E 25
Cherbury St. N1—1F 25
Cheriton Ct. SE12—5C 72
Cheriton Sq. SW17—2C 78
Cherry Garden St. SE16—3D 41
Cherry Laurel Wlk. SW2—4B 66
Cherry Orchard. SE7—2E 59
Cherrytree Dri. SW16—3A 80
Cherry Tree Rd. E15—2A 16

Cherry Tree Wlk. EC1—3E 25
Cherrywood Dri. SW15—3F 61
Chertsey St. SW17—5C 78
Cheryls Clo. SW6—4D 49
Cheseman St. SE26—3D 83
Chesham Pl. SW1—4C 36
Chesham Pl. SW19—5F 77
Chesham St. SW1—4C 36
Cheshire Clo. SE4—5B 56
Cheshire St. E2—3C 26
Cheshunt Rd. E7—3D 17
Chesilton Rd. SW6—4B 48
Chesley Gdns. E6—1F 31
Chesney St. SW11—4C 50
Chessington Clo. N16—2A 12
Chesson Rd. W14—2B 48
Chester Clo. SW1—3D 37
Chester Clo. SW15—1D 61
Chester Clo. N. NW1—2D 23
Chester Clo. S. NW1—2D 23
Chester Ct. NW1—2D 23
Chester Cres. E8—4B 12
Chesterfield Clo. SE13—1F 71
Chesterfield Gdns. W1—2D 37
Chesterfield Gro. SE22—3B 68
Chesterfield Hill. W1—2D 37
Chesterfield St. W1—2D 37
Chesterfield Wlk. SE10—4F 57
Chesterfield Way. SE15—3E 55
Chesterford Gdns. NW3—1D 7
Chester Ga. NW1—2D 23
Chester M. SW1—4D 37
Chester Pl. NW1—2C 23
Chester Rd. E7—4F 17
Chester Rd. E16—3A 30
Chester Rd. NW1—2C 22
Chester Rd. SW19—5E 75
Chester Row. SW1—5C 36
Chester Sq. SW1—5C 36
Chester Sq. E2—3C 26
Chester St. E2—3C 26
Chester St. SW1—4C 36
Chester Ter. NW1—2D 23
Chester Way. SE11—5C 38
Chesterton Clo. SW18—3C 62
Chesterton Rd. E13—2C 30
Chesterton Rd. W10—4F 19
Chesterton Ter. E13—2C 30
Chester Way. SE11—5C 38
Chestnut All. SW6—2B 48
Chestnut Av. E7—1D 17
Chestnut Clo. SE6—5E 85
Chestnut Clo. SW6—2B 48
Chestnut Gro. SW12—5C 64
Chestnut Rd. SE27—3E 81
Chestnuts, The. SW16—4C 80
Chetwode Rd. SW17—3C 78
Chetwynd Rd. NW5—1D 9
Cheval Pl. SW7—4A 36

Cheval St. E14—4C 42
Chevening Rd. NW6—1F 19
Chevening Rd. SE10—1B 58
Chevet St. E9—2A 14
Cheviot Rd. SE27—5C 80
Cheyne Ct. SW3—2B 50
Cheyne Gdns. SW3—2A 50
Cheyne M. SW3—2A 50
Cheyne Row. SW3—2A 50
Cheyne Wlk.—3F 49
    SW3 1-90
    SW10 remainder
Chichele Rd. NW2—2F 5
Chicheley St. SE1—3B 38
Chichester Clo. SE3—4E 59
Chichester Rd. NW6—1C 20
Chichester Rd. W02—4D 21
Chichester St. SW1—1E 51
Chichester Way. E14—5F 43
Chicksand St. E1—4C 26
Chiddingstone St. SW6—5C 48
Chigwell Hill. E1—1D 41
Childebert Rd. SW17—2D 79
Childeric Rd. SE14—3A 56
Childerley St. SW6—4A 48
Childers St. SE8—2A 56
Child's Pl. SW5—5C 34
Child's St. SW5—5C 34
Child's Wlk. SW5—5C 34
Chiliot Clo. E14—5D 29
Chillerton Rd. SW17—5D 79
Chillingworth Rd. N7—2C 10
Chiltern Rd. E3—3C 28
Chiltern St. W1—4C 22
Chilthorne Clo. SE6—5B 70
Chilton Gro. SE8—5A 42
Chilton St. E2—3B 26
Chilver St. SE10—1B 58
Chilworth Ct. SW19—1F 75
Chilworth M. W2—5F 21
Chilworth St. W2—5E 21
Chinbrook Cres. SE12—3D 87
Chinbrook Rd. SE12—3D 87
Chingly Clo. Brom—5A 86
Chipka St. E14—3E 43
    (in two parts)
Chipley St. SE14—2A 56
Chippenham Gdns. NW6—2C 20
Chippenham M. W9—3C 20
Chippenham Rd. W9—3C 20
Chipstead St. SW6—5C 48
Chip St. SW4—2F 65
Chisenhale Rd. E3—1A 28
Chiswell Sq. SE3—5D 59
Chiswell St. EC1—4F 25
Chiswick High Rd. W4—5A 32
Chiswick La. N. W4—1A 46
Chiswick La. S. W4—2B 46

Chiswick Mall. W4 & W6
—2B 46
Chiswick Sq. W4—2A 46
Chiswick Wharf. W4—2B 46
Chitty St. W1—4E 23
Chivalry Rd. SW11—3A 64
Chobham Gdns. SW19—2F 75
Chobham Rd. E15—2F 15
Cholmeley Gdns. NW6—2C 6
Cholmondeley Av. NW10—1C 18
Choppin's Ct. E1—2D 41
Choumert Gro. SE15—5C 54
Choumert Rd. SE15—1B 68
Choumert Sq. SE15—5C 54
Crisp St. E14—5D 29
Christchurch Av. NW6—5F 5
Christchurch Pl. SW8—5F 51
Christchurch Rd. SW2—1B 80
Christchurch Rd. SW3—2B 50
Christchurch Way. SE10—1A 58
Christian St. E1—5C 26
Christie Rd. E9—3A 14
Christina St. EC2—3A 26
Christopher Pl. NW1—2F 23
Christopher St. EC2—3F 25
Chryssell Rd. SW9—3C 52
Chubworthy St. SE14—2A 56
Chudleigh Rd. NW6—4F 5
Chudleigh Rd. SE4—3B 70
Chudleigh St. E1—5F 27
Chulsa Rd. SE26—5D 83
Chumleigh St. SE5—2A 54
Church App. SE21—3F 81
Church Av. NW1—3D 9
Churchbury Rd. SE9—5F 73
Church Cres. E9—4F 13
Churchcroft Clo. SW12—5C 64
Churchdown. Brom—4A 86
Churchfields. SE10—2E 57
Church Ga. SW6—1A 62
Church Gro. SE13—3D 71
Church Hill. SW19—5B 76
Churchill Gdns. SW1—1E 51
Churchill Gdns. Rd. SW1—1D 51
Churchill Rd. E16—5E 31
Churchill Rd. NW2—3D 5
Churchill Rd. NW5—1D 9
Churchill Wlk. E9—2E 13
Church La. SW17—5B 78
Churchley Rd. SE26—4D 83
Churchmead Rd. NW10—3C 4
Church Path. N5—2D 11
Church Path. NW10—4A 4
Church Pl. SW1—1E 37
Church Rise. SE23—2F 83
Church Rd. NW10—4A 4
Church Rd. SW13—5B 46

Church Rd. SW19—5A 76
Church Row. NW3—1E 7
Church Sq. E9—5E 13
Church St. E15—5A 16
Church St.—4F 21
    NW8 1-127 & 2-142
    W2 remainder
Church St. W4—2B 46
Church St. NW8—3F 21
Church St. N. E15—5A 16
Church St. Pas. E15—5A 16
Church Ter. SE13—1A 72
Church Vale. SE23—2F 83
Church Wlk. N16—1F 11
Church Wlk. SW13—4C 46
Church Wlk. SW15—3D 61
Churchway. NW1—2F 23
Churchwell Path. E9—2E 13
Churchyard Row. SE11—5D 39
Churston Av. E13—5D 17
Churston Clo. SW2—1C 80
Churton Pl. SW1—5E 37
Churton St. SW1—5E 37
Chusan Pl. E14—5B 28
Cibber Rd. SE23—2F 83
Cicada Rd. SW18—4E 63
Cicely Rd. SE15—4C 54
Cinderford Way. Brom—4A 86
Cinnamon Row. SW11—1E 63
Cinnamon St. E1—2D 41
  (in two parts)
Circus Pl. EC2—4F 25
Circus Rd. NW8—2F 21
Circus St. SE10—3E 57
Cirencester St. W2—4D 21
Cissbury Ho. SE26—5C 82
Citizen Rd. N7—1C 10
City Garden Row. N1—1D 25
City Rd. EC1—1D 25
Clabon M. SW1—4B 36
Clack St. SE16—3E 41
Clacton Rd. E6—2F 31
Claire Pl. E14—4C 42
Clairview Rd. SW16—5D 79
Clancarty Rd. SW6—5C 48
Clandon St. SE8—5C 56
Clanfield Way. SE15—3B 54
Clanricarde Gdns. W2—1C 34
Clapham Comn. N. Side. SW4
    —2C 64
Clapham Comn. S. Side. SW4
    —4D 65
Clapham Comn. W. Side. SW4
    —2B 64
  (in three parts)
Clapham Cres. SW4—2F 65
Clapham High St. SW4—2F 65

Clapham Junct. Est. SW11
    —2A 64
Clapham Junct. App. SW11
    —2A 64
Clapham Mnr. St. SW4—1E 65
Clapham Pk. Est. SW4—4F 65
Clapham Pk. Rd. SW4—2F 65
Clapham Rd. SW9—1A 66
Clapham Rd. Est. SW4—1A 66
Clapton Pk. Est. E5—1F 13
Clapton Pas. E5—2E 13
Clapton Sq. E5—2E 13
Clapton Way. E5—1C 12
Claredale St. E2—1C 26
Clare Gdns. E7—1C 16
Clare Gdns. W11—5A 20
Clare La. N1—4E 11
Clare Mkt. WC2—5B 24
Claremont Clo. N1—1C 24
Claremont Clo. SW2—1C 80
Claremont Gro. W4—3A 46
Claremont Rd. E7—2D 17
Claremont Rd. W9—1B 20
Claremont Sq. N1—1C 24
Claremont St. SE10—2D 57
Clarence Av. SW4—5F 65
Clarence Cres. SW4—4F 65
Clarence Gdns. NW1—2D 23
Clarence La. SW15—4A 60
Clarence M. E5—2D 13
Clarence Pas. NW1—1A 24
Clarence Pl. E5—2D 13
Clarence Rd. E5—1D 13
Clarence Rd. E12—2F 17
Clarence Rd. E16—3A 30
Clarence Rd. NW6—4B 6
Clarence Rd. SW19—5D 77
Clarence Ter. NW1—3B 22
Clarence Wlk. SW4—5A 52
Clarence Way. NW1—4D 9
Clarendon Clo. W2—1A 36
Clarendon Cross. W11—1A 34
Clarendon Dri. SW15—2E 61
Clarendon Gdns. W9—3E 21
Clarendon Gro. NW1—2F 23
Clarendon M. W2—1A 36
Clarendon Pl. W2—1A 36
Clarendon Rise. SE13—2E 71
Clarendon Rd. W11—1A 34
Clarendon St. SW1—1D 51
Clarendon Ter. W9—3E 21
Clarendon Wlk. W11—5A 20
Clarens St. SE6—2B 84
Clare Pl. SW15—5B 60
Clare Rd. NW10—4C 4
Clare Rd. SE14—5B 56
Clare St. E2—1D 27

Clareville Gro. SW7—5E 35
Clareville St. SW7—5E 35
Clarewood Wlk. SW9—2C 66
Clarges M. W1—2D 37
Clarges St. W1—2D 37
Claribel Rd. SW9—5D 53
Clarissa St. E8—5B 12
Clarkson Rd. E16—5B 30
Clarkson St. E2—2D 27
Clark's Pl. EC2—5A 26
Clark St. E1—4E 27
Claude Rd. E13—5D 17
Claude Rd. SE15—5D 55
Claude St. E14—5C 42
Claudia Jones Way. SW2
            —4A 66
Claudia Pl. SW19—1A 76
Claughton Rd. E13—1E 31
Clavell St. SE10—2E 57
Claverdale Rd. SW2—5B 66
Clavering Av. SW13—2D 47
Claverton St. SW1—1E 51
Clave St. E1—2E 41
Claxton Gro. W6—1F 47
Claybank Gro. SE13—1D 71
Claybridge Rd. SE12—4E 87
Claybrook Rd. W6—2F 47
Clayhill Cres. SE9—4F 87
Claylands Pl. SW8—3C 52
Claylands Rd. SW8—2B 52
Claypole Rd. E15—1E 29
Clays La. E15—2D 15
Clays La. Clo. E15—2D 15
Clay St. W1—4B 22
Clayton Rd. SE15—4C 54
Clayton St. SE11—2C 52
Clearbrook Way. E1—5E 27
Clearwell Dri. W9—3D 21
Cleaver Sq. SE11—1C 52
Cleaver St. SE11—1C 52
Cleeve Hill. SE23—1D 83
Clegg St. E1—2D 41
Clegg St. E13—1C 30
Clematis St. W12—1C 32
Clem Attlee Ct. SW6—2B 48
Clemence St. E14—4B 28
Clement Clo. NW6—4F 5
Clement Rd. SW19—5A 76
Clement's Av. E16—1C 44
Clement's Inn. WC2—5B 24
Clement's La. EC4—1F 39
Clement's Rd. SE16—4C 40
Clennam St. SE1—3E 39
Clenston M. W1—5B 22
Clephane Rd. N1—3E 11
Clere Pl. EC2—2F 25
Clere St. EC2—3F 25

Clerkenwell Clo. EC1—3C 24
Clerkenwell Grn. EC1—3D 25
Clerkenwell Rd. EC1—3C 24
Clermont Rd. E9—5E 13
Cleveland Av. W4—5B 32
Cleveland Gdns. SW13—5B 46
Cleveland Gdns. W2—5E 21
Cleveland Gro. E1—3E 27
Cleveland M. W1—4E 23
Cleveland Pl. SW1—2E 37
Cleveland Rd. N1—4F 11
Cleveland Rd. SW13—5B 46
Cleveland Row. SW1—2E 37
Cleveland Sq. W2—5E 21
Cleveland St. W1—3D 23
Cleveland Ter. W2—5E 21
Cleveland Way. E1—3E 27
Cleveley Clo. SE7—5F 45
Cleverley Est. W12—2C 32
Cleve Rd. NW6—4D 7
Cleves Rd. E6—5F 17
Clichy Est. E1—4E 27
Clifden Rd. E5—2E 13
Clifford Dri. SW9—2D 67
Clifford Gdns. NW10—1E 19
Clifford Rd. E16—3B 30
Clifford's Inn Pas. EC4—5C 24
Clifford St. W1—1E 37
Clifford Way. NW10—1B 4
Cliff Rd. NW1—3F 9
Cliff Ter. SE8—5C 56
Cliffview Rd. SE13—1C 70
Cliff Vs. NW1—3F 9
Cliff Wlk. E16—4B 30
Clifton Av. W12—2B 32
Clifton Cres. SE15—3E 55
  (in two parts)
Clifton Est. SE15—4D 55
Clifton Gdns. W9—3E 21
Clifton Gro. E8—3C 12
Clifton Hill. NW8—1D 21
Clifton Pl. SE16—3E 41
Clifton Pl. W2—5F 21
Clifton Rise. SE14—3A 56
Clifton Rd. E7—3F 17
Clifton Rd. E16—4A 30
Clifton Rd. NW10—1C 18
Clifton Rd. SW19—5F 75
Clifton Rd. W9—3E 21
Clifton St. EC2—4A 26
Clifton Vs. W9—4E 21
Cliftonville Ct. SE12—1C 86
Clifton Way. SE15—3E 55
Clinger Ct. N1—5A 12
Clink St. SE1—2F 39
Clinton Rd. E3—2A 28
Clinton Rd. E7—1C 16

Clipper Clo. SE16—3F 41
Clipper Way. SE13—2E 71
Clipstone M. W1—4E 23
Clipstone St. W1—4E 23
Clissold Cres. N5—1F 11
Clitheroe Rd. SW9—5A 52
Cliveden Pl. SW1—5C 36
Clive Pas. SE21—3F 81
Clive Rd. SE21—3F 81
Cloak La. EC4—1E 39
Clockhouse Clo. SW19—2E 75
Clock Tower M. N1—5E 11
Clock Tower Pl. N7—3A 10
Cloisters, The. SW9—4C 52
Clonbrook Rd. N16—1A 12
Cloncurry St. SW6—5F 47
Clonmel Rd. SW6—4B 48
Clonmore St. SW18—1B 76
Cloth Fair. EC1—4D 25
Cloth St. EC1—4E 25
Cloudesdale Rd. SW17—2D 79
Cloudesley Pl. N1—5C 10
Cloudesley Rd. N1—5C 10
Cloudesley Sq. N1—5C 10
Cloudesley St. N1—5C 10
Clova Rd. E7—3B 16
Clove Hitch Quay. SW11—1E 63
Clovelly Way. E1—5E 27
Clover M. SW3—2B 50
Clove St. E13—3C 30
Clowders Rd. SE6—3B 84
Cloysters Grn. E1—2C 40
Club Row—3B 26
  E1 1-11 & 2-10
  E2 remainder
Clunbury St. N1—1F 25
Cluny Est. SE1—4A 40
Cluny M. SW5—5C 34
Cluny Pl. SE1—4A 40
Clutton St. E14—4D 29
Clydesdale Rd. W11—5B 20
Clyde St. SE8—2B 56
Clyde Ter. SE23—2E 83
Clyde Vale. SE23—2E 83
Clyston St. SW8—5E 51
Coach & Horses Yd. W1—1E 37
Coach Ho. La. N5—1D 11
Coach Ho. La. SW19—4F 75
Coach Ho. M. SE23—4F 69
Coaldale Wlk. SE21—5E 67
Coalecroft Rd. SW15—2E 61
Coal Wharf Rd. W12—3F 33
Coate St. E2—1C 26
Cobbett St. SW8—3B 52
Cobbold Est. NW10—3B 4
Cobbold Rd. NW10—3B 4
Cobbold Rd. W12—3A 32
Cobb St. E1—4B 26

Cobden St. E14—4D 29
Cobham Clo. SW11—4A 64
Cobland Rd. SE12—4E 87
Coborn Rd. E3—2B 28
Coborn St. E3—2B 28
Cobourg Rd. SE5—2B 54
Cobourg St. NW1—2E 23
Coburg Cres. SW2—1B 80
Cochrane M. NW8—1F 21
Cochrane St. NW8—1F 21
Cockayne Way. SE8—5A 42
Cock Hill. E1—4A 26
Cock La. EC1—4D 25
Cockpit Yd. WC1—4B 24
Cockspur Ct. SW1—2F 37
Cockspur St. SW1—2F 37
Code St. E1—3B 26
Codling Clo. E1—2C 40
Codrington Hill. SE23—5A 70
Codrington M. W11—5A 20
Cody Rd. E16—3A 30
Coin St. SE1—2C 38
Coity Rd. NW5—3C 8
Cokers La. SE21—1F 81
Coke St. E1—5C 26
Colas M. NW6—5C 6
Colbeck M. SW7—5D 35
Colby Rd. SE19—5A 82
Colchester St. E1—5B 26
Coldbath Sq. EC1—3C 24
Coldbath St. SE13—4D 57
Cold Blow La. SE14—3F 55
Coldharbour. E14—2E 43
Coldharbour La.—2C 66
　SE5 1-199 & 2-200
　SW9 remainder
Coldharbour Pl. SE5—5F 53
Coldstream Gdns. SW18—4B 62
Colebeck M. N1—3D 11
Colebert Av. E1—3E 27
Colebrook Clo. SW15—5F 61
Colebrooke Pl. N1—5D 11
Colebrooke Row. N1—1D 25
Coleford Rd. SW18—3E 63
Colegrave Rd. E15—2F 15
Colegrove Rd. SE15—2B 54
Coleherne Ct. SW5—1D 49
Coleherne M. SW10—1D 49
Coleherne Rd. SW10—1D 49
Colehill Gdns. SW6—4A 48
Colehill La. SW6—4A 48
Coleman Fields. N1—5E 11
Coleman Rd. SE5—3A 54
Coleman St. EC2—5F 25
Colenso Rd. E5—1E 13
Coleraine Rd. SE3—2B 58

Coleridge Clo. SW8—5D 51
Coleridge Gdns. NW6—4E 7
Colestown St. SW11—5A 50
Cole St. SE1—3E 39
Colet Gdns. W14—5F 33
Coley St. WC1—3B 24
Colfe Rd. SE23—1A 84
Colinette Rd. SW15—2E 61
Colin Rd. NW10—3C 4
Coliston Pas. SW18—5C 62
Coliston Rd. SW18
Collamore Av. SW18—1A 78
College App. SE10—2E 57
College Clo. E9—2E 19
College Cres. NW3—3F 7
College Cross. N1—4C 10
College Gdns. SE21—1A 82
College Gdns. SW17—2A 78
College Gro. NW1—5F 9
College Hill. EC4—1E 39
College La. NW5—1D 9
College Pk. Clo. SE13—2F 71
College Pl. NW1—5E 9
College Rd. NW10—1E 19
College Rd.—5A 68
　SE21 1-111 & 2-120
　SE19 remainder
College Row. E9—2F 13
College St. EC4—1E 39
College Ter. E3—2B 28
College View. SE9—1F 87
College Yd. NW5—1D 9
Collent St. E9—3E 13
Collett Rd. SE16—4D 41
Collier St. N1—1B 24
Collingbourne Rd. W12—2D 33
Collingham Gdns. SW5—5D 35
Collingham Pl. SW5—5D 35
Collingham Rd. SW5—5D 35
Collingtree Rd. SE26—4E 83
Collingwood St. E1—3D 27
Collins Ct. E8—3C 12
Collinson St. SE1—3E 39
Collinson Wlk. SE1—3E 39
Collins Rd. N5—1E 11
Collins St. SE3—5A 58
Collin's Yd. N1—5D 11
Colls Rd. SE15—4E 55
Collyer Pl. SE15—4B 54
Colman Rd. E16—4E 31
Colmar Clo. E1—3F 27
Colnbrook St. SE1—4D 39
Colne Rd. E5—1A 14
Colne St. E13—2C 30
Cologne Rd. SW11—2F 63
Colombo Rd. SE1—2D 39
Colomb St. SE10—1A 58

Colonnade. WC1—3A 24
Colonnade, The. SE8—5B 42
Colson Way. SW16—4E 79
Colston Pas. SW18—5C 62
Colston Rd. E7—3F 17
Columbia Rd. E2—2B 26
Columbia Rd. E13—3B 30
Columbia Wharf. SE16—2B 42
Columbine Way. SE13—5E 57
Colvestone Cres. E8—2B 12
Colview Ct. SE9—1F 87
Colville Gdns. W11—5B 20
Colville Houses. W11—5B 20
Colville M. W11—5B 20
Colville Pl. W1—4F 23
Colville Rd. W11—5B 20
Colville Sq. W11—5B 20
Colville Sq. M. W11—5B 20
Colville Ter. W11—5B 20
Colvin Clo. SE26—5E 83
Colwell Rd. SE22—3B 68
Colwith Rd. W6—2E 47
Colworth Gro. SE17—5E 39
Colyer Clo. N1—1B 24
Colyton Rd. SE22—3D 69
Combe Av. SE3—3B 58
Combedale Rd. SE10—1C 58
Combe Lodge. SE7—2E 59
Combemartin Rd. SW18—5A 62
Combe M. SE3—3B 58
Comber Gro. SE5—3E 53
Combermere Rd. SW9—1B 66
Comeragh M. W14—1A 48
Comeragh Rd. W14—1A 48
Comerford Rd. SE4—2A 70
Comet Pl. SE8—3C 56
Comet St. SE8—3C 56
Commercial Rd.—5C 26
　E1 1-601a & 2-554
　E14 remainder
Commercial St. E1—4B 26
Commercial Way. SE15—3B 54
Commerell St. SE10—1A 58
Commodity Quay. E1—1B 40
Commodore Sq. SW10—4E 49
Commodore St. E1—3A 28
Commondale. SW15—1E 61
Commonfield La. SW17—5A 78
Common Rd. SW13—1D 61
Commonwealth Av. W12
　　　　　　　　　　—1D 33
Community Rd. E15—2F 15
Como Rd. SE23—2A 84
Compayne Gdns. NW6—4D 7
Compton Av. E6—1F 31
Compton Av. N1—3D 11
Compton Ct. SE17—5A 82

Compton Pas. EC1—3D 25
Compton Pl. WC1—3A 24
Compton Rd. N1—3D 11
Compton Rd. NW10—2F 19
Compton Rd. SW19—5B 76
Compton St. EC1—3D 25
Compton Ter. N1—3D 11
Comus Pl. SE17—5A 40
Comyn Rd. SW11—2A 64
Comyns Clo. E16—4B 30
Concanon Rd. SW2—2B 66
Concert Hall App. SE1—2B 38
Condell Rd. SW8—4E 51
Conder St. E14—5A 28
Conderton Rd. SE5—1E 67
Condray Pl. SW11—3A 50
Conduit M. W2—5F 21
Conduit Pl. W2—5F 21
Conduit St. W1—1D 37
Coney Acre. SE21—1E 81
Coney Way. SW8—2B 52
Congreve Ct. SE11—5C 38
Congreve St. SE17—5A 40
Conifer Gdns. SW16—3B 80
Coniger Rd. SW6—5C 48
Coningham M. W12—2C 32
Coningham Rd. W12—3D 33
Conington Rd. SE13—5E 57
Conisborough Cres. SE6—3E 85
Coniston Clo. SW13—3B 46
Conistone Way. N7—4A 10
Coniston Rd. Brom—5A 86
Coniston Wlk. E9—2E 13
Conlan St. W10—3A 20
Conley Rd. NW10—3A 4
Conley St. SE10—1A 58
Connaught Pl. W2—1B 36
Connaught Rd. E16—2F 45
Connaught Rd. NW10—5A 4
Connaught Sq. W2—5B 22
Connaught St. W2—5A 22
Connor St. E9—5F 13
Cons St. SE1—3C 38
Constable Wlk. SE21—3A 82
Constantine Rd. NW3—1B 8
Constitution Hill. SW1—3D 37
Content St. SE17—5F 39
Convent Gdns. W11—5A 20
Conway St. W1—3E 23
(in two parts)
Conybeare. NW3—5A 8
Conyer's Rd. SW16—5F 79
Conyer St. E3—1A 28
Cookham Cres. SE16—3F 41
Cook's Rd. E15—1D 29
Cook's Rd. SE17—2D 53

Coolfin Rd. E16—5C 30
Coomassie Rd. W9—3B 20
Coombe Rd. SE26—4D 83
Coombe Rd. W4—1A 46
Coombs St. N1—1D 25
Coomer M. SW6—2B 48
Coomer Pl. SW6—2B 48
Coomer Rd. SW6—2B 48
Cooper Clo. SE1—3C 38
Cooper Ct. E15—2D 15
Cooper Rd. NW10—2C 4
Coopersale Rd. E9—2F 13
Coopers Clo. E1—3E 27
Coopers Cope Rd. Beck—5C 84
Coopers La. NW1—1F 23
Cooper's La. SE12—2D 87
Cooper's Rd. SE1—1B 54
Cooper's Row. EC3—1B 40
Cooper St. E16—4B 30
Cooper's Yd. SE19—5A 82
Copeland Dri. E14—5C 42
Copeland Rd. SE15—5C 54
Copeman Clo. SE26—5E 83
Copenhagen Pl. E14—5B 28
Copenhagen St. N1—5A 10
Cope Pl. W8—4C 34
Cope St. SE16—5F 41
Copleston Pas. SE15—5A 54
Copleston Rd. SE15—1B 68
Copley Clo. SE17—2E 53
Copley Pk. SW16—5B 80
Copley St. E1—4F 27
Copner Way. S15—3B 54
Coppelia Rd. SE3—2B 72
Copperas St. SE8—2D 57
Copperbeech Clo. NW3—2F 7
Copperfield Rd. E3—4A 28
Copperfield St. SE1—3D 39
Copper Mill La. SW17—4E 77
Coppice Dri. SW15—4D 61
Coppock Clo. SW11—5A 50
Copse Clo. SE7—2D 59
Copthall Av. EC2—5F 25
(in two parts)
Copthall Clo. EC2—5F 25
Copthorne Av. SW12—5F 65
Coptic St. WC1—4A 24
Coral Row. LE1—1F 63
Coral St. SE1—3C 38
Coram St. WC1—3A 24
Corbet Ct. EC3—5F 25
Corbet Pl. E1—4B 26
Corbett Ct. SE26—4B 84
Corbett's La. SE16—5E 41
Corbett's Pas. SE16—5E 41
Corbridge Cres. E2—1D 27
Corby Way. E3—3C 28

Cordelia St. E14—5D 29
Cording St. E14—4D 29
Cordova Rd. E3—2A 28
Cordwainers Wlk. E13—1C 30
Cord Way. E14—4C 42
Cordwell Rd. SE13—3A 72
Corfield St. E2—2D 27
Corinne Rd. N19—1E 9
Cork Sq. E1—2D 41
Cork St. W1—1E 37
Corlett St. NW1—4A 22
Cormont Rd. SE5—4D 53
Cornelia St. N7—3B 10
Corner Grn. SE3—5C 58
Corney Rd. W4—2A 46
Cornflower Ter. SE22—4D 69
Cornford Gro. SW12—2D 79
Cornhill. EC3—5F 25
Cornmill La. SE13—1E 71
Cornwall Av. E2—2E 27
Cornwall Cres. W11—5A 20
Cornwall Gdns. NW10—3D 5
Cornwall Gdns. SW7—4D 35
Cornwall Gdns. Wlk. SW7
                    —4D 35
Cornwall Gro. W4—1A 46
Cornwall M. S. SW7—4E 35
Cornwall M. W. SW7—4D 35
Cornwall Rd. SE1—2C 38
Cornwall St. E1—1D 41
Cornwall Ter. NW1—3B 22
Cornwood Dri. E1—5E 27
Corona Rd. SE12—5C 72
Coronation Av. N16—1B 12
Coronation Rd. E13—2E 31
Coronet St. N1—2A 26
Corporation Row. EC1—3C 24
Corporation St. E15—1A 30
Corporation St. N7—2A 10
Corrance Rd. SW2—2A 66
Corsham St. N1—2F 25
Corsica St. N5—3D 11
Corsley Way. E9—3B 14
Cortayne Rd. SW6—5B 48
Cortis Rd. SW15—4D 61
Cortis Ter. SW15—4D 61
Corunna Rd. SW8—4E 51
Corunna Ter. SW8—4E 51
Corvette Sq. SE10—2F 57
Coryton Path. W9—3B 20
Cosbycote Av. SE24—3F 67
Cosmo Pl. WC1—4A 24
Cosmur Clo. W12—4B 32
Cossall Wlk. SE15—5D 55
Cosser St. SE1—4C 38
Costa St. SE15—5C 54
Cosway St. NW1—4A 22

Cotall St. E14—4C 28
Coteford St. SW17—4B 78
Cotham St. SE17—5E 39
Cotherstone Rd. SW2—1B 80
Cotleigh Rd. NW6—4C 6
Cotman Clo. SW15—4F 61
Cotswold Gdns. E6—2F 31
Cotswold M. SW11—4F 49
Cotswold St. SE27—4D 81
Cottage Grn. SE5—3F 53
Cottage Gro. SW9—1A 66
Cottage Pl. SW3—4A 36
Cottage St. E14—1D 43
Cottage Wlk. SE15—4B 54
Cottage Wlk. SW1—4B 36
Cottesbrook St. SE14—3A 56
Cottesmore Gdns. W8—4D 35
Cottingham Rd. SW8—3B 52
Cottington Clo. SE11—1D 53
Cottington St. SE11—1D 53
Cotton Hill. Brom—4E 85
Cotton Row. SW11—1F 63
Cottons Centre. SE1—2A 40
Cotton's Gdns. E2—2A 26
Cottons La. SE1—2A 40
Cotton St. E14—1E 43
Coulgate St. SE4—1A 70
Coulson St. SW3—1B 50
Coulston Rd. SW18—5C 62
Coulter Rd. W6—4D 33
Councillor St. SE5—3E 53
Countess Rd. NW5—2E 9
County Gro. SE5—4E 53
County St. SE1—4E 39
Courland Gro. SW8—4F 51
Courland St. SW8—4F 51
(in two parts)
Courtenay Sq. SE11—1C 52
Courtenay St. SE11—1C 52
Court Farm Rd. SE9—2F 87
Courtfield Gdns. SW5—5D 35
Courtfield M. SW7—5E 35
Courtfield Rd. SW7—5E 35
Courthill Rd. SE13—2E 71
Courthope Rd. NW3—1B 8
Courthope Rd. SW19—5A 76
Courtlands Av. SE12—3D 73
Court La. SE21—4A 68
Court La. Gdns. SE21—5A 68
Courtmead Clo. SE24—4E 67
Courtnell St. W2—5C 20
Courtney Rd. N7—2C 10
Courtrai Rd. SE23—4A 70
Courtside. SE26—3D 83
Court St. E1—4D 27
Courtyard, The. N1—4B 10
Courtyard, The. NW1—4C 8

Cousin La. EC4—1F 39
Couthurst Rd. SE3—3D 59
Covent Garden. WC2—1A 38
Coventry Clo. NW6—1C 20
Coventry Rd. E1 & E2—3D 27
Coventry St. W1—1F 37
Coverdale Rd. NW2—4F 5
Coverdale Rd. W12—3D 33
Coverley Clo. E1—4C 26
Coverton Rd. SW17—5A 78
Covington Way. SW16—5B 80
Cowcross St. EC1—4D 25
Cowden St. SE6—4C 84
Cowdrey Rd. SW19—5E 77
Cowdry Rd. E9—3A 14
Cowick Rd. SW17—4B 78
Cowley Rd. SW9—4C 52
Cowley Rd. SW14—1A 60
Cowley Rd. W3—2B 32
Cowley St. SW1—4A 38
Cowling Clo. W11—2A 34
Cowper Rd. N16—2A 12
(in two parts)
Cowper Rd. SW19—5E 77
Cowper St. EC2—2F 25
Cowper Ter. W10—4F 19
Cowthorpe Rd. SW8—4F 51
Coxmount Rd. SE7—1F 59
Coxson Pl. SE1—3B 40
Cox's Wlk. SE21 & SE26—1C 82
Crabtree Ct. E15—2D 15
Crabtree La. SW6—3E 47
(in two parts)
Crace St. NW1—2F 23
Craddock St. NW5—3C 8
Craigerne Rd. SE3—3D 59
Craignair Rd. SW2—5C 66
Craig's Ct. SW1—2A 38
Crail Row. SE17—5F 39
Cramer St. W1—4C 22
Cramond Clo. W6—2A 48
Crampton St. SE17—5E 39
Cranbourne Rd. E15—1E 15
Cranbourn Pas. SE16—3D 41
Cranbourn St. WC2—1F 37
Cranbrook Est. E2—1F 27
Cranbrook Point. E16—2D 45
Cranbrook Rd. SE8—4C 56
Cranbrook Rd. W4—1A 46
Cranbrook St. E2—1F 27
Cranbury Rd. SW6—5D 49
Crane Ct. EC4—5C 24
Crane Gro. N7—3C 10
Cranemead. SE16—5F 41
Crane St. SE10—1F 57
Cranfield Clo. SE27—3E 81
Cranfield Rd. SE4—1B 70

Cranford St. E1—1F 41
Cranhurst Rd. NW2—2F 5
Cranleigh M. SW11—1C 64
Cranleigh St. NW1—1E 23
Cranley Gdns. SW7—1E 49
Cranley M. SW7—1E 49
Cranley Pl. SW7—5F 35
Cranley Rd. E13—4D 31
Cranmer Ct. SW3—5A 36
Cranmer Ct. SW4—1F 65
Cranmer Rd. E7—1D 17
Cranmer Rd. SW9—3C 52
Cranmer Ter. SW17—5F 77
Cranmore Rd. Brom—3B 86
Cranston Est. N1—1F 25
Cranston Rd. SE23—1A 84
Cranswick Rd. SE16—1D 55
Crantock Rd. SE6—2D 85
Cranwell Clo. E3—3D 29
Cranwood St. EC1—2F 25
Cranworth Gdns. SW9—4C 52
Craster Rd. SW2—5B 66
Crathie Rd. SE12—4D 73
Crathorn St. SE13—1E 71
Craven Gdns. SW19—5D 77
Craven Hill. W2—1E 35
Craven Hill Gdns. W2—1E 35
Craven Hill M. W2—1E 35
Craven M. SW11—1C 64
Craven Park. NW10—5A 4
Craven Pk. M. NW10—5A 4
Craven Pk. Rd. NW10—5A 4
Craven Rd. W2—5F 21
Craven St. WC2—2A 38
Craven Ter. W2—1E 35
Crawford Est. SE5—5E 53
Crawford M. W1—4B 22
Crawford Pas. EC1—3C 24
Crawford Pl. W1—5A 22
Crawford Rd. SE5—4E 53
Crawford St. W1—4B 22
Crawshaw Ct. SW9—4C 52
Crawthew Gro. SE22—2B 68
Crayford Rd. N7—1A 10
Crealock St. SW18—4D 63
Creasy St. SE1—4A 40
Crebor St. SE22—4C 68
Credenhill Way. SE15—3D 55
Crediton Hill. NW6—2D 7
Crediton Rd. E16—5C 30
Crediton Rd. NW10—5F 5
Credon Rd. E13—1E 31
Credon Rd. SE16—1D 55
Creechurch La. EC3—5A 26
Creed La. EC4—5D 25
Creek Rd.—2C 56
     SE8 1-201 & 2-194
     SE10 remainder

Creekside. SE8—3D 57
Creeland Gro. SE6—1B 84
Crefeld Clo. W6—2A 48
Creighton Av. E6—1F 31
Creighton Rd. NW6—1F 19
Cremer St. E2—1B 26
Cremorne Est. SW10—2F 49
Cremorne Rd. SW10—3F 49
Crescent Gdns. SW19—3C 76
Crescent Gro. SW4—2E 65
Crescent La. SW4—2E 65
Crescent Pl. SW3—5A 36
Crescent Rd. E6—5E 17
Crescent Rd. E13—5C 16
Crescent Row. EC1—3E 25
Crescent Stables. SW15—3A 62
Crescent St. N1—4B 10
Crescent, The. SW13—5C 46
Crescent, The. SW19—3C 76
Crescent, The. W3—5A 18
Crescent Way. SE4—1C 70
Crescent Wood Rd. SE26—3C 82
Cresford Rd. SW6—4D 49
Cresset Rd. E9—3E 13
Cresset St. SW4—1F 65
Cressfield Clo. NW5—2C 8
Cressingham Gdns. Est. SW2
—5C 66
Cressingham Rd. SE13—1E 71
Cresswell Gdns. SW5—1E 49
Cresswell Pk. SE3—1B 72
Cresswell Pl. SW10—1E 49
Cressy Ct. E1—4E 27
Cressy Ct. W6—4D 33
Cressy Pl. E1—4E 27
Cressy Rd. NW3—2B 8
Crestfield St. WC1—1A 24
Crestway. SW15—4C 60
Creswick Wlk. E3—2C 28
Crewdson Rd. SW9—3C 52
Crewe Pl. NW10—2B 18
Crews St. E14—5C 42
Crewys Rd. SE15—5D 55
Cricketfield Rd. E5—1D 13
Cricklade Av. SW2—2A 80
Cricklewood B'way. NW2—1F 5
Cricklewood La. NW2—1F 5
Crieff Rd. SW18—4E 63
Criffel Av. SW2—2F 79
Crimscott St. SE1—4A 40
Crimsworth Rd. SW8—3F 51
Crinan St. N1—1A 24
Cringle St. SW8—3E 51
Cripplegate St. EC2—4E 25
Crispian Clo. NW10—1A 4
Crispin St. E1—4B 26
Crisp Rd. W6—1E 47

Cristowe Rd. SW6—5B 48
Crockerton Rd. SW17—2B 78
Crofters Way. NW1—5F 9
Croftongate Way. SE4—3A 70
Crofton Pk. Rd. SE4—4B 70
Crofton Rd. E13—3D 31
Crofton Rd. SE5—4A 54
Crofton Ter. E5—2A 14
Crofts St. E1—1C 40
Croft St. SE8—5A 42
Croft, The. NW10—1B 18
Croftway. NW3—1C 6
Crogsland Rd. NW1—4C 8
Cromer St. WC1—2A 24
Cromer Ter. E8—2C 12
Cromer Vs. Rd. SW18—4B 62
Cromford Path. E5—1F 13
Cromford Rd. SW18—3C 62
Crompton St. W2—3F 21
Cromwell Clo. E1—2C 40
Cromwell Cres. SW5—5C 34
Cromwell Gdns. SW7—4F 35
Cromwell Gro. W6—4E 33
Cromwell La. W6—1D 47
Cromwell M. SW7—5F 35
Cromwell Pl. SW7—5F 35
Cromwell Rd. E7—4E 17
Cromwell Rd. SW5—5D 35
      SW7 1-147 & 2-156
      SW5 remainder
Cromwell Rd. SW9—4D 53
Cromwell Rd. SW19—5C 76
Crondace Rd. SW6—4C 48
Crondall St. N1—1A 26
Crooked Billet Yd. E2—2A 26
Crooke Rd. SE8—1F 55
Crookham Rd. SW6—4B 48
Croombs Rd. E16—4E 31
Croom's Hill. SE10—3E 57
Croom's Hill Gro. SE10
—3E 57
Cropley St. N1—1F 25
Crosby Ct. SE1—3F 39
Crosby Row. SE1—3F 39
Crosby Sq. EC3—5A 26
Crosby Wlk. E8—3B 12
Crosby Wlk. SW2—5C 66
Crosland Pl. SW11—1C 64
Cross Av. SE10—2A 58
Cross Clo. SE15—5D 55
Crossfield Rd. NW3—3F 7
Crossfield St. SE8—3C 56
Crossford St. SW9—5B 52
Crossharbour. E14—4D 43
Cross Keys Clo. W1—4C 22
Cross La. EC3—1A 40
Crosslet St. SE17—5F 39
Crossley St. N7—3C 10
Cross Rd. SE5—5A 54

Cross St. N1—5D 11
Cross St. SW13—5A 46
Crossthwaite Av. SE5—2F 67
Crosswall. EC3—1B 40
Crossway. N16—2A 12
Crossway, The. SE9—2F 87
Croston Rd. E8—5C 12
Crouchman's Clo. SE26—3B 82
Crowborough Rd. SW17—5C 78
Crowder St. E1—1D 41
Crowhurst Clo. SW9—5C 52
Crowland Ter. N1—4F 11
Crowlin Wlk. N1—4F 11
Crowmarsh Gdns. SE23—5E 69
Crown Clo. E3—5C 14
Crown Clo. NW6—3D 7
Crown Ct. SE12—4D 73
Crown Ct. WC2—5A 24
Crowndale Rd. NW1—1E 23
Crownfield Rd. E15—1F 15
Crown Hill Rd. NW10—5B 4
Crown La. SW16—5C 80
Crown La. Gdns. SW16—5C 80
Crown Office Row. EC4—1C 38
Crown Pas. SW1—2E 37
Crown Pl. NW5—3D 9
Crownstone Rd. SW2—3C 66
Crown St. SE5—3E 53
Crows Rd. E15—2F 29
Crowthorne Clo. SW18—1B 76
Crowthorne Rd. W10—5F 19
Croxley Rd. W9—2B 20
Croxted Clo. SE21—5E 67
Croxted Rd.—5E 67
      SE21 1-293 & 2-198
      SE24 remainder
Croydon Rd. E13—3B 30
Crozier Ter. E9—2F 13
Crucifix La. SE1—3A 40
Cruden St. N1—5D 11
Cruikshank Rd. E15—1A 16
Cruikshank St. WC1—2C 24
Crutched Friars. EC3—1A 40
Crutchley Rd. SE6—2A 86
Crystal Pal. Pde. SE19—5B 82
Crystal Pal. Pk. Rd. SE26
—5C 82
Crystal Pal. Rd. SE22—4B 68
Crystal Ter. SE19—5F 81
Cuba St. E14—3C 42
Cubitt St. WC1—2B 24
Cubitt Ter. SW4—1E 65
Cudham St. SE6—5E 71
Cudworth St. E1—3D 27
Cuff Cres. SE9—4F 73
Culford Gdns. SW3—5B 36
Culford Gro. N1—3A 12

116

Culford M. N1—3A 12
Culford Rd. N1—4A 12
Culling Rd. SE16—4E 41
Cullingworth Rd. NW10—2D 5
Culloden St. E14—5E 29
Cullum St. EC3—1A 40
Culmore Rd. SE15—3E 55
Culmstock Rd. SW11—3C 64
Culross St. W1—1C 36
Culverden Rd. SW12—7E 79
Culverhouse Gdns. SW16
—3B 80
Culverley Rd. SE6—1D 85
Culvert Pl. SW11—5C 50
Culvert Rd. SW11—5B 50
(in two parts)
Culworth St. NW8—1A 22
Cumberland Clo. E8—3B 12
Cumberland Cres. W14—5A 34
(in two parts)
Cumberland Gdns. WC1—2C 24
Cumberland Ga. W1—1B 36
Cumberland Mkt. NW1—2D 23
Cumberland Mills Sq. E14
—1F 57
Cumberland Pl. NW1—2D 23
Cumberland Rd. E12—1F 17
Cumberland Rd. E13—4D 31
Cumberland Rd. SW13—4B 46
Cumberland St. SW1—1D 51
Cumberland Ter. NW1—1D 23
Cumming St. N1—1B 24
Cunard St. SE5—2A 54
Cunard Wlk. SE16—5F 41
Cuncliffe St. SW16—5E 79
Cundy Rd. E16—5E 31
Cundy St. SW1—5C 36
Cunningham Pl. NW8—3F 21
Cupar Rd. SW11—4C 50
Cureton St. SW1—1F 51
Curlew St. SE1—3B 40
Curnick's La. SE27—4E 81
Curricle St. W3—2A 32
Currie Hill Clo. SW19—4B 76
Cursitor St. EC4—5C 24
Curtain Rd. EC2—3A 26
Curtis Field Rd. SW16—4B 80
Curtis St. SE1—5B 40
Curtis Way. SE1—5B 40
Curve, The. W12—1C 32
Curwen Av. E7—1D 17
Curwen Rd. W12—3C 32
Curzon Cres. NW10—4A 4
Curzon Ga. W1—2C 36
Curzon Pl. W1—2C 36
Curzon St. W1—2D 37

Cutcombe Rd. SE5—5E 53
Cuthbert St. W2—3F 21
Cutler St. E1—5A 26
Cut, The. SE1—3D 39
Cyclops M. E14—5C 42
Cyclops Wharf Development. E14
—5C 42
Cygnet St. E1—3B 26
Cygnus Business Centre. NW10
—3B 4
Cynthia St. N1—1B 24
Cypress Pl. W1—3E 23
Cyprus Pl. E2—1E 27
Cyprus St. E2—1E 27
(in two parts)
Cyrena Rd. SE22—4B 68
Cyrus St. EC1—3D 25
Czar St. SE8—2C 56

Dabin Cres. SE10—4E 57
Dacca St. SE8—2B 56
Dace Rd. E3—5C 14
Dacre Gdns. SE13—2A 72
Dacre Pk. SE13—1A 72
Dacre Pl. SE13—1A 72
Dacre Rd. E13—5D 17
Dacres Est. SE23—3F 83
Dacres Rd. SE23—2F 83
Dacre St. SW1—4F 37
Daffodil St. W12—1B 32
Dafforne Rd. SW17—3C 78
Dagmar Gdns. NW10—1F 19
Dagmar Rd. SE5—4A 54
Dagmar Ter. N1—5D 11
Dagnall St. SW11—5B 50
Dagnan Rd. SW12—5D 65
Dagonet Gdns. Brom—3C 86
Dagonet Rd. Brom—3C 86
Dahomey Rd. SW16—5E 79
Daintry Way. E9—3B 14
Dairy M. SW9—1A 66
Dairy Wlk. SW19—4A 76
Daisy La. SW6—1C 62
Dalberg Rd. SW2—3C 66
Dalby Rd. SW18—2C 61
Dalby St. NW5—3D 9
Dalebury Rd. SW17—2B 78
Dale Clo. SE3—1C 72
Daleham Gdns. NW3—2F 7
Daleham M. NW3—3F 7
Dale Rd. NW5—2C 8
Dale Rd. SE17—2D 53
Dale Row. W11—5A 20
Daleside Rd. SW16—5D 79
Dale St. W4—1A 46

Daley St. E9—3F 13
Daley Thompson Way. SW8—1D 65
Dalgarno Gdns. W10—4E 19
Dalgarno Way. W10—3E 19
Dalgleish St. E14—5A 28
Daling Way. E3—1A 28
Dalkeith Rd. SE21—1E 81
Dallas Rd. SE26—3D 83
Dallinger Rd. SE12—4B 72
Dalling Rd. W6—5D 33
Dallington St. EC1—3D 25
Dalmain Rd. SE23—1F 83
Dalmeny Av. N7—1F 9
Dalmore Rd. SE21—2E 81
Dalrymple Rd. SE4—2A 70
Dalston La. E8—3B 12
Dalton St. SE27—3D 81
Dalwood St. SE5—4A 54
Daly Ct. E15—2E 15
Dalyell Rd. SW9—1B 66
Dalmeny Rd. N7—1F 9
Damer Ter. SW10—3E 49
Dames Rd. E7—1C 16
Dame St. N1—1E 25
Damien St. E1—5D 27
Danbury St. N1—1D 25
Danby St. SE15—1B 68
Dancer Rd. SW6—4B 48
Dando Cres. SE3—1D 73
Dandridge Clo. SE10—1B 58
Danebury Av. SW15—4A 60
Daneby Rd. SE6—3D 85
Danecroft Rd. SE24—3E 67
Danehurst St. SW6—4A 48
Danemere St. SW15—1E 61
Dane Pl. E3—1A 28
Danescombe. SE12—1C 86
Danesdale Rd. E9—3A 14
Dane St. WC1—4B 24
Daneswood Av. SE6—3E 85
Daneville Rd. SE5—4F 53
Daniel Bolt Clo. E14—4D 29
Daniel Clo. SW19—5A 78
Daniel Gdns. SE15—3B 54
Daniel's Rd. SE15—1E 69
Dan Leno Wlk. SW6—3D 49
Dante Rd. SE11—5D 39
Danube St. SW3—1A 50
Danvers St. SW3—2F 49
Daphne St. SW18—4E 63
Daplyn St. E1—4C 26
D'Arblay St. W1—5E 23
Darfield Rd. SE4—3B 70
Darfield Way. W10—5F 19
Darfur St. SW15—1F 61
Darien Rd. SW11—1F 63
Darlan Rd. SW6—3B 48
Darley Rd. SW11—4B 64

Darling Rd. SE4—1C 70
Darling Row. E1—3D 27
Darlington Rd. SE27—5D 81
Darnley Rd. E9—3E 13
Darnley Ter. W11—2F 33
Darrell Rd. SW22—3C 68
Darsley Dri. SW8—4F 51
Dartford St. SE17—2E 53
Dartmouth Clo. W11—5C 20
Dartmouth Gro. SE10—4E 57
Dartmouth Hill. SE10—4E 57
Dartmouth Pk. Rd. NW5—1D 9
Dartmouth Pl. SE23—2E 83
Dartmouth Pl. W4—2A 46
Dartmouth Rd. E16—5C 30
Dartmouth Rd. NW2—2F 5
Dartmouth Rd.—3D 83
    SE23 1-147 & 2-104
    SE26 remainder
Dartmouth Row. SE10—4E 57
Dartmouth St. SW1—3F 37
Dartmouth Ter. SE10—4F 57
Dartrey Wlk. SW10—3E 49
Dart St. W10—2A 20
Darwin St. SE17—5F 39
    (in two parts)
Dassett Rd. SE27—5D 81
Datchelor Pl. SE5—4F 53
Datchet Rd. SE6—2B 84
Date St. SE17—1F 53
Daubeney Rd. E5—1A 14
Dault Rd. SW18—4E 63
Davenant St. E1—4C 26
Davenport Rd. SE6—4D 71
Daventry St. NW1—4A 22
Davern Clo. SE10—5B 44
Davey Clo. N7—3B 10
Davey Rd. E9—4C 14
Davey St. SE15—2B 54
Davidge St. SE1—3D 39
David M. W1—4B 22
Davidson Gdns. SW8—3A 52
David's Rd. SE23—1E 83
David St. E15—3F 15
Davies M. W1—1D 37
Davies St. W1—5D 23
Davis Rd. W3—2B 32
Davis St. E13—1D 31
Davisville Rd. W12—3C 32
Dawes Rd. SW6—3A 48
Dawes St. SE17—1F 53
Dawlish Av. SW18—2D 77
Dawlish Rd. NW2—2F 5
Dawnay Gdns. SW18—2F 77
Dawnay Rd. SW18—2E 77
Dawson Pl. W2—1C 34
Dawson Rd. NW2—2E 5

Dawson St. E2—1B 26
Daylesford Rd. SW15—2C 60
Daysbrook Rd. SW2—1B 80
Dayton Gro. SE15—4E 55
Deacon Rd. NW2—2C 4
Deacon Way. SE17—5E 39
Deal Porters Way. SE16—4E 41
Deal's Gateway. SE10—4C 56
Deal St. E1—4C 26
Dealtry Rd. SW15—2E 61
Deancross St. E1—5E 27
Deanery Rd. E15—3A 16
Deanery St. W1—2C 36
Dean Farrar St. SW1—4F 37
Dean Rd. NW2—3E 5
Dean Ryle St. SW1—5A 38
Dean's Bldgs. SE17—5F 39
Deans Ct. EC4—5D 25
Deans Ga. Clo. SE23—3F 83
Dean's M. W1—5D 23
Dean's Pl. SW1—1F 51
Dean Stanley St. SW1—4A 38
Dean St. E7—2C 16
Dean St. W1—5F 23
Dean's Yd. SW1—4F 37
Dean Trench St. SW1—4A 38
Deason St. E15—5E 15
De Beauvoir Cres. N1—5A 12
De Beauvoir Est. N1—5A 12
De Beauvoir Rd. N1—4A 12
De Beauvoir Sq. N1—4A 12
Debnams Rd. SE16—5E 41
De Bruin Ct. E14—1E 57
Decima St. SE1—4A 40
Deck Clo. SE16—2F 41
De Crespigny Pk. SE5—5F 53
Deeley Rd. SW8—4F 51
Deepdale. SW19—4F 75
Deepdene Gdns. SW2—5B 66
Deepdene Rd. SE5—2F 67
Deerbrook Rd. SE24—1D 81
Deerdale Rd. SE24—2E 67
Deerhurst Rd. NW2—3F 5
Deerhurst Rd. SW16—5B 80
Deeside Rd. SW17—3F 77
Dee St. E14—5E 29
Defoe Clo. SW19—5A 78
De Frene Rd. SE26—4F 83
Dekker Rd. SE21—4A 68
Delacourt Rd. SE3—3D 59
Delafield Rd. SE7—1D 59
Delaford Rd. SE16—1D 55
Delaford St. SW6—3A 48
Delamere Ter. W2—4D 21

Delancey St. NW1—5D 9
De Laune St. SE17—1D 53
Delaware Rd. W9—3D 21
Delawyk Cres. SE24—4E 67
Delft Way. SE22—3A 68
Delhi St. N1—5A 10
Delia St. SW18—5D 63
Dell Clo. E15—5F 15
Dellow St. E1—1D 41
Delmare Clo. SW9—2B 66
Delme Cres. SE3—5D 59
Delorme St. W6—2F 47
Delta St. E2—2C 26
Delverton Rd. SE17—1D 53
Delvino Rd. SW6—4C 48
De Montfort Rd. SW16—2A 80
De Morgan Rd. SW6—1D 63
Dempster Rd. SW18—3E 63
Denbigh Clo. NW10—4A 4
Denbigh Clo. W11—1B 34
Denbigh Pl. SW1—1E 51
Denbigh Rd. E6—2F 31
Denbigh Rd. W11—1B 34
Denbigh St. SW1—5E 37
Denbigh Ter. W11—1B 34
Dendy St. SW12—1C 78
Dene Clo. SE4—1A 70
Denham St. SE10—1B 58
Denholme Rd. W9—2B 20
Denison Rd. SW19—5F 77
Denman Rd. SE15—4B 54
Denman St. W1—1F 37
Denmark Hill. SE5—2F 67
Denmark Hill Est. SE5—2F 67
Denmark Pl. WC2—5F 23
Denmark Rd. NW6—1B 20
    (in two parts)
Denmark Rd. SE5—4E 53
Denmark St. E13—4D 31
Denmark St. WC2—5F 23
Denmark Wlk. SE27—4E 81
Denne Ter. E8—5B 12
Dennett's Gro. SE14—4E 55
Dennett's Rd. SE14—5F 55
Denning Clo. NW8—2E 21
Denning Rd. NW3—1F 7
Dennington Pk. Rd. NW6—3C 6
Denny Cres. SE11—5C 52
Denny St. SE11—1C 52
Densham Rd. E15—5A 16
Denton St. SW18—4D 63
Dents Rd. SW11—4B 64
Denyer St. SW3—5A 36
Denzil Rd. NW10—2B 4
Deodar Rd. SW15—2A 62
Deptford Bri. SE8—4C 56
Deptford B'way. SE8—4C 56

Deptford Chu. St. SE8—3C 56
Deptford Ferry Rd. E14—5C 42
Deptford Grn. SE8—2C 56
Deptford High St. SE8—2C 56
Deptford Strand. SE8—5B 42
Deptford Wharf. SE8—5B 42
Derby Ga. SW1—3A 38
Derby Hill. SE23—2E 83
Derby Hill Cres. SE23—2E 83
Derby Rd. E7—4F 17
Derby Rd. E9—5F 13
Derbyshire St. E2—2C 26
Derby St. W1—2C 36
Dereham Pl. EC2—2A 26
Dericote St. E8—5D 13
Dering St. W1—5D 23
Dering Yd. W1—5D 23
Derinton Rd. SW17—4B 78
Dermody Gdns. SE13—3F 71
Dermody Rd. SE13—3F 71
Deronda Est. SW2—1D 81
Deronda Rd. SE24—1D 81
Derrick Gdns. SE7—5E 45
Derry St. W8—3D 35
Derwent Av. SW15—4A 74
Derwent Gro. SE22—2B 68
Derwent St. SE10—1A 58
Desenfans Rd. SE21—4A 68
Desford Rd. E16—3A 30
Desmond St. SE14—3A 56
Detling Rd. Brom—5C 86
Devas St. E3—3D 29
Devenay Rd. E15—4B 16
Deventer Cres. SE22—3A 68
De Vere Gdns. W8—3E 35
Deverell St. SE1—4F 39
Devereux Rd. SW11—4B 64
Devonia Rd. N1—1D 25
Devonport M. W12—2D 33
Devonport Rd. W12—3D 33
Devonport St. E1—5E 27
Devons Est. E3—2D 29
Devonshire Clo. E15—1A 16
Devonshire Clo. W1—4D 23
Devonshire Dri. SE10—3D 57
Devonshire Gro. SE15—2D 55
Devonshire M. W4—1A 46
Devonshire M. N. W1—4D 23
Devonshire M. S. W1—4D 23
Devonshire M. W. W1—3C 22
Devonshire Pas. W4—1A 46
Devonshire Pl. W1—3C 22
Devonshire Pl. W4—1A 46
Devonshire Pl. M. W1—4C 22
Devonshire Rd. E15—1A 16
Devonshire Rd. E16—5D 31
Devonshire Rd. SE23—1E 83

Devonshire Rd. W4—1A 46
Devonshire Row. EC2—4A 26
Devonshire Sq. EC2—5A 26
Devonshire St. W1—4C 22
Devonshire St. W4—1A 46
Devonshire Ter. W2—5E 21
Devons Rd. E3—4C 28
Devon St. SE15—2D 55
De Walden St. W1—4C 22
Dewar St. SE15—1C 68
Dewey Rd. N1—1C 24
Dewey St. SW17—5B 78
Dewhurst Rd. W14—4F 33
Dewsberry St. E14—4E 29
Dewsbury Rd. NW10—2C 4
Dewsbury Ter. NW1—5D 9
D'Eynsford Rd. SE5—4F 53
Diamond Est. SW17—3A 78
Diamond St. SE15—3A 54
Diamond Ter. SE10—4E 57
Diana Ho. SW13—4B 46
Diana Pl. NW1—3D 23
Dibden St. N1—5E 11
Dibden Row. SE1—4C 38
Dicey Av. NW2—1E 5
Dickens St. SE16—4C 40
Dickenson St. NW5—3D 9
Dickens Rd. E6—1F 31
Dickens Sq. SE1—4E 39
Dickens St. SW8—5D 51
Digby Rd. E9—3F 13
Digby St. E2—2E 27
Diggon St. E1—4F 27
Dighton Rd. SW18—3E 63
Dignum St. N1—1C 24
Digswell St. N7—3C 10
Dilhorne Clo. SE12—3D 87
Dilke St. SW3—2B 50
Dillwyn Clo. SE26—4A 84
Dilton Gdns. SW15—1D 75
Dimes Pl. W6—5D 33
Dimond Clo. E7—1C 16
Dimsdale Wlk. E13—1C 30
Dingle Gdns. E14—1C 42
Dingley La. SW16—2F 79
Dingley Pl. EC1—2E 25
Dingley Rd. EC1—2E 25
Dingwall Rd. SW18—5E 63
Dinmont Est. E2—1C 26
Dinmont St. E2—1D 27
Dinsdale Rd. SE3—2B 58
Dinsmore Rd. SW12—5D 65
Dinton Rd. SW19—2F 77
Dirleton Rd. E15—5B 16
Disbrowe Rd. W6—2A 48
Discovery Wlk. E1—1D 41
Disney Pl. SE1—3E 39

Disney St. SE1—3E 39
Disraeli Rd. E7—3C 16
Disraeli Rd. SW15—2A 62
Diss St. E2—2B 26
Distaff La. EC4—1E 39
Distillery La. W6—1E 47
Distillery Rd. W6—1E 47
Distin St. SE11—5C 38
Ditch All. SE10—4D 57
Ditchburn St. E14—1E 43
Divis Way. SW15—4D 61
Dixon Rd. SE14—4A 56
Dixon's All. SE16—3D 41
Dobree Av. NW10—4D 5
Dobson Clo. NW6—4F 7
Dockhead. SE1—3B 40
Dock Hill Av. SE16—3F 41
Dockley Rd. SE16—4C 40
Dock Rd. E16—1B 44
Dock St. E1—1C 40
Doctor Johnson Av. SW17
—3D 79
Doctors Clo. SE26—5E 83
Docwra's Bldgs. N1—3A 12
Dodbrooke Rd. SE27—3C 80
Doddington Gro. SE17—1D 53
Doddington Pl. SE17—2D 53
Dodson St. SE1—3C 38
Dod St. E14—5C 28
Doggett Rd. SE6—5C 70
Dog Kennel Hill. SE22—1A 68
Dog Kennel Hill Est. SE22
—1A 68
Dog La. NW10—1A 4
Doherty Rd. E13—3C 30
Dolben St. SE1—2D 39
(in two parts)
Dolby Rd. SW6—5B 48
Dolland St. SE11—1B 52
Dollis Hill La. NW2—1B 4
Dolman Rd. SW4—2B 66
Dolphin Clo. SE16—3F 41
Dolphin La. E14—1D 43
Dolphin Sq. SW1—1E 51
Dombey St. WC1—4B 24
Dome Hill Pk. SE26—4B 82
Domett Clo. SE5—2F 67
Domfe Way. E5—1E 13
Domingo St. EC1—3E 25
Dominion St. EC2—4F 25
Domville Gro. SE5—1B 54
Donald Rd. E13—5D 17
Donaldson Rd. NW6—5B 6
Donegal St. N1—1B 24
Doneraile St. SW6—5F 47
Dongola Rd. E13—2D 31
Dongola Rd. W. E13—2D 31

Donne Ct. SE24—4E 67
Donne Pl. SW3—5A 36
Donnington Rd. NW10—4D 5
Don Phelan Clo. SE5—4F 53
Doon St. SE1—2C 38
Doran Wlk. E15—4E 15
Dora Rd. SW19—5C 76
Dora St. E14—5B 28
Dorchester Dri. SE24—3E 67
Dorchester Gro. W4—1A 46
Dordrecht Rd. W3—3A 32
Doria Rd. SW6—5B 48
Doric Way. NW1—2F 23
Dorinda St. N7—3C 10
Doris Emmerton Ct. SW11
—2E 63
Doris Rd. E7—4C 16
Dorking Clo. SE8—2B 56
Dorlcote Rd. SW18—5A 64
Dorman Way. NW8—5F 7
Dormay St. SW18—3D 63
Dormer Clo. E15—3B 16
Dornberg Clo. SE3—3C 58
Dorncliffe Rd. SW6—5A 48
Dornfell St. NW6—2B 6
Dornton Rd. SW12—2D 79
Dorothy Rd. SW11—1B 64
Dorrell Pl. SW9—2C 66
Dorrien Wlk. SW16—2F 79
Dorrington St. EC1—4C 24
Dorryn Ct. SE26—5F 83
Dorset Bldgs. EC4—5D 25
Dorset Clo. NW1—4B 22
Dorset M. SW1—4D 37
Dorset Pl. E15—3F 15
Dorset Rise. EC4—5D 25
Dorset Rd. E7—4E 17
Dorset Rd. SW8—3A 52
Dorset Sq. NW1—3B 22
Dorset St. W1—4B 22
Dorville Cres. W6—4D 33
Dorville Rd. SE12—3B 72
Doughty M. WC1—3B 24
Doughty St. WC1—3B 24
Douglas Pl. E14—1E 57
Douglas Rd. E16—4C 30
Douglas Rd. N1—4E 11
Douglas Rd. NW6—5B 6
Douglas St. SW1—5F 37
Douglas Way. SE8—3B 56
Dounesforth Gdns. SW18
—1D 77
Douro Pl. W8—4D 35
Douro St. E3—1C 28
Douthwaite Sq. E1—2C 40
Dove Commercial Centre. NW5
—2E 9

Dovedale Rd. SE22—3D 69
Dovehouse St. SW3—1F 49
Dove M. SW5—5E 35
Dovercourt Est. N1—3F 11
Dovercourt Rd. SE22—4A 68
Doverfield Rd. SW2—5A 66
Dover Ho. Rd. SW15—2C 60
Dove Rd. N1—3F 11
Dove Row. E2—5C 12
Dover Pk. Dri. SW15—4D 61
Dover Rd. SE19—5F 81
Dover St. W1—1D 37
Doveton St. E1—3E 27
Dove Wlk. SW1—1C 50
Downahill Rd. SE6—1F 85
Dowdeswell Clo. SW15—2A 60
Dowgate Hill. EC4—1F 39
Dowland St. W10—2A 20
Dowlas St. SE5—3A 54
Downderry Rd. Brom—3F 85
Downers Cotts. SW4—2E 65
Downes Pl. SE15—2C 54
Downfield Clo. W9—3D 21
Downham Rd. N1—4F 11
Downham Way. Brom—5F 85
Downing St. SW1—3A 38
Down Pl. W6—5D 33
Downsell Rd. E15—1F 15
Downshire Hill. NW3—1F 7
Downside Cres. NW3—2A 8
Downs La. E5—1D 13
Downs Pk. Rd.—2B 12
    E8 1-73 & 2-90
    E5 remainder
Downs Rd. E5—1C 12
Down St. W1—2D 37
Down St. M. W1—2D 37
Downton Av. SW2—2A 80
Downtown Rd. SE16—3A 42
Dowrey St. N1—5C 10
Dowson Clo. SE5—2F 67
Doyce St. SE1—3E 39
Doyle Gdns. NW10—5C 4
D'Oyley St. SW1—5C 36
Draco St. SE17—2E 53
Dragoon Rd. SE8—1B 56
Drake Clo. SE16—3B 41
Drakefell Rd.—5F 55
    SE14 1-87 & 2-134
    SE4 remainder
Drakefield Rd. SW17—3C 78
Drakeley Ct. N5—1D 11
Drake Rd. SE4—1C 70
Drakes Courtyard. NW6—4B 6
Drake St. WC1—4B 24
Draper's Gdns. EC2—5F 25
Drapers Rd. E15—1F 15

Drappers Way. SE16—5C 40
Drawdock Rd. SE10—3F 43
Draycott Av. SW3—5A 36
Draycott Pl. SW3—5B 36
Draycott Ter. SW3—5B 36
Drayford Clo. W9—3B 20
Dray Gdns. SW2—3B 66
Drayson M. W8—3C 34
Drayton Gdns. NW1—1E 49
Drayton Pk. N5—1C 10
Drayton Rd. NW10—5B 4
Dreadnought St. SE10—4A 44
Dresden Clo. NW6—3D 7
Dresden M. NW6—3D 7
Dressington Av. SE4—4C 70
Drewstead Rd. SW16—2F 79
Driffield Rd. E3—1A 28
Drive, The. N7—3B 10
Drive, The. NW10—5B 4
Droitwich Clo. SE26—3C 82
Dromore Rd. SW15—4A 62
Droop St. W10—2A 20
Druce Rd. SE21—4A 68
Druid St. SE1—3A 40
Drummond Cres. NW1—2F 23
Drummond Ga. SW1—1F 51
Drummond Rd. SE16—4D 41
Drummond St. NW1—3D 23
Drum St. E1—5B 26
Drury La. WC2—5A 24
Dryad St. SW15—1F 61
Dryburgh Rd. SW15—1D 61
Dryden Ct. SE11—5D 39
Dryden Rd. SW19—5E 77
Dryden St. WC2—5A 24
Dryfield Wlk. SE8—2C 56
Drysdale Pl. N1—2A 26
Drysdale St. N1—2A 26
Ducal St. E2—2B 26
Du Cane Ct. SW12—1C 78
Du Cane Rd. W12—5B 18
Duchess M. W1—4D 23
Duchess of Bedford's Wlk. W8
—3C 34
Duchess St. W1—4D 23
Duchy Pl. SE1—2C 38
Duchy St. SE1—2C 38
Ducie St. SW4—2B 66
Duckett St. E1—3F 27
Du Cros Rd. W3—2A 32
Dudden Hill La. NW10—1B 4
Duddington Clo. SE9—4F 87
Dudley Rd. NW6—1A 20
Dudley Rd. SW19—5C 76
Dudley St. W2—4F 21
Dufferin St. EC1—3E 25
Duff St. E14—5D 29

Dufour's Pl. W1—5E 23
Duke Humphrey Rd. SE3—4A 58
Duke of Wellington Pl. SW1
—3C 36
Duke of York St. SW1—2E 37
Duke Shore Pl. E14—1B 42
Duke's La. W8—3D 35
Duke's Pl. EC3—5A 26
Duke's Rd. WC1—2F 23
Dukesthorpe Rd. SE26—4F 83
Duke St. W1—5C 22
Duke St. Hill. SE1—2F 39
Duke St. Saint James's. SW1
—2E 37
Duke's Yd. W1—1C 36
Dulford St. W11—1A 34
Dulka Rd. SW11—3B 64
Dulwich Comn. SE21—1A 82
Dulwich Rd. SE24—3C 66
Dulwich Village. SE21—4A 66
Dulwich Wood Av. SE19—4A 82
Dulwich Wood Pk. SE19—4A 82
Dumbarton Rd. SW2—4A 66
Dumpton Pl. NW1—4C 8
Dunbar Rd. E7—3C 16
Dunbar St. SE27—3E 81
Dunboyne Rd. NW3—2B 8
Dunbridge St. E2—3C 26
Duncan Grn. W3—5A 18
Duncannon St. WC2—1A 38
Duncan Rd. E8—5D 13
Duncan St. N1—1D 25
Duncan Ter. N1—1D 25
Dunch St. E1—5D 27
Duncombe Hill. SE23—5A 70
Duncrievie Rd. SE13—4F 71
Dundalk Rd. SE4—1A 70
Dundas Rd. SE15—5E 55
Dundee Rd. E13—1D 31
Dundee St. E1—2D 41
Dundonald Rd. NW10—5F 5
Dundry Ho. SE26—3C 82
Dunelm St. E1—5F 27
Dunfield Gdns. SE6—5D 85
Dunfield Rd. SE6—5D 85
(in two parts)
Dunford St. N7—1B 10
Dungarvan Av. SW15—2C 60
Dunkery Rd. SE9—4F 87
Dunkirk St. SE27—4E 81
Dunlace Rd. E5—1E 13
Dunlem Gro. SE27—3E 81
Dunloe St. E2—1B 26
Dunlop Pl. SE16—4B 40
Dunlop Point. E16—2D 45
Dunmore Rd. NW6—5A 6
Dunmow Rd. E15—1F 15

Dunn St. E8—2B 12
Dunollie Pl. NW5—2E 9
Dunollie Rd. NW5—2E 9
Dunoon Rd. SE23—5E 69
Dunraven Rd. W12—2C 32
Dunraven St. W1—1B 36
Dunsany Rd. W14—4F 33
Dunstable M. W1—4C 22
Dunstan's Gro. SE22—4D 69
Dunstan's Rd. SE22—5C 68
Dunster Ct. EC3—1A 40
Dunster Gdns. NW6—4B 6
Dunster Ho. SE6—3D 85
Dunsterville Way. SE1—3F 39
Dunston Pl. E8—5B 12
Dunston Rd. SW11—1C 64
Dunston St. E8—5B 12
Dunton Rd. SE1—5B 40
Dunthill Rd. SW18—1D 77
Dunworth M. W11—5B 20
Duplex Ride. SW1—3B 36
Dupont St. E14—4A 28
Dupree Rd. SE7—1D 59
Durand Gdns. SW9—4B 52
Durands Wlk. SE16—3A 42
Durant St. E2—2C 26
Durban Rd. E15—2A 30
Durban Rd. SE27—4E 81
Durford Cres. SW15—1D 75
Durham Hill. Brom—4B 85
Durham Rd. E12—1F 17
Durham Rd. E16—3A 30
Durham Row. E1—4F 27
Durham St. SE11—2B 52
Durham Ter. W2—5D 21
Durnford Ho. SE6—3D 85
Durnford St. SE10—2E 57
Durning Rd. SE19—5F 81
Durnsford Av. SW19—2C 76
Durnsford Rd. SW19—2C 76
Durrell Rd. SW6—4B 48
Durrington Rd. E5—1A 14
Dursley Clo. SE3—5E 59
Dursley Gdns. SE3—4F 59
Dursley Rd. SE3—5E 59
Durward St. E1—4D 27
(in two parts)
Durweston St. W1—4B 22
Dutch Yd. SW18—3C 62
Duthie St. E14—1E 43
Dutton St. SE10—4E 57
Dye Ho. La. E3—5C 14
Dyer's Bldgs. EC1—4C 24
Dyers La. SW15—1D 61
Dylways. SE5—2F 67
Dymes Path. SW19—2F 75
Dymock St. SW6—1D 63

Dyneley Rd. SE12—3E 87
Dyne Rd. NW6—4A 6
Dynham Rd. NW6—4C 6
Dyott St. WC1—5F 23
Dysart St. EC2—3A 26
Dyson Rd. E15—3B 16

Eagle Ct. EC1—4D 25
Eagle Wlk. WC1—4B 24
Eagle Wharf Rd. N1—1E 25
Ealdham Sq. SE9—2E 73
Eamont St. NW8—1A 22
Eardley Cres. SW5—1C 48
Eardley Rd. SW16—5E 79
Earldom Rd. SW15—2E 61
Earlham Gro. E7—2B 16
Earlham St. WC2—5A 24
Earl Rd. SE1—1B 54
Earls Ct. Gdns. SW5—5D 35
Earls Ct. Rd.—4C 34
W8 1-109 & 4-138
SW5 remainder
Earls Ct. Sq. SW5—1D 49
Earlsferry Way. N1—4B 10
Earlsfield Rd. SW18—1E 77
Earlsmead Rd. NW10—2E 19
Earls Ter. W8—4B 34
Earlsthorpe M. SW12—4C 64
Earlsthorpe Rd. SE26—4F 83
Earlstoke St. EC1—2D 25
Earlston Gro. E9—5D 13
Earl St. EC2—4F 25
Earls Wlk. W8—4C 34
Earlswood Clo. SE10—1A 58
Earlswood St. SE10—1A 58
Early M. NW1—5D 9
Earnshaw St. WC2—5F 23
Earsby St. W14—5A 34
E. Acton La. W3—2A 32
E. Arbour St. E1—5F 27
Eastbourne M. W2—5E 21
Eastbourne Rd. E15—5A 16
Eastbourne Ter. W2—5E 21
Eastbrook Rd. SE3—4D 59
Eastbury Gro. W4—1A 46
Eastbury Ter. E1—3F 27
Eastcastle St. W1—5E 23
Eastcheap. EC3—1A 40
Eastcombe Av. SE7—2D 59
Eastcote St. SW9—5B 52
Eastdown Pk. SE13—2F 71
E. Dulwich Gro. SE22—3A 68
E. Dulwich Rd. SE22—2B 68
(in two parts)
Eastern Rd. E13—1D 31
Eastern Rd. SE4—2C 70

E. Ferry Rd. E14—4D 43
(in two parts)
East Gdns. SW19—5A 78
E. Harding St. EC4—5C 24
E. Heath Rd. NW3—1A 8
East Hill. SW18—3D 63
E. India Dock Rd. E14—5C 28
E. India Dock Wall Rd. E14
—1F 43
Eastlake Rd. SE5—5E 53
Eastlands Cres. SE21—4B 68
East La. SE16—3C 40
Eastleigh Wlk. SW15—5C 60
Eastmearn Rd. SE21—2E 81
Eastmoor Pl. SE7—4F 45
Eastmoor St. SE7—4F 45
E. Mount St. E1—4D 27
Eastney St. SE10—1F 57
Easton St. WC1—3C 24
East Pier. E1—2D 41
East Pl. SE27—4E 81
E. Poultry Av. EC1—4D 25
East Rd. E15—5C 16
East Rd. N1—2F 25
East Row. W10—3A 20
E. Smithfield. E1—1B 40
East St. SE17—1E 53
E. Surrey Gro. SE15—3B 54
E. Tenter St. E1—5B 26
Eastway. E9—3B 14
Eastway Commercial Centre. E15
—2C 14
Eaton Clo. SW1—5C 36
Eaton Dri. SW9—2D 67
Eaton Ga. SW1—5C 36
Eaton La. SW1—4D 37
Eaton M. N. SW1—4C 36
Eaton M. S. SW1—4D 37
Eaton M. W. SW1—5C 36
Eaton Pl. SW1—4C 36
Eaton Row. SW1—4D 37
Eaton Sq. SW1—5C 36
Eaton Ter. SW1—2A 28
Eaton Ter. SW1—5C 36
Eatonville Rd. SW17—2B 78
Eatonville Vs. SW17—2B 78
Ebbisham Dri. SW8—2B 52
Ebbsfleet Rd. NW2—2A 6
Ebdon Way. SE3—1D 73
Ebenezer St. N1—2F 25
Ebley Clo. SE15—2B 54
Ebner St. SW18—3D 63
Ebor Cotts. SW15—3A 74
Ebor St. E1—3B 26
Ebsworth St. SE23—5F 69
Ebury Bri. SW1—1D 51
Ebury Bri. Rd. SW1—1C 50
Ebury M. SW1—5D 37

Ebury M. E. SW1—4D 37
Ebury Sq. SW1—5D 37
Ebury St. SW1—5C 36
Ecclesbourne Rd. N1—4E 11
Eccles Rd. SW11—2B 64
Eccleston Bri. SW1—5D 37
Ecclestone Ho. SW2—4C 66
Eccleston M. SW1—4C 36
Eccleston Pl. SW1—5D 37
Eccleston Sq. SW1—5D 37
Eccleston Sq. M. SW1—5E 37
Eccleston St. SW1—4D 37
Eckersley St. E1—3B 26
Eckford St. N1—1C 24
Eckstein Rd. SW11—2A 64
Eclipse Rd. E13—4D 31
Ector Rd. SE6—2A 86
Edbrooke Rd. W9—3C 20
Eddisbury Ho. SE26—3C 82
Eddiscombe Rd. SW6—5B 48
Eddystone Rd. SE4—3A 70
Edenbridge Rd. E9—4F 13
Edencourt Rd. SW16—5D 79
Eden Gro. N7—2B 10
Edenham Way. W10—3B 20
Edenhurst Av. SW6—1B 62
Eden M. SW17—3E 77
Eden Rd. SE27—5D 81
Edensor Gdns. W4—3A 46
Edensor Rd. W4—3A 46
Edenvale St. SW6—5E 49
Edgarley Ter. SW6—4A 48
Edgar Rd. E3—2D 29
Edgeley La. SW4—1F 65
Edgeley Rd. SW4—1F 65
Edgel St. SW18—2D 63
Edgepoint Clo. SE27—5D 81
Edge St. W8—2C 34
Edgeworth Rd. SE9—2E 73
Edgware Rd. W2—3F 21
Edinburgh Ga. SW1—3B 36
Edinburgh Rd. E13—1D 31
Edis St. NW1—5C 8
Edith Gro. SW10—2E 49
Edithna St. SW9—1A 66
Edith Rd. E6—4F 17
Edith Rd. E15—2F 15
Edith Rd. W14—5A 34
Edith Rd. SW19—5D 77
Edith Row. SW6—4D 49
Edith Ter. SW10—3E 49
Edith Vs. W14—5B 34
Edith Yd. SW10—3E 49
Edmund St. SE5—3F 53
Edna St. SW11—4A 50
Edric Rd. SE14—3F 55
Edward Ct. E16—4C 30

Edwardes Sq. W8—4B 34
Edward M. NW1—2D 23
Edward M. W1—5C 22
Edward Pl. SE8—2B 56
Edward's Cotts. N1—3D 11
Edward Sq. N1—5B 10
Edward St. E16—3C 30
Edward St.—3A 56
SE8 1-95 & 2-86
SE14 remainder
Edward Temme Av. E15—4B 16
Edwin's Mead. E9—1A 14
Edwin St. E1—3E 27
Edwin St. E16—4C 30
Effie Pl. SW6—3C 48
Effie Rd. SW6—3C 48
Effingham Rd. SE12—3A 72
Effort St. SW17—5A 78
Effra Pde. SW2—3C 66
Effra Rd. SW2—3C 66
Effra Rd. SW19—5D 77
Egan Way. SE16—1D 55
Egbert St. NW1—5C 8
Egerton Cres. SW3—5A 36
Egerton Dri. SE10—4D 57
Egerton Gdns. NW10—5E 5
Egerton Gdns. SW3—4A 36
Egerton Gdns. M. SW3—4A 36
Egerton Pl. SW3—4A 36
Egerton Ter. SW3—4A 36
Egham Clo. SW19—2A 76
Egham Rd. E13—4D 31
Eglantine Rd. SW18—3E 63
Egliston M. SW15—1E 61
Egliston Rd. SW15—1E 61
Egmont St. SE14—3F 55
Egremont Rd. SE27—3C 80
Eiaine Gro. NW5—2C 8
Elam Clo. SE5—5D 53
Elam St. SE5—5D 53
Eland Rd. SW11—1B 64
Elba Pl. SE17—5E 39
Elbe St. SW6—5E 49
Elborough St. SW18—1C 76
Elbury Dri. E16—5C 30
Elcho St. SW11—3A 50
Elcot Av. SE15—3D 55
Elderberry Grn SE27—4E 81
Elderfield Rd. E5—1E 13
Elder Rd. SE27—5E 81
Elder St. E1—3B 26
Elderton Rd. SE26—4A 84
Elderwood Pl. SE27—5E 81
Eldon Gro. NW3—2F 7
Eldon Rd. W8—4D 35
Eldon St. EC2—4F 25
Eleanor Gro. SW13—1A 60

Eleanor Rd. E8—3D 13
Eleanor Rd. E15—3B 16
Eleanor St. E3—2C 28
Electric Av. SW9—2C 66
Electric La. SW9—2C 66
Elephant & Castle. SE1—5D 39
Elephant La. SE16—3E 41
Elephant Rd. SE17—5E 39
Elfindale Rd. SE24—3E 67
Elford Clo. SE3—2E 73
Elford M. SW4—3E 65
Elfort Rd. N5—1C 10
Elfrida Cres. SE6—4C 84
Elf Row. E1—1E 41
Elgar Clo. SE8—3C 56
Elgar St. SE16—4A 42
Elgin Av. W9—3C 20
Elgin Ct. W9—3D 21
Elgin Cres. W11—1A 34
Elgin Est. W9—3C 20
Elgin M. W11—5A 20
Elgin M. N. W9—2D 21
Elgin M. S. W9—2D 21
Elgood Clo. W11—1A 34
Elia M. N1—1D 25
Elias Pl. SW8—2C 52
Elia St. N1—1D 25
Elim Est. SE1—4A 40
Elim Way. E13—2B 30
Eliot Bank. SE23—2D 83
Eliot Cotts. SE3—5A 58
Eliot Gdns. SW15—2C 60
Eliot Hill. SE13—5E 57
Eliot Pk. SE13—5E 57
Eliot Pl. SE3—5A 58
Eliot Vale. SE3—5F 57
Elizabeth Av. N1—4F 11
Elizabeth Bri. SW1—5D 37
Elizabeth Clo. E14—5D 29
Elizabeth Clo. W9—3E 21
Elizabeth Fry Rd. E8—4D 13
Elizabeth Gdns. W3—2B 32
Elizabeth M. NW3—3B 8
Elizabeth Rd. E6—5F 17
Elizabeth St. SW1—5C 36
Elkington Rd. E13—3D 31
Elkstone Rd. W10—4B 20
Ellaline Rd. W6—2F 47
Elland Rd. SE15—2E 69
Ellenborough Pl. SW15—2C 60
Ellen St. E1—5C 26
Ellerby St. SW6—4F 47
Ellerdale Clo. NW3—1E 7
Ellerdale Rd. NW3—2E 7
Ellerdale St. SE13—2D 71
Ellerslie Gdns. NW10—5C 4
Ellerslie Rd. W12—2D 33

Ellerslie Sq. Industrial Est. SW2
—3A 66
Ellerton Rd. SW13—4C 46
Ellerton Rd. SW18—1F 77
Ellery St. SE15—5D 55
Ellesmere Rd. E3—1A 28
Ellesmere Rd. NW10—2C 4
Ellesmere St. E14—5D 29
Ellingfort Rd. E8—4D 13
Ellingham Rd. E15—1F 15
Ellingham Rd. W12—3C 32
Ellington St. N7—3C 10
Elliot Clo. E15—4A 16
Elliott Rd. SW9—3D 53
Elliott Rd. W4—5A 32
Elliott's Pl. N1—5D 11
Elliott Sq. NW3—4A 8
Elliotts Row. SE11—5D 39
Elliscombe Rd. SE7—2E 59
Ellisfield Dri. SW15—5C 60
Ellis M. SE7—2E 59
Ellison Rd. SW13—5B 46
Ellis St. SW1—5C 36
Ellora Rd. SW16—5F 79
Ellsworth St. E2—2D 27
Elm Bank Gdns. SW13—5A 46
Elmbourne Rd. SW17—3D 79
Elmbridge Wlk. E8—4C 12
Elmcourt Rd. SE27—2D 81
Elmcroft St. E5—1E 13
Elmer Rd. SE6—5E 71
Elmfield Rd. SW17—2C 78
Elm Friars Wlk. NW1—4F 9
Elm Grn. W3—5A 18
Elm Grn. Clo. E15—5A 16
Elm Gro. NW2—1F 5
Elm Gro. SE15—5B 54
Elm Gro. Rd. SW13—5C 46
Elmhurst Rd. E7—4D 17
Elmhurst St. SW4—1F 65
Elmington Est. SE5—3F 53
Elmington Rd. SE5—3F 53
Elmira St. SE13—1D 71
Elm La. SE6—2B 84
Elm Lodge. SW6—4F 47
Elmore St. N1—4F 11
Elm Pk. SW2—4B 66
Elm Pk. Gdns. SW10—1F 49
Elm Pk. La. SW10—1F 49
Elm Pk. Rd. SW3—2F 49
Elm Pl. SW7—1F 49
Elm Rd. E7—3B 16
Elmscott Rd. Brom—5B 86
Elms Cres. SW4—4E 65
Elmshaw Rd. SW15—3C 60
Elms M. W2—1F 35
Elms Rd. SW4—3E 65

Elms, The. SW13—1B 60
Elmstone Rd. SW6—4C 48
Elm St. WC1—3B 24
Elm Ter. NW3—1A 8
Elm Tree Clo. NW8—2F 21
Elm Tree Rd. NW8—2F 21
Elm Way. NW10—1A 4
Elmwood Rd. SE24—3F 67
Elmworth Gro. SE21—2F 81
Elnathan M. W9—3D 21
Elphinstone St. N5—1D 11
Elrington Rd. E8—3C 12
Elsa St. E1—4A 28
Elsdale St. E9—3E 13
Elsden M. E2—1E 27
Elsenham St. SW18—1B 76
Elsham Rd. E11—1A 16
Elsham Rd. W14—3A 34
Elsiemaud Rd. SE4—3B 70
Elsie Rd. SE22—2B 68
Elsinore Rd. SE23—1A 84
Elsley Rd. SW11—1B 64
Elspeth Rd. SW11—2B 64
Elsted St. SE17—5F 39
Elswick Rd. SE13—5D 57
Elswick St. SW6—5E 49
Elsworthy Rise. NW3—4A 8
Elsworthy Rd. NW3—5A 8
Elsworthy Ter. NW3—4A 8
Elsynge Rd. SW18—3F 63
Eltham Grn. SE9—3F 73
Eltham Grn. Rd. SE9—2E 73
Eltham Hill. SE9—3F 73
Eltham Pal. Rd. SE9—4E 73
Eltham Rd.—3C 72
 SE12 1-101 & 2-120
 SE9 remainder
Elthiron Rd. SW6—4C 48
Elthruda Rd. SE13—4F 71
Elton Pl. N16—2A 12
Eltringham St. SW18—2E 63
Elvaston M. SW7—4E 35
Elvaston Pl. SW7—4E 35
Elverson Rd. SE8—5D 57
Elverton St. SW1—5F 37
Elvino Rd. SE26—5A 84
Elvis Rd. NW2—3E 5
Elwin St. E2—2C 26
Elwyn Gdns. SE12—5C 72
Ely Pl. EC1—4C 24
Elysium St. SW6—5B 48
Elystan Pl. SW3—1B 50
Elystan St. SW3—5A 36
Elystan Wlk. N1—5C 10
Embankment. SW15—5F 47
Embankment Gdns. SW3
—2B 50

Embankment Pl. WC2—2A 38
Emba St. SE16—3C 40
Embleton Rd. SE13—2D 71
Emden St. SW6—4D 49
Emerald St. WC1—4B 24
Emerson St. SE1—2E 39
Emery Hill St. SW1—4E 37
Emery St. SE1—4C 38
Emily Pl. N7—1C 10
Emlyn Gdns. W12—3A 32
Emlyn Rd. W12—3A 32
Emmanuel Rd. SW12—1E 79
Emma Rd. E13—1B 30
Emma St. E2—1D 27
Emmett St. E14—1B 42
Emmott Clo. E1—3A 28
Emperor's Ga. SW7—4E 35
Empire Wharf Rd. E14—5F 43
Empire Works Development. E14
—3C 42
Empress Pl. SW6—1C 48
Empress St. SE17—2E 53
Empson St. E3—3D 29
Emsworth St. SW2—2B 80
Enbrook St. W10—2A 20
Endeavour Way. SW19—4D 77
Endell St. WC2—5A 24
Enderby St. SE10—1A 58
Endlesham Rd. SW12—5C 64
Endsleigh Gdns. WC1—3F 23
Endsleigh Pl. WC1—3F 23
Endsleigh St. WC1—3F 23
Endwell Rd. SE4—5A 56
Endymion Rd. SW2—4B 66
Enfield Rd. N1—4A 12
Enford St. W1—4B 22
Engadine St. SW18—1C 76
Engate St. SE13—2E 71
England's La. NW3—3B 8
Englefield Rd. N1—4F 11
Engleheart Rd. SE6—5D 71
Englewood Rd. SW12—4D 65
English Grounds. SE1—2A 40
Enid St. SE16—4B 40
Enmore Rd. SW15—2E 61
Ennersdale Rd. SE13—3F 71
Ennismore Av. W4—5B 32
Ennismore Gdns. SW7—3A 36
Ennismore Gdns. M. SW7
—4A 36
Ennismore M. SW7—4A 36
Ennismore St. SW7—4A 36
Ensign St. E1—1C 40
Ensor M. SW7—1F 49
Enterprise Business Pk. E14
—3D 43

Enterprise Ho. E14—3D 43
Enterprise Industrial Est. SE16
—1E 55
Enterprise Way. NW10—2C 19
Enterprise Way. SW18—2C 62
Enterprize Way. SE8—5B 42
Epcot M. NW10—2F 19
Epirus M. SW6—3C 48
Epirus Rd. SW6—3B 48
Epping Clo. E14—5C 42
Epping Pl. N1—3C 10
Epple Rd. SW6—4B 48
Epworth St. EC2—3F 25
Erasmus St. SW1—5F 37
Erconwald St. W12—5B 18
Eresby Pl. NW6—4C 6
Erica St. W12—1C 32
Ericsson Clo. SW18—3C 62
Eric Rd. NW10—3B 4
Eric Clo. E7—1C 16
Eric Rd. E7—1C 16
Eric St. E3—3B 28
Erlanger Rd. SE14—4F 55
Ermine Rd. SE13—2D 71
Ernest Av. SE27—4D 81
Ernest St. E1—3F 27
Ernshaw Pl. SW15—3A 62
Erpingham Rd. SW15—1E 61
Errington Rd. W9—3B 20
Errol St. EC1—3E 25
Erskine Rd. NW3—4B 8
Esam Way. SW16—5C 80
Esher Gdns. SW19—2F 75
Esk Rd. E13—3D 31
Esmeralda Rd. SE1—5C 40
Esmond Rd. NW6—5B 6
Esmond St. SW15—2A 62
Esparto St. SW18—5D 63
Essendine Rd. W9—2C 20
Essex Ct. SW13—5B 46
Essex Gro. SE19—5F 81
Essex Pk. M. W3—3C 18
Essex Rd. N1—5D 11
Essex Rd. NW10—4A 4
Essex St. E7—2C 16
Essex St. WC2—1C 38
Essex Vs. W8—3C 34
Essian St. E1—4A 28
Estcourt Rd. SW6—3B 48
Estelle Rd. NW3—1B 8
Esterbrooke St. SW1—5F 37
Este Rd. SW11—1A 64
Estreham Rd. SW16—5F 79
Eswyn Rd. SW17—4B 78
Etchingham Rd. E15—1E 15
Eternit Wlk. SW6—4F 47
Ethelbert St. SW12—1D 79

Ethelburga St. SW11—4A 50
Ethelden Rd. W12—2D 33
Ethel Rd. E16—5D 31
Ethel St. SE17—5E 39
Etherow St. SE22—5C 68
Etherstone Grn. SW16—4C 80
Etherstone Rd. SW16—4C 80
Ethnard Rd. SE15—2D 55
Eton Av. NW3—4F 7
Eton College Rd. NW3—3B 8
Eton Garages. NW3—3A 8
Eton Gro. SE13—1A 72
Eton Pl. NW3—4C 8
Eton Rd. NW3—4B 8
Eton Vs. NW3—3B 8
Etta St. SE8—2A 56
Ettrick St. E14—5E 29
(in two parts)
Eugenia Rd. SE16—5E 41
Europa Pl. EC1—2E 25
Eustace Rd. SW6—3C 48
Euston Rd. NW1—2F 23
Euston Sq. NW1—2F 23
Euston Sta. Colonnade. NW1
—2F 23
Euston St. NW1—2E 23
Evandale Rd. SW9—5C 52
Evangelist Rd. NW5—1D 9
Evans Clo. E8—3B 12
Evans Rd. SE6—2A 86
Evelina Rd. SE15—1E 69
Evelyn Ct. E8—1C 12
Evelyn Fox Ct. W10—4E 19
Evelyn Gdns. SW7—1F 49
Evelyn Lowe Est. SE16—5C 40
Evelyn Rd. SW19—5D 77
Evelyn St. SE8—1A 56
Evelyn Wlk. N1—1F 25
Evelyn Yd. W1—5F 23
Evenwood Clo. SW15—3A 62
Everatt Clo. SW18—4B 62
Everdon Rd. SW13—2C 46
Everest Pl. E14—4E 29
Everilda St. N1—5B 10
Everington St. W6—2F 47
Eve Rd. E11—1A 16
Eve Rd. E15—1A 30
Eversholt St. NW1—1E 23
Eversleigh Rd. E6—5F 17
Eversleigh Rd. SW11—1B 64
Eversley Pk. SW19—5D 75
Eversley Rd. SE7—2D 59
Everthorpe Rd. SE15—1B 68
Evesham Rd. E15—4B 16
Evesham Rd. N11—1F 33
Evesham St. W11—1A 34
Evesham Wlk. SE5—5F 53
Evesham Wlk. SW9—5C 52

Evesham Way. SW11—1C 64
Ewald Rd. SW6—5B 48
Ewart Rd. SE23—5F 69
Ewe Clo. N7—3A 10
Ewelme Rd. SE23—1E 83
Ewen Cres. SW2—1C 80
Ewer St. SE1—2E 39
Ewhurst Rd. SE4—4B 70
Exbury Rd. SE6—2C 84
Excelsior Gdns. SE13—5E 57
Exchange Ct. WC2—1A 38
Exchange Pl. EC2—4A 26
Exchange Sq. EC2—4A 26
Exeter M. NW6—3D 7
Exeter Rd. E16—4C 30
Exeter Rd. NW2—2A 6
Exeter Rd. SE15—4B 54
Exeter St. WC2—1A 38
Exeter Way. SE14—3B 56
Exford Gdns. SE12—1D 87
Exford Rd. SE12—2D 87
Exhibition Clo. W12—1E 33
Exhibition Rd. SW7—3F 35
Exmoor St. W10—4F 19
Exmouth Mkt. EC1—3C 24
Exmouth M. NW1—2E 23
Exmouth Pl. E8—4D 13
Exmouth St. E1—5E 27
Exning Rd. E16—3B 30
Exon St. SE17—1A 54
Exton St. SE1—2C 38
Eylewood Rd. SE27—5E 81
Eynella Rd. SE22—5B 68
Eynham Rd. W12—5E 19
Eyot Gdns. W6—1B 46
Eyot Grn. W4—1B 46
Eyre Ct. NW8—1F 21
Eyre St. Hill. EC1—3C 24
Eythorne Rd. SW9—4C 52
Ezra St. E2—2B 26

Fabian Rd. SW6—3B 48
Factory Pl. E14—1D 57
Fairacres. SW15—2C 60
Fairbairn Grn. SW9—4D 53
Fairburn Ct. SW15—3A 62
Fairby Rd. SE12—3D 73
Fairchild St. EC2—3A 26
Fairclough St. E1—5C 26
Fairdale Gdns. SW15—2D 61
Fairfax Gdns. SE3—4E 59
Fairfax Pl. NW6—4E 7
Fairfax Rd. NW6—4E 7
Fairfax Rd. W4—4A 32
Fairfield Ct. NW10—5C 4
Fairfield Dri. SW18—3D 63

Fairfield Gro. SE7—2F 59
Fairfield Rd. E3—1C 28
Fairfield St. SW18—3D 63
Fairfoot Rd. E3—3C 28
Fairhazel Gdns. NW6—3D 7
Fairholme Rd. W14—1A 48
Fairholt St. SW7—4A 36
Fairland Rd. E15—4B 16
Fairlawn. SE7—2E 59
Fairlawn Pk. SE26—5A 84
Fairlie Gdns. SE23—5E 69
Fairlight Av. NW10—1A 18
Fairlight Rd. SW17—4F 79
Fairlop Pl. NW8—2F 21
Fairmile Av. SW16—5F 79
Fairmount Rd. SW2—4B 66
Fair St. SE1—3A 40
Fairthorn Rd. SE7—1C 58
Fairview Pl. SW2—5B 66
Fairway, The. W3—5A 18
Fairwyn Rd. SE26—4A 84
Fakruddin St. E1—3C 26
Falconberg Ct. W1—5F 23
Falconberg M. W1—5F 23
Falcon Clo. SE1—2D 39
Falcon Ct. EC4—5C 24
Falcon Gro. SW11—1A 64
Falcon La. SW11—1B 64
Falcon Rd. SW11—5A 50
Falcon St. E13—3C 30
Falcon Ter. SW11—1A 64
Falcon Way. E14—5D 43
Falconwood Ct. SE3—5B 58
Falkirk St. N1—1A 26
Falkland Rd. NW5—2E 9
Falmouth Clo. SE12—3B 72
Falmouth Rd. SE1—4E 39
Falmouth St. E15—2F 15
Fambridge Rd. SE26—4B 84
Fane St. W14—2B 48
Fann St. EC1—3E 25
Fanshaw St. N1—2A 26
Fanthorpe St. SW15—1E 61
Faraday Clo. N7—3B 10
Faraday Rd. E15—3B 16
Faraday Rd. SW19—5D 77
Faraday Rd. W10—4A 20
Faraday Way. SE18
            —4F 45
Fareham St. W1—5F 23
Faringford Rd. E15—4A 16
Farjeon Rd. SE3—4F 59
Farleigh Pl. N16—1B 12
Farleigh Rd. N16—1B 12
Farley Ho. SE26—3B 83
Farley Rd. SE6—5D 71
Farlington Pl. SW15—5D 61
Farlow Rd. SW15—1F 61

Farlton Rd. SW18—1D 77
Farm Av. SW16—4A 80
Farmcote Rd. SE12—1C 86
Farmdale Rd. SE10—1C 58
Farmer's Rd. SE5—3D 53
Farmer St. W8—2C 34
Farmfield Rd. Brom—5A 86
Farm Av. NW2—1B 6
Farm La. SW6—3C 48
Farm Pl. W8—2C 34
Farmstead Rd. SE6—4D 85
Farm St. W1—1D 37
Farnaby Rd. SE9—2E 73
Farnan Rd. SW16—5A 80
Farnborough Way. SE15—3B 54
Farncombe St. SE16—3C 40
Farnell M. SW5—1D 49
Farnham Pl. SE1—2D 39
Farnham Royal. SE11—1B 52
Faroe Rd. W14—4F 33
Farquhar Rd. SE19—5B 82
Farquhar Rd. SW19—3C 76
Farrance St. E14—5C 28
Farren Rd. SE23—2A 84
Farrier St. NW1—4D 9
Farringdon La. EC1—3C 24
Farringdon Rd. EC1—3C 24
Farringdon St. EC4—4D 25
Farrins Rents. SE16—2A 42
Farrow Pl. SE16—4A 42
Farthing All. SE1—3C 40
Farthing Fields. E1—2D 41
Fashion St. E1—4B 26
Fassett Rd. E8—3C 12
Fassett Sq. E8—3C 12
Faulkner's All. EC1—4D 25
Faulkner St. SE14—4E 55
Faunce St. SE17—1D 53
Favart Rd. SW6—4C 48
Faversham Rd. SE6—1B 84
Fawcett Clo. SW11—5F 49
Fawcett Rd. NW10—4B 4
Fawcett St. SW10—2E 49
Fawe Pk. Rd. SW15—2B 62
Fawe St. E14—4D 29
Fawley Rd. NW6—2D 7
Fawnbrake Av. SE24—3E 67
Fawn Rd. E13—1E 31
Faygate Rd. SW2—2B 80
Fayland Av. SW16—5E 79
Fearon St. SE10—1C 58
Feathers Pl. SE10—2F 57
Featherstone Av. SE23—2D 83
Featherstone St. EC1—3F 25
Featley Rd. SW9—1D 67
Felbridge Clo. SW16—4C 80
Felday Rd. SE13—4D 71
Felden St. SW6—4B 48

Felgate M. W6—5D 33
Felixstowe Rd. NW10—2D 19
Felix St. E2—1D 27
Fellbrigg Rd. SE22—3B 68
Fellbrigg St. E1—3D 27
Fellows Rd. NW3—4F 7
Felltram Way. SE7—1C 58
Felmersham Clo. SW4—2A 66
Felsberg Rd. SW2—5A 66
Felsham Rd. SW15—1E 61
Felstead Gdns. E14—1E 57
Felstead St. E9—3B 14
Felstead Wharf. E14—1E 57
Felsted Rd. E16—5F 31
Felton St. N1—5F 11
Fenchurch Av. EC3—5A 26
Fenchurch Bldgs. EC3—5A 26
Fenchurch Pl. EC3—1A 40
Fenchurch St. EC3—1A 40
Fen Ct. EC3—5A 26
Fendall St. SE1—4A 40
Fendt Clo. E16—5B 30
Fenelon Pl. W14—5B 34
Fenham Rd. SE15—3C 54
Fenner Clo. SE16—5D 41
Fenner Sq. SW11—1F 63
Fenning St. SE1—3A 40
Fen St. E9—2E 13
Fen St. E16—1B 44
Fentiman Rd. SW8—2A 52
Fenton Clo. E8—3B 12
Fenton Clo. SW9—5B 52
Fentons Av. E13—2D 31
Fenwick Gro. SE15—1C 68
Fenwick Pl. SW9—1A 66
Fenwick Rd. SE15—1C 68
Ferdinand Pl. NW1—4C 8
Ferdinand St. NW1—4C 8
Ferguson's & Roses' Wharves
    Development. E14—5C 42
Fergus Rd. N5—2D 11
Fermor Rd. SE23—1A 84
Fermoy Rd. W9—3B 20
Fernbrook Rd. SE13—4A 72
Ferncliff Rd. E8—2C 12
Ferncroft Av. NW3—1C 6
Ferndale Rd. E7—4D 17
Ferndale Rd.—2A 66
    SW4 1-169 & 2-172
    SW9 remainder
Ferndene Rd. SE24—2E 67
Ferndown Rd. SE9—5F 73
Fernhead Rd. W9—2B 20
Fernholme Rd. SE15—3F 69
Fernhurst Rd. SW6—4A 48
Fernlea Rd. SW12—1D 79
Fernsbury St. WC1—2C 24
Fernshaw Rd. SW10—2E 49

Ferhside Rd. SW12—1B 78
Ferns Rd. E15—3B 16
Fern St. E3—3C 28
Fernthorpe Rd. SW16—5E 79
Ferntower Rd. N5—2F 11
Fernwood Av. SW16—4F 79
Ferranti Clo. SE18—5F 45
Ferrers Rd. SW16—5F 79
Ferriby Clo. N1—4C 10
Ferrier St. SW18—2D 63
Ferrings. SE21—3A 82
Ferris Rd. SE22—2C 68
Ferry La. SW13—2B 46
Ferry Rd. SW13—3C 46
Ferry St. E14—1E 57
Festing Rd. SW15—1F 61
Fetter La. EC4—5C 24
Ffinch St. SE8—3C 56
Field Ct. SW19—3C 76
Field Ct. WC1—4B 24
Fieldgate St. E1—4C 26
Fieldhouse Rd. SW12—1E 79
Fielding Rd. W14—4F 33
Fieldings, The. SE23—1E 83
Fielding St. SE17—2E 53
Field Rd. E7—1C 16
Field Rd. W6—1A 48
Fieldside Rd. Brom—5D 87
Field St. WC1—2B 24
Fieldview. SW18—1F 77
Fieldway Cres. N5—2C 10
Fife Rd. E16—4C 30
Fife Ter. N1—1B 24
Fifield Path. SE23—3F 83
Fifth Av. W10—2A 20
Fig Tree Clo. NW10—5A 4
Filmer Rd. SW6—4B 48
Finborough Rd. SW10—2D 49
Finch Av. SE27—1F 81
Finchdean Way. SE15—3A 54
Finch La. EC3—5F 25
Finchley Pl. NW8—1F 21
Finchley Rd. NW3 & NW8—1C 6
Finck St. SE1—3B 38
Finden Rd. E7—2E 17
Findhorn St. E14—5E 29
Findon Clo. SW18—4C 62
Findon Rd. W12—3C 32
Fingal St. SE10—1B 58
Finland Rd. SE4—1A 70
Finland St. SE16—4A 42
Finlay St. SW6—4F 47
Finnis St. E2—3D 27
Finsbury Av. EC2—4F 25
Finsbury Cir. EC2—4F 25
Finsbury Est. EC1—2C 24
Finsbury Mkt. EC2—3A 26
    (in two parts)

Finsbury Pavement. EC2—4F 25
Finsbury Sq. EC2—4F 25
Finsbury St. EC2—4F 25
Finsen Rd. SE5—1E 67
Finstock Rd. W10—5F 19
Firbank Clo. E16—4F 31
Firbank Rd. SE15—5D 55
Fircroft Rd. SW17—2B 78
Firhill Rd. SE6—4C 84
Firs Clo. SE23—5A 70
First Av. E13—2C 30
First Av. SW14—1A 60
First Av. W3—2B 32
First Av. W10—3B 20
First St. SW3—5A 36
Firth Gdns. SW6—4A 48
Fir Tree Clo. SW16—5E 79
Fir Trees Clo. SE16—2A 42
Fishermans Dri. SE16—3F 41
Fisherman's Pl. W4—2B 46
Fishers Ct. SE14—4F 55
Fisher St. E16—4C 30
Fisher St. WC1—4B 24
Fisherton St. NW8—3F 21
Fishponds Rd. SW17—4A 78
Fish St. Hill. EC3—1F 39
Fisons Rd. E16—2C 44
Fitzalan St. SE11—5C 38
Fitzgeorge Av. W14—5A 34
Fitzgerald Av. SW14—1A 60
Fitzhardinge St. W1—5C 22
Fitzhugh Gro. SW18—4F 63
Fitzjames Av. W14—5A 34
Fitzjohn's Av. NW3—1E 7
Fitzmaurice Pl. W1—2D 37
Fitzneal St. W12—5B 18
Fitzroy Rd. NW1—5C 8
Fitzroy Sq. W1—3E 23
Fitzroy St. W1—3E 23
    (in two parts)
Fitzwilliam Rd. SW4—1E 65
Fiveways Rd. SW9—5C 52
Flamborough St. E14
        —5A 28
Flanchford Rd. W12—4B 32
Flanders Rd. W4—5A 32
Flanders Way. E9—3F 13
Flank St. E1—1C 40
Flask Wlk. NW3—1E 7
Flaxman Rd. SE5—5D 53
Flaxman Ter. WC1—2F 23
Fleece Wlk. N7—3A 10
Fleet La. EC4—5D 25
Fleet Rd. NW3—2A 8
Fleet Sq. WC1—2D 24
Fleet St. EC4—5C 24
Fleet St. Hill. E1—3C 26
Fleetwood Clo. E16—4F 31

Fleetwood Rd. NW10—2C 4
Fleming Rd. SE17—2D 53
Fletcher Path. SE8—3C 56
Fletcher St. E1—1C 40
Fletching Rd. SE7—2F 59
Fleur de Lis St. E1—3B 26
Fleur Gates. SW19—5F 61
Flimwell Clo. Brom—5A 86
Flinton St. SE17—1A 54
Flint St. SE17—5F 39
Flitcroft St. WC2—5F 23
Flockton St. SE16—3C 40
Flodden Rd. SE5—4E 53
Flood St. SW3—1A 50
Flood Wlk. SW3—2A 50
Flora Clo. E14—5D 29
Floral St. WC2—1A 38
Florence Rd. E6—5E 17
Florence Rd. E13—1C 30
Florence Rd. SE14—4B 56
Florence Rd. SW19—5D 77
Florence St. E16—3B 30
Florence St. N1—4D 11
Florence Ter. SE14—4B 56
Florence Ter. SW15—3A 74
Florfield Rd. E8—3D 13
Florian Rd. SW15—2A 62
Florida St. E2—2C 26
Floss St. SW15—5E 47
Flower & Dean Wlk. E1
—4B 26
Flowersmead. SW17—2C 78
Flower Wlk, The. SW7—3E 35
Floyd Rd. SE7—1E 59
Fludyer St. SE13—2A 72
Folair Way. SE16—1D 55
Foley St. W1—4E 23
Folgate St. E1—4A 26
Foliot St. W12—5B 18
Follett St. E14—5E 29
Folly M. W11—5B 20
Folly Wall. E14—3E 43
Fontarabia Rd. SW11—2C 64
Fontenoy Rd. SW12—2D 79
Fontley Way. SW15—5C 60
Footpath, The. SW15—3C 60
Forbes St. E1—5C 26
Fordel Rd. SE6—1F 85
Fordham St. E1—5C 26
Fordingley Rd. W9—2B 20
Fordington Ho. SE26—3D 83
Ford Rd. E3—1B 28
Fords Pk. Rd. E16—5C 30
Ford Sq. E1—4D 27
Ford St. E3—5A 14
(in two parts)
Ford St. E16—5B 30

Fordwych Rd. NW2—2A 6
Fordyce Rd. SE13—4E 71
Foreign St. SE5—5D 53
Foreman Ct. W6—5E 33
Foreshore. SE8—5B 42
Forester Rd. SE15—1D 69
Forest Gro. E8—4B 12
Forest Hill Rd.—4D 69
SE22 3-41 & 2-128
SE23 remainder
Forestholme Clo. SE23—2E 83
Forest La.—2A 16
E15 1-91
E7 remainder
Fore St. EC2—4E 25
Fore St. Av. EC2—4F 25
Forest Rd. E7—1C 16
Forest Rd. E8—3B 12
Forest Side. E7—1D 17
Forest St. E7—2C 16
Forfar Rd. SW11—4C 50
Forge Pl. NW1—3C 8
Forman Pl. N16—1B 12
Formosa St. W9—3D 21
Formunt Clo. E16—4B 30
Forrester Path. SE26—4E 83
Forset St. W1—5A 22
Forster Rd. SW2—5A 66
Forston St. N1—1E 25
Forsyth Gdns. SE17—2D 53
Fortescue Av. E8—4D 13
(in two parts)
Fortess Gro. NW5—2E 9
Fortess Rd. NW5—2D 9
Fortess Wlk. NW5—2D 9
Forthbridge Rd. SW11—2C 64
Fortis Clo. E16—5E 31
Fort Rd. SE1—5B 40
Fortrose Gdns. SW2—1A 80
Fort St. E1—4A 26
Fort St. E16—2D 45
Fortuna Clo. N7—3B 10
Fortunegate Rd. NW10
—5A 4
Fortune Grn. Rd. NW6—1C 6
Fortune St. EC1—3E 25
Fortune Way. NW10—2C 18
Forty Acre La. E16—4C 30
Fosbury M. W2—1D 35
Foscote M. W9—3C 20
Foskett Rd. SW6—5B 48
Fossdene Rd. SE7—1D 59
Fossil Rd. SE13—1C 70
Foss Rd. SW17—4F 77
Foster La. EC2—5E 25
Foster Rd. E13—3C 30
Foster Rd. W3—1A 32

Fothergill Clo. E13—1C 30
Foubert's Pl. W1—5E 23
Foulden Rd. N16—1B 12
Foulis Ter. SW7—1F 49
Foulser Rd. SW17—3B 78
Foundry Clo. SE16—2A 42
Fountain Ct. EC4—1C 38
Fountain Dri. SE19—4B 82
Fountain Pl. SW9—4C 52
Fountain Rd. SW17—5F 77
Fount St. SW8—3F 51
Fournier St. E1—4B 26
Fourth Av. W10—3A 20
Fowey Clo. E1—2D 41
Fowler Clo. SW11—1F 63
Fowler Rd. E7—1C 16
Fowler Rd. N1—5D 11
Fownes St. SW11—1A 64
Foxberry Rd. SE4—1A 70
Foxborough Gdns. SE4—3C 70
Foxbourne Rd. SW17—2C 78
Fox Clo. E1—3E 27
Fox Clo. E16—4C 30
Foxcombe Clo. E6—1F 31
Foxcombe Rd. SW15—1C 74
Foxes Dale. SE3—1C 72
Foxglove St. W12—1B 32
Foxley Clo. E8—2C 12
Foxley Rd. SW9—3C 52
Foxley Sq. SW9—4D 53
Foxmore St. SW11—4B 50
Fox Rd. E16—4B 30
Foxwell St. SE4—1A 70
Foxwood Rd. SE3—2B 72
Foyle Rd. SE3—2B 58
Framfield Rd. N5—2D 11
Frampton Pk. Est. E9—4E 13
Frampton Pk. Rd. E9—3E 13
Frampton St. NW8—3F 21
Francemary Rd. SE4—3C 70
Franche Ct. Rd. SW17—3E 77
Francis Barber Clo. SW16
—4B 80
Franciscan Rd. SW17—5B 78
Francis Chichester Way. SW11
—4C 50
Francis Clo. E14—5F 43
Francis St. E15—2A 16
Francis St. SW1—5E 37
Francis Wlk. N1—5A 10
Franconia Rd. SW4—3F 65
Frank Dixon Clo. SE21—1A 82
Frank Dixon Way. SE21—1A 82
Frankfurt Rd. SE24—3E 67
Frankham St. SE8—3C 56
Frankland Clo. SE16—5D 41
Frankland Rd. SW7—4F 35
Franklin Clo. SE27—3D 81

Franklin Sq. W14—1B 48
Franklin's Row. SW3—1B 50
Franklin St. E3—2D 29
Franklyn Rd. NW10—3B 4
Frank St. E13—3C 30
Fransfield Gro. SE26—3D 83
Frans Hals Ct. E14—4F 43
Franthorne Way. SE6—3D 85
Fraser St. W4—1A 46
Frazier St. SE1—3C 38
Frean St. SE16—4C 40
Freda Corbett Clo. SE15—3C 54
Frederica St. N7—4B 10
Frederick Clo. W2—1A 36
Frederick Cres. SW9—3D 53
Frederick Rd. SE17—2D 53
Frederick's Pl. EC2—5F 25
Frederick's Row. EC1—2D 25
Frederick St. WC1—2B 24
Frederick Ter. E8—4B 12
Freedom St. SW11—5B 50
Freegrove Rd. N7—2A 10
Freeling St. N1—4A 10
 (in two parts)
Freemasons Rd. E16—4D 31
Free Trade Wharf. E1—1F 41
Freightliner Depot Rd. NW10
 —2A 18
Freke Rd. SW11—1C 64
Fremantle St. SE17—1A 54
Fremont St. E9—5E 13
French Pl. E1—2A 26
Frendsbury Rd. SE4—2A 70
Frensham Dri. SW15—3B 74
Frensham St. SE15—2C 54
Frere St. SW11—5A 50
Freshfield Clo. SE13—1F 71
Freshfield Clo. SE13
Freshford St. SW18—3E 77
Freshwater Rd. SW17—5C 78
Freston Rd. W10 & W11—1F 33
Frewin Rd. SW18—1F 77
Friar M. SE27—3D 81
Friars Av. SW15—3B 74
Friars Clo. SE1—2E 39
Friars Rd. E6—5F 17
Friar St. EC4—5D 26
Friary Est. SE15—2C 54
 (in two parts)
Friary Rd. SE15—3C 54
Friday St. EC4—1E 39
Frideswide Pl. NW5—2E 9
Friendly St. SE8—5C 56
Friendly St. M. SE8—5C 56
Friend St. EC1—2D 25
Friern Rd. SE22—5C 68
Frigate M. SE8—2C 56

Frimley Clo. SW19—2A 76
Frimley Way. E1—3F 27
Frinton Rd. E6—2F 31
Friston St. SW6—5D 49
Frith Rd. E11—1E 15
Frith St. W1—5F 23
Frithville Gdns. W12—2E 33
Frobisher St. SE10—2A 58
Frogley Rd. SE22—2B 68
Frogmore. SW18—3C 62
Frognal. NW3—2E 7
Frognal Clo. NW3—2E 7
Frognal Ct. NW3—3E 7
Frognal Gdns. NW3—1E 7
Frognal La. NW3—2D 7
Frognal Pde. NW3—3E 7
Frognal Rise. NW3—1E 7
Frognal Way. NW3—1E 7
Froissart Rd. SE9—3F 73
Frome St. N1—1E 25
Frostic Wlk. E1—4C 26
Froude St. SW8—5D 51
Fryatt St. E14—5A 30
Frye's Bldgs. N1—1C 24
Fry Rd. E6—4F 17
Fry Rd. NW10—5B 4
Fulbourne St. E1—4D 27
Fulbrook M. N19—1E 9
Fulbrook Rd. N19—1E 9
Fulford St. SE16—3D 41
Fulham B'way. SW6—3C 48
Fulham High St. SW6—5A 48
Fulham Pal. Rd.—1E 47
 W6 55-211 & 2-284
 SW6 remainder
Fulham Pk. Gdns. SW6—5B 48
Fulham Pk. Rd. SW6—5B 48
Fulham Rd.—5A 48
 SW3 77-267 & 6-132
 SW10 273-459 & 134-366
 SW6 remainder
Fuller St. E2—3C 26
Fullerton Rd. SW18—3E 63
Fullwood's M. N1—2F 25
Fulmead St. SW6—4D 49
Fulmer Rd. E16—4F 31
Fulthorp Rd. SE3—5C 58
Fulwood Pl. WC1 1B 24
Fulwood Wlk. SW19—1A 76
Furber St. W6—4D 33
Furley Rd. SE15—3C 54
Furlong Rd. N7—3C 10
Furmage St. SW18—5D 63
Furneaux Av. SE27—5D 81
Furness Rd. NW10—1C 18
Furness Rd. SW6—5D 49
Furnival St. EC4—5C 24

Furrow La. E9—2E 13
Further Grn. Rd. SE6—5A 72
Furzedown Dri. SW17—5D 79
Furzedown Rd. SW17—5D 79
Furzefield Rd. SE3—3D 59
Furze St. E3—4C 28
Fyfield Rd. SW9—1C 66
Fynes St. SW1—5F 37

Gable Ct. SE26—4D 83
Gables Clo. SE12—1C 86
Gabrielle Ct. NW3—3F 7
Gabriel St. SE23—5F 69
Gage Rd. E16—4A 30
Gage St. WC1—4A 24
Gainford St. N1—5C 10
Gainsborough M. SE26—3D 83
Gainsborough Rd. E15—2A 30
Gainsborough Rd. W4—5B 32
Gainsford St. SE1—3B 40
Gairloch Rd. SE5—5A 54
Gaisford St. NW5—3E 9
Galahad Rd. Brom—4C 86
Galata Rd. SW13—3C 46
Galatea Sq. SE15—1D 69
Galbraith St. E14—4E 43
Galena Rd. W6—5D 33
Galesbury Rd. SW18—4E 63
Gales Gdns. E2—2D 27
Gale St. E3—4C 28
Galgate Clo. SW19—1A 76
Galleon Clo. SE16—3F 41
Gallery Rd. SE21—1F 81
Galleywall Rd. SE16—5D 41
Galleywall Rd. Trading Est. SE16
 —5D 41
Gallia Rd. N5—2D 11
Gallions Rd. SE7—5D 49
Gulliver Pl. E5—1D 13
Gallon Clo. SE7—5E 45
Galloway Rd. W12—2C 32
Gallus Sq. SE3—1D 73
Galsworthy Cres. SE3—4E 59
Galsworthy Rd. NW2—1A 6
Galton St. W10—2A 20
Galveston Rd. SW15—3B 62
Galway St. EC1—2E 25
Gambetta St. SW8—5D 51
Gambia St. SE1—2D 39
Gambole Rd. SW17—4A 78
Gamlen Rd. SW15—2F 61
Ganton St. W1—1E 37
Gap Rd. SW19—5C 76
Garbutt Pl. W1—4C 22
Garden Clo. SE12—3D 87
Garden Clo. SW15—5D 61

Gardener's Rd. E3—1F 27
Garden La. SW2—1B 80
Garden M. W2—1C 34
Garden Rd. NW8—2E 21
Garden Row. SE1—4D 39
Gardens, The. SE22—2C 68
Garden St. E1—4F 27
Garden Ter. SW1—1F 51
Garden Wlk. EC2—2A 26
Gardiner Av. NW10—2E 5
Gardiners Rd. N1—4A 12
Gardner Rd. E13—3D 31
Gardners La. EC4—1E 39
Gardnor Rd. NW3—1F 7
Gard St. EC1—2D 25
Gareth Gro. Brom—4C 86
Garfield Rd. E13—3B 30
Garfield Rd. SW11—1C 64
Garfield Rd. SW19—5E 77
Galford St. E14—1C 42
Garlick Hill. EC4—1E 39
Garlies Rd. SE23—3A 84
Garlinge Rd. NW2—3B 6
Garnault Pl. EC1—2C 24
Garner St. E2—1C 26
Garnet Rd. NW10—3A 4
Garnet St. E1—1E 41
Garnett Rd. NW3—2B 8
Garnies Clo. SE15—3B 54
Garrad's Rd. SW16—3F 79
Garratt La.—4D 63
   SW18 1-643 & 2-480
   SW17 remainder
Garratt Ter. SW17—4A 78
Garrett St. EC1—3E 25
Garrick Clo. SW18—2E 63
Garrick St. WC2—1A 38
Garsington M. SE4—1B 70
Garthorne Rd. SE23—5F 69
Gartmoor Gdns. SW19—1B 76
Garton Pl. SW18—4E 63
Gartons Way. SW11—1E 63
Garvary Rd. E16—5D 31
Garway Rd. W2—5D 21
Gascoigne Pl. E2—2B 26
Gascony Av. NW6—4C 6
Gascoyne Rd. E9—4F 13
Gaselee St. E14—1E 43
Gasholder Pl. SE11—1B 52
Gaskarth Rd. SW12—4D 65
Gaskell St. SW4—5A 52
Gaskin St. N1—5D 11
Gaspar M. SW5—5D 35
Gassiot Rd. SW17—4B 78
Gastein Rd. W6—2F 47
Gateforth St. NW8—3A 22

Gateley Rd. SW9—1B 66
Gatesborough St. EC2—2A 26
Gateside Rd. SW17—3B 78
Gate St. WC2—5B 24
Gateway. SE17—2E 53
Gateway Trading Est. NW10
   —2B 18
Gathorne St. E2—1F 27
Gatliff Rd. SW1—1D 51
Gatton Rd. SW17—4A 78
Gatwick Rd. SW18—5B 62
Gauden Clo. SW4—1F 65
Gauden Rd. SW4—5F 51
Gaunt St. SE1—4E 39
Gautrey Rd. SE15—5E 55
Gavel St. SE17—5F 39
Gaverick St. E14—5C 42
Gavestone Cres. SE12—5D 73
Gavestone Rd. SE12—5D 73
Gawber St. E2—2E 27
Gawsworth Clo. E15—2B 16
Gay Clo. NW2—2D 5
Gayfere St. SW1—4A 38
Gayford Rd. W12—3B 32
Gayhurst Rd. E8—4C 12
Gaynesford Rd. SE23—2F 83
Gay Rd. E15—1F 29
Gay St. SW15—1F 61
Gayton Cres. NW3—1F 7
Gayton Rd. NW3—1F 7
Gayville Rd. SW11—4B 64
Gaywood Clo. SW2—1B 80
Gaywood St. SE1—4D 39
Gaza St. SE17—1D 53
Geary Rd. NW10—2C 4
Geary St. N7—2B 10
Gedling Pl. SE1—4B 40
Geere Rd. E15—5B 16
Gees Ct. W1—5C 22
Gee St. EC1—3E 25
Geffrye Ct. N1—1A 26
Geffrye St. E2—1B 26
Geldart Rd. SE15—3D 55
Gellatly Rd. SE14—5E 55
General Wolfe Rd. SE10—4F 57
Geneva Dri. SW9—2C 66
Genoa Av. SW15—3E 61
Gentian Row. SE13—4E 57
Gentry Gdns. E13—3C 30
Geoffrey Rd. SE4—1B 70
George & Catherine Wheel All.
   EC2—4A 26
George Beard Rd. SE8—5B 42
George Inn Yd. SE1—2F 39
George La. SE13—4E 71
George Row. SE16—3C 40
George's Rd. N7—2B 10

George St. E16—5B 30
George St. W1—5B 22
Georgetown Clo. SE19—5A 82
Georgette Pl. SE10—3E 57
George Wyver Clo. SW19
   —5A 62
George Yd. EC3—5E 25
George Yd. W1—1C 36
Georgiana St. NW1—5E 9
Georgina Gdns. E2—2B 26
Geraint Rd. Brom—4C 86
Geraldine Rd. SW18—3E 63
Geraldine St. SE11—4D 39
Gerald Rd. E16—3B 30
Gerald Rd. SW1—5C 36
Gerard Rd. SW13—4B 46
Germander Way. E15—2A 30
Gernon Rd. E3—1A 28
Gerrard Pl. W1—1F 37
Gerrard Rd. N1—1D 25
Gerrard St. W1—1F 37
Gerridge St. SE1—4C 38
Gerry Raffles Sq. E15—4F 15
Gertrude St. SW10—2E 49
Gervase St. SE15—3D 55
Ghent St. SE6—2C 84
Ghent Way. E8—3B 12
Gibbins Rd. E15—4E 15
Gibbon Rd. SE15—5E 55
Gibbon Rd. W3—1A 32
Gibbons Rd. NW10—3A 4
Gibbon Wlk. SW15—2C 60
Gibbs Av. SE19—5F 81
Gibbs Clo. SE19—5F 81
Gibbs Grn. W14—1B 48
Gibbs Sq. SE19—5F 81
Gibraltar Wlk. E2—2B 26
Gibson Clo. E1—3E 27
Gibson Rd. SE11—5B 38
Gibson Sq. N1—5C 10
Gibson St. SE10—1A 58
Gideon Rd. SW11—1C 64
Giffin St. SE8—3C 56
Gifford St. N1—4A 10
Gift La. E15—5B 16
Gilbert Pl. WC1—4A 24
Gilbert Rd. SE11—5C 38
Gilbert St. E15—1A 16
Gilbert St. W1—5C 22
Gilbey Rd. SW17—4A 78
Gildea St. W1—4D 23
Gilden Cres. NW5—2C 8
Giles Coppice. SE19—4B 82
Gilkes Cres. SE21—4A 68
Gilkes Pl. SE21—4A 68
Gill Av. E16—5C 30
Gillender St.—3E 29

E14 43-50
E3 remainder
Gillett St. N16—2A 12
Gillian St. SE13—3D 71
Gillies St. NW5—2C 8
Gilling Ct. NW3—3A 8
Gillingham M. SW1—5E 37
Gillingham Row. SW1—5E 37
Gillingham St. SW1—5E 37
Gillison Wlk. SE16—4C 40
Gillman Dri. E15—5B 16
Gill St. E14—5B 28
Gilmore Rd. SE13—2F 71
Gilpin Rd. E5—1A 14
Gilstead Rd. SW6—5D 49
Gilton Rd. SE6—3A 86
Giltspur St. EC1—5D 25
Gipsy Hill. SE19—5A 82
Gipsy La. SW15—1D 61
Gipsy Rd. SE27—4E 81
Gipsy Rd. Gdns. SE27—4E 81
Giralda Clo. E16—4F 31
Giraud St. E14—5D 29
Girdler's Rd. W14—5F 33
Girdwood Rd. SW18—5A 62
Gironde Rd. SW6—3B 48
Girton Rd. SE26—5F 83
Girton Vs. W10—5F 19
Given Wilson Wlk. E13—1B 30
Gladding Rd. E12—1F 17
Glade, The. SE7—3E 59
Gladiator St. SE23—5A 70
Gladstone Pl. E3—1B 28
Gladstone St. SE1—4D 39
Gladstone Ter. SW8—4D 51
Gladwell Rd. Brom—5C 86
Gladwyn Rd. SW15—1F 61
Gladys Rd. NW6—4C 6
Glaisher St. SE10—3E 57
Glamis Pl. E1—1E 41
Glamis Rd. E1—1E 41
Glanville Rd. SW2—3A 66
Glasbrook Rd. SE9—5F 73
Glasford St. SW17—5B 78
Glasgow Rd. E13—1D 31
Glasgow Ter. SW1—1E 51
Glasshill St. SE1—3D 39
Glasshouse Fields. E1—1F 41
Glasshouse St. W1—1E 37
Glasshouse Wlk. SE11—1B 52
Glasshouse Yd. EC1—3E 25
Glass St. E2—3D 27
Glastonbury St. NW6—2B 6
Glaucus St. E3—4D 29
Glazbury Rd. W14—5A 34
Glazebrook Clo. SE21—2F 81

Glebe Clo. W4—1A 46
Glebe Hyrst. SE19—4A 82
Glebelands Clo. SE5—1A 68
Glebe Pl. SW3—2A 50
Glebe Rd. E8—4B 12
Glebe Rd. NW10—3B 4
Glebe Rd. SW13—5C 46
Glebe St. W4—1A 46
Glebe Ter. E3—2D 29
Glebe, The. SE3—1A 72
Glebe, The. SW16—4A 80
Gledhow Gdns. SW5—5E 35
Gledstanes Rd. W14—1A 48
Glegg Pl. SW15—2F 61
Glenaffric Av. E14—5F 43
Glen Albyn Rd. SW19—2F 75
Glenarm Rd. E5—1E 13
Glenavon Rd. E15—4A 16
Glenbow Rd. Brom—5A 86
Glenbrook Rd. NW6—2C 6
Glenburnie Rd. SW17—3B 78
Glencairne Clo. E16—4F 31
Glendale Dri. SW19—5B 76
Glendall St. SW9—2B 66
Glendarvon St. SW15—1F 61
Glendower Pl. SW7—5F 35
Glendun Rd. W3—1A 32
Gleneagle M. SW16—5F 79
Gleneagle Rd. SW16—5F 79
Gleneldon M. SW16—4A 80
Gleneldon Rd. SW16—4A 80
Glenelg Rd. SW2—3A 66
Glenfarg Rd. SE6—1E 85
Glenfield Rd. SW12—1E 79
Glenfinlas Way. SE5—3D 53
Glenforth St. SE10—1B 58
Glengall Causeway. E14—4C 42
Glengall Gro. E14—4E 43
Glengall Rd. NW6—5B 6
Glengall Rd. SE15—1B 54
Glengall Ter. SE15—2B 54
Glengarnock Av. E14—5F 43
Glengarry Rd. SE22—3A 68
Glenhurst Av. NW6—1C 8
Glenilla Rd. NW3—3A 8
Glenister Rd. SE10—1B 58
Glenloch Rd. NW3—3A 8
Glenluce Rd. SE3—2C 58
Glenmore Rd. NW3—3A 8
Glennie Rd. SE27—3C 80
Glenparke Rd. E7—3D 17
Glen Rd. E13—3E 31
Glenrosa St. SW6—5E 49
Glenroy St. W12—5E 19
Glensdale Rd. SE4—1B 70
Glentanner Way. SW17—3F 77
Glen Ter. E14—3E 43

Glentham Gdns. SW13—2D 47
Glentham Rd. SW13—2D 47
Glenthorne Rd. W6—5D 33
Glenton Rd. SE13—2A 72
Glentworth St. NW1—3B 22
Glenville Gro. SE8—3B 56
Glenville M. SW18—5D 63
Glenwood Rd. SE6—1B 84
Glenworth Av. E14—5F 43
Gliddon Rd. W14—5A 34
Global App. E3—1D 29
Globe Pond Rd. SE16—2A 42
Globe Rd.—2E 27
E1 1-123 & 2-154a
E2 remainder
Globe Rd. E15—2B 16
Globe St. SE1—4F 39
Globe Ter. E2—2E 27
Globe Town Mkt. E2—2F 27
Gloucester Av. NW1—4C 8
Gloucester Cir. SE10—3E 57
Gloucester Ct. EC3—1A 40
Gloucester Cres. NW1—5D 9
Gloucester Gdns. W2—5E 21
Gloucester Ga. NW1—1D 23
(in two parts)
Gloucester Ga. M. NW1—1D 23
Gloucester M. W2—5E 21
Gloucester M. W. W2—5E 21
Gloucester Pl.—3B 22
W1 1-127 & 10-118
NW1 remainder
Gloucester Pl. M. W1—4B 22
Gloucester Rd. SW7—4E 35
Gloucester Sq. W2—5F 21
Gloucester St. SW1—1E 51
Gloucester Ter. W2—5D 21
Gloucester Wlk. W8—3C 34
Gloucester Way. EC1—2C 24
Glycena Rd. SW11—1B 64
Glynde St. SE4—4B 70
Glynfield Rd. NW10—4A 4
Glyn Rd. E5—1F 13
Glyn St. SE11—1B 52
Glynwood Dri. SE23—2E 83
Godalming Rd. E14—4D 29
Godbold Rd. E15—2A 30
Godfrey St. E15—1E 29
Godfrey St. SW3—1A 50
Goding St. SE11—1B 52
Godley Rd. SW18—1F 77
Godliman St. EC4—5E 25
Godman Rd. SE15—5D 55
Godolphin Rd. W12—3D 33
Godson St. N1—1C 24
Godwin Rd. E7—1D 17
Goffers Rd. SE3—4A 58
Golborne Gdns. W10—3A 20

Golborne M. W10—4A 20
Golborne Rd. W10—4A 20
Goldcrest Clo. E16—4F 31
Golden La. EC1 & EC2—3E 25
Golden La. Est. EC1—3E 25
Golden Sq. W1—1E 37
Goldhawk M. W12—3D 33
Goldhawk Rd.—5B 32
  W12 1-309 & 2-310
  W6 remainder
Goldhurst Ter. NW6—4D 7
Golding St. E1—5C 26
Goldington Cres. NW1—1F 23
Goldington St. NW1—1F 23
Goldman Clo. E2—3C 26
Goldney Rd. W9—3C 20
Goldsborough Rd. SW8—3F 51
Goldsmith Rd. SE15—4C 54
Goldsmith's Row. E2—1C 26
Goldsmith's Sq. E2—1C 26
Goldsmith St. EC2—5E 25
Goldsworthy Gdns. SE16
  —1E 55
Goldwin Clo. SE14—4E 55
Gollogly Ter. SE7—2E 59
Gomm Rd. SE16—4E 41
Gondar Gdns. NW6—2B 6
Gonson St. SE8—2D 57
Gonston Clo. SW19—2A 76
Gonville St. SW6—1A 62
Goodge Pl. W1—4E 23
Goodge St. W1—4E 23
Goodhall St. NW10—2B 18
  (in two parts)
Goodinge Clo. N7—3A 10
Goodman Cres. SW2—2F 79
Goodman's Ct. E1—1B 40
Goodman's Stile. E1—5C 26
Goodman's Yd. E1—1B 40
Goodrich Rd. SE22—4B 68
Goodson Rd. NW10—4A 4
Goods Way. NW1—5F 9
Goodway Gdns. E14—5F 29
Goodwin Clo. SE16—4C 40
Goodwin Rd. W12—3C 32
Goodwins Ct. WC2—1A 38
Goodwood Rd. SE14—3A 56
Goodyear Pl. SE5—2E 53
Gophir La. EC4—1F 39
Gopsall St. N1—5F 11
Gordon Av. SW14—2A 60
Gordonbrock Rd. SE4—3C 70
Gordon Ct. W12—5E 19
Gordondale Rd. SW19—2C 76
Gordon Gro. SE5—5D 53
Gordon Ho. Rd. NW5—1C 8
Gordon Pl. W8—3C 34

Gordon Rd. E15—1E 15
Gordon Rd. SE15—5D 55
Gordon Sq. WC1—3F 23
Gordon St. E13—2C 30
Gordon St. WC1—3F 23
Gorefield Pl. NW6—1C 20
Gore Rd. E9—5E 13
Gore St. SW7—4E 35
Gorham Pl. W11—1A 34
Gorleston St. W14—5A 34
Gorse Rise. SW17—5C 78
Gorst Rd. SW11—4B 64
Gorsuch Pl. E2—2B 26
Gorsuch St. E2—2B 26
Gosberton Rd. SW12—1C 78
Gosfield St. W1—4E 23
Goslett Yd. WC2—5F 23
Gosling Way. SW9—4C 52
Gospel Oak Est. NW5—2B 8
Gosport Way. SE15—3B 54
Gosset St. E2—2B 26
Gosterwood St. SE8—2A 56
Goswell Rd. EC1—2D 25
Goudhurst Rd. Brom—5A 86
Gough Rd. E15—1B 16
Gough Sq. EC4—5C 24
Gough St. WC1—3B 24
Gough Wlk. E14—5C 28
Gould Ter. E8—2D 13
Goulston St. E1—5B 26
Goulton Rd. E5—1D 13
Govan St. E2—5C 12
Govier Clo. E15—4A 16
Gowan Av. SW6—4A 48
Gowan Rd. NW10—3D 5
Gower Ct. WC1—3F 23
Gower M. WC1—4F 23
Gower Pl. WC1—3F 23
Gower Rd. E7—3C 16
Gower St. WC1—3E 23
Gowers Wlk. E1—5C 26
Gowlett Rd. SE15—1C 68
Gowrie Rd. SW11—1C 64
Gracechurch St. EC3—1F 39
Grace Clo. SE9—3F 87
Gracedale Rd. SW16—5D 79
Gracefield Gdns. SW16—3A 80
Grace Jones Clo. E8—3C 12
Grace Path. SE26—4E 83
Grace Pl. E3—2D 29
Grace's All. E1—1C 40
Grace's M. SE5—5A 54
Grace's Rd. SE5—5A 54
Grace St. E3—2D 29
Gradient, The. SE26—4C 82
Grafton Cres. NW1—3D 9
Grafton M. W1—3E 23

Grafton Pl. NW1—2F 23
Grafton Rd. NW5—2C 8
Grafton Sq. SW4—1E 65
Grafton St. W1—1D 37
Grafton Ter. NW5—2B 8
Grafton Way—3E 23
  WC1 1-29 & 2-46
  W1 remainder
Grafton Yd. NW5—3D 9
Graham Rd. E8—3C 12
Graham Rd. E13—3C 30
Graham St. N1—1D 25
Graham Ter. SW1—5C 36
Granada St. SW17—5B 78
Granard Av. SW15—3D 61
Granard Rd. SW12—5B 64
Granary St. NW1—5F 9
Granby St. E2—3B 26
Granby Ter. NW1—1E 23
Grand Av. EC1—4D 25
Grandison Rd. SW11—3B 64
Grand Pde. M. SW15—3A 62
Grand Wlk. E1—3A 28
Granfield St. SW11—4F 49
Grange Ct. WC2—5B 24
Grange Gro. N1—3E 11
Grange La. SE21—2B 82
Grangemill Rd. SE6—3C 84
Grangemill Way. SE6—2C 84
Grange Pl. NW6—4C 6
Grange Rd. E13—2B 30
Grange Rd. NW10—3D 5
Grange Rd. SE1—4A 40
Grange Rd. SW13—4C 46
Grange, The. SE1—4B 40
Grange, The. SW19—5F 75
Grange Wlk. SE1—4A 40
Grange Way. NW6—4C 6
Grangewood St. E6—5F 17
Grange Yd. SE1—4B 40
Gransden Av. E8—4D 13
Gransden Rd. W12—3B 32
Grantbridge St. N1—1D 25
Grantham Pl. W1—2D 37
Grantham Rd. SW9—5A 52
Grantham Rd. W4—3A 46
Grantley St. E1—2F 27
Grant Rd. SW11—2F 63
Grant St. E13—2C 30
Grant St. N1—1C 24
Grantully Rd. W9—2D 21
Granville Gro. SE13—1E 71
Granville Pk. SE13—1E 71
Granville Pl. W1—5C 22
Granville Rd. NW6—1C 20
  (in two parts)
Granville Rd. SW18—5B 62

Granville Sq. SE15—3A 54
Granville Sq. WC1—2B 24
Granville St. WC1—2B 24
Grape St. WC2—5A 24
Grasmere Rd. E13—1C 30
Grasmere Rd. SW16—5B 80
Grassmount SE23—2D 83
Grateley Way. SE15—3B 54
Gratton Rd. W14—4A 34
Gravel La. E1—5B 26
Graveney Rd. SW17—4A 78
Gravesend Rd. W12—1C 32
Grayshott Rd. SW11—1C 64
Gray's Inn Ct. WC1—4B 24
Gray's Inn Rd. WC1—2B 24
Gray's Inn Sq. WC1—4B 24
Gray St. SE1—3F 38
(in two parts)
Grazeley Ct. SE19—5A 82
Gt. Bell All. EC2—5F 25
Gt. Brownings. SE21—4B 82
Gt. Castle St. W1—5E 23
Gt. Central St. NW1—4B 22
Gt. Central Way. NW10—2A 4
Gt. Chapel St. W1—5F 23
Gt. Church La. W6—5F 33
Gt. College St. SW1—4A 38
Gt. Cross Av. SE10—3A 58
Gt. Cumberland M. W1—5B 22
Gt. Cumberland Pl. W1—5B 22
Gt. Dover St. SE1—4F 39
Gt. Eastern Enterprise Centre.
    E14—3D 43
Gt. Eastern Rd. E15—4F 15
Gt. Eastern St. EC2—3A 26
Greatfield Clo. N19—1E 9
Gt. Field Clo. SE4—2C 70
Gt. George St. SW1—3F 37
Gt. Guildford St. SE1—2E 39
Greatham Wlk. SW15—1C 74
Gt. James St. WC1—4B 24
Gt. Marlborough St. W1—5E 23
Gt. Maze Pond. SE1—3F 39
(in two parts)
Gt. Newport St. WC2—1A 38
Gt. New St. EC4—5C 24
Greatorex St. E1—4C 26
Gt. Ormond St. WC1—4A 24
Gt. Percy St. WC1—2B 24
Gt. Peter St. SW1—4F 37
Gt. Portland St. W1—3D 23
Gt. Pulteney St. W1—1E 37
Gt. Queen St. WC2—5A 24
Gt. Russell St. WC1—5F 23
Gt. Saint Helen's. EC3—5A 26
Gt. Saint Thomas Apostle. EC4
    —1E 39
Gt. Scotland Yd. SW1—2A 38

Gt. Smith St. SW1—4F 37
Gt. Spilmans. SE22—3A 68
Gt. Suffolk St. SE1—2D 39
Gt. Sutton St. EC1—3D 25
Gt. Swan All. EC2—5F 25
Gt. Titchfield St. W1—4E 23
Gt. Tower St. EC3—1A 40
Gt. Trinity La. EC4—1E 39
Gt. Turnstile. WC1—4B 24
Gt. Western Rd.—4B 20
    W9 1-59 & 2-56
    W11 remainder
Gt. West Rd. W4 & W6—1B 46
Gt. Winchester St. EC2—5F 25
Gt. Windmill St. W1—1F 37
Greaves Pl. SW17—4A 78
Grecian Cres. SE19—5D 81
Greek Ct. W1—5F 23
Greek St. W1—5F 23
Greenacre Sq. SE16—3F 41
Greenaway Gdns. NW3—1D 7
Green Bank. E1—2C 40
Greenbay Rd. SE7—3F 59
Greenberry St. NW8—1A 22
Greencoat Pl. SW1—5E 37
Greencoat Row. SW1—4E 37
Greencroft Gdns. NW6—4D 7
Grn. Dale. SE22 & SE5—3A 68
Green Dale Clo. SE22—3A 68
Green Dragon Yd. E1—4C 26
Greenend Rd. W4—3A 32
Greenfell St. SE10—4A 44
Greenfield Rd. E1—5C 26
Greengate St. E13—1D 31
Greenham Clo. SE1—3C 38
Greenhill. NW3—1F 7
Greenhill Pk. NW10—5A 4
Greenhill Rd. NW10—5A 4
Greenhill's Rents. EC1—4D 25
Greenhills Ter. N1—3F 11
Green Hundred Rd. SE15—2C 54
Greenhurst Rd. SE27—5C 80
Greenland M. SE8—1F 55
Greenland Pl. NW1—5D 9
Greenland Quay. SE16—5F 41
Greenland Rd. NW1—5D 9
Greenland St. NW1—5D 9
Green Lanes. N5—1F 11
Greenleaf Rd. E6—5E 17
Greenman St. N1—5E 11
Greenoak Way. SW19—4F 75
Green Shield Industrial Est. E16
    —3D 45
Greenside Rd. W12—4C 32
Greenstead Gdns. SW15—3D 61
Green St.—3D 17
    E7 1-283 & 2-304
    E13 remainder

Green St. W1—1C 36
Green, The. E15—3B 16
Green, The. SW19—5F 75
Green, The. W3—5A 18
Green, The. Brom—3C 86
    (Grove Park)
Green Wlk. SE1—4A 40
Green Way. SE9—3F 73
Greenwell St. W1—3D 23
Greenwich Chu. St. SE10—2E 57
Greenwich High Rd. SE10
    —3D 57
Greenwich Mkt. SE10—2E 57
Greenwich Pk. St. SE10—2F 57
Greenwich S. St. SE10—4D 57
Greenwich View Pl. E14—4D 43
Greenwood Pl. NW5—2D 9
Greenwood Rd. E8—3C 12
Greenwood Rd. E13—1B 30
Greet St. SE1—2C 38
Gregory Cres. SE9—5F 73
Gregory M. SE3—3C 58
Gregory Pl. W8—3D 35
Greig Ter. SE17—2D 53
Grenada Rd. SE7—3E 59
Grenade St. E14—1B 42
Grendon St. NW8—3A 22
Grenfell Rd. W11—1F 33
Grenfell Tower. W11—1F 33
Grenfell Wlk. W11—1F 33
Grenville Pl. SW7—4E 35
Grenville St. WC1—3A 24
Gresham Rd. E16—5D 31
Gresham Rd. SW9—1C 66
Gresham St. EC2—5E 25
Gresham Way. SW19—3D 77
Gressenhall Rd. SW18—4B 62
Gresse St. W1—5F 23
Greswell St. SW6—4F 47
Greville Pl. NW6—1D 21
Greville Rd. NW6—5D 7
Greville St. EC1—4C 24
Greycoat Pl. SW1—4F 37
Greycoat St. SW1—4F 37
Greycot Rd. Beck—5C 84
Grey Eagle St. E1—3B 26
Greyfriars Pas. EC1—5D 25
Greyhound La. WC2—1B 38
Greyhound Rd. NW10—2D 19
Greyhound Rd.—2F 47
    W6 1-183 & 2-136
    W14 remainder
Greystead Rd. SE23—5E 69
Greystoke Pl. EC4—5C 24
Greyswood St. SW16—5D 79
Grierson Rd. SE23—4F 69
Griffin Clo. NW10—2D 5

Grimsby St. E2—3B 26
Grimsell Path. SE5—3D 53
Grimston Rd. SW6—5B 48
Grindal St. SE1—3C 38
Grinling Pl. SE8—2C 56
Grinstead Rd. SE8—1A 56
Grittleton Rd. W9—3C 20
Grizedale Ter. SE23—2D 83
Grocer's Hall Ct. EC2—5F 25
Groombridge Rd. E9—4F 13
Groom Cres. SW18—5F 63
Groomfield Clo. SW17—4C 78

Groom Pl. SW1—4C 36
Grosse Way. SW15—4D 61
Grosvenor Av. N5—2E 11
Grosvenor Av. SW14—1A 60
Grosvenor Cotts. SW1—5C 36
Grosvenor Cres. SW1—3C 36
Grosvenor Cres. M. SW1—3C 36
Grosvenor Est. SW1—5F 37
Grosvenor Gdns. E6—2F 31
Grosvenor Gdns. NW2—3E 5
Grosvenor Gdns. SW1—4D 37
Grosvenor Gdns. SW14—1A 60
Grosvenor Ga. W1—1C 36
Grosvenor Hill. W1—1D 37
Grosvenor Pk. SE5—3E 53
Grosvenor Pl. SW1—3D 37
Grosvenor Rd. E6—5F 17
Grosvenor Rd. E7—3D 17
Grosvenor Rd. SW1—2D 51
Grosvenor Sq. W1—1C 36
Grosvenor St. W1—1D 37
Grosvenor Ter. SE5—2E 53
Grosvenor Wharf Rd. E14
—5F 43
Grote's Bldgs. SE3—5A 58
Grote's Pl. SE3—5A 58
Groton Rd. SW18—2D 77
Grotto Ct. SE1—3E 39
Grotto Pas. W1—4C 22
Grove Clo. SE23—1A 84
Grove Cres. SE5—5A 54
Grove Cres. Rd. E15—3F 15
Grove End Rd. NW8—2F 21
Grove Gdns. E15—3A 16
Grove Gdns. NW8—2A 22
Grove Hall Ct. NW8—2E 21
Grove Hill Rd. SE5—1A 68
Grovelands Clo. SE5—5A 54
Grove La. SE5—4F 53
Grove M. W6—4E 33
Grove M. W11—5B 20
Grove Pk. SE5—5A 54
Grove Pk. Rd. SE9—3E 87
Grove Pas. E2—1D 27
Grove Rd. E3—5F 13

Grove Rd. NW2—3E 5
Grove Rd. SW13—5B 46
Grove St. SE8—5B 42
Grove, The. E15—3A 16
Grove Vale. SE22—2B 68
Grove Vs. E14—1D 43
Groveway. SW9—4B 52
Grummant Rd. SE15—4B 54
Grundy St. E14—5D 29
Gubyon Av. SE24—3D 67
Guerin Sq. E3—2B 28
Guernsey Gro. SE24—5E 67
Guernsey Ho. N1—3E 11
Guibal Rd. SE12—5D 73
Guildford Gro. SE10—4D 57
Guildford Rd. SW8—4A 52
Guildhall Yd. EC2—5E 25
Guildhouse St. SW1—5E 37
Guild Rd. SE7—1F 59
Guilford Pl. WC1—3B 24
Guilford St. WC1—3A 24
Guilsborough Clo. NW10—4A 4
Guinness Clo. E9—4A 14
Guinness Ct. NW8—5A 8
Guinness Sq. SE1—5A 40
Guion Rd. SW6—5B 48
Gulliver St. SE16—4B 42
Gunmaker's La. E3—5A 14
Gunners Rd. SW18—2F 77
Gunstor Rd. N16—1A 12
Gun St. E1—4B 26
Gunter Gro. SW10—2E 49
Gunterstone Rd. W14—5A 34
Gunthorpe St. E1—4B 26
Gunwhale Clo. SE16—2F 41
Gurdon Rd. SE7—1C 58
Gurney Clo. E15—2A 16
Gurney Rd. E15—2A 16
Guthrie St. SW3—1F 49
Gutter La. EC2—5E 25
Guyscliff Rd. SE13—3E 71
Guy St. SE1—3F 39
Gwalior Rd. SW15—2F 61
Gwendolen Av. SW15—2F 61
Gwendolen Clo. SW15—3F 61
Gwendoline Av. E13—5D 17
Gwendwr Rd. W14—1A 48
Gwyn Clo. SW6—3E 49
Gwynne Pl. WC1—2B 24
Gwynne Rd. SW11—5F 49
Gylcote Clo. SE5—2F 67

Haarlem Rd. W14—4F 33
Haberdasher Pl. N1—2F 25
Haberdasher St. N1—2F 25
Hackford Rd. SW9—4B 52

Hackington Cres. Beck—5C 84
Hackney Gro. E8—3D 13
Hackney Rd. E2—2B 26
Haddington Rd. Brom—3F 85
Haddonfield. SE8—5F 41
Haddo St. SE10—2E 57
Hadleigh Clo. E1—3E 27
Hadleigh St. E2—2E 27
Hadley St. NW1—3D 9
Hadrian St. SE10—1A 58
Hadyn Pk. Rd. W12—3C 32
Hafer Rd. SW11—2B 64
Hafton Rd. SE6—1A 86
Haggerston Rd. E8—4B 12
Hague St. E2—2C 26
Haig Rd. E. E13—2E 31
Haig Rd. W. E13—2E 31
Hailsham Av. SW2—2B 80
Haimo Rd. SE9—3F 73
Haines St. SW8—3E 51
Hainthorpe Rd. SE27—3D 81
Hainton Path. E1—5D 27
Halcomb St. N1—5A 12
Halcrow St. E1—4D 27
Haldane Pl. SW18—1D 77
Haldane Rd. E6—2F 31
Haldane Rd. SW6—3B 48
Haldon Rd. SW18—4B 62
Hale Path. SE27—4D 81
Hales St. SE8—3C 56
Hale St. E14—1D 43
Halesworth Rd. SE13—1D 71
Half Moon Cres. N1—1B 24
Half Moon La. SE24—4E 67
Half Moon Pas. E1—5B 26
Half Moon St. W1—2D 37
Halford Rd. SW6—2C 48
Halidon Clo. E9—2E 13
Halifax St. SE26—3D 83
Halkin Arc. SW1—4C 36
Halkin M. SW1—4C 36
Halkin Pl. SW1—4C 36
Halkin St. SW1—3C 36
Hallam M. W1—4D 23
Hallam St. W1—4D 23
Hall Dri. SE26—5E 83
Halley Gdns. SE13—2F 71
Halley Pl. E14—4A 28
Halley Rd.—3E 17
E7 1-207 & 2-188
E12 remainder
Halley St. E14—4A 28
Hallfield Est. W2—5E 21
Hall Ga. NW8—2F 21
Halliford St. N1—4E 11
Halliwell Rd. SW2—4B 66
Hall Oak Wlk. NW6—3B 6

Hall Pl. W2—3F 21
Hall Rd. E15—1F 15
Hall Rd. NW8—2E 21
Hall St. EC1—2D 25
Hallsville Rd. E16—5B 30
Hall, The. SE3—1C 72
Hall View. SE9—2F 87
Halpin Pl. SE17—5F 39
Halsbrook Rd. SE3—1F 73
Halsbury Rd. W12—2D 33
Halsey M. SW3—5B 36
Halsey St. SW3—5B 36
Halsmere Rd. SE5—4D 53
Halston Clo. SW11—4B 64
Halstow Rd. NW10—2F 19
Halstow Rd. SE10—1C 58
Halton Rd. N1—4D 11
Hambalt Rd. SW4—3E 65
Hambleden Pl. SE21—1B 82
Hambledon Rd. SW18—5B 62
Hamble St. SW6—1D 63
Hambridge Way. SW2—5C 66
Hamelin St. E14—5E 29
Hamfrith Rd. E15—3B 16
Hamilton Clo. NW8—2F 21
Hamilton Clo. SE16—3A 42
Hamilton Gdns. NW8—2E 21
Hamilton La. N5—1D 11
Hamilton M. W1—3D 37
Hamilton Pk. N5—1D 11
Hamilton Pk. W. N5—1D 11
Hamilton Pl. W1—2C 36
Hamilton Rd. E15—2A 30
Hamilton Rd. NW10—2C 4
Hamilton Rd. SE27—4F 81
Hamilton Rd. W4—3A 32
Hamilton St. SE8—2C 56
Hamilton Ter. NW8—1E 21
Hamlea Clo. SE12—3C 72
Hamlet Clo. SE13—2A 72
Hamlet Gdns. W6—5C 32
Hamlet Industrial Est. E9
—4C 14
Hamlets Way. E3—3B 28
Hamlet, The. SE5—1F 67
Hammelton Grn. SW9—4D 53
Hammersmith Bri. SW13 & W6
—2D 47
Hammersmith Bri. Rd. W6
—1E 47
Hammersmith B'way. W6
—5E 33
Hammersmith Flyover. W6
—1E 47
Hammersmith Gro. W6—4E 33
Hammersmith Rd.—5F 33
W14 1-155 & 2-92
W6 remainder

Hammersmith Ter. W6—1C 46
Hammett St. EC3—1B 40
Hammond St. NW5—3E 9
Ham Pk. Rd.—4B 16
E15 1-111 & 2-66
E7 remainder
Hampden Clo. NW1—1F 23
Hampden Gurney St. W1—5B 22
Hampden Ho. SW9—5C 52
Hampshire Hog La. W6—5D 33
Hampshire St. NW5—3F 9
Hampson Way. SW8—4B 52
Hampstead Grn. NW3—2A 8
Hampstead High St. NW3—1E 7
Hampstead Hill Gdns. NW3
—1F 7
Hampstead Rd. NW1—1E 23
Hampton Clo. NW6—2C 20
Hampton Ct. N1—3D 11
Hampton Rd. E7—2D 17
Hampton St. SE17 & SE1
—5E 39
Ham Yd. W1—1F 37
Hanameel St. E16—2D 45
Hanbury M. N1—5E 11
Hanbury St. E1—4B 26
Hancock Rd. E3—2E 29
Handa Wlk. N1—3F 11
Hand Ct. WC1—4B 24
Handel St. WC1—3A 24
Handen Rd. SE12—3A 72
Handforth Rd. SW9—3C 52
Handley Rd. E9—5E 13
Hands Wlk. E16—5C 30
Hanford Clo. SE4—2F 69
Hanford Rd. SW18—1C 76
Hankey Pl. SE1—3F 39
Hannah Mary Way. SE1—5C 40
Hannay Wlk. SW16—2F 79
Hannell Rd. SW6—3A 48
Hannen Rd. SE27—3D 81
Hannibal Rd. E1—4E 27
Hannington Rd. SW4—1D 65
Hanover Clo. SE11—2C 52
Hanover Ga. NW1—2A 22
Hanover Pk. SE15—4C 54
Hanover Pl. WC2—5A 24
Hanover Rd. NW10—4E 5
Hanover Sq. W1—5D 23
Hanover St. W1—5D 23
Hanover Ter. NW1—2B 22
Hanover Ter. M. NW1—2B 22
Hansard M. W14—3F 33
Hans Cres. SW1—4B 36
Hansler Rd. SE22—3B 68
Hanson Clo. SW12—5D 65
Hanson St. W1—4E 23

Hans Pl. SW1—4B 36
Hans Rd. SW3—4B 36
Hans St. SW1—4B 36
Hanway Pl. W1—5F 23
Hanway St. W1—5F 23
Harad's Pl. E1—1C 40
Harben Rd. NW6—4E 7
Harberson Rd. E15—5B 16
Harberson Rd. SW12—1D 79
Harbet Rd. W2—4F 21
Harbinger Rd. E14—5D 43
Harbledown Rd. SW6—4C 48
Harbord Clo. SE5—5F 53
Harbord St. SW6—4F 47
Harborough Rd. SW16—4B 80
Harbour Av. SW10—4E 49
Harbour Exchange. E14—3D 43
Harbour Exchange Sq. E14
—3D 43
Harbour Quay. E14—2E 43
Harbour Rd. SE5—1E 67
Harbour Yd. SW10—4E 49
Harbridge Av. SW15—5C 60
Harbut Rd. SW11—2F 63
Harcourt Rd. E15—1B 30
Harcourt Rd. SE4—1B 70
Harcourt St. W1—4A 22
Harcourt Ter. SW10—1D 49
Hardel Rise. SW2—1D 81
Hardel Wlk. SW2—1C 80
Harden's Mnr. Way. SE7—4F 45
Harders Rd. SE15—4D 55
(in two parts)
Harders Rd. M. SE15—4D 55
Hardess St. SE24—1E 67
Harding Clo. SE17—2E 53
Hardinge Rd. NW10—5D 5
Hardinge St. E1—5E 27
(in two parts)
Hardman Rd. SE7—1D 59
Hardwick St. EC1—2C 24
Hardwick's Way. SW18—3C 62
Hardwidge St. SE1—3A 40
Hardy Clo. SE16—3F 41
Hardy Rd. SE3—2B 58
Hare & Billet Rd. SE3—4F 57
Hare Ct. EC4—5C 24
Harecourt Rd. N1—3E 11
Haredale Rd. SE24—2E 67
Haredon Clo. SE23—5F 69
Harefield Rd. SE4—1B 70
Hare Marsh. E2—3C 26
Hare Row. E2—1D 27
Hare Wlk. N1—1A 26
Harewood Av. NW1—3A 22
Harewood Pl. W1—5D 23
Harewood Row. NW1—4A 22

Harfield Gdns. SE5—1A 68
Harford St. E1—3A 28
Hargood Rd. SE3—4E 59
Hargrave Pl. N7—2F 9
Hargwyne St. SW9—1B 66
Harland Rd. SE12—1C 86
Harlescott Rd. SE15—2F 69
Harlesden Gdns. NW10—5B 4
Harlesden La. NW10—5C 4
Harlesden Rd. NW10—5C 4
Harleyford Rd. SE11—2B 52
Harleyford St. SE11—2C 52
Harley Gdns. SW10—1E 49
Harley Gro. E3—2B 28
Harley Pl. W1—4D 23
Harley Rd. NW3—4F 7
Harley Rd. NW10—1A 18
Harley St. W1—4D 23
Harlowe Clo. E8—5C 12
Harmood Gro. NW1—4D 9
Harmood Pl. NW1—4D 9
Harmood St. NW1—3D 9
Harmsworth St. SE17—2D 53
Harold Est. SE1—4A 40
Harold Pl. SE11—1C 52
Harold Rd. E13—5D 17
Harp All. EC4—5D 25
Harpenden Rd. SE27—2D 81
Harper Rd. SE1—4E 39
Harpley Sq. E1—3F 27
Harpsden St. SW11—4C 50
Harpur M. WC1—4B 24
Harpur St. WC1—4B 24
Harraden Rd. SE3—4E 59
Harriet Clo. E8—5C 12
Harriet St. SW1—3B 36
Harriet Wlk. SW1—3B 36
Harrington Gdns. SW7—5E 35
Harrington Rd. SW7—5F 35
Harrington Sq. NW1—1E 23
Harrington St. NW1—2E 23
Harrington Way. SE18—4F 45
Harriott Clo. SE10—5B 44
Harrison St. WC1—2A 24
Harris St. SE5—3F 53
Harroway Rd. SW11—5F 49
Harrowby St. W1—5A 22
Harrowgate Rd. E9—4A 14
Harrow La. E14—1E 43
Harrow Pl. E1—5B 26
Harrow Rd.—2D 19
  W2 1-281 & 2-322
  W9 283-421a & 283-570
  W10 421-625 & 572-742
  NW10 remainder

Harrow Rd. Bri. W2—4E 21
Hartfield Ter. E3—1C 28

Hartham Clo. N7—2A 10
Hartham Rd. N7—2A 10
Hartington Rd. E16—5D 31
Hartington Rd. SW8—4A 52
Hartismere Rd. SW6—3B 48
Hartlake Rd. E9—3F 13
Hartland Rd. E15—4B 16
Hartland Rd. NW1—4D 9
Hartland Rd. NW6—1B 20
Hartley St. E2—2E 27
Hartnoll St. N7—2B 10
Harton St. SE8—4C 56
Hart's La. SE14—4A 56
Hart St. EC3—1A 40
Hartswood Rd. W12—3B 32
Hartsworth Clo. E13—1B 30
Hartwell St. E8—3B 12
Harvard Rd. SE13—3E 71
Harvey Gdns. SE7—5F 45
Harvey Rd. SE5—4F 53
(in two parts)
Harvey's Bldgs. WC2—1A 38
Harvey St. N1—5F 11
Harvington Rd. E8—4C 12
Harvist Est. N7—1C 10
Harvist Rd. NW6—1F 19
Harwood Rd. SW6—3C 48
Harwood Ter. SW6—4D 49
Haseley End. SE23—5E 69
Haselrigge Rd. SW4—2F 65
Haseltine Rd. SE26—4B 84
Hasker St. SW3—5A 36
Haslam Clo. N1—4C 10
Haslemere Av. SW18—2D 77
Hassard St. E2—1B 26
Hassendean Rd. SE3—3D 59
Hassett Rd. E9—3F 13
Hassocks Clo. SE26—3D 83
Hassop Rd. NW2—1F 5
Hasted Rd. SE7—1F 59
Hastings Clo. SE15—3C 54
Hastings St. WC1—2A 24
Hatcham Pk. M. SE14—4F 55
Hatcham Pk. Rd. SE14—4F 55
Hatcham Rd. SE15—2E 55
Hatcliffe Clo. SE3—1B 72
Hatfield Clo. SE14—3F 55
Hatfield Rd. E15—2A 16
Hatfields. SE1—2C 38
Hatherley Gdns. E6—2F 31
Hatherley Gro. W2—5D 21
Hatherley St. SW1—5E 37
Hathorne Clo. SE15—5E 55
Hathway St. SE15—5F 55
Hatteraick St. SE16—3E 41
Hatton Garden. EC1—4C 24

Hatton Pl. EC1—4C 24
Hatton St. NW8—3F 21
Hatton Wall. EC1—4C 24
Haunch of Venison Yd. W1
                      —5D 23
Havana Rd. SW19—2C 76
Havannah St. E14—3C 42
Havant Way. SE15—3B 54
Havelock Rd. SW19—5E 77
Havelock St. N1—5A 10
Havelock Ter. SW8—4D 51
Havelock Wlk. SE23—1E 83
Haven Clo. SW19—3F 75
Haven M. E3—4B 28
Haven St. NW1—4D 9
Haverfield Rd. E3—2A 28
Haverhill Rd. SW12—1E 79
Havering St. E1—5F 27
Haverstock Hill. NW3—2A 8
Haverstock Rd. NW5—2C 8
Haverstock St. N1—1A 10
Havil St. SE5—3A 54
Hawarden Gro. SE24—5E 67
Hawes St. N1—4D 11
Hawgood St. E3—4C 28
Hawke Rd. SE19—5F 81
Hawkesbury Rd. SW15—3D 61
Hawkesfield Rd. SE23—2A 84
Hawkesmoor M. E1—1D 41
Hawkley Gdns. SE27—2D 81
Hawkshaw Clo. SW2—1A 80
Hawkshead Rd. NW10—4B 4
Hawkshead Rd. W4—3A 32
Hawkslade Rd. SE15—3F 69
Hawks M. SE10—3E 57
Hawksmoor St. W6—2F 47
Hawkstone Rd. SE16—5E 41
Hawley Cres. NW1—4D 9
Hawley M. NW1—4D 9
Hawley Rd. NW1—4D 9
Hawley St. NW1—4D 9
Hawstead Rd. SE6—4D 71
Hawthorn Clo. N1—3A 12
Hawthorne Rd. NW10—4C 4
Hawthorn Wlk. W10—3A 20
Hawtrey Rd. NW3—4A 8
Hay Clo. E15—4A 16
Haycroft Gdns. NW10—5C 4
Haycroft Rd. SW2—3A 66
Hay Currie St. E14—5D 29
Hayday Rd. E16—4C 30
Hayden's Pl. W11—5B 20
Haydon Pk. Rd. SW19—5C 76
Haydons Rd. SW19—5D 77
Haydon St. EC3—1B 40
Haydon Wlk. E1—5B 26
Hayes Pl. NW1—3A 22

Hayfield Pas. E1—3E 27
Hayfield Yd. E1—3E 27
Haygarth Pl. SW19—5F 75
Hay Hill. W1—1D 37
Hayles St. SE11—5D 39
Hayling Clo. N16—2A 12
Hayman St. N1—4D 11
Haymarket. SW1—1F 37
Haymerle Rd. SE15—2C 54
Haynes Clo. SE3—1A 72
Hayne St. EC1—4D 25
Hay's Galleria. SE1—2A 40
Hay's La. SE1—2A 40
Hay's M. W1—2D 37
Hay St. E2—5C 12
Hayter Rd. SW2—3A 66
Hayton Clo. E8—3B 12
Hayward Gdns. SW15—4E 61
Hayward's Pl. EC1—3D 25
Hazelbank Rd. SE6—2F 85
Hazelbourne Rd. SW12—4D 65
Hazel Clo. SE15—5C 54
Hazeldon Rd. SE4—3A 70
Hazel Gro. SE26—4F 83
Hazelhurst Rd. SW17—4F 77
Hazelmere Rd. NW6—5B 6
Hazel Rd. E15—2A 16
Hazel Rd. NW10—2E 19
Hazel Way. SE1—5B 40
Hazlebury Rd. SW6—5D 49
Hazlewell Rd. SW15—3E 61
Hazlewood Cres. W10—3A 20
Hazlitt M. W14—4A 34
Hazlitt Rd. W14—4A 34
Headcorn Rd. Brom—5B 86
Headfort Pl. SW1—3C 36
Headington Rd. SW18—2E 77
Headlam Rd. SW4—5F 65
Headlam St. E1—3D 27
Headley Ct. SE26—5E 83
Head's M. W11—5C 20
Head St. E1—5F 27
   (in two parts)
Heald St. SE14—4C 56
Healey St. NW1—3D 9
Hearn St. EC2—3A 26
Hearnville Rd. SW12—1C 78
Heathcote St. WC1—3B 24
Heath Dri. NW3—1D 7
Heathedge. SE26—2D 83
Heather Clo. SW8—1D 65
Heather Rd. SE12—1C 86
Heather Wlk. W10—3A 20
Heathfield Av. SW18—5F 63
Heathfield Clo. E16—4F 31
Heathfield Gdns. SW18—4F 63
Heathfield Pk. NW2—3E 5

Heathfield Rd. SW18—4F 63
Heathfield Sq. SW18—5F 63
Heath Hurst Rd. NW3—1A 8
Heath La. SE3—5F 57
Heathlee Rd. SE3—2B 72
Heathmans Rd. SW6—4B 48
Heath Mead. SW19—3F 75
Heath Rise. SW15—4F 61
Heath Side. NW3—1F 7
Heathstan Rd. W12—5C 18
Heath St. NW3—1E 7
Heathview Gdns. SW15—5E 61
Heathwall St. SW11—1B 64
Heathway. SE3—3C 58
Heaton Rd. SE15—5D 55
Heaver Rd. SW11—1F 63
Hebdon Rd. SW17—3A 78
Heber Rd. NW2—2F 5
Heber Rd. SE22—4B 68
Hebron Rd. W6—4E 33
Heckfield Pl. SW6—3C 48
Heckford St. E1—1F 41
Heddington Gro. N7—2B 10
Heddon St. W1—1E 37
Hedgers Gro. E9—3A 14
Hedgley St. SE12—3B 72
Hedingham Clo. N1—4E 11
Hedley Row. N5—2F 11
Helby Rd. SW4—4F 65
Heldar Ct. SE1—3F 39
Helder Gro. SE12—5B 72
Helena Rd. E13—1B 30
Helena Rd. NW10—2D 5
Helen's Pl. E2—2E 27
Helix Gdns. SW2—4B 66
Helix Rd. SW2—4B 66
Hellings St. E1—2C 40
Helme Clo. SW19—5B 76
Helmet Row. EC1—3E 25
Helmsley Pl. E8—4D 13
Helmsley St. E8—4D 13
Helvetia St. SE6—2B 84
Hemans St. SW8—3F 51
Hemans St. Est. SW8—3F 51
Hemberton Rd. SW9—1A 66
Hemingford Rd. N1—5B 10
Hemlock Rd. W12—1B 32
Hemming St. E1—3C 26
Hemp Walk. SE17—5F 39
Hemstal Rd. NW6—4C 6
Hemsworth Ct. N1—1A 26
Hemsworth St. N1—1A 26
Hemus Pl. SW3—1A 50
Henchman St. W12—5B 18
Henderson Dri. NW8—3F 21
Henderson Rd. E7—3E 17

Henderson Rd. SW18—5A 64
Hendham Rd. SW17—2A 78
Hendre Rd. SE1—5A 40
Hendrick Av. SW12—5B 64
Heneage La. EC3—5A 26
Heneage Pl. EC3—5A 26
Heneage St. E1—4B 26
Hengist Rd. SE12—5D 73
Hengrave Rd. SE23—5E 69
Henley Dri. SE1—5B 40
Henley Rd. NW10—5E 5
Henley St. SW11—5C 50
Hennel Clo. SE23—3E 83
Henniker Gdns. E6—2F 31
Henniker M. SW3—2F 49
Henniker Rd. E15—2F 15
Henning St. SW11—4A 50
Henrietta M. WC1—3A 24
Henrietta Pl. W1—5D 23
Henrietta St. E15—2E 15
Henrietta St. WC2—1A 38
Henriques St. E1—5C 26
Henry Cooper Way. SE9—4F 87
Henry Dickens Ct. W11—1F 33
Henry Jackson Rd. SW15
                    —1F 61
Henryson Rd. SE4—3C 70
Hensford Gdns. SE26—4D 83
Henshall St. N1—3F 11
Henshaw St. SE17—5F 39
Henslowe Rd. SE22—3C 68
Henson Av. NW2—2E 5
Henstridge Pl. NW8—5A 8
Henty Clo. SW11—3A 50
Henty Wlk. SW15—3D 61
Henwood Rd. SE16—4E 41
Hepburn M. SW11—3B 64
Hepplestone Clo. SW15—4D 61
Hepscott Rd. E9—4C 14
Hepworth Ct. NW3—2A 8
Herald St. E2—3D 27
Herbal Hill. EC1—3C 24
Herbert Cres. SW1—4B 36
Herbert Gdns. NW10—1D 19
Herbert Rackley Way. E3
                    —3D 29
Herbert St. E13—1C 30
Herbert St. NW5—3C 8
Herbrand St. WC1—3A 24
Hercules Pl. SE1—4B 38
Hereford M. W2—5C 20
Hereford Pl. SE14—3B 56
Hereford Retreat. SE15—3C 54
Hereford Rd. W2—5C 20
Hereford Sq. SW7—5E 35
Hereford St. E2—3C 26
Hereward Rd. SW17—4B 78

Herlwyn Gdns. SW17—4B 78
Hermes St. N1—1C 24
Herm Ho. N1—3E 11
Hermitage Rd. SE19—5F 81
Hermitage St. W2—4F 21
Hermitage, The. SE23—1E 83
Hermitage, The. SW13—4B 46
Hermitage Wall. E1—2C 40
Hermit Pl. NW6—5D 7
Hermit Rd. E16—4B 30
Hermit St. EC1—2D 25
Herndon Rd. SW18—3E 63
Herne Hill. SE24—3E 67
Herne Hill Rd. SE24—1E 67
Herne Pl. SE24—3D 67
Heron Clo. NW10—3A 4
Herondale Av. SW18—1F 77
Heron Industrial Est. E15
—1D 29
Heron Pl. SE16—2A 42
Heron Quays. E14—2C 42
Heron Quays Development. E14
—2D 43
Heron Rd. SE24—2E 67
Heron St. SE17—2D 53
Herrick St. SW1—5F 37
Herries St. W10—2A 20
Herringham Rd. SE7—4E 45
Herring St. SE5—2A 54
Hersant Clo. NW10—5C 4
Herschell Rd. SE23—5A 70
Hersham Clo. SW15—5C 60
Hertford Av. SW14—2A 60
Hertford Pl. W1—3E 23
Hertford Rd. N1—4A 12
(in two parts)
Hertford St. W1—2D 37
Hervey Rd. SE3—4D 59
Hesketh Pl. W11—1A 34
Heslop St. SW12—1B 78
Hesper M. SW5—5D 35
Hesperus Cres. E14—5D 43
Hessel St. E1—5D 27
Hestercombe Av. SW6—4A 48
Hester Rd. SW11—3A 50
Heston St. SE14—4C 56
Hetherington Rd. SW4—2A 66
Hetley Rd. W12—2D 33
Hevelius Clo. SE10—1B 58
Hewer St. W10—4F 19
Hewett St. EC2—3A 26
Hewlett Rd. E3—1A 28
Hexal Rd. SE6—3A 86
Hexham Rd. SE27—2E 81
Heyford Av. SW8—3A 52
Heygate St. SE17—5E 39
Heylyn Sq. E3—2B 28

Heythorp St. SW18—1B 76
Heyworth Rd. E5—1D 13
Heyworth Rd. E15—1B 16
Hibbert St. SW11—1F 63
Hichisson Rd. SE15—3E 69
Hickin Clo. SE7—5F 45
Hickin St. E14—4E 43
Hickman Clo. E16—4F 31
Hickmore Wlk. SW4—1F 65
Hicks Clo. SW11—1A 64
Hicks St. SE8—1A 56
Hide Pl. SW1—5F 37
Hides St. N7—3B 10
High Bri. SE10—1F 57
Highbrook Rd. SE3—1F 73
Highbury Cres. N5—2D 11
Highbury Est. N5—2E 11
Highbury Grange. N5—1E 11
Highbury Gro. N5—2D 11
Highbury Hill. N5—1D 11
Highbury M. N7—3C 10
Highbury New Pk. N5—2E 11
Highbury Pk. N5—5D 11
Highbury Pk. M. N5—1E 11
Highbury Pl. N5—3D 11
Highbury Rd. SW19—5A 76
Highbury Sta. Rd. N1—3C 10
Highbury Ter. N5—2D 11
Highbury Ter. M. N5—2D 11
Highclere St. SE26—4A 84
Highcliffe Dri. SW15—4B 60
Highcombe. SE7—2D 59
Highcross Way. SW15—1C 74
Highdown Rd. SW15—4D 61
Highgate Ho. SE26—3C 82
Highgate Rd. NW5—1D 9
High Holborn. WC1—5A 24
Highland Croft. Beck.—5D 85
Highland Rd. SE19—5A 82
Highlands Heath. SW15—5E 61
High Level Dri. SE26—4C 82
Highlever Rd. W10—4E 19
High Meads Rd. E16—5F 31
Highmore Rd. SE3—3A 58
High Rd. Leyton. E15—1E 15
High Rd. Leytonstone, E11
—1A 16
High Rd. Willesden, NW10—3B 4
Highshore Rd. SE15—5B 54
High St. Colliers Wood, SW19
—5A 78
High St. Harlesden, NW10—1B 18
High St. Plaistow, E13—1C 30
High St. Stratford, E15—1E 29
High St. Wimbledon. SW19
—5F 75
High St. M. SW19—5A 76

High Timber St. EC4—1E 39
High Trees. SW2—1C 80
Highway, The—1F 41
E1 1-485 & 2-388
E14 remainder
Highway Trading Centre, The. E1
—1F 41
Hilary Clo. SW6—3D 49
Hilary Rd. W12—1B 32
Hilda Rd. E6—4F 17
Hilda Rd. E16—3A 30
(in two parts)
Hilda Ter. SW9—5C 52
Hildenborough Gdns. Brom
—5A 86
Hildreth St. SW12—1D 79
Hildyard Rd. SW6—2C 48
Hiley Rd. NW10—2E 19
Hilgrove Rd. NW6—4E 7
Hillbeck Clo. SE15—3E 55
Hillbrook Rd. SW17—3B 78
Hillbury Rd. SW17—3D 79
Hillcourt Rd. SE22—4D 69
Hillcrest Clo. SE26—4C 82
Hillcrest Rd. Brom—5C 86
Hilldrop Cres. N7—2F 9
Hilldrop Est. N7—1A 10
Hilldrop La. N7—2F 9
Hilldrop Rd. N7—2F 9
Hilldrop Rd. Brom—5D 87
Hillersdon Av. SW13—5C 46
Hillery Clo. SE17—5F 39
Hill Farm Rd. W10—4E 19
Hillfield Ct. NW3—2A 8
Hillfield Rd. NW6—2B 6
Hillgate Pl. W8—2C 34
Hillgate St. W8—2C 34
Hill Ho. Rd. SW16—5B 80
Hilliards Ct. E1—2E 41
Hillier Rd. SW11—4B 64
Hillingdon St.—2D 53
SE17 1-237 & 2-244
SE5 remainder
Hillman St. E8—3D 13
Hillmarton Rd. N7—2A 10
Hillmead Dri. SW9—2D 67
Hillmore Gro. SE26—5A 84
Hill Path. SW16—5B 80
Hill Rise. SE23—1D 83
Hill Rd. NW8—1E 21
Hillsborough Rd. SE22—3A 68
Hillside Clo. NW8—1D 21
Hillside Pas. SW2—2B 80
Hillside Rd. SW2—2C 80
Hillsleigh Rd. W8—2B 34
Hills Pl. W1—5E 23
Hill St. W1—2C 36

Hilltop Rd. NW6—4C 6
Hillworth Rd. SW2—5C 66
Hillyard St. SW9—4C 52
Hilly Fields Cres. SE4—1C 70
Hilsea St. E5—1E 13
Hilversum Cres. SE22—3A 68
Himley Rd. SW17—5A 78
Hinckley Rd. SE15—2C 68
Hind Ct. EC4—5C 24
Hinde St. W1—5C 22
Hind Gro. E14—5C 28
Hindmans Rd. SE22—3C 68
Hindmarsh Clo. E1—1C 40
Hindrey Rd. E5—2D 13
Hindsley's Pl. SE23—2F 83
Hinton Rd. SE24—1D 67
Hippodrome Pl. W11—1A 34
Hitchin Sq. E3—1A 28
Hitherfield Rd. SW16—3C 80
Hither Grn. La. SE13—3B 71
Hitherwood Dri. SE19—4B 82
Hoadly Rd. SW16—3F 79
Hobart Pl. SW1—4D 37
Hobbes Wlk. SW15—3D 61
Hobbs Rd. SE27—4E 81
Hobday St. E14—5D 29
Hobury St. SW10—2F 49
Hocker St. E2—2B 26
Hockett Clo. SE8—5A 42
Hodister Clo. SE5—3E 53
Hodnet Gro. SE16—5F 41
Hoever Ho. SE6—4E 85
Hofland Rd. W14—4A 34
Hogan M. W2—4F 21
Hogarth Clo. E16—4F 31
Hogarth Ct. EC3—5A 26
Hogarth Ct. SE19—4B 82
Hogarth La. W4—2A 46
Hogarth Rd. SW5—5D 35
Hogsden Clo. N1—1E 25
Holbeach M. SW12—1D 79
Holbeach Rd. SE6—5C 70
Holbeck Row. SE15—3C 54
Holbein M. SW1—1C 50
Holbein Pl. SW1—5C 36
Holberton Gdns. NW10
　　　　　　　—2D 19
Holborn. EC1—4C 24
Holborn Cir. EC1—4C 24
Holborn Rd. E13—4D 31
Holborn Viaduct. EC1—4D 25
Holbrook Rd. E15—1B 30
Holburne Clo. SE3—4E 59
Holburne Gdns. SE3—4F 59
Holburne Rd. SE3—4E 59
Holcombe St. W6—5D 33
Holcroft Rd. E9—4E 13

Holdenby Rd. SE4—3A 70
Holden St. SW11—5C 50
Holdernesse Rd. SW17—2C 78
Holderness Way. SE27—5D 81
Holdgate St. SE7—4F 45
Holford Pl. WC1—2B 24
Holford St. WC1—2C 24
Holgate Av. SW11—1F 63
Holland Dri. SE23—3A 84
Holland Gdns. W14—4A 34
Holland Gro. SW9—3C 52
Holland La. W14—4B 34
Holland Pk. W11—2A 34
Holland Pk. Av. W11—2A 34
Holland Pk. Gdns. W14—3A 34
Holland Pk. M. W11—2B 34
Holland Pk. Rd. W14—4B 34
Holland Rd. E15—2A 30
Holland Rd. NW10—5C 4
Holland Rd. W14—3A 34
Holland St. SE1—2D 39
Holland St. W8—3C 34
Holland Vs. Rd. W14—3A 34
Holland Wlk. W8—2B 34
Hollen St. W1—5F 23
Holles St. W1—5D 23
Holley Rd. W3—3A 32
Hollies Way. SW12—5C 64
Hollingbourne Rd. SE24—3E 67
Holloway Rd. N7—1B 10
Holly Berry La. NW3—1E 7
Holly Bush Hill. NW3—1E 7
Hollybush Hill. NW3—1E 7
Hollybush Pl. E2—2D 27
Hollybush St. E13—2D 31
Holly Bush Vale. NW3—1E 7
Holly Clo. NW10—4A 4
Hollydale Rd. SE15—5E 55
Holly Dene. SE15—4D 55
Holly Gro. SE15—5B 54
Holly Hedge Ter. SE13—3F 71
Holly Hill. NW3—1E 7
Holly Mt. NW3—1E 7
Hollymount Clo. SE10—4E 57
Holly St. E8—4B 12
Holly St. Est. E8—4B 12
Holly Tree Clo. SW19—1F 75
Holly Wlk. NW3—1E 7
Hollywood M. SW10—2E 49
Hollywood Rd. SW10—2E 49
Holman Rd. SW11—5F 49
Holmbury Ct. SW17—3B 78
Holmbush Rd. SW15—4A 62
Holmcote Gdns. N5—2E 11
Holmdale Rd. NW6—2C 6
Holmdene Av. SE24—4E 67
Holmead Rd. SW6—3D 49
Holme Lacey Rd. SE12—4B 72

Holmesley Rd. SE23—4A 70
Holmes Pl. SW10—2E 49
Holmes Rd. NW5—2D 9
Holmewood Gdns. SW2—5B 66
Holmewood Rd. SW2—5B 66
Holmfield Ct. NW3—3A 8
Holmoak Clo. SW15—4B 62
Holm Oak M. SW4—3A 66
Holmshaw Clo. SE26—4A 84
Holmside Rd. SW12—4C 64
Holm Wlk. SE3—5C 58
Holmwood Vs. SE7—1C 58
Holness Rd. E15—3B 16
Holroyd Rd. SW15—2E 61
Holt Ct. E15—2E 15
Holt Ho. SW2—4C 66
Holton St. E1—3F 27
Holwood Pl. SW4—2F 65
Holybourne Av. SW15—5C 60
Holybush Wlk. SW9—2D 67
Holyhead Clo. E3—2C 28
Holyoake Ct. SE16—3B 42
Holyoak Rd. SE11—5D 39
Holyport Rd. SW6—3F 47
Holyrood St. SE1—2A 40
Holywell Clo. SE3—2C 58
Holywell La. EC2—3A 26
Holywell Row. EC2—3A 26
Homecroft Rd. SE26—5E 83
Homefield Rd. W4—1B 46
Homefield Rd. SW19—5A 76
Homefield St. N1—1A 26
Homeleigh Rd. SE15—3F 69
Home Pk. Rd. SW19—4B 76
Homer Dri. E14—5C 42
Home Rd. SW11—5A 50
Homer Rd. E9—3A 14
Homer Row. W1—4A 22
Homer St. W1—4A 22
Homerton Gro. E9—2F 13
Homerton High St. E9
　　　　　　　—2F 13
Homerton Rd. E9—2B 14
Homerton Row. E9—2E 13
Homerton Ter. E9—3E 13
(in two parts)
Homestall Rd. SE22—3E 69
Homestead Rd. SW6—3B 48
Homildon Ho. SE26—3C 82
Honduras St. EC1—3E 25
Honeybourne Rd. NW6—2D 7
Honeybrook Rd. SW12—5E 65
Honeyman Clo. NW6—4F 5
Honeywell Rd. SW11—4B 64
Honeywood Rd. NW10—1B 18
Honiton Rd. NW6—1B 20
Honley Rd. SE6—5D 71
Honor Oak Pk. SE23—4E 69

Honor Oak Rise. SE23—4E 69
Honor Oak Rd. SE23—1E 83
Hooks Clo. SE15—4D 55
Hooks Way. SE22—1C 82
Hooper Rd. E16—5C 30
Hooper's Ct. SW3—3B 36
Hooper St. E1—5C 26
Hope Clo. SE12—3D 87
Hopedale Rd. SE7—2D 59
Hopefield Av. NW6—1A 20
Hope St. SW11—1F 63
Hopetown St. E1—4B 26
Hopewell St. SE5—3F 53
Hop Gdns. WC2—1A 38
Hopgood St. W12—2E 33
Hopkinsons Pl. NW1—5C 8
Hopkins St. W1—5E 23
Hopping La. N1—3D 11
Hopton Rd. SW16—5A 80
Hopton St. SE1—2D 39
Hopwood Rd. SE17—2F 53
Hopwood Wlk. E8—4C 12
Horace Rd. E7—1D 17
Horatio St. E2—1C 26
Horbury Cres. W11—1C 34
Horbury M. W11—1B 34
Horder Rd. SW6—4A 48
Hordle Promenade E. SE15
—3B 54
Hordle Promenade N. SE15
—3B 54
Hordle Promenade S. SE15
—3B 54
Hordle Promenade W. SE15
—3A 54
Horizon Way. SE7—5D 45
Hormead Rd. W9—3B 20
Hornbeam Clo. SE11—5C 38
Hornblower Clo. SE16—5A 42
Hornby Clo. NW3—4A 8
Horncastle Clo. SE12—5C 72
Horncastle Rd. SE12—5C 72
Horndean Clo. SW15—1C 74
Horne Way. SW15—5E 43
Hornfair Rd. SE7—2F 59
Horniman Dri. SE23—1D 83
Horn La. SE10—5C 44
Horn Pk. Clo. SE12—3D 73
Hornpark La. SE12—3D 73
Hornsey St. N7—2B 10
Hornsey Rd. N7—1C 10
Hornshay St. SE15—2E 55
Hornton Pl. W8—3D 35
Hornton St. W8—3C 34
Horsa Rd. SE12—5E 73
Horseferry Pl. SE10—2E 57
Horseferry Rd. SW1—5F 37
Horseguards Av. SW1—2A 38
Horse Guards Rd. SW1—2F 37

Horsell Rd. N5—2C 10
Horselydown La. SE1—2B 40
Horseshoe Clo. E14—1E 57
Horsfeld Rd. SE9—3F 73
Horsford Rd. SW2—3B 66
Horsley St. SE17—2F 53
Horsman St. SE5—2C 53
Horsmonden Rd. SE4—4B 70
Hortensia Rd. SW10—3E 49
Horton Av. NW2—1A 6
Horton Rd. E8—3D 13
Horton St. SE13—1D 71
Hosack Rd. SW17—2C 78
Hoser Av. SE12—2C 86
Hosier La. EC1—4D 25
Hoskins Clo. E16—5E 31
Hoskins St. SE10—1F 57
Hospital Rd. E9—2E 13
Hotham Rd. SW15—1E 61
Hotham St. E15—5A 16
Hothfield Pl. SE16—4E 41
Hotspur St. SE11—1C 52
Houghton Clo. E8—3B 12
Houghton St. WC2—5B 24
Houndsditch. EC3—5A 26
Housman Way. SE5—3F 53
Houston Rd. SE23—2A 84
Hoveden Rd. NW2—2A 6
Howard Clo. NW2—1A 6
Howard M. N5—1D 11
Howard Pl. SW1—4E 37
Howard Rd. N16—1F 11
Howard Rd. NW2—1F 5
Howard's La. SW15—2D 61
Howards Rd. E13—2C 30
Howard Way. SE22—1C 82
Howbury Rd. SE15—1E 69
Howden St. SE15—1C 68
Howell Wlk. SE17—5D 39
Howick Pl. SW1—4E 37
Howie St. SW11—3A 50
Howitt Rd. NW3—3A 8
Howland M. E. W1—4E 23
Howland St. W1—4E 23
Howland Way. SE16—3A 42
Howlett's Rd. SE24—4E 67
Howley Pl. W2—4E 21
Howsman Rd. SW13—2C 46
Howson Rd. SE4—2A 70
How's St. E2—1B 26
Hoxton Sq. N1—2A 26
Hoxton St. N1—5A 12
Hoylake Rd. W3—5A 18
Hoyland Clo. SE15—3D 55
Hoyle Rd. SW17—5A 78
Hoy St. E16—5B 30
Hubbard Rd. SE27—4E 81
Hubbard St. E15—5A 16

Hubert Gro. SW9—1A 66
Hubert Rd. E6—2F 31
Huddart St. E3—4B 28
(in two parts)
Huddlestone Rd. E7—1B 16
Huddlestone Rd. N7—1E 9
Huddlestone Rd. NW2—3D 5
Hudson's Pl. SW1—5D 37
Huggin Hill. EC4—1E 39
Hughan Rd. E15—2F 15
Hughendon Ter. E15—1E 15
Hugh M. SW1—5D 37
Hugh St. SW1—5D 37
Hugon Rd. SW6—1D 63
Hugo Rd. N19—1E 9
Huguenot St. SW18—3E 63
Huguenot Sq. SE15—1D 69
Hullbridge M. N1—5F 11
Hull Clo. SE16—2F 41
Hull St. EC1—2E 25
Hulme Pl.—3E 39
Humber Rd. SE3—2B 58
Humberstone Rd. E13—2E 31
Humberton Clo. E9—2A 14
Humbolt Rd. W6—2A 48
Humphrey St. SE1—1B 54
Hungerford St. N7—3F 9
Hungerford St. E1—5D 27
Hunsdon Rd. SE14—3F 55
Hunslett St. E2—2E 27
Hunter Clo. SE1—4F 39
Hunters Clo. SW12—1C 78
Hunters Meadows. SE19—4A 82
Hunter St. WC1—3A 24
Hunter Wlk. E13—1C 30
Huntingdon St. E16—5B 30
Huntingdon St. N1—4B 10
Huntingfield Rd. SW15—2C 60
Huntley St. WC1—3E 23
Hunton St. E1—4C 26
Hunt's Clo. SE3—5C 58
Hunt's Ct. WC2—1F 37
Hunts La. E15—1E 29
Huntsman St. SE17—5A 40
Huntspill St. SW17—3E 77
Hunts Slip Rd. SE21—3A 82
Hunt St. W11—2F 33
Huntsworth M. NW1—3B 22
Hunt Way. SE22—1C 82
Hurley Cres. SE16—3F 41
Hurlingham Ct. SW6—1B 62
Hurlingham Gdns. SW6—1B 62
Hurlingham Rd. SW6—5B 48
Hurlingham Sq. SW6—1D 63
Huron Rd. SW17—2C 78
Hurren Clo. SE3—1A 72
Hurry Clo. E15—4A 16
Hurstbourne Rd. SE23—1A 84
Hurst St. SE24—4D 67

Hurstway Wlk. W11—1F 33
Huson Clo. NW3—4A 8
Hutchings St. E14—3C 42
Hutchings Wharf Development.
  E14—3C 42
Hutchins Clo. E15—4E 15
Hutton St. EC4—5D 25
Huxbear St. SE4—3B 70
Huxley St. W10—2A 20
Hyacinth Rd. SW15—1C 74
Hyde Clo. E13—1C 30
Hyde La. SW11—4A 50
Hyde Pk. Corner. SW1 & W1
  —3C 36
Hyde Pk. Cres. W2—5A 22
Hyde Pk. Gdns. W2—1F 35
Hyde Pk. Gdns. M. W2—1F 35
Hyde Pk. Ga. SW7—3E 35
  (in two parts)
Hyde Pk. Ga. M. SW7—3E 35
Hyde Pk. Pl. W2—1A 36
Hyde Pk. Sq. W2—5A 22
Hyde Pk. St. W2—5A 22
Hyde Rd. N1—5F 11
  (in two parts)
Hydes Pl. N1—4D 11
Hyde St. SE8—2C 56
Hydethorpe Rd. SW12—1E 79
Hyde Vale. SE10—3E 57
Hyndewood. SE23—3F 83
Hyndman St. SE15—2D 55
Hyson Rd. SE16—1D 55
Hythe Rd. NW10—2B 18

Ibbotson Av. E16—5B 30
Ibbott St. E1—3E 27
Ibsley Gdns. SW15—1C 74
Iceland Rd. E3—5C 14
Ida St. E14—5E 29
  (in two parts)
Idmiston Rd. E15—1B 16
Idmiston Rd. SE27—3E 81
Idol La. EC3—1A 40
Idonia St. SE8—3C 56
Iffley Rd. W6—4D 33
Ifield Rd. SW10—2D 49
Ilbert St. W10—2F 19
Ilchester Gdns. W2—1D 35
Ilchester Pl. W14—4B 33
Ildersley Gro. SE21—2F 81
Ilderton Rd.—1E 55
  SE16 1-187 & 2-132
  SE15 remainder
Ilex Rd. NW10—3B 4
Ilex Way. SW16—5C 80
Ilfracombe Rd. Brom—3B 86
Iliffe St. SE17—1D 53

Ilkley Rd. E16—4E 31
Ilminster Gdns. SW11—2A 64
Imber St. N1—5F 11
Imperial Av. N16—1A 12
Imperial College Rd. SW7
  —4F 35
Imperial M. E6—1F 31
Imperial Rd. SW6—4D 49
Imperial Sq. SW6—4D 49
Imperial St. E3—2E 29
Inchmery Rd. SE6—2D 85
Independents Rd. SE3—1B 72
Indescon Ct. E14—3D 43
India St. EC3—5B 26
India Way. W12—1D 33
Indus Rd. SE7—3E 59
Industry Ter. SW9—1C 66
Ingal Rd. E13—3C 30
Ingate Pl. SW8—4D 51
Ingelow Rd. SW8—5D 51
Ingersoll Rd. W12—2D 33
Ingestre Pl. W1—5E 23
Ingestre Rd. E7—1C 16
Ingestre Rd. NW5—1D 9
Ingham Rd. NW6—1C 6
Inglebert St. EC1—2C 24
Ingleborough St. SW9—5C 52
Ingleby Rd. SE23—3F 83
Inglesham Wlk. E9—3B 14
Ingleside Gro. SE3—2B 58
Inglethorpe St. SW6—4F 47
Ingleton St. SW9—5C 52
Inglewood Clo. E14—5C 42
Inglewood Rd. NW6—2C 6
Inglis St. SE5—4D 53
Ingram Clo. SE11—5B 38
Ingrave St. SW11—1F 63
Ingress St. W4—1A 46
Inkerman Rd. NW5—3D 9
Inman Rd. NW10—5A 4
Inman Rd. SW18—5E 63
Inner Circ. NW1—2C 22
Inner Pk. Rd. SW19—2F 75
Inner Temple La. EC4—5C 24
Innes Gdns. SW15—4D 61
Inniskilling Rd. E13—1E 31
Institute Pl. E8—2D 13
Insurance St. WC1—2C 24
Inver Ct. W2—5D 21
Inverine Rd. SE7—1D 59
Inverness Gdns. W8—2D 35
Inverness M. W2—1D 35
Inverness Pl. W2—1D 35
Inverness St. NW1—5D 9
Inverness Ter. W2—5D 21
Inverton Rd. SE15—2F 69
Invicta Rd. SE3—3C 58
Inville Rd. SE17—1F 53

Inville Wlk. SE17—1F 53
Inworth St. SW11—5A 50
Iona Clo. SE6—5C 70
Ion Sq. E2—1C 26
Ireland Yd. EC4—5D 25
Irene Rd. SW6—4C 48
Ireton Ho. SW9—5C 52
Ireton Rd. SW9—5C 52
Iron Mill Pl. SW18—4D 63
Iron Mill Rd. SW18—4D 63
Ironmonger La. EC2—5F 25
Ironmonger Row. EC1—2F 25
Ironmongers Pl. E14—5C 42
Ironside Clo. SE16—3F 41
Irving Gro. SW9—5B 52
Irving Rd. W14—4F 33
Irving St. WC2—1F 37
Irwin Gdns. NW10—5D 5
Isabella Rd. E9—2E 13
Isabella St. SE1—2D 39
Isabel St. SW9—4B 52
Isambard M. E14—4E 43
Isambard Pl. SE16—2E 41
Isel Way. SE22—3A 68
Isis Clo. SW15—2E 61
Isis St. SW18—2E 77
Island Quay. E14—2C 42
Island Row. E14—5B 28
Islay Wlk. N1—3E 11
Islington Grn. N1—5D 11
Islington High St. N1—1C 24
  (in two parts)
Islington Pk. St. N1—4C 10
Islip St. NW5—2E 9
Ismailia Rd. E7—4D 17
Isom Clo. E13—2D 31
Ivanhoe Rd. SE5—1B 68
Ivatt Pl. W14—1B 48
Iveagh Clo. E9—5F 13
Iveley Rd. SW4—5E 51
Iverna Ct. W8—4C 34
Iverna Gdns. W8—4C 34
Iverson Rd. NW6—3B 6
Ives Rd. E16—4A 30
Ives St. SW3—5A 36
Ivestor Ter. SE23—5E 69
Ivimey St. E2—2C 26
Ivor Pl. NW1—3B 22
Ivor St. NW1—4E 9
Ivorydown. Brom—4C 86
Ivory Ho. E1—2B 40
Ivory Sq. SW11—1E 63
Ivybridge La. WC2—1A 38
Ivychurch La. SE17—1B 54
Ivy Cotts. E14—1D 43
Ivydale Rd. SE15—1F 69
Ivyday Gro. SW16—3B 80
Ivymount Rd. SE27—3C 80
Ivy Rd. E16—5C 30

Ivy Rd. NW2—1E 5
Ivy Rd. SE4—2B 70
Ivy St. N1—1A 26
Ixworth Pl. SW3—1A 50

Jackman St. E8—5D 13
Jackson Rd. N7—1B 10
Jack Walker Ct. N5—1D 11
Jacob St. SE1—3C 40
Jacob's Well M. W1—5C 22
Jade Clo. E16—5F 31
Jaggard Way. SW12—5B 64
Jago Wlk. SE5—3F 53
Jamaica Rd. SE1 & SE16—3B 40
Jamaica St. E1—4E 27
James Av. NW2—2E 5
James Boswell Clo. SW16
—4C 80
James Clo. E13—1C 30
James Collins Clo. W9—3B 20
Jameson St. W8—2C 34
James St. W1—5C 22
James St. WC2—1A 38
Jamestown Rd. NW1—5D 9
Jane St. E1—5D 27
Janet St. E14—4C 42
Janeway Pl. SE16—3D 41
Janeway St. SE16—3C 40
Jansen Wlk. SW11—1F 63
Janson Clo. E15—2A 16
Janson Rd. E15—2A 16
Jarrett Clo. SW2—1D 81
Jarrow Rd. SE16—5E 41
Jarrow Way. E9—1B 14
Jarvis Rd. SE22—2A 68
Jasmine Ct. SW19—5C 76
Jasper Pas. SE19—5B 82
Jasper Rd. E16—5F 31
Jasper Rd. SE19—5B 82
Jay M. SW7—3E 35
Jebb Av. SW2—4A 66
Jebb St. E3—1C 28
Jedburgh Rd. E13—2E 31
Jedburgh St. SW11—2C 64
Jeddo Rd. W12—3B 32
Jeffrey Row. SE12—3D 73
Jeffrey's Pl. NW1—4E 9
Jeffreys Rd. SW4—5A 52
Jeffrey's St. NW1—4E 9
Jeffreys Wlk. SW4—5A 52
Jeken Rd. SE9—2E 73
Jelf Rd. SW2—3C 66
Jellicoe Rd. E13—3C 30
Jenkins Rd. E13—3D 31
Jenner Pl. SW13—2D 47
Jennifer Rd. Brom—3B 86
Jennings Rd. SE22—4B 68

Jephson Rd. E7—4E 17
Jephson St. SE5—4F 53
Jephtha Rd. SW18—4C 62
Jerdan Pl. SW6—3C 48
Jeremiah St. E14—5D 29
Jermyn St. SW1—2E 37
Jerningham Rd. SE14—5A 56
Jerome Cres. NW8—3A 22
Jerome St. E1—3B 26
Jerrard St. SE13—1D 71
Jerrold St. N1—1A 26
Jersey Ho. N1—3E 11
Jersey Rd. E16—5D 31
Jersey St. E2—2D 27
Jerusalem Pas. EC1—3D 25
Jerviston Gdns. SW16—5C 80
Jessica Rd. SW18—4E 63
Jessop Rd. SE24—2E 67
Jessop Sq. E14—2C 42
Jevington Way. SE12—1D 87
Jewry St. EC3—5B 26
Jew's Row. SW18—2E 63
Jews Wlk. SE26—4D 83
Jeymer Av. NW2—2D 5
Jeypore Pas. SW18—4E 63
Jeypore Rd. SW18—4E 63
Joan Cres. SE9—5F 73
Joan St. SE1—2D 39
Jockey's Fields. WC1—4B 24
Jodrell Rd. E3—5B 14
Joe Hunte Ct. SE27—5D 81
Johanna St. SE1—3C 38
John Adam St. WC2—1A 38
John Ashby Clo. SW2—4A 66
John Baird Ct. SE23—4F 83
John Barnes Wlk. E15—3B 16
John Campbell Rd. N16—2A 12
John Carpenter St. EC4—1D 39
John Felton Rd. SE16—3C 40
John Fisher St. E1—1C 40
John Islip St. SW1—5F 37
John McKenna Wlk. SE16
—4C 40
John Parker Sq. SW11—1F 63
John Penn St. SE13—4D 57
John Prince's St. W1—5D 23
John Rennie Wlk. E1—2D 41
John Roll Way. SE16—4C 40
John Ruskin St. SE5—3D 53
John's M. WC1—3B 24
Johnson Clo. E8—5C 12
Johnson's Ct. EC4—5C 24
Johnson's Pl. SW1—1E 51
Johnson St. E1—1E 41
John Spencer Sq. N1—3D 11
John's Pl. E1—5D 27
John St. E15—5B 16
John St. WC1—3B 24

John Woolley Clo. SE13—2F 71
Joiner St. SE1—2F 39
Jonathan St. SE11—1B 52
Jones Rd. E13—3D 31
Jones St. W1—1D 37
Joram Way. SE16—1D 55
Josephine Av. SW2—3B 66
Joseph Powell Clo. SW12
—4D 65
Joseph St. E3—3B 28
Joshua St. E14—5E 29
Joubert St. SW11—5B 50
Jowett St. SE15—3B 54
Joyce Page Clo. SE7—2F 59
Jubilee Cres. E14—4E 43
Jubilee Pl. SW3—1A 50
Jubilee St. E1—5E 27
Jubilee Ter. N1—1F 25
Judd St. WC1—2A 24
Jude St. E16—5B 30
Juer St. SW11—3A 50
Julian Pl. E14—1D 57
Julia St. NW5—1C 8
Junction App. SE13—1E 71
Junction App. SW11—1A 64
Junction M. W2—5A 22
Junction Rd. E13—1D 31
Juniper St. E1—1E 41
Juno Way. SE14—2F 55
Jupiter Way. N7—3B 10
Jupp Rd. E15—4F 15
Jupp Rd. W. E15—5F 15
Jutland Rd. E13—3C 30
Jutland Rd. SE6—5E 71
Juxon St. SE11—5B 38

Kambala Rd. SW11—1F 63
Kangley Bri. Rd. SE26—5B 84
Kashmir Rd. SE7—3F 59
Kassala Rd. SW11—4B 50
Katherine Gdns. SE9—2F 73
Katherine Rd.—3E 17
 E6 1-239 & 2-224
 E7 remainder
Kathleen Rd. SW11—1B 64
Kay Rd. SW9—5A 52
Kay St. E2—1C 26
Kay St. E15—4F 15
Kean St. WC2—5B 24
Kearsley M. SW11—4B 50
Keats Clo. NW3—1A 8
Keats Clo. SW19—5F 77
Keat's Gro. NW3—1A 8
Keble St. SW17—4E 77
Kedleston Wlk. E2—2D 27
Keedonwood Rd. Brom—5A 86
Keel Clo. SE16—2F 41

Keeley St. WC2—5B 24
Keeling Rd. SE9—3F 73
Keen's Yd. N1—3D 11
Keep, The. SE3—5C 58
Keeton's Rd. SE16—4D 41
Keevil Dri. SW19—5F 61
Keighley Clo. N7—1A 10
Keildon Rd. SW11—2B 64
Keith Connor Clo. SW8—1D 65
Keith Gro. W12—3C 32
Kelfield Gdns. W10—5E 19
Kelfield M. W10—5F 19
Kelland Rd. E13—3C 30
Kellaway Rd. SE3—5F 59
Kellerton Rd. SE13—3A 72
Kellett Rd. SW2—2C 66
Kellino St. SW17—4B 78
Kell St. SE1—4D 39
Kelly St. NW1—3D 9
Kelman Clo. SW4—5F 51
Kelmore Gro. SE22—2C 68
Kelmscott Gdns. W12—4C 32
Kelmscott Rd. SW11—3A 64
Kelross Rd. N5—1E 11
Kelsall Clo. SE3—5D 59
Kelsey St. E2—3C 26
Kelso Pl. W8—4D 35
Kelvedon Rd. SW6—3B 48
Kelvin Gro. SE26—3D 83
Kelvington Rd. SE15—3F 69
Kelvin Rd. N5—1E 11
Kember St. N1—4B 10
Kemble Rd. SE23—1F 83
Kemble St. WC2—5B 24
Kemerton Rd. SE5—1E 67
Kemeys St. E9—2A 14
Kempe Rd. NW6—1F 19
Kempis Way. SE22—3A 68
Kemplay Rd. NW3—1F 7
Kemps Dri. E14—1C 42
Kempsford Gdns. SW5—1C 48
Kempsford Rd. SE11—5C 38
Kemps Gdns. SE13—3E 71
Kempson Rd. SW6—3C 48
Kempthorne Rd. SE8—5B 42
Kemsing Rd. SE10—1C 58
Kenbury St. SE5—5E 53
Kenchester Clo. SW8—3A 52
Kendal Clo. SW9—3D 53
Kendale Rd. Brom—5A 86
Kendall Pl. W1—4C 22
Kendal Pl. SW15—3B 62
Kendal Rd. NW10—1C 4
Kendal St. W2—5A 22
Kender St. SE14—3E 55
Kendoa Rd. SW4—2F 65
Kendrick M. SW7—5F 35
Kendrick Pl. SW7—5F 35

Kenilford Rd. SW12—5D 65
Kenilworth Av. SW19—5C 76
Kenilworth Rd. E3—1A 28
Kenilworth Rd. NW6—5B 6
Kenley Wlk. W11—2A 34
Kenlor Rd. SW17—5F 77
Kenmont Gdns. NW10—2D 19
Kenmure Rd. E8—2D 13
Kenmure Yd. E8—2D 13
Kennard Rd. E15—4F 15
Kennard St. SW11—4C 50
Kennedy Clo. E13—1C 30
Kennet Clo. SW11—2F 63
Kenneth Cres. NW2—2D 5
Kennet Rd. W9—3B 20
Kennet St. E1—2C 40
Kenning St. SE16—3E 41
Kennings Way. SE11—1C 52
Kenning Ter. N1—5A 12
Kennington Grn. SE11—1C 52
Kennington Gro. SE11—2B 52
Kennington La. SE11—1B 52
Kennington Oval. SE11—2B 52
Kennington Pk. Gdns. SE11
—2D 53
Kennington Pk. Pl. SE11—2C 52
Kennington Pk. Rd. SE11
—2C 52
Kennington Rd.—4C 38
SE1 1-69 & 2-64
SE11 remainder
Kenrick Pl. W1—4C 22
Kensal Rd. W10—3A 20
Kensington Chu. St. W8—2C 34
Kensington Ct. W8—3D 35
Kensington Ct. Pl. W8—4D 35
Kensington Gdns. Sq. W2
—5D 21
Kensington Ga. W8—4E 35
Kensington Gore. SW7—3F 35
Kensington Hall Gdns. W14
—1B 48
Kensington High St.—4B 34
W8 1-353 & 2-280
W14 remainder
Kensington Mall. W8—2C 34
Kensington Pal. Gdns. W8
—2D 35
Kensington Pk. Gdns. W11
—1B 34
Kensington Pk. M. W11—5B 20
Kensington Pk. Rd. W11—5B 20
Kensington Pl. W8—2C 34
Kensington Rd. W8 & SW7
—3E 35
Kensington Sq. W8—3D 35
Kent Ho. La. Beck—5A 84
Kent Ho. Rd.—5A 84

SE26 1-95 & 2-72
Beck remainder
Kentish Town Rd.—4D 9
NW1 1-187 & 2-158
NW5 remainder
Kenton Rd. E9—3F 13
Kenton St. WC1—3A 24
Kent Pas. NW1—3B 22
Kent St. E2—1B 26
Kent St. E13—2E 31
Kent Ter. NW1—2A 22
Kent Wlk. SW9—2D 67
Kent Way. SE15—4B 54
Kentwode Grn. SW13—3C 46
Kent Yd. SW7—3A 36
Kenward Rd. SE9—3E 73
Kenway Rd. SW5—5D 35
Kenwood Av. SE14—4F 55
Kenworthy Rd. E9—2A 14
Kenwyn Rd. SW4—2F 65
Kenya Rd. SE7—3F 59
Kenyon St. SW6—4F 47
Keogh Rd. E15—3A 16
Kepler Rd. SW4—2A 66
Keppel Row. SE1—2E 39
Keppel St. WC1—4F 23
Kerbela St. E2—3C 26
Kerby St. E14—5D 29
Kerfield Cres. SE5—4F 53
Kerfield Pl. SE5—4F 53
Kerrison Rd. E15—5F 15
Kerrison Rd. SW11—1A 64
Kerry Clo. E16—5D 31
Kerry Path. SE14—2B 56
Kersfield Rd. SW15—4F 61
Kershaw Clo. SW18—4F 63
Kersley St. SW11—5B 50
Kerwick Clo. N7—4A 10
Keslake Rd. NW6—1F 19
Keston Rd. SE15—1C 68
Kestrel Av. SE24—3E 67
Keswick Av. SW15—5A 74
Keswick Rd. SW15—3A 62
Kett Gdns. SW2—3B 66
Key Clo. E1—3E 27
Keyes Rd. NW2—2F 5
Keymer Rd. SW2—2B 80
Keynsham Rd. SE9—3F 73
Keyse Rd. SE1—4B 40
Keystone Cres. N1—1A 24
Keyworth St. SE1—4D 39
Kezia St. SE8—1A 56
Khama Rd. SW17—4A 78
Khartoum Rd. E13—2D 31
Khartoum Rd. SW17—4F 77
Khyber Rd. SW11—5A 50
Kibworth St. SW8—3B 52
Kidbrooke Gdns. SE3—5C 58

Kidbrooke Gro. SE3—4C 58
Kidbrooke Pk. Clo. SE3—4D 59
Kidbrooke Pk. Rd. SE3—4D 59
Kidbrooke Way. SE3—5D 59
Kidderpore Av. NW3—1C 6
Kidderpore Gdns. NW3—1C 6
Kidron Way. E9—5E 13
Kiffen St. EC2—3F 25
Kilburn High Rd. NW6—4B 6
Kilburn La.—2F 19
  W10 1-271 & 2-300
  W9 remainder
Kilburn Pk. Rd. NW6—2C 20
Kilburn Pl. NW6—5C 6
Kilburn Priory. NW6—5D 7
Kilburn Sq. NW6—5C 6
Kilburn Vale. NW6—5D 7
Kildare Gdns. W2—5C 20
Kildare Rd. E16—4C 30
Kildare Ter. W2—5C 20
Kildare Wlk. E14—5C 28
Kildoran Rd. SW2—3A 66
Kilgour Rd. SE23—4A 70
Kilkie St. SW6—5E 49
Killarney Rd. SW18—4E 63
Killearn Rd. SE6—1F 85
Killick St. N1—1B 24
Killieser Av. SW2—2A 80
Killip Clo. E16—5B 30
Killowen Rd. E9—3F 13
Killyon Rd. SW8—5E 51
Killyon Ter. SW8—5E 51
Kilmaine Rd. SW6—3A 48
Kilmarsh Rd. W6—5E 33
Kilmeston Way. SE15—3B 54
Kilmington Rd. SW13—2C 46
Kilmorie Rd. SE23—1A 84
Kilner St. E14—4C 28
Kiln Pl. NW5—2C 8
Kilravock St. W10—2A 20
Kimbell Gdns. SW6—4A 48
Kimberley Av. SE15—5E 55
Kimberley Rd. E16—3B 30
Kimberley Rd. NW6—5A 6
Kimberley Rd. SW9—1A 66
Kimber Rd. SW18—5C 62
Kimbolton Clo. SE12—4B 72
Kimpton Rd. SE5—4F 53
Kinburn St. SE16—3F 41
Kincaid Rd. SE15—3D 55
Kincardine Gdns. W9—3C 20
Kinder St. E1—5D 27
Kinfauns Rd. SW2—2C 80
King Alfred Av. SE6—4C 84
King & Queen St. SE17—1E 53
King Arthur Clo. SE15—3E 55
King Charles St. SW1—3A 38
King Charles Wlk. SW19—1A 76

King David La. E1—1E 41
Kingdon Rd. NW6—3C 6
King Edward M. SW13—4C 46
King Edward's Rd. E9—5D 13
King Edward St. EC1—5E 25
King Edward Wlk. SE1—4C 38
Kingfield St. E14—5E 43
Kingfisher Ct. SW19—2A 76 `
King Frederick II Tower. SE16
      —4B 42
King George Av. E16—5F 31
King George St. SE10—3E 57
Kingham Clo. SW18—5E 63
Kingham Clo. W11—3A 34
King Henry's Rd. NW3—4F 7
King Henry St. N16—2A 12
King Henry's Wlk. N1—3A 12
Kinghorn St. EC1—4E 25
King James St. SE1—3D 39
King John Ct. EC2—3A 26
King John St. E1—4F 27
Kinglake Est. SE17—1A 54
Kinglake St. SE17—1A 54
Kingly St. W1—5E 23
Kingsand Rd. SE12—2C 86
Kings Arms Yd. EC2—5F 25
Kings Av.—5F 65
  SW4 1-147 & 2-118
  SW12 remainder
Kings Av. Brom—5B 86
King's Bench St. SE1—3D 39
King's Bench Wlk. EC4—1C 38
Kingsbridge Rd. W10—5E 19
Kingsbury Rd. N1—3A 12
Kingsbury Ter. N1—3A 12
Kingsclere Clo. SW15—5C 60
Kingscliffe Gdns. SW19—1B 76
King's College Rd. NW3—4A 8
Kingscote Rd. SE4—1D 69
King's Ct. E13—5D 17
Kingscourt Rd. SW16—3F 79
Kingscroft Rd. NW2—3B 6
Kingsdale Gdns. W11—2F 33
Kingsdown Av. W3—1A 32
Kingsdown Clo. W10—5F 19
Kingsford St. NW5—2B 8
Kings Garth M. SE23—2E 83
Kingsgate Pl. NW6—4C 6
Kingsgate Rd. NW6—4C 6
Kingsground. SE9—5D 73
King's Gro. SE15—4D 55
  (in two parts)
King's Head Yd. SE1—2F 39
Kingshold Rd. E9—4E 13
Kingsholm Gdns. SE9—2F 73
Kingshurst Rd. SE12—5C 72
Kingsland Grn. E8—3A 12

Kingsland High St. E8—3B 12
Kingsland Pas. E8—3A 12
Kingsland Rd.—2A 26
  E2 1-283 & 2-240 E8 remainder
Kingsland Rd. E13—2E 31
Kingslawn Clo. SW15—3D 61
Kingsley M. W8—4D 35
Kingsley Rd. E7—4C 16
Kingsley Rd. NW6—5B 6
Kingsley Rd. SW19—5D 77
Kingsley St. SW11—1B 64
Kings Mall. W6—5E 33
Kingsmead Rd. SW2—2C 80
King's Mead Way. E9—1A 14
Kingsmere Clo. SW15—1F 61
Kingsmere Rd. SW19—2F 75
King's M. SW4—3A 66
King's M. WC1—3B 24
Kingsmill Ter. NW8—1F 21
King's Pl. SE1—3E 39
King's Rd. SW19—5C 76
King Sq. EC1—2E 25
Kingsridge. SW19—2A 76
King's Rd. E6—5E 17
King's Rd. NW10—4D 5
King's Rd.—3D 49
  SW3 1-363 & 2-392
  SW10 365-539 & 394-552
  SW6 remainder
King Stairs Clo. SE16—3D 41
King's Ter. NW1—5E 9
Kingsthorpe Rd. SE26—4F 83
Kingston Rd. SW15—2C 74
Kingston Sq. SW19—5F 81
Kingston Vale. SW3A 74
Kingstown St. NW1—5C 8
King St. E13—3C 30
King St. EC2—5E 25
King St. SW1—2E 37
King St. W6—5C 32
King St. WC2—1A 38
Kingswater Pl. SW11—3A 50
Kingsway. WC2—5B 24
Kingswood Av. NW6—5A 6
Kingswood Clo. SW8—3A 52
Kingswood Dri. SE19—4A 82
Kingswood Est. SE21—4A 82
Kingswood Pl. SE13—2A 72
Kingswood Rd. SW2—4A 66
Kingswood Rd. SE13—2A 72
King William St. EC4—1F 39
King William Wlk. SE10—2E 57
Kingwood Rd. SW6—4A 48
Kinnaird Av. Brom—5B 86
Kinnear Rd. W12—3B 32
Kinnerton St. SW1—3C 36
Kinnoul Rd. W6—2A 48
Kinross St. SE1—3A 40
Kinsale Rd. SE15—1C 68

Kintal Dri. E14—5C 42
Kintore Way. SE1—5B 40
Kinver Rd. SE26—4E 83
Kipling Dri. SW19—5F 77
Kipling Est. SE1—3F 39
Kipling St. SE1—3F 39
Kippington Dri. SE9—1F 87
Kirby Gro. SE1—3A 40
Kirby St. EC1—4C 24
Kirkdale. SE26—2D 83
Kirkland Wlk. E8—3B 12
Kirkmichael Rd. E14—5E 29
Kirkside Rd. SE3—2C 58
Kirk's Pl. E14—4B 28
Kirkstall Gdns. SW2—1A 80
Kirkstall Rd. SW2—1F 79
Kirkwall Pl. E2—2E 27
Kirkwood Pl. NW1—4C 8
Kirkwood Rd. SE15—5D 55
Kirtley Rd. SE26—4A 84
Kirtling St. SW8—3E 51
Kirton Gdns. E2—2B 26
Kirton Rd. E13—1E 31
Kirwyn Way. SE5—3E 53
Kitcat Ter. E3—2C 28
Kitchener Rd. E7—3D 17
Kitson Rd. SE5—3F 53
Kitson Rd. SW13—4C 46
Kitto Rd. SE14—5F 55
Klea Av. SW4—4E 65
Knapdale Clo. SE23—2D 83
Knapmill Rd. SE6—2C 84
Knapmill Way. SE6—2D 85
Knapp Clo. NW10—3A 4
Knapp Rd. E3—3C 28
Knaresborough Pl. SW5—5D 35
Knatchbull Rd. SE5—5D 53
Knebworth Rd. N16—1A 12
Kneller Rd. SE4—2A 70
Knighten St. E1—2D 41
Knighton Pk. Rd. SE26—5F 83
Knightrider St. EC4—5D 25
Knightsbridge—3B 36
  SW1 1-161 & 2-124
  SW7 remainder
Knightsbridge Grn. SW1—3B 36
Knight's Clo. SE9—2E 13
Knights Hill. SE27—5D 81
Knights Hill Sq. SE27—4D 81
Knight's Pl. E16—3C 44
Knight's Wlk. SE11—5D 39
Knivet Rd. SW6—2C 48
Knobs Hill Rd. E15—5D 15
Knockholt Rd. SE9—3F 73
Knoll Rd. SW18—3E 63
Knollys Clo. SW16—3C 80
Knollys Rd. SW16—3C 80
Knottisford St. E2—2E 27

Knowle Clo. SW9—1C 66
Knowles Hill Cres. SE13—3F 71
Knowles Wlk. SW4—1E 65
Knowsley Rd. SW11—5B 50
Knox Rd. E7—3B 16
Knox St. W1—4B 22
Knoyle St. SE14—2A 56
Kohat Rd. SW19—5D 77
Kossuth St. SE10—1A 58
Kotree Way. SE1—5C 40
Kramer M. SW5—1C 48
Kuhn Way. E7—2C 16
Kylemore Clo. E6—1F 31
Kylemore Rd. NW6—4C 6
Kynance M. SW7—4E 35
Kynance Pl. SW7—4E 35
Kynaston Rd. Brom—5C 86
Kyrle Rd. SW11—4C 64

Laburnum Clo. SE15—3E 55
Laburnum St. E2—5B 12
Lacey Wlk. E3—1C 28
Lackington St. EC2—4F 25
Lacon Rd. SE22—2C 68
Lacy Rd. SW15—2F 61
Ladas Rd. SE27—4E 81
Ladbroke Cres. W11—5A 20
Ladbroke Gdns. W11—1B 34
Ladbroke Gro—3F 19
  W11 1-137 & 2-108
  W10 remainder
Ladbroke M. W11—2A 34
Ladbroke Rd. W11—2B 34
Ladbroke Sq. W11—1B 34
Ladbroke Ter. W11—1B 34
Ladbroke Wlk. W11—2B 34
Ladycroft Rd. SE13—1D 71
Lady Dock Wlk. SE16—3A 42
Lady Margaret Rd.—2E 9
  NW5 1-83 & 2-70
  N19 remainder
Ladyship Ter. SE22—5C 68
Ladysmith Rd. E16—2B 30
Lady Somerset Rd. NW5—1D 9
Ladywell Rd. SE13—3C 70
Ladywell St. E15—5B 16
Lafone St. SE1—3B 40
Lagado M. SE16—2F 41
Lainson St. SW18—5C 62
Lairdale Clo. SE21—1E 81
Lairs Clo. N7—2A 10
Laitwood Rd. SW12—1D 79
Lake Av. Brom—5C 86
Lake Rd. SW19—5B 76
Laker Pl. SW15—4A 62
Lakeside Rd. W14—4F 33
Lakeview Rd. SE27—5C 80

Lakis Clo. NW3—1E 7
Laleham Rd. SE6—5E 71
Lalor St. SW6—5A 48
Lamberhurst Rd. SE27—4C 80
Lambert Rd. E16—5D 31
Lambert Rd. SW2—3A 66
Lambert St. N1—4C 10
Lambeth Bri. SW1 & SE1
                  —5A 38
Lambeth High St. SE1—5B 38
Lambeth Hill. EC4—1E 39
Lambeth Pal. Rd. SE1—4B 38
Lambeth Rd. SE1—4B 38
Lambeth Wlk. SE11—5B 38
  (in two parts)
Lamb La. E8—4D 13
Lamble St. NW5—2C 8
Lambolle Pl. NW3—3A 8
Lambolle Rd. NW3—3A 8
Lambourne Av. SW19—4B 76
Lambourne Pl. SE3—4D 59
Lambourn Rd. SW4—1D 65
Lambrook Ter. SW6—4A 48
Lamb's Bldgs. EC1—3F 25
Lamb's Conduit Pas. WC1
                  —4B 24
Lamb's Conduit St. WC1—3B 24
Lambscroft Av. SE9—3E 87
Lamb's M. N1—5D 11
Lamb's Pas. EC1—3F 25
Lamb St. E1—4B 26
Lambton Pl. W11—1B 34
Lamb Wlk. SE1—3A 40
Lamerock Rd. Brom—4B 86
Lamerton St. SE8—2C 56
Lamington St. W6—5D 33
Lamlash St. SE11—5D 39
Lammas Grn. SE26—3D 83
Lammas Rd. E9—4F 13
Lammermoor Rd. SW12—5D 65
Lamont Rd. SW10—2E 49
Lampern Sq. E2—2C 26
Lampeter Sq. W6—2A 48
Lamplighter Clo. E1—3E 27
Lampmead Rd. SE12—3B 72
Lampton Ho. Clo. SW19—4F 75
Lanark Pl. W9—3E 21
Lanark Rd. W9—1D 21
Lanark Sq. E14—4D 43
Lanbury Rd. SE15—2F 69
Lancaster Av. SE27—2D 81
Lancaster Av. SW19—5F 75
Lancaster Clo. N1—4A 12
Lancaster Clo. SW20—2D 81
Lancaster Ct. SW6—3B 48
Lancaster Dri. E14—2E 43
Lancaster Dri. NW3—3A 8
Lancaster Gdns. SW19—5A 76

Lancaster Ga. W2—1E 35
Lancaster Gro. NW3—3F 7
Lancaster M. W2—1E 35
Lancaster Pl. SW19—5F 75
Lancaster Pl. WC2—1B 38
Lancaster Rd. E7—4C 16
Lancaster Rd. NW10—2C 4
Lancaster Rd. SW19—5F 75
Lancaster Rd. W11—5A 20
Lancaster Stables. NW3—3A 8
Lancaster St. SE1—3D 39
Lancaster Ter. W2—1F 35
Lancaster Wlk. W2 & SW7
—2E 35
Lancefield St. W10—2B 20
(in two parts)
Lancelot Pl. SW7—3B 36
Lancing St. NW1—2F 23
Landcroft Rd. SE22—3B 68
Landells Rd. SE22—4B 68
Landford Rd. SW15—1E 61
Landgrove Rd. SW19—5C 76
Landmann Way. SE14—1F 55
Landon Pl. SW1—4B 36
Landon's Clo. E14—2E 43
Landon Wlk. E14—1D 43
Landor Rd. SW9—1A 66
Landor Wlk. W12—3C 32
Landport Way. SE15—3B 54
Landridge Rd. SW6—5B 48
Lanercost Clo. SW2—2C 80
Lanercost Rd. SW2—2C 80
Lane, The. NW8—1E 21
Lane, The. SE3—1C 72
Laneway. SW15—3D 61
Lanfranc Rd. E3—1A 28
Lanfrey Pl. W14—1B 48
Langbrook Rd. SE3—1F 73
Langdale Clo. SE17—2E 53
Langdale Rd. SE10—3E 57
Langdale St. E1—5D 27
Langdon Ct. NW10—5A 4
Langdon Way. SE1—5C 40
Langford Clo. E8—2C 12
Langford Clo. NW8—1E 21
Langford Grn. SE5—1A 68
Langford Pl. NW8—1E 21
Langford Rd. SW6—5B 48
Langham Pl. W1—4D 23
Langham Pl. W4—2A 46
Langham St. W1—4D 23
Langholm Clo. SW12—5F 65
Langland Gdns. NW3—2D 7
Langler Rd. NW10—1E 19
Langley Ct. WC2—1A 38
Langley La. SW8—2B 52
Langley St. WC2—5A 24
Langmead St. SE27—4E 81
Langroyd Rd. SW17—2B 78

Langside Av. SW15—2C 60
Lang St. E1—3E 27
Langthorn Ct. EC2—5F 25
Langthorne St. SW6—3F 47
Langton Clo. WC1—3B 24
Langton Rise. SE23—5D 69
Langton Rd. SW9—3D 53
Langton St. SW10—2E 49
Langton Way. SE3—4C 58
Langtry Rd. NW8—5D 7
Langtry Wlk. NW8—5E 7
Lanhill Rd. W9—3C 20
Lanier Rd. SE13—4F 71
Lanrick Rd. E14—5F 29
Lansbury Est. E14—5D 29
Lansbury Gdns. E14—5F 29
Lanscombe Wlk. SW8—4A 52
Lansdowne Cres. W11—1A 34
Lansdowne Dri. E8—4C 12
Lansdowne Gdns. SW8—4A 52
Lansdowne Gro. NW10—1A 4
Lansdowne Hill. SE27—3D 81
Lansdowne La. SE7—1F 59
Lansdowne M. SE7—1F 59
Lansdowne M. W11—2B 34
Lansdowne Pl. SE1—4F 39
Lansdowne Rise. W11—1A 34
Lansdowne Row. W1—2D 37
Lansdowne Ter. WC1—3A 24
Lansdowne Wlk. W11—2B 34
Lansdowne Way. SW8—4F 51
Lansdowne Wood. SE27—3D 81
Lansdown Rd. E7—4E 17
Lantern Clo. SW15—2C 60
Lanterns Ct. E14—4D 43
Lant St. SE1—3E 39
Lanvanor Rd. SE15—5E 55
Lapford Clo. W9—3B 20
Lapse Wood Wlk. SE23—2D 83
Lara Clo. SE13—4E 71
Larch Av. W3—2A 32
Larch Clo. SE8—2B 56
Larch Clo. SW12—2D 79
Larden Rd. W3—3A 32
Larkbere Rd. SE26—4A 84
Larkhall La. SW4—5F 51
Larkhall Rise. SW4—1E 65
Lark Row. E2—5E 13
Larnach Rd. W6—2F 47
Larpent Av. SW15—3E 61
Lassell St. SE10—1F 57
Latchmere Pas. SW11—5B 50
Latchmere Rd. SW11—5B 50
Latchmere St. SW11—5B 50
Latimer Pl. W10—5E 19
Latimer Rd. E7—1D 17

Latimer Rd. W10—4E 19
Latimer St. E1—4F 27
Latona Rd. SE15—2C 54
Latymer Ct. W6—5F 33
Lauderdale Rd. W9—2D 21
Laud St. SE11—1B 52
Launcelot Rd. Brom—4C 86
Launcelot St. SE1—3C 38
Launceston Pl. W8—4E 35
Launch St. E14—4E 43
Laundry Rd. W6—2A 48
Laura Pl. E5—1E 13
Laurel Bank Gdns. SW6—5B 48
Laurelbrook. SE6—3A 86
Laurel Gro. SE26—4F 83
Laurel Gro. SW13—5C 46
Laurel St. E8—3B 12
Laurence M. W12—3C 32
Laurence Pountney Hill. EC4
—1F 39
Laurence Pountney La. EC4
—1F 39
Laurie Gro. SE14—4A 56
Lauriston Rd. E9—4E 13
Lauriston Rd. SW19—5F 75
Lausanne Rd. SE15—4E 55
Lavell St. N16—1F 11
Lavender Clo. SW3—2F 49
Lavender Gdns. SW11—2B 64
Lavender Gro. E8—4C 12
Lavender Hill. SW11—1B 64
Lavender Rd. SE16—2A 42
Lavender Rd. SW11—1F 63
Lavender St. E15—3A 16
Lavender Sweep. SW11—2B 64
Lavender Ter. SW11—1A 64
Lavender Wlk. SW11—2B 64
Lavengro Rd. SE27—2E 81
Lavenham Rd. SW18—2B 76
Laverstoke Gdns. SW15—5B 60
Laverton M. SW5—5D 35
Laverton Pl. SW5—5D 35
Lavina Gro. N1—1B 24
Lavington St. SE1—2D 39
Lawford Rd. N1—4A 12
Lawford Rd. NW5—3E 9
Lawless St. E14—1D 43
Lawley St. E5—1E 13
Lawn La. SW8—2B 52
Lawn Rd. NW3—2B 8
Lawnside. SE3—2B 72
Lawns, The. SE3—1B 72
Lawn Ter. SE3—1A 72
Lawrence Clo. E3—2C 28
Lawrence La. EC2—5E 25
Lawrence Rd. E13—5D 17
Lawrence St. E16—4B 30
Lawrence St. SW3—2A 50
Lawrence Wharf Development.
SE16—2B 42

Lawrie Pk. Av. SE26—5D 83
Lawrie Pk. Cres. SE26—5D 83
Lawrie Pk. Gdns. SE26—4D 83
Lawrie Pk. Rd. SE26—5D 83
Lawson Clo. E16—4E 31
Lawson Clo. SW19—3F 75
Law St. SE1—4F 39
Lawton Rd. E3—2A 28
Laxley Clo. SE5—3D 53
Laxton Pl. NW1—3D 23
Layard Rd. SE16—5D 41
Layard Sq. SE16—5D 41
Laycock St. N1—3C 10
Laystall St. EC1—3C 24
Layton Rd. N1—1C 24
Layton's Bldgs. SE1—3F 39
Layzell Wlk. SE9—1F 87
Leacroft Av. SW12—5B 64
Leadenhall Pl. EC3—5A 26
Leadenhall St. EC3—5A 26
Leadenham Ct. E3—3C 28
Leaf Gro. SE27—5C 80
Leafy Oak Rd. SE12—4E 87
Leahurst Rd. SE13—3F 71
Leake Ct. SE1—3B 38
Leake St. SE1—3B 38
Leamington Av. Brom—5E 87
Leamington Clo. Brom—5E 87
Leamington Rd. Vs. W11
—4B 20
Leamore St. W6—5E 33
Leamouth Rd. E14—1F 43
Leander Ct. SE8—4C 56
Leander Ct. SE16—2B 42
Leander Rd. SW2—4B 66
Leatherdale St. E1—3E 27
(in two parts)
Leather Gdns. E15—5A 16
Leather La. EC1—4C 24
Leathermarket St. SE1—3A 40
Leathwaite Rd. SW11—2B 64
Leathwell Rd. SE8—5D 57
Lebanon Gdns. SW18—4C 62
Lebanon Rd. SW18—3C 62
Lebrun Sq. SE3—2D 73
Lechmere Rd. NW2—3D 5
Leckford Rd. SW18—2E 77
Lecky St. SW7—1F 49
Leconfield Av. SW13—1B 60
Leconfield Rd. N5—1F 11
Ledbury M. N. W11—1C 34
Ledbury M. W. W11—1C 34
Ledbury Rd. W11—5B 20
Ledbury St. SE15—3C 54
Lee Bri. SE13—1E 71
Lee Chu. St. SE13—2A 72
Lee Conservancy Rd. E9—2B 14
Leefern Rd. W12—3C 32
Lee Ga. SE12—3B 72

Lee Grn. SE12—3B 72
Lee High Rd.—1E 71
SE13 1-231 & 2-332
SE12 remainder
Leeke St. WC1—2B 24
Leeland Way. NW10—1B 4
Lee Pk. SE3—2B 72
Leerdam Rd. E14—4E 43
Lee Rd. SE3—1B 72
Leeson Rd. SE24—2C 66
Lees Pl. W1—1C 36
Lee St. E8—5B 12
Lee Ter. SE3—1A 72
Leeward Gdns. SW19—5A 76
Leeway. SE8—1B 56
Lefevre Wlk. E3—5B 14
Lefroy Rd. W12—3B 32
Legatt Rd. SE9—3F 73
Leggatt Rd. E15—1E 29
Legge St. SE13—3E 71
Leghorn Rd. NW10—1B 18
Legion Rd. N1—4C 10
Leicester Pl. WC2—1F 37
Leicester Sq. WC2—1F 37
Leicester St. WC2—1F 37
Leigham Av. SW16—3A 80
Leigham Ct. Rd. SW16—2A 80
Leigham Vale—3B 80
SW16 8-91
SW2 remainder
Leigh Gdns. NW10—1E 19
Leigh Hunt St. SE1—3E 39
Leigh Orchard Clo. SW16
—3B 80
Leigh Pl. EC1—4C 24
Leigh Rd. N5—1D 11
Leigh St. WC1—2A 24
Leighton Cres. NW5—2E 9
Leighton Gdns. NW10—1D 19
Leighton Gro. NW5—2E 9
Leighton Pl. NW5—2E 9
Leighton Rd. NW5—2E 9
Leinster Gdns. W2—5E 21
Leinster M. W2—1E 35
Leinster Pl. W2—5E 21
Leinster Rd. NW6—2C 20
Leinster Sq. W2—5D 21
Leinster Ter. W2—1E 35
Leithcote Gdns. SW16—4B 80
Leithcote Path. SW16—3B 80
Letitia Clo. E8—5C 12
Leman St. E1—5B 26
Le May Av. SE12—3D 87
Lemmon Rd. SE10—2A 58
Lemuel St. SW18—4E 63
Lena Gdns. W6—4E 33
Lendal Ter. SW4—1F 65
Lenham Rd. SE12—2B 72
Lennard Rd.—5F 83

SE20 1-89 & 2-98
Beck remainder
Lennon Rd. NW2—2E 5
Lennox Gdns. NW10—1B 4
Lennox Gdns. SW1—5B 36
Lennox Gdns. M. SW1—5B 36
Lens Rd. E7—4E 17
Lenthall Rd. E8—4C 12
Lenthorp Rd. SE10—5B 44
Lentmead Rd. Brom—3B 86
Lenville Way. SE16—1C 54
Leof Cres. SE6—5D 85
Leonard Rd. E7—1C 16
Leonard St. EC2—2F 25
Leontine Clo. SE15—3C 54
Leopold Av. SW19—5B 76
Leopold Rd. NW10—4A 4
Leopold Rd. SW19—4B 76
Leopold St. E3—4B 28
Leo St. SE15—3D 55
Leppoc Rd. SW4—3F 65
Leroy St. SE1—5A 40
Lescombe Clo. SE23—3A 84
Lescombe Rd. SE23—3A 84
Leslie Rd. E11—1E 15
Leslie Rd. E16—5D 31
Lessar Av. SW4—4E 65
Lessingham Av. SW17—4B 78
Lessing St. SE23—5A 70
Lester Av. E15—2A 30
Letchford Gdns. NW10—2C 18
Letchford M. NW10—2C 18
Letchworth St. SW17—4B 78
Lethbridge Clo. SE13—4E 57
Letterstone Rd. SW6—3B 48
Lettice St. SW6—4B 48
Lett Rd. E15—4F 15
Lettsom St. SE5—5A 54
Lettsom Wlk. E13—1C 30
Levana Clo. SW19—1A 76
Levehurst Way. SW4—5A 52
Levendale Rd. SE23—2A 84
Leven Rd. E14—4E 29
Leverett St. SW3—5A 36
Lever St. EC1—2D 25
Leverton Pl. NW5—2E 9
Leverton St. NW5—2E 9
Lewesdon Clo. SW19—1F 75
Lewin Rd. SW16—5F 79
Lewis Gro. SE13—1E 71
Lewisham High St. SE13
—4D 71
Lewisham Hill. SE13—5E 57
Lewisham Pk. SE13—3E 71
Lewisham Rd. SE13—4D 57
Lewisham St. SW1—3F 37
Lewisham Way.—4B 56
SE14 1-169 & 2-158a
SE4 remainder

Lewis St. NW1—4D 9
(in two parts)
Lexham Gdns. W8—5C 34
Lexham Gdns. M. W8—4D 35
Lexham M. W8—5C 34
Lexington St. W1—1E 37
Lexton Gdns. SW12—1F 79
Leybourne Rd. NW1—4D 9
(in two parts)
Leybourne St. NW1—4D 9
Leybridge Ct. SE12—3C 72
Leyden St. E1—4B 26
Leydon Clo. SE16—2F 41
Leyes Rd. E16—5E 31
Leyland Rd. SE12—3C 72
Leylang Rd. SE14—3F 55
Leysfield Rd. W12—4C 32
Leyton Ct. SE23—1E 83
Leyton Rd. E15—2E 15
Leytonstone Rd. E15—2A 16
Leywick St. E15—1A 30
Liardet St. SE14—2A 56
Liberia Rd. N5—3D 11
Liberty M. SW12—4D 65
Liberty St. SW9—4B 52
Libra Rd. E3—1B 28
Libra Rd. E13—1C 30
Library Pl. E1—1D 41
Library St. SE1—3D 39
Lichfield Rd. E3—2A 28
Lichfield Rd. E6—2F 31
Lichfield Rd. NW2—1A 6
Lidcote Gdns. SW9—5C 52
Liddell Gdns. NW10—1E 19
Liddell Rd. NW6—3C 6
Liddington Rd. E15—5B 16
Liddon Rd. E13—2D 31
Lidfield Rd. N16—1F 11
Lidiard Rd. SW18—2E 77
Lidlington Pl. NW1—1E 23
Liffords Pl. SW13—5B 46
Lifford St. SW15—2F 61
Lightermans Rd. E14—3C 42
Ligonier St. E2—3B 26
Lilac Pl. SE11—5B 38
Lilac St. W12—1C 32
Lilestone St. NW8—3A 22
Lilford Rd. SE5—5D 53
Lillian Rd. SW13—2D 47
Lillie Rd. SW6—2A 48
Lillieshall Rd. SW4—1D 65
Lillie Yd. SW6—2C 48
Lillington Gdns. Est. SW1
—5E 37
Liliput Ct. SE12—3D 73
Lillyville Rd. SW6—4B 48
Lily Clo. W14—5F 33
Lily Pl. EC1—4C 24
Limburg Rd. SW11—2A 64

Lime Clo. E1—?C 40
Lime Gro. W12—3E 33
Limeharbour. E14—4D 43
Limeharbour Ct. E14—4D 43
Limehouse Causeway. E14
—1B 42
Limehouse Fields Est. E14
—4A 28
Limerick Clo. SW12—5E 65
Limerston St. SW10—2E 49
Limes Av. SW13—5B 46
Limes Field Rd. SW14—1A 60
Limesford Rd. SE15—2F 69
Limes Gdns. SW18—4C 62
Limes Gro. SE13—2E 71
Lime St. EC3—1A 40
Lime St. Pas. EC3—5A 26
Limes Wlk. SE15—2E 69
Limetree Clo. SW2—1B 80
Lime Wlk. E15—5A 16
Limpsfield Av. SW19—2F 75
Linacre Rd. NW2—3D 5
Linberry Wlk. SE8—5B 42
Linchmere Rd. SE12—5C 72
Lincoln Av. SW19—3F 75
Lincoln M. NW6—5B 6
Lincoln M. SE21—2F 81
Lincoln Rd. E7—3F 17
Lincoln Rd. E13—3D 31
Lincoln's Inn Fields. WC2
—5B 24
Lincoln St. SW3—5B 36
Lincombe Rd. Brom—3B 86
Lindal Rd. SE4—3B 70
Linden Av. NW10—1F 19
Linden Ct. W12—2E 33
Linden Gdns. W2—1C 34
Linden Gdns. W4—1A 46
Linden Gro. SE15—1D 69
Linden M. W2—1C 34
Lindfield Gdns. NW3—2E 7
Lindfield St. E14—5C 28
Lindisfarne Way. E9—1A 14
Lindley St. SE15—3C 54
Lindley St. E1—4E 27
Lindore Rd. SW11—2B 64
Lindrop St. SW6—5E 49
Lindsay Sq. SW1—1F 51
Lindsell St. SE10—4E 57
Lindsey M. N1—4E 11
Lindsey St. EC1—4D 25
Lind St. SE8—5C 56
Lindway. SE27—5D 81
Linford St. SW8—4E 51
Lingards Rd. SE13—2E 71
Lingfield Rd. SW19—5F 75
Lingham St. SW9—5A 52
Ling Rd. E16—4C 30
Lings Coppice. SE21—2F 81

Lingwell Rd. SW17—3A 78
Linhope St. NW1—3B 22
Link St. E9—3E 13
Linnell Rd. SE5—5A 54
Linnet M. SW12—5C 64
Linom Rd. SW4—2A 66
Linscott Rd. E5—1E 13
Linsey St. SE16—5C 40
(in two parts)
Linstead St. NW6—4C 6
Linstead Way. SW18—5A 62
Lintaine Clo. W6—2A 48
Linton Gro. SE27—5E 81
Linton St. N1—5E 11
Linver Rd. SW6—5C 48
Linwood Clo. SE5—5B 54
Lionel Gdns. SE9—3F 73
Lionel M. W10—4A 20
Lionel Rd. SE9—3F 73
Lions Clo. SE9—3F 87
Liphook Cres. SE23—5E 69
Lipton Rd. E1—5F 27
Lisburne Rd. NW3—1B 8
Lisford St. SE15—4B 54
Lisgar Ter. W14—5B 34
Liskeard Gdns. SE3—4C 58
Lisle St. WC2—1F 37
Lissenden Gdns. NW5—1C 8
Lisson Gro.—3F 21
    NW1 1-135 & 2-116
    NW8 remainder
Lisson St. NW1—4A 22
Liss Way. SE15—3B 54
Listergate Ct. SW15—2E 61
Lister M. N7—1B 10
Lister St. E13—2C 30
Liston Rd. SW4—1E 65
Listowel Clo. SW9—3D 53
Litchfield Av. E15—3A 16
Litchfield Gdns. NW10—3C 4
Litchfield St. WC2—1F 37
Lithos Rd. NW3—3D 7
Lit. Argyll St. W1—5E 23
Lit. Boltons, The. SW10—1D 49
Lit. Bornes. SE21—4A 82
Lit. Britain. EC1—4D 25
Lit. Brownings. SE23—2D 83
Littlebury Rd. SW4—1F 65
Lit. Chester St. SW1—4D 37
Lit. College St. SW1—4A 38
Littlecombe. SE7—2D 59
Littlecombe Clo. SW15—4F 61
Littlecote Clo. SW19—5A 62
Lit. Dimocks. SW12—2D 79
Lit. Dorrit Ct. SE1—3E 39
Lit. Edward St. NW1—2D 23
Littlefield Clo. N19—1E 9
Lit. George St. SW1—3A 38
Lit. Green St. NW5—1D 9

Lit. Newport St. WC2—1F 37
Lit. New St. EC4—5C 24
Lit. Portland St. W1—5E 23
Lit. Russell St. WC1—4A 24
Lit. Saint James's St. SW1
—2E 37
Lit. Sanctuary. SW1—3F 37
Lit. Smith St. SW1—4F 37
Lit. Somerset St. E1—5B 26
Lit. Titchfield St. W1—4E 23
Littleton St. SW18—2E 77
Lit. Trinity La. EC4—1E 39
Lit. Turnstile. WC1—4B 24
Lit. Venice. W2—4E 21
Littlewood. SE13—4E 71
Livermere Rd. E8—5B 12
Liverpool Gro. SE17—1F 53
Liverpool Rd. E16—4A 30
Liverpool Rd.—3C 10
N1 1-393 & 2-296
N7 remainder
Liverpool St. EC2—4A 26
Livesey Pl. SE15—2C 54
Livingstone Pl. E14—1E 57
Livingstone Rd. E15—5E 15
Livingstone Rd. SW11—1F 63
Livonia St. W1—5E 23
Lizard St. EC1—2E 25
Lizban St. SE3—3D 59
Llewellyn St. SE16—3C 40
Lloyd Baker St. WC1—2C 24
Lloyd's Av. EC3—5A 26
Lloyd's Pl. SE3—5A 58
Lloyd Sq. WC1—2C 24
Lloyd's Row. EC1—2C 24
Lloyd St. WC1—2C 24
Loampit Hill. SE13—5C 56
Loampit Vale. SE13—1D 71
Loanda Clo. E8—5B 12
Loats Rd. SW2—4A 66
Lochaber Rd. SE13—2A 72
Lochaline St. W6—2E 47
Lochinvar St. SW12—5D 65
Lochnagar St. E14—4E 29
Lock Chase. SE3—1A 72
Lockesfield Pl. E14—1D 57
Locke's Wharf Development. E14
—1D 57
Lockhart Clo. N7—3B 10
Lockhart St. E3—3B 28
Lockhurst St. E5—1F 13
Lockington Rd. SW8—4D 51
Lockmead Rd. SE13—1E 71
Locksley Est. E14—5B 28
Locksley St. E14—4B 28
Lockwood Clo. SE26—4F 83
Lockwood Sq. SE16—4D 41
Lockyer St. SE1—3F 39
Loddiges Rd. E9—4E 13

Loder St. SE15—3E 55
Lodge Av. SW14—1A 60
Lodge Rd. NW8—2F 21
Lodore St. E14—5E 29
Loftie St. SE16—3C 40
Lofting Rd. N1—4C 10
Loftus Rd. W12—2D 33
Logan M. W8—5C 34
Logan Pl. W8—5C 34
Loggetts. SE21—2A 82
Lolesworth Clo. E1—4B 26
Lollard St. SE11—5B 38
(in two parts)
Loman St. SE1—3D 39
Lomas St. E1—4C 26
Lombard Business Centre, The.
SW11—5F 49
Lombard Ct. EC3—1F 39
Lombard La. EC4—5C 24
Lombard Rd. SW11—5F 49
Lombard St. EC3—5F 25
Lombard Wall. SE7—4D 45
(in two parts)
Lombardy Pl. W2—1D 35
Lomond Gro. SE5—3F 53
Lomond Ho. SE15—3B 54
Loncroft Rd. SE5—2A 54
Londesborough Rd. N16—1A 12
London Bri. SE1 & EC4—2F 39
London Bri. St. SE1—2F 39
London Fields E. Side. E8
—4D 13
London Fields W. Side. E8
—4C 12
London La. E8—4D 13
London M. W2—5F 21
London Rd. E13—1C 30
London Rd. SE1—4D 39
London Rd. SE23—1D 83
London St. EC3—1A 40
London St. W2—5F 21
London Ter. E2—1C 26
London Wall. EC2—4F 25
Long Acre. WC2—1A 38
Longbeach Rd. SW11—1B 64
Longbridge Way. SE13—3E 71
Longdown Rd. SE6—4C 84
Long Dri. W3—5A 18
Longfellow Rd. E3—2A 28
Longfield Cres. SE26—2E 83
Longfield Est. SE1—5B 40
Longfield St. SW18—5C 62
Longford St. NW1—3D 23
Longford Wlk. SW2—5C 66
Longhedge St. SW11—5C 50
Longhill Rd. SE6—2F 85
Longhope Clo. SE15—2A 54
Longhope Gdns. SE15—2A 54
Longhurst Rd. SE13—3F 71

Longland Ct. SE1—1C 54
Long La. EC1—4D 25
Long La. SE1—3F 39
Longley Rd. SW17—5A 78
Longley St. SE1—5C 40
Long Mark Rd. E16—4F 31
Longmead Ho. SE27—5E 81
Long Meadow. NW5—2F 9
Longmead Rd. SW17—5B 78
Longmoore St. SW1—5E 37
Longnor Est. E1—2F 27
Longnor Rd. E1—2F 27
Long Pond Rd. SE3—4A 58
Longridge Rd. SW5—5C 34
Long Rd. SW4—2E 65
Longshore. SE8—5B 42
Longstaff Cres. SW18—5C 62
Longstaff Rd. SW18—4C 62
Longstone Av. NW10—4B 4
Longstone Rd. SW17—5D 79
Long St. E2—2B 26
(in two parts)
Longton Av. SE26—4C 82
Longton Gro. SE26—4D 83
Longville Rd. SE11—5D 39
Long Wlk. SE1—4A 40
Long Wlk. SW13—5B 46
Long Wall. E15—2F 29
Longwood Dri. SW15—4C 60
Long Yd. WC1—3B 24
Lonsdale Av. E6—3F 31
Lonsdale Clo. SE9—3F 87
Lonsdale Pl. N1—4C 10
Lonsdale Rd. NW6—5B 6
Lonsdale Rd. W4—5B 32
Lonsdale Rd. W11—5B 20
Lonsdale Sq. N1—4C 10
Lonsdale Yd. W11—1C 35
Loraine Rd. N7—1B 10
Lorden Wlk. E2—2C 26
Lord Hills Bri. W2—4D 21
Lord Hill's Rd. W2—4D 21
Lord Holland La. SW9—5C 52
Lord Napier Pl. W6—1C 46
Lord North St. SW1—4A 38
Lord Roberts M. SW6—3D 49
Lord's Clo. SE21—2E 81
Lordship La. SE22—3B 68
Lordship La. Est. SE22—1C 82
Lordship Pl. SW3—2A 50
Lords View. NW8—2A 22
Lorenzo St. WC1—2B 24
Loris Rd. W6—4E 33
Lorn Ct. SW9—4C 52
Lorne Clo. NW8—2A 22
Lorne Gdns. W11—3A 34
Lorne Rd. E7—1D 17
Lorn Rd. SW9—5B 52

Lorrimore Rd. SE17—2D 53
Lorrimore Sq. SE17—2D 53
Losberne Way. SE16—1C 54
Lothbury. EC2—5F 25
Lothian Rd. SW9—4D 53
Lothrop St. W10—2A 20
Lots Rd. SW10—3E 49
Loubet St. SW17—5B 78
Loudoun Rd. NW8—5E 7
Loughborough Est. SW9—1D 67
Loughborough Pk. SW9—2D 67
Loughborough Rd. SW9—5C 52
Loughborough St. SE11—1B 52
Lough Rd. N7—2B 10
Louisa Gdns. E1—3F 27
Louisa St. E1—3F 27
Louise Rd. E15—3A 16
Louisville Rd. SW17—3C 78
Louvaine Rd. SW11—2F 63
Lovat La. EC3—1A 40
Lovegrove St. SE1—1C 54
Lovegrove Wlk. E14—2E 43
Lovelace Rd. SE21—2E 81
Love La. EC2—5E 25
Lovelinch Clo. SE15—2E 55
Lovell Pl. SE16—4A 42
Loveridge M. NW6—3B 6
Loveridge Rd. NW6—3B 6
Lovers Wlk. SE10—2F 57
Love Wlk. SE5—5F 53
Low Cross Wood La. SE21
—3B 82
Lowden Rd. SE24—2D 67
Lowe Av. E16—4C 30
Lowell St. E14—5A 28
Lwr. Addison Gdns. W14—3A 34
Lwr. Belgrave St. SW1—4D 37
Lwr. Clapton. E5—1D 13
Lwr. Common S. SW15—1D 61
Lwr. Grosvenor Pl. SW1—4D 37
Lwr. James St. W1—1E 37
Lwr. John St. W1—1E 37
Lwr. Mall. W6—1D 47
Lwr. Marsh. SE1—3C 38
Lwr. Merton Rise. NW3—4A 8
Lwr. Richmond Rd. SW15—1D 61
Lower Rd.—4E 41
 SE16 1-245 & 2-196
 SE8 remainder
Lwr. Sloane St. SW1—5C 36
Lwr. Sydenham Industrial Est.
 SE26—5B 84
Lwr. Thames St. EC3—1A 40
Lowfield Rd. NW6—4C 6
Lowman Rd. N7—1B 10
Lowndes Clo. SW1—4C 36
Lowndes Ct. SW1—4B 36
Lowndes Pl. SW1—4C 36
Lowndes Sq. SW1—3B 36

Lowndes St. SW1—4C 36
Lowood St. E1—1D 41
Lowther Gdns. SW7—4F 35
Lowther Hill. SE23—5A 70
Lowther Rd. N7—2C 10
Lowther Rd. SW13—4B 46
Lowth Rd. SE5—5E 53
Loxford Av. E6—1F 31
Loxham St. WC1—2A 24
Loxley Clo. SE26—5F 83
Loxley Rd. SW18—1F 77
Loxton St. SE23—1F 83
Lubbock St. SE14—3E 55
Lucan Pl. SW3—5A 36
Lucas Av. E13—5D 17
Lucas St. SE8—4C 56
Lucerne M. W8—2C 34
Lucerne Rd. N5—1D 11
Lucey Rd. SE16—4C 40
Lucey Way. SE16—4C 40
Lucien Rd. SW17—4C 78
Lucien Rd. SW19—2D 77
Lucorn Clo. SE12—4B 72
Ludgate B'way. EC4—5D 25
Ludgate Cir. EC4—5D 25
Ludgate Hill. EC4—5D 25
Ludgate Sq. EC4—5D 25
Ludlow St. EC1—3E 25
Ludovick Wlk. SW15—2A 60
Ludwick M. SE14—3A 56
Luffman Rd. SE12—3D 87
Lugard Rd. SE15—5D 55
Luke St. EC2—3A 26
Lukin St. E1—5E 27
Lulworth Rd. SE15—5D 55
Lumley Ct. WC2—1A 38
Lumley St. W1—5C 22
Lundy Wlk. N1—3E 11
Lunham Rd. SE19—5A 82
Lupin Clo. SW2—2D 81
Lupton Clo. SE12—3D 87
Lupton St. NW5—1E 9
Lupus St. SW1—1D 51
Luralda Gdns. E14—1F 57
Lurgan Av. W6—2F 47
Lurline Gdns. SW11—4C 50
Luscombe Way. SW8—3A 52
Lushington Rd. NW10—1D 19
Lushington Rd. SE6—5D 85
Lushington Ter. E8—2C 12
Luton Pl. SE10—3E 57
Luton Rd. E13—3C 30
Luton St. NW8—3F 21
Luttrell Av. SW15—3D 61
Lutwyche Rd. SE6—2B 84
Luxborough St. W1—4C 22
Luxemburg Gdns. W6—5F 33
Luxford St. SE16—5F 41
Luxmore Gdns. SE4—5B 56

Luxmore St. SE4—4B 56
Luxor St. SE5—1E 67
Lyall Av. SE21—4A 82
Lyall M. SW1—4C 36
Lyall M. W. SW1—4C 36
Lyall St. SW1—4C 36
Lyal Rd. E3—1A 28
Lycett Pl. W12—3C 32
Lydden Gro. SW18—5D 63
Lydden Rd. SW18—5D 63
Lydford Rd. NW2—3F 5
Lydford Rd. W9—3B 20
Lydhurst Av. SW2—2B 80
Lydney Clo. SE15—3A 54
Lydney Clo. SW19—2A 76
Lydon Rd. SW4—1E 65
Lyford Rd. SW18—5F 63
Lygon Pl. SW1—4D 37
Lyham Clo. SW2—4A 66
Lyham Rd. SW2—3A 66
Lyme Farm Rd. SE12—2C 72
Lyme Gro. E9—4E 13
Lymer Av. SE19—5B 82
Lyme St. NW1—4E 9
Lyme Ter. NW1—4E 9
Lyminge Gdns. SW18—1A 78
Lymington Rd. NW6—3D 7
Lympstone Gdns. SE15—3C 54
Lynbrook Clo. SE15—3A 54
Lynch Wlk. SE8—2B 56
Lyncott Cres. SW4—2D 65
Lyncroft Gdns. NW6—2C 6
Lyndale. NW2—1B 6
Lyndale Clo. SE3—2B 58
Lyndhurst Gdns. NW3—2F 7
Lyndhurst Gro. SE15—5A 54
Lyndhurst Rd. NW3—2F 7
Lyndhurst Sq. SE15—4B 54
Lyndhurst Ter. NW3—2F 7
Lyndhurst Way. SE15—4B 54
Lyneham Wlk. E5—2A 14
Lynette Av. SW4—4E 65
Lynne Way. NW10—3A 4
Lyn Rd. SW12—5D 65
Lynsted Gdns. SE9—2F 73
Lynton Rd. NW6—1B 20
Lynton Rd. SE1—5B 40
Lynwood Rd. SW17—4B 78
Lyons Pl. NW8—3F 21
Lyon St. N1—4B 10
Lyons Wlk. W14—5A 34
Lyric Rd. SW13—4B 46
Lysias Rd. SW12—4D 65
Lysia St. SW6—3F 47
Lysons Wlk. SW15—2C 60
Lytcott Gro. SE22—3B 68
Lytham St. SE17—1F 53
Lyttelton Clo. NW3—4A 8
Lytton Gro. SW15—3F 61

Lyveden Rd. SE3—3D 59

Mabledon Pl. WC1—2F 23
Mablethorpe Rd. SW6—3A 48
Mabley St. E9—2A 14
Macarthur Ter. SE7—2F 59
Macaulay Rd. E6—1F 31
Macaulay Rd. SW4—1D 65
Macaulay Sq. SW4—2D 65
McAuley Clo. SE1—4C 38
Macbeth St. W6—1D 47
McCall Clo. SW4—5A 52
Macclesfield Rd. EC1—2E 25
Macclesfield St. W1—1F 37
MacCoid Way. SE1—3E 39
McCrone M. NW3—3F 7
McCullum Rd. E3—1B 28
McDermott Clo. SW11—1A 64
McDermott Rd. SE15—1C 68
Macdonald Rd. E7—1C 16
McDowall Clo. E16—4B 30
McDowall Rd. SE5—4E 53
Macduff Rd. SW11—4C 50
Mace Clo. E1—2D 41
Mace St. E2—1F 27
McEwan Way. E15—5F 15
Macfarlane Rd. W12—2E 33
Macfarren Pl. NW1—3C 22
McGrath Rd. E15—3B 16
Macgregor Rd. E16—4E 31
McGregor Rd. W11—4B 20
Machell Rd. SE15—1C 68
Mackay Rd. SW4—1D 65
Mackennal St. NW8—1A 22
Mackenzie Rd. N7—3B 10
McKerrell Rd. SE15—4C 54
Mackeson Rd. NW3—1B 8
Mackie Rd. SW2—5C 66
Mackintosh La. E9—2F 13
Macklin St. WC2—5A 24
Mackrow Wlk. E14—1E 43
Mack's Rd. SE16—5C 40
Mackworth St. NW1—2E 23
Maclean Rd. SE23—4A 70
McLeod's M. SW7—5D 35
McLeod St. SE17—1E 53
Maclise Rd. W14—4A 34
McMillan St. SE8—2C 56
McNeil Rd. SE5—5A 54
Macquarie Way. E14—5D 43
Macready Pl. N7—1A 10
Macroom Rd. W9—2B 20
Maddams St. E3—3D 29
Maddock Way. SE17—2D 53
Maddox St. W1—1D 37
Madeira Rd. SW16—5A 80
Madras Pl. N7—3C 10

Madrid Rd. SW13—4C 46
Madron St. SE17—1A 54
Mafeking Rd. E16—3B 30
Magdalene Clo. SE15—5D 55
Magdalen Pas. E1—1B 40
Magdalen Rd. SW18—1E 77
Magdalen St. SE1—2A 40
Magee St. SE11—2C 52
Magnin Clo. E8—5C 12
Magnolia Ct. SW4—3A 66
Magpie All. EC4—5C 24
Magri Wlk. E1—4E 27
Maguire St. SE1—3B 40
Mahatma Gandhi Industrial Est.
                  SE24—2D 67
Mahogany Clo. SE16—2A 42
Maida Av. W2—4E 21
Maida Vale. W9—1D 21
Maiden La. NW1—4F 9
Maiden La. WC2—1A 38
Maiden Rd. E15—4A 16
Maidenstone Hill. SE10—4E 57
Maidstone Bldgs. SE1—2E 39
Mail Coach Yd. N1—2A 26
Maismore St. SE15—2C 54
Maitland Pk. Est. NW3—3B 8
Maitland Pk. Rd. NW3—3B 8
Maitland Pk. Vs. NW3—3B 8
Maitland Pl. E5—1D 13
Maitland Rd. E15—3B 16
Maitland Rd. SE26—5F 83
Maize Row. E14—1B 42
Major Rd. E15—2F 15
Major Rd. SE16—4C 40
Makins St. SW3—5A 36
Malabar St. E14—4C 42
Malam Gdns. E14—1D 43
Malbrook Rd. SW15—2D 61
Malcolm Ct. E7—3B 16
Malcolm Pl. E2—3E 27
Malcolm Rd. E1—3E 27
Malden Cres. NW1—3C 8
Malden Pl. NW5—2C 8
Malden Rd. NW5—2C 8
Maldon Clo. N1—5E 11
Maldon Clo. SE5—1A 68
Malet Pl. WC1—3F 23
Malet St. WC1—3F 23
Maley Av. SE27—2D 81
Malfort Rd. SE5—1A 68
Malham Rd. SE23—1F 83
Malham Rd. Industrial Centre.
                  SE23—1F 83
Mallams M. SW9—1D 67
Mallard Clo. E9—4B 14
Mallet Rd. SE13—4F 71
Mallinson Rd. SW11—3A 64
Mallord St. SW3—2F 49
Mallory Clo. SE4—2A 70

Mallory St. NW8—3A 22
Mallow St. EC1—3F 25
Mall Rd. W6—1D 47
Mall, The. E15—4F 15
Mall, The. SW1—2F 37
Malmesbury Rd. E3—2B 28
Malmesbury Rd. E16—4A 30
Malmesbury Ter. E16—4B 30
Malpas Rd. E8—2D 13
Malpas Rd. SE4—5B 56
Malta St. EC1—3D 25
Maltby St. SE1—3B 40
Maltings Clo. SW13—5B 46
Maltings Pl. SW6—4D 49
Malton M. W10—5A 20
Malton Rd. W10—5A 20
Maltravers St. WC2—1B 38
Malt St. SE1—2C 54
Malva Clo. SW18—3D 63
Malvern Clo. W10—4B 20
Malvern Gdns. NW6—1B 20
Malvern M. NW6—2C 20
Malvern Pl. NW6—2B 20
Malvern Rd. E8—4C 12
Malvern Rd. NW6—2C 20
Malvern Ter. N1—5C 10
Malwood Rd. SW12—4D 65
Malyons Rd. SE13—3D 71
Malyons Ter. SE13—3D 71
Managers St. E14—2E 43
Manaton Clo. SE15—1D 69
Manbey Gro. E15—3A 16
Manbey Pk. Rd. E15—3A 16
Manbey Rd. E15—3A 16
Manbey St. E15—3A 16
Manbre Rd. W6—2E 47
Manchester Dri. W10—3A 20
Manchester Gro. E14—1E 57
Manchester Rd. E14—1E 57
Manchester Sq. W1—5C 22
Manchester St. W1—4C 22
Manchuria Rd. SW11—4C 64
Manciple St. SE1—3F 39
Manconochies Rd. E14—1D 57
Mandalay Rd. SW4—3E 65
Mandarin St. E14—1C 42
Mandela Rd. E16—5C 30
Mandela St. NW1—5E 9
Mandela St. SW9—3C 52
Mandela Way. SE1—5A 40
Mandeville Clo. SE3—5C 58
Mandeville Pl. W1—5C 22
Mandeville St. E5—1A 14
Mandrake Rd. SW17—3B 78
Mandrell Rd. SW2—3A 66
Manette St. W1—5F 23
Manfred Rd. SW15—3B 62
Manger Rd. N7—3A 10
Manilla St. E14—3C 42
Manley St. NW1—5C 8

Manning Av. SW4—2A 66
Manningford Clo. EC1—2D 25
Manningtree Clo. SW19—1A 76
Manningtree St. E1—5C 26
Manor Av. SE4—5B 56
Manor Brook. SE3—2C 72
Manor Ct. SW6—4D 49
Manor Est. SE16—5D 41
Manor Fields. SW15—4F 61
Manor Gdns. W4—1A 46
Manor Gro. SE15—2E 55
Manor Ho. Dri. NW6—4F 5
Manor La.—3A 72
  SE13 1-59 & 2-86
  SE12 remainder
Manor La. Ter. SE13—3A 72
Manor M. SE4—5B 56
Manor Mt. SE23—1E 83
Manor Pk. SE13—2F 71
Manor Pk. Rd. E12—1F 17
Manor Pk. Rd. NW10—5B 4
Manor Pl. SE17—1D 53
Manor Rd.—3A 30
  E15 1-347 & 2-118
  E16 remainder
Manor Way. SE3—2B 72
Manresa Rd. SW3—1A 50
Mansard Beeches. SW17—5C 78
Mansell Rd. SW19—5A 76
Mansell St. E1—5B 26
Mansfield M. W1—4D 23
Mansfield Pl. NW3—1E 7
Mansfield Rd. NW3—2B 8
Mansfield St. W1—4D 23
Mansford St. E2—1C 26
Mansion Ho. Pl. EC4—5F 25
Manson M. SW7—3E 35
Manson Pl. SW7—5F 35
Manstone Rd. NW2—2A 6
Mantilla Rd. SW17—4C 78
Mantle Rd. SE4—1A 70
Mantua St. SW11—1F 63
Mantus Clo. E1—3E 27
Mantus Rd. E1—3E 27
Manville Gdns. SW17—3D 79
Manville Rd. SW17—2C 78
Manwood Rd. SE4—3B 70
Manygates. SW12—2D 79
Mapesbury Rd. NW2—4A 6
Mape St. E2—3D 27
Maple Av. W3—2A 32
Maple Clo. SW4—4F 65
Mapledene Rd. E8—4C 12
Maple Leaf Sq. SE16—3F 41
Maple M. NW6—1D 21
Maple M. SW16—5B 80
Maple Pl. W1—4E 23
Maples Pl. E1—4D 27
Maplestead Rd. SW2—5B 66

Maple St. W1—4E 23
Mapleton Cres. SW18—4D 63
Mapleton Rd. SW18—4D 63
Maple Wlk. W10—2F 19
Maplin Rd. E16—5C 30
Maplin St. E3—3B 28
Marban Rd. W9—2B 20
Marble Arch. W1—1B 36
Marble Quay. E1—2C 40
Marbrook Ct. SE12—2E 87
Marchbank Rd. W14—2B 48
Marchmont St. WC1—3A 24
Marchwood Clo. SE5—3A 54
Marcia Rd. SE1—5A 40
Marcilly Rd. SW18—3F 63
Marcon Pl. E8—2D 13
Marco Rd. W6—4E 33
Marcus Ct. E15—5A 16
Marcus Garvey Way. SE24
  —2C 66
Marcus St. E15—5A 16
Marcus St. SW18—4D 63
Marcus Ter. SW18—4D 63
Marden Ct. SE8—2A 56
Marden Sq. SE16—4D 41
Maresfield Gdns. NW3—2E 7
Mare St. E8—5D 13
Margaret St. W1—5E 23
Margaretta Ter. SW3—2A 50
Margate Rd. SW2—3A 66
Margery Pk. Rd. E7—3C 16
Margery St. WC1—2C 24
Margin Dri. SW19—5F 75
Margravine Gdns. W6—1F 47
Margravine Rd. W6—1F 47
Marham Gdns. SW18—1A 78
Marian Pl. E2—1D 27
Marian St. E2—1D 27
Marian Way. NW10—4B 4
Maria Ter. E1—4F 27
Marie Lloyd Wlk. E8—3C 12
Marigold St. SE16—3D 41
Marinefield Rd. SW6—5D 49
Mariners M. E14—5F 43
Marine St. SE16—4C 40
Marion Sq. E2—1D 27
Marischal Rd. SE13—1F 71
Maritime St. E3—3B 28
Marius Pas. SW17—2C 78
Marius Rd. SW17—2C 78
Marjorie Gro. SW11—2B 64
Market Entrance. SW8—3E 51
Market M. W1—2D 37
Market Pl. SE16—5C 40
Market Pl. W1—5E 23
Market Rd. N7—3A 10
Market Sq. E14—5D 29
Market Way. E14—5D 29
Markham Pl.—1B 50

Markham Sq. SW3—1B 50
Markham St. SW3—1A 50
Mark La. EC3—1A 40
Mark St. E15—4A 16
Mark St. EC2—3A 26
Markwell Clo. SE26—4D 83
Marlborough Av. E8—5C 12
  (in three parts)
Marlborough Clo. SE17—5E 39
Marlborough Cres. W4—4A 32
Marlborough Gro. SE1—1C 54
Marlborough Hill. NW8—5E 7
Marlborough La. SE7—3E 59
Marlborough Pl. NW8—1E 21
Marlborough Rd. E7—4E 17
Marlborough Rd. E15—1A 16
Marlborough Rd. SW1—2E 37
Marlborough Rd. SW3—5A 36
Marler Rd. SE23—1A 84
Marley Wlk. NW2—2E 5
Marloes Rd. W8—4D 35
Marlowes, The. NW8—5E 7
Marlow Way. SE16—3F 41
Marl Rd. SW18—2D 63
Marlton St. SE10—1B 58
Marmion M. SW11—1C 64
Marmion Rd. SW11—2C 64
Marmont Rd. SE15—4C 54
Marmora Rd. SE22—4E 69
Marne St. W10—2A 20
Marney Rd. SW11—2C 64
Marnham Av. NW2—1A 6
Marnock Rd. SE4—3B 70
Maroon St. E14—4A 28
Maroons Way. SE6—5C 84
Marquess Rd. N1—3F 11
Marquis Rd. NW1—3F 9
Marrick Clo. SW15—2C 60
Marriett Ho. SE6—4E 85
Marriott Rd. E15—5A 16
Marryat Pl. SW19—4A 76
Marryat Rd. SW19—5F 75
Marsala Rd. SE13—2D 71
Marsden St. SE15—1B 68
Marsden St. NW5—3C 8
Marshall Clo. SW18—4E 63
Marshall's Pl. SE16—4B 40
Marshall St. W1—5E 23
Marshalsea Rd. SE1—3E 39
Marsham Ct. SW1—5F 37
Marsham St. SW1—4F 37
Marshbrook Clo. SE3—1F 73
Marsh Ct. E8—4C 12
Marshfield St. E14—4E 43
Marshgate La. E15—5D 15
Marsh Hill. E9—2A 14
Marsh St. E14—5D 43
Marsh Wall. E14—2C 42
Marsland Clo. SE17—1D 53

Marston Clo. NW6—4E 7
Marston Ho. SW9—5C 52
Martello St. E8—4D 13
Martello Ter. E8—4D 13
Martell Rd. SE21—3F 81
Martel Pl. E8—3B 12
Martha Ct. E2—1D 27
Martha Rd. E15—3A 16
Martha St. E1—5E 27
Martinau Est. E1—5E 27
Martinau St. E1—5E 27
Martindale Rd. SW12—5D 65
Martineau Rd. N5—1D 11
Martin La. EC4—1F 39
Martlett Ct. WC2—5A 24
Marton Clo. SE6—3C 84
Mart St. WC2—1A 38
Marvels Clo. SE12—2D 87
Marvels La. SE12—2D 87
Marville Rd. SW6—3B 48
Marvin St. E8—3D 13
Marwood Way. SE16—1D 55
Mary Adelaide Clo. SW15
—4A 74
Mary Ann Gdns. SE8—2C 56
Mary Datchelor Clo. SE5—4F 53
Maryland Pk. E15—2A 16
(in two parts)
Maryland Rd. E15—2F 15
Maryland Rd. W9—3C 20
Maryland Sq. E15—2A 16
Maryland St. E15—2F 15
Mary Lawrenson Pl. SE3—3C 58
Marylebone Fly-over. W2 & NW1
—4A 22
Marylebone High St. W1—4C 22
Marylebone La. W1—5C 22
Marylebone M. W1—4D 23
Marylebone Pas. W1—5E 23
Marylebone Rd. NW1—4A 22
Marylebone St. W1—4C 22
Marylee Way. SE11—5B 38
Maryon M. NW3—1A 8
Mary Pl. W11—1A 34
Mary Seacole Clo. E8—5B 12
Mary St. E16—4B 30
Mary St. N1—5E 11
Mary Ter. NW1—5E 9
Masbro Rd. W14—4F 33
Mascalls Rd. SE7—2E 59
Mascotte Rd. SW15—2F 61
Mashie Rd. W3—5A 18
Maskell Clo. SW2—1C 80
Maskell Rd. SW17—3E 77
Maskelyne Clo. SW11—4A 50
Mason Clo. E16—1C 44
Mason's Arms M. W1—5D 23
Mason's Av. EC2—5F 25
Mason's Pl. EC1—2E 25

Mason St. SE17—5F 39
Mason's Yd. SW1—2E 37
Mason's Yd. SW19—5F 75
Massie Rd. E8—3C 12
Massinger St. SE17—5A 40
Massingham St. E1—3F 27
Master's St. E1—4F 27
Mast Ho. Ter. E14—5C 42
Masthouse Ter. Development.
E14—5C 42
Mastmaker Ct. E14—3C 42
Mastmaker Rd. E14—3C 42
Matham Gro. SE22—2B 68
Matheson Rd. W14—5B 34
Mathews Pk. Av. E15—3B 16
Mathews Yd. WC2—5A 24
Matilda St. N1—5B 10
Matlock Clo. SE24—2E 67
Matlock St. E14—5A 28
Matrimony Pl. SW4—5E 51
Matthew Clo. W10—3F 19
Matthew Parker St. SW1
—3F 37
Matthews St. SW11—5B 50
Matthias Rd. N16—2A 12
Maude Rd. SE5—4A 54
Maud Gdns. E13—1B 30
Maudlin's Grn. E1—2C 40
Maud Rd. E13—1B 30
Maud St. E16—4B 30
Mauleverer Rd. SW2—3A 66
Maughty Wlk. NW10—3A 4
Maunsel St. SW1—5F 37
Maurice St. W12—5D 19
Mauritius Rd. SE10—5A 44
Maverton Rd. E3—5C 14
Mawbey Pl. SE1—1B 54
Mawbey Rd. SE1—1B 54
Mawbey St. SW8—3A 52
Mawson La. W4—2B 46
Maxilla Wlk. W10—5F 19
Maxted Rd. SE15—1B 68
Maxwell Rd. SW6—3D 49
Mayall Rd. SE24—3D 67
Maybury Gdns. NW10—3D 5
Maybury Rd. E13—3E 31
Maybury St. SW17—5A 78
Mayerne Rd. SE9—3F 73
Mayeswood Rd. SE12—4E 87
Mayfair Pl. W1—2D 37
Mayfield Av. W4—5A 32
Mayfield Clo. E8—4B 12
Mayfield Clo. SW4—3F 65
Mayfield Rd. E8—4B 12
Mayfield Rd. E13—3B 30
Mayfield Rd. W12—3A 32
Mayflower Clo. SE16—5F 41
Mayflower Ct. SE16—3E 41
Mayflower Rd. SW9—1A 66

Mayflower St. SE16—3E 41
Mayford Clo. SW12—5B 64
Mayford Rd. SW12—5B 64
Maygood St. N1—1C 24
Maygrove Rd. NW6—3B 6
Mayhill Rd. SE7—2D 59
Maynard Clo. SW6—3D 49
Maynard Clo. SW6—3D 49
Maynards Quay. E1—1E 41
Mayola Rd. E5—1E 13
Mayo Rd. NW10—3A 4
Mayow Rd.—4F 83
SE23 1-69 & 2-24
SE26 remainder
May Rd. E13—1C 30
Mays Ct. WC2—1A 38
Maysoule Rd. SW11—2F 63
May St. W14—1B 48
May Tree Wlk. SW2—2C 80
Mayville Est. N16—2A 12
May Wlk. E13—1D 31
Maze Hill—2A 58
SE10 1-119 & 2-40
SE3 remainder
Mazenod Av. NW6—4C 6
Meadcroft Rd. SE11—2D 53
Meadcroft St. SE17—2D 53
Meader Ct. SE14—3F 55
Meadowbank. NW3—4B 8
Meadow Bank. SE3—1B 72
Meadowbank Clo. SW6—3E 47
Meadow Clo. SE6—5C 84
Meadowcourt Rd. SE3—2B 72
Meadow M. SW8—2B 52
Meadow Pl. SW8—3A 52
Meadow Rd. SW8—3B 52
Meadow Row. SE1—4E 39
Meadowside. SE9—2E 73
Meadowsweet Clo. E16—4F 31
Meadowview Rd. SE6—5C 84
Mead Path. SW17—4E 77
Mead Pl. E9—3E 13
Mead Row. E1—4C 38
Meads Ct. E15—3B 16
Meadway, The. SE3—5F 57
Meakin Est. SE1—4A 40
Meard St. W1—5F 23
Meath Rd. E15—1B 30
Meath St. SW11—4D 51
Mechanic's Path. SE18—3C 56
Mecklenburgh Pl. WC1—3B 24
Mecklenburgh Sq. WC1—3B 24
Mecklenburgh St. WC1—3B 24
Medburn St. NW1—1F 23
Medcalfe Pl. N1—1C 24
Medebourne Clo. SE3—1C 72
Medfield St. SW15—5D 61
Medhurst Clo. E3—1A 28
Median Rd. E5—2E 13
Medlar St. SE5—4E 53

Medley Rd. NW6—3C 6
Medora Rd. SW2—5B 66
Medusa Rd. SE6—4D 71
Medway M. E3—1A 28
Medway Rd. E3—1A 28
Medway St. SW1—4F 37
Medwin St. SW4—2B 66
Meerbrook Rd. SE3—1E 73
Meeson Rd. E15—4B 16
Meeson St. E5—1A 14
Meeting Field Path.E9—3E 13
Meetinghouse All. E1—2D 41
Meeting Ho. La. SE15—4D 55
Mehetabel Rd. E9—2E 13
Melba Way. SE13—4D 57
Melbourne Gro. SE22—2A 68
Melbourne M. SE6—5E 71
Melbourne M. SW9—4C 52
Melbourne Pl. WC2—5B 24
Melbourne Sq. SW9—4C 52
Melbury Ct. W8—4C 34
Melbury Dri. SE5—3A 54
Melbury Rd. W14—4B 34
Melbury Ter. NW1—3A 22
Melcombe Pl. NW1—4B 22
Melcombe St. NW1—3B 22
Meldon Clo. SW6—4D 49
Melfield Gdns. SE6—5E 85
Melford Rd. SE22—5C 68
Melgund Rd. N5—2C 10
Melina Ct. SW15—1C 60
Melina Pl. NW8—2F 21
Melina Rd. W12—3D 33
Melior Pl. SE1—3A 40
Melior St. SE1—3A 40
Meliot Rd. SE6—2F 85
Mellish St. E14—4C 42
Mellison Rd. SW17—5A 78
Mellitus St. W12—5B 18
Mell St. SE10—1A 58
Melody Rd. SW18—3E 63
Melon Pl. W8—3C 34
Melon Rd. SE15—4C 54
Melrose Av. NW2—2D 5
Melrose Av. SW19—2B 76
Melrose Clo. SE12—1C 86
Melrose Gdns. W6—4E 33
Melrose Rd. SW13—5B 46
Melrose Rd. SW18—4B 62
Melrose Ter. W6—4E 33
Meltham Way. SE16—1D 55
Melton Ct. SW7—5F 35
Melton St. NW1—2F 23
Melville Rd. SW13—4C 46
Melville St. N1—4E 11
Melyn Clo. N7—1E 9
Memel St. EC1—3E 25
Memorial Av. E15—2A 30
Mendip Clo. SE26—4E 83

Mendip Clo. SW19—2A 76
Mendip Rd. SW11—1E 63
Mendora Rd. SW6—3A 48
Menelik Rd. NW2—1A 6
Menotti St. E2—3C 26
Mentmore Ter. E8—4D 13
Mepham St. SE1—2C 38
Merbury Clo. SE13—3E 71
Mercator Rd. SE13—2F 71
Merceron St. E1—3D 27
Mercers Clo. SE10—5B 44
Mercers Pl. W6—5E 33
Mercer St. WC2—5A 24
Merchant St. E3—2B 28
Merchiston Rd. SE6—2F 85
Mercia Gro. SE13—2E 71
Mercier Rd. SW15—3A 62
Mercury Way. SE14—2F 55
Mercy Ter. SE13—3D 71
Mere Clo. SW15—5F 61
Meredith Av. NW2—2E 5
Meredith St. E13—2C 30
Meredith St. EC1—2D 25
Meredyth Rd. SW13—5C 46
Meretone Clo. SE4—2A 70
Meridian Ga. E14—3E 43
Meridian Rd. SE7—3F 59
Merifield Rd. SE9—2E 73
Merivale Rd. SW15—2A 62
Merlin Gdns. Brom—3C 86
Merlin St. WC1—2C 24
Mermaid Ct. SE1—3F 39
Merredene St. SW2—4B 66
Merrick Sq. SE1—4F 39
Merriman Rd. SE3—4E 59
Merrington Rd. SW6—2C 48
Merritt Rd. SE4—3B 70
Merrow St. SE17—1F 53
Merrow Wlk. SE17—1F 53
Merryfield. SE3—5B 58
Merthyr Ter. SW13—2D 47
Merton Av. W4—5B 32
Merton Rise. NW3—4A 8
Merton Rd. SW18—4C 62
Merttins Rd. SE15—3F 69
Mervan Rd. SW2—2C 66
Messent Rd. SE3—5E 73
Messina Av. NW6—4C 6
Meteor St. SW11—2C 64
Methley St. SE11—1C 52
Metwold Rd. W10—4F 19
Mews St. E1—2C 40
Mews, The. N1—5E 11
Mexfield Rd. SW15—3B 62
Meymott St. SE1—2D 39
Meynell Cres. E9—4F 13
Meynell Gdns. E9—4F 13
Meynell Rd. E9—4F 13
Meyrick Rd. NW10—3C 4

Meyrick Rd. SW11—1F 63
Miall Wlk. SE26—4A 84
Micawber St. N1—2E 25
Michael Rd. SW6—4D 49
Michael's Clo. SE13—2A 72
Micheldever Rd. SE12—4B 72
Michigan Ho. E14—4C 42
Micklethwaite Rd. SW6—2C 48
Middle Field. NW8—5F 7
Middle Pk. Av. SE9—4F 73
Middle Rd. E13—1C 30
Middle Row. W10—3A 20
Middlesex St. W4—1B 46
Middlesex St. E1—4A 26
Middle St. EC1—4E 25
Middle Temple La. EC4—5C 24
Middleton Dri. SE16—3F 41
Middleton Gro. N7—2A 10
Middleton M. N7—2A 10
Middleton Rd. E8—4B 12
Middleton St. E2—2D 27
Middleton Way. SE13—2F 71
Middle Yd. SE1—2A 40
Midford Pl. W1—3E 23
Midhope St. WC1—2A 24
Midland Pl. E14—1E 57
Midland Rd. NW1—1F 23
Midland Ter. NW10—3A 18
Midlothian Rd. E3—3B 28
Midmoor Rd. SW12—1E 79
Midship Clo. SE16—2F 41
Midstrath Rd. NW10—1A 4
Milborne Gro. SW10—1E 49
Milborne St. E9—3E 13
Milborough Cres. SE12—4A 72
Milcote St. SE1—3D 39
Mildenhall Rd. E5—1E 13
Mildmay Av. N1—3F 11
Mildmay Gro. N1—2F 11
(in two parts)
Mildmay Pk. N1—2F 11
Mildmay Rd. N1—2F 11
Mildmay St. N1—3F 11
Mile End Pl. E1—3F 27
Mile End Rd.—4E 27
  E1 1-357 & 2-510
  E3 remainder
Miles St. SW8—2A 52
(in two parts)
Milfoil St. W12—1C 32
Milford La. WC2—1C 38
Milford M. SW16—3B 80
Milford Towers. SE6—5D 71
Milford Way. SE15—4B 54
Milk St. EC2—5A 26
Milk St. Brom—5D 87
Milkwell Yd. SE5—4F 51
Milkwood Rd. SE24—3D 67
Milk Yd. E1—1E 41

Millais Rd. E11—1E 15
Millard Clo. N16—2A 12
Millbank. SW1—5A 38
Millbank Way. SE12—3C 72
Millbrook Rd. SW9—1D 67
Millender Wlk. SE16—5E 41
Miller Rd. SW19—5F 77
Millers Av. E8—2B 12
Miller's Ct. W6—1B 46
Millers Ter. E8—2B 12
Miller St. NW1—1E 23
Millers Way. W6—3F 33
Millfields Rd. E5—1E 13
Mill Gdns. SE26—3D 83
Millgrove St. SW11—5C 50
Millharbour. E14—4D 43
Mill Hill Rd. SW13—5C 46
Millhouse Pl. SE27—4D 81
Milligan St. E14—1B 42
Mill La. NW6—2B 6
Millman M. WC1—3B 24
Millman St. WC1—3B 24
Millmark Gro. SE14—5A 56
Mill Pl. E14—5A 28
Mill Quay Development. E14
—5D 43
Mill Rd. E16—2D 45
Mill Rd. SE13—1E 71
Mill Row. N1—5A 12
Mills Gro. E14—5E 29
Mill Shot Clo. SW6—4E 47
Millstream Rd. SE1—3B 40
Mill St. SE1—3B 40
Mill St. W1—1E 37
Millwall Dock Rd. E14—4C 42
Millwall Wharf Development.
E14—4F 43
Millwood St. W10—4A 20
Milman Rd. NW6—1A 20
Milman's St. SW10—2F 49
Milner Pl. N1—5D 11
Milner Rd. E15—2A 30
Milner Sq. N1—4D 11
Milner St. SW3—5B 36
Milo Rd. SE22—4B 68
Milroy Wlk. SE1—2D 39
Milson Rd. W14—4F 33
Milton Av. E6—4F 17
Milton Ct. EC2—4F 25
Milton Ct. Rd. SE14—2A 56
Milton Garden Est. N16—1A 12
Milton Gro. N16—1A 12
Milton Pl. N7—2C 10
Milton Rd. SE24—3D 67
Milton Rd. SW19—5E 77
Milton St. EC2—4F 25
Milverton Rd. NW6—4E 5
Milverton St. SE11—1C 52
Milward St. E1—4D 27

Mimosa St. SW6—4B 48
Minard Rd. SE6—5A 72
Mina Rd. SE17—1A 54
Mincing La. EC3—1A 40
Minehead Rd. SW16—5B 80
Minera M. SW1—5C 36
Minerva Clo. SW9—3C 52
Minerva St. E2—1D 27
Minet Av. NW10—1A 18
Minet Gdns. NW10—1A 18
Minet Rd. SW9—5D 53
Minford Gdns. W14—3F 33
Ming St. E14—1C 42
Minnow Wlk. SE17—5A 40
Minories. EC3—5B 26
Minshull St. SW8—4F 51
Minson Rd. E9—5F 13
Minstead Gdns. SW15—5B 60
Minster Rd. NW2—2A 6
Mintern St. N1—1F 25
Minton M. NW6—3D 7
Mint St. SE1—3E 39
Mirabel Rd. SW6—3B 48
Mirfield St. SE7—5F 45
Mirror Path. SE9—3E 87
Mission Pl. SE15—4C 54
Mitcham La. SW16—5E 79
Mitcham Rd. SW17—5B 78
Mitchell St. EC1—3E 25
Mitchison Rd. N1—3F 11
Mitre Ct. EC4—5C 24
Mitre Rd. E15—1A 30
Mitre Rd. SE1—3C 38
Mitre Sq. EC3—5A 26
Mitre St. EC3—5A 26
Mitre, The. E14—1B 42
Mitre Way. NW10—4D 19
Moat Dri. E13—1E 31
Moat Pl. SW9—1B 66
Moberley Rd. SW4—5F 65
Modbury Gdns. NW5—3C 8
Modder Pl. SW15—2F 61
Moelwyn Hughes Ct. N7—2F 9
Moffat Rd. SW17—4B 78
Moiety Rd. E14—3C 42
Moland Mead. SE16—1F 55
Molasses Row. SW11—1E 63
Molesford Rd. SW6—4C 48
Molesworth St. SE13—1E 71
Molly Huggins Clo. SW12
—5E 65
Molyneux St. W1—4A 22
Monarch Dri. E16—4F 31
Monarch M. SW16—5C 80
Mona Rd. SE15—5E 55
Mona St. E16—4B 30
Monck St. SW1—4F 37
Monclar Rd. SE5—2F 67
Moncorvo Clo. SW7—3A 36

Moncrieff St. SE15—5C 54
(in two parts)
Monega Rd.—3E 17
E7 1-203 & 2-204
E12 remainder
Monier Rd. E3—4C 14
Monk Dri. E16—1C 44
Monkton St. SE11—5C 38
Monkwell Sq. EC2—4E 25
Monmouth M. W2—5C 20
Monmouth St. WC2—5A 24
Monnow Rd. SE1—5C 40
Monson Rd. NW10—1C 18
Monson Rd. SE14—3F 55
Montacute Rd. SE6—5B 70
Montagu Av. SE4—2B 70
Montague Clo. SE1—2F 39
Montague Pl. WC1—4F 23
Montague Rd. E8—2C 12
Montague Sq. SE15—3E 55
Montague St. WC1—4A 24
Montagu Mans. W1—4B 22
Montagu M. N. W1—4B 22
Montagu M. S. W1—5B 22
Montagu M. W. W1—5B 22
Montagu Pl. W1—4B 22
Montagu Row. W1—4B 22
Montagu Sq. W1—4B 22
Montagu St. W1—5B 22
Montana Rd. SW17—3C 78
Montcalm Ho. E14—5C 42
Montcalm Rd. SE7—3F 59
Montclare St. E2—3B 26
Monteagle Ct. N1—1A 26
Monteagle Way. SE15—1D 69
Montefiore St. SW8—5D 51
Monteith Rd. E3—5B 14
Montem Rd. SE23—5B 70
Montford Pl. SE11—1C 52
Montford Pl. SW19—1F 75
Montholme Rd. SW11—4B 64
Monthope Rd. E1—4C 26
Montolieu Gdns. SW15—3D 61
Montpelier Gdns. E6—2F 31
Montpelier Gro. NW5—2C 9
Montpelier M. SW7—4A 36
Montpelier Pl. SW7—4A 36
Montpelier Rd. SE15—4D 55
Montpelier Row. SE3—5B 58
Montpelier Sq. SW7—3A 36
Montpelier St. SW7—4A 36
Montpelier Ter. SW7—3A 36
Montpelier Vale. SE3—5B 58
Montpelier Wlk. SW7—4A 36
Montreal Pl. WC2—1B 38
Montrell Rd. SW2—1A 80
Montrose Av. NW6—1A 20
Montrose Ct. SW7—3F 35
Montrose Ho. E14—4C 42

154

Montrose Pl. SW1—3C 36
Montrose Way. SE23—1F 83
Montserrat Clo. SE19—5F 81
Montserrat Rd. SW15—2A 62
Monument Gdns. SE13—3E 71
Monument St. EC3—1F 39
Monza St. E1—1E 41
Moodkee St. SE16—4E 41
Moody St. E1—2F 27
Moon St. N1—5D 11
Moorcroft Rd. SW16—3A 80
Moorehead Way. SE3—1D 73
Moore Pk. Rd. SW6—3D 49
Moore St. SW3—5B 36
Moore Wlk. E7—1C 16
Moore Way. SE22—1C 82
Moorey Clo. E15—5B 16
Moorfields. EC2—4F 25
Moorgate. EC2—5F 25
Moorhouse Rd. W2—5C 20
Moorland Rd. SW9—2D 67
Moor La. EC2—4F 25
Moor Pl. EC2—4F 25
Moorside Rd. Brom—3A 86
Moor St. W1—5F 23
Morant St. E14—1C 42
Mora Rd. NW2—1E 5
Mora St. EC1—2E 25
Morat St. SW9—4B 52
Moravian Pl. SW10—2F 49
Moravian St. E2—2E 27
Mordaunt St. SW9—1B 66
Morden Hill. SE13—5E 57
Morden La. SE13—4E 57
Morden Rd. SE3—5C 58
Morden Rd. M. SE3—5C 58
Morden St. SE13—4D 57
Morden Wharf Rd. SE10—4A 44
Mordred Rd. SE6—2A 86
Morecambe Clo. E1—4F 27
Morecambe St. SE17—1E 53
More Clo. E16—5B 30
More Clo. W14—5F 33
Moreland St. EC1—2D 25
Morella Rd. SW12—5B 64
Moremead Rd. SE6—4B 84
Morena St. SE6—5D 71
Moresby Wlk. SW8—5E 51
Moreton Pl. SW1—1E 51
Moreton St. SW1—1E 51
Moreton Ter. SW1—1E 51
Moreton Ter. M. N. SW1—1E 51
Moreton Ter. M. S. SW1—1E 51
Morgan Rd. N7—2C 10
Morgan Rd. W10—4B 20
Morgan's La. SE1—2A 40
Morgan St. E3—2A 28
Morgan St. E16—4B 30

Morie St. SW18—3D 63
Moring Rd. SW17—4C 78
Morkyns Wlk. SE21—3A 82
Morland M. N1—4C 10
Morley Rd. E15—1B 30
Morley Rd. SE13—2E 71
Morley St. SE1—4C 38
Morna Rd. SE5—5E 53
Morning La. E9—3E 13
Mornington Av. W14—5B 34
Mornington Cres. NW1—1E 23
Mornington Gro. E3—2C 28
Mornington M. SE5—4E 53
Mornington Pl. NW1—1E 23
Mornington Rd. SE8—3B 56
Mornington St. NW1—1D 23
Mornington Ter. NW1—1D 23
Morocco St. SE1—3A 40
Morpeth Gro. E9—5F 13
Morpeth Rd. E9—5F 13
Morpeth St. E2—2F 27
Morpeth Ter. SW1—4E 37
Morris Gdns. SW18—5C 62
Morrish Rd. SW2—5A 66
Morrison St. SW11—1C 64
Morris Rd. E14—4D 29
Morris Rd. E15—1A 16
Morris St. E1—5D 27
Morse Clo. E13—2C 30
Morshead Rd. W9—2C 20
Morten Clo. SW4—4F 65
Mortham St. E15—5A 16
Mortimer Clo. NW2—5B 6
Mortimer Cres. NW6—5D 7
Mortimer Est. NW6—5D 7
Mortimer Mkt. WC1—3E 23
Mortimer Pl. NW6—5D 7
Mortimer Rd. N1—4A 12
Mortimer Rd. NW10—2E 19
Mortimer Sq. W11—1F 33
Mortimer St. W1—4E 23
Mortimer Ter. NW5—1D 9
Mortlake High St. SW14—5A 46
Mortlake Rd. E16—5D 31
Mortlock Clo. SE15—4D 55
Mortlock Ct. E12—1F 17
Morton M. SW5—5D 35
Morton Pl. SE1—4C 38
Morton Rd. E15—4B 16
Morton Rd. N1—4E 11
Morval Rd. SW2—3C 66
Morven Rd. SW17—3B 78
Morville St. E3—1B 28
Morwell St. WC1—4F 23
Moscow Pl. W2—1D 35
Moscow Rd. W2—1C 34
Mossbury Rd. SW11—1A 64
Moss Clo. E1—4C 26
Mossford St. E3—3B 28
Mossington Gdns. SE16—5E 41

Mossop St. SW3—5A 36
Mostyn Gdns. NW10—2F 19
Mostyn Gro. E3—1C 28
Mostyn Rd. SW9—4C 52
Motcomb St. SW1—4C 36
Motley St. SW8—5E 51
Mottingham Gdns. SE9—1F 87
Mottingham La.—1E 87
SE12 2-48 SE9 remainder
Moulins Rd. E9—4F 13
Mountacre Clo. SE26—4C 82
Mt. Adon Pk. SE22—5C 68
Montague Pl. E14—1E 43
Mt. Angelus Rd. SW15—5B 60
Mt. Ash Rd. SE26—3D 83
Mountbatten Clo. SE19—5A 82
Mountbatten M. SW18—5E 63
Mount Ct. SW15—1A 62
Mountearl Gdns. SW16—3B 80
Mt. Ephraim La. SW16—3F 79
Mt. Ephraim Rd. SW16—3F 79
Mountford St. E1—5C 26
Mountfort Cres. N1—4C 10
Mountfort Ter. N1—4C 10
Mount Gdns. SE26—3D 83
Mt. Mills. EC1—2D 25
Mt. Nod Rd. SW16—3B 80
Mt. Pleasant. SE27—4E 81
Mt. Pleasant. WC1—3C 24
Mt. Pleasant Rd. NW10—4E 5
Mt. Pleasant Rd. SE13—4D 71
Mount Rd. SW19—2C 76
Mount Row. W1—1D 37
Mountsfield Ct. SE13—4F 71
Mounts Pond Rd. SE3—5F 57
(in two parts)
Mount St. W1—1C 36
Mount Ter. E1—4D 27
Mount, The. NW3—1E 7
Mt. Vernon. NW3—1E 7
Mount Vs. SE27—3D 81
Mowbray Rd. NW6—4A 6
Mowlem St. E2—1D 27
Mowll St. SW9—3C 52
Moxon Clo. E13—1B 30
Moxon St. W1—4C 22
Moye Clo. E2—1C 26
Moylan Rd. W6—2A 48
Moyser Rd. SW16—5D 79
Mozart St. W10—2B 20
Mudlarks Way. SE10 & SE7
—4B 44
Muirfield. W3—5A 18
Muirkirk Rd. SE6—1E 85
Muir Rd. E5—1C 12
Mulberry Business Centre. SE16
—3F 41
Mulberry Business Pk. SE16
—3F 41

Mulberry Clo. NW3—1F 7
Mulberry Clo. SW16—4E 79
Mulberry Pl. W6—1C 46
Mulberry St. E1—5C 26
Mulberry Wlk. SW3—2F 49
Mulgrave Rd. NW10—1B 4
Mulgrave Rd. SW6—2B 48
Muller Rd. SW4—4F 65
Mullet Gdns. E2—2C 26
Mulready St. NW8—3A 22
Multi Way. W3—3A 32
Multon Rd. SW18—5F 63
Mulvaney Way. SE1—3F 39
Mumford Ct. EC2—5E 25
Mumford Rd. SE24—3D 67
Muncaster Rd. SW11—3B 64
Muncies M. SE6—2E 85
Mundania Rd. SE22—4D 69
Munday Rd. E16—1C 44
Munden St. W14—5A 34
Mund St. W14—1B 48
Mundy St. N1—2A 26
Munro M. W10—4A 20
Munro Ter. SW10—2F 49
Munster Rd. SW6—3A 48
Munster Sq. NW1—3D 23
Munton Rd. SE17—5E 39
Murdock Clo. E16—5B 30
Murdock St. SE15—2D 55
Murfett Clo. SW19—2A 76
Muriel St. N1—1B 24
    (in two parts)
Murillo Rd. SE13—2F 71
Murphy St. SE1—3C 38
Murray Gro. N1—1E 25
Murray M. NW1—4F 9
Murray Rd. SW19—5F 75
Murray Sq. E16—5C 30
Murray St. NW1—4F 9
Murray Ter. NW3—1F 7
Mursell Est. SW8—4B 52
Musard Rd. W6—2A 48
Musbury St. E1—5E 27
Muscatel Pl. SE5—4A 54
Muschamp Rd. SE15—1B 68
Muscovy St. EC3—1A 40
Museum Pas. E2—2E 27
Museum St. WC1—4A 24
Musgrave Cres. SW6—4C 48
Musgrove Rd. SE14—4F 55
Musjid Rd. SW11—5F 49
Mustow Pl. SW6—5B 48
Mutrix Rd. NW6—5C 6
Mutton Pl. NW1—3C 8
Myatt Rd. SW9—4D 53
Mycenae Rd. SE3—3C 58
Myddelton Pas. EC1—2C 24
Myddelton Sq. EC1—2C 24
Myddelton St. EC1—2C 24

Mylis Clo. SE26—4D 83
Mylne St. EC1—2C 24
Myrdle St. E1—4C 26
Myron Pl. SE13—1E 71
Myrtle Wlk. N1—1A 26
Mysore Rd. SW11—2B 64
Myton Rd. SE21—3F 81

Nadine St. SE7—1E 59
Nairne Gro. SE24—3F 67
Nairn St. E14—4E 29
Naish Ct. N1—5A 10
Naldera Gdns. SE3—2C 58
Nankin St. E14—5C 28
Nansen Rd. SW11—1C 64
Nantes Clo. SW18—2E 63
Nantes Pas. E1—4B 26
Nant St. E2—2D 27
Napier Av. E14—1C 56
Napier Av. SW6—1B 62
Napier Clo. SE8—3B 56
Napier Clo. W14—4B 34
Napier Gro. N1—1E 25
Napier Pl. W14—4B 34
Napier Rd. E11—1A 16
Napier Rd. E15—1A 30
Napier Rd. NW10—2D 19
Napier Rd. W14—4B 34
Napier Ter. N1—4D 11
Narbonne Av. SW4—3E 65
Narborough St. SW6—5D 49
Narcissus Rd. NW6—2C 6
Narrow St. E14—1A 42
Nascot St. W12—5E 19
Naseby Clo. NW6—4E 7
Naseby Rd. SE19—5F 81
Nash Rd. SE4—3A 70
Nash St. NW1—2D 23
Nasmyth St. W6—4D 33
Nassau Rd. SW13—4B 44
Nassau St. W1—4E 23
Nassington Rd. NW3—1B 8
Natal Rd. SW16—5F 79
Nathaniel Clo. E1—4B 26
Naval Row. E14—1E 43
Navarino Gro. E8—3C 12
Navarino Rd. E8—3C 12
Navarre St. E2—3B 26
Navenby Wlk. E3—3C 28
Navy St. SW4—1F 65
Naylor Rd. SE15—3D 55
Nazrul St. E2—2B 26
Nealden St. SW9—1B 66
Neal St. WC2—5A 24
Neal's Yd. WC2—5A 24
Neasden Clo. NW10—2A 4
Neasden La. NW10—1A 4
    (in two parts)

Neate St. SE5—2A 54
Neathouse Pl. SW1—5E 37
Nebraska St. SE1—3F 39
Neckinger. SE1—4B 40
Neckinger St. SE1—3B 40
Nectarine Way. SE13—5D 57
Needham Rd. W11—5C 20
Needleman St. SE16—3F 41
Nelgarde Rd. SE6—5C 70
Nella Rd. W6—2F 47
Nelldale Rd. SE16—5E 41
Nello James Gdns. SE27—4F 81
Nelson Gdns. E2—2C 26
Nelson Mandela Rd. SE3—1E 73
Nelson Pas. E1—2E 25
Nelson Pl. N1—1D 25
Nelson Rd. SE10—2E 57
Nelson Sq. SE1—3D 39
Nelson's Row. SW4—2F 65
Nelson St. E1—5D 27
Nelson St. E16—1B 44
    (in two parts)
Nelson Ter. N1—1D 25
Nelson Wlk. SE16—2A 42
Nepaul Rd. SW11—1A 64
Nepean St. SW15—4C 60
Neptune St. SE16—4E 41
Nesbit Clo. SE3—1A 72
Nesbit Rd. SE9—2F 73
Nesham St. E1—1C 40
Ness St. SE16—4C 40
Netheravon Rd. N. W4—5B 32
Netheravon Rd. S. W4—1B 46
Netherby Rd. SE23—5E 69
Netherfield Rd. SW17—3C 78
Netherford Rd. SW4—5E 51
Netherhall Gdns. NW3—3E 7
Netherhall Way. NW3—2E 7
Netherton Gro. SW10—2E 49
Netherwood Rd. W14—4F 33
Netherwood St. NW6—4B 6
Netley St. NW1—2E 23
Nettlefold Pl. SE27—3D 81
Nettleton Rd. SE14—4F 55
Neuchatel Rd. SE6—2B 84
Nevada St. SE10—2E 57
Nevern Pl. SW5—5C 34
Nevern Rd. SW5—5C 34
Nevern Sq. SW5—5C 34
Neville Clo. NW1—1F 23
Neville Clo. NW6—1B 20
Neville Clo. SE15—4C 54
Neville Gill Clo. SW18—4C 62
Neville Rd. E7—4C 16
Neville Rd. NW6—1B 20
Neville St. SW7—1F 49
Neville Ter. SW7—1F 49
Nevill Rd. N16—1A 12
Nevis Rd. SW17—2C 78

Newark St. E1—4D 27
(in two parts)
New Barn St. E13—3C 30
New Bond St. W1—5D 23
New Bri. St. EC4—5D 25
New Broad St. EC2—4A 26
Newburgh St. W1—5E 23
New Burlington M. W1—1E 37
New Burlington Pl. W1—1E 37
New Burlington St. W1—1E 37
New Burn St. SE11—1B 52
Newbury M. NW5—3C 8
Newbury St. EC1—4E 25
New Butt La. SE8—3C 56
Newby St. E14—1E 43
Newby St. SW8—1D 65
New Caledonian Wharf. SE16
—4B 42
Newcastle Clo. EC4—5D 25
Newcastle Pl. W2—4F 21
Newcastle Row. EC1—3C 24
New Cavendish St. W1—4C 22
New Change. EC4—5E 25
New Chu. Rd. SE5—3F 53
(in two parts)
New City Rd. E13—2E 31
New College M. N1—4C 10
Newcombe Gdns. SW16—4A 80
Newcombe St. W8—2C 34
Newcomen Rd. SW11—1F 63
Newcomen St. SE1—3F 39
New Compton St. WC2—5F 23
Newcourt St. NW8—1A 22
New Coventry St. W1—1F 37
New Cross Rd. SE14—3F 55
Newell St. E14—5B 28
Newent Clo. SE15—3A 54
New Fetter La. EC4—5C 24
Newgate St. EC1—5D 25
New Goulston St. E1—5B 26
Newham's Row. SE1—3A 40
Newham Way—4B 30
   E16 55-413
   E6 remainder
Newhaven Gdns. SE9—2F 73
Newick Rd. E5—1D 13
Newington Butts—5D 39
   SE1 2-22
   SE11 remainder
Newington Causeway. SE1
—4E 39
Newington Grn. N1 & N16
—2F 11
Newington Grn. Rd. N1—2F 11
Newington Industrial Est. SE17
—5E 39
New Inn B'way. EC2—3A 26
New Inn St. EC2—3A 26

New Inn Yd. EC2—3A 26
New Kent Rd. SE1—5E 39
New Kings Rd. SW6—5B 48
New King St. SE8—2C 56
Newlands Pk. SE26—5E 83
Newlands Quay. E1—1E 41
New Lydenburgh St. SE7—4E 45
New Lyndenburgh Commercial
   Est. SE7—4E 45
Newman Pas. W1—4E 23
Newman Rd. E13—2D 31
Newman's Row. WC2—4B 24
Newman St. W1—4E 23
Newman Yd. W1—5F 23
Newmarket Grn. SE9—5F 73
New Mount St. E15—4F 15
Newnes Path. SW15—2D 61
Newnham Ter. SE1—4C 38
Newnham Ter. SE1—4C 38
Newport Av. E13—3D 31
Newport Ct. WC2—1F 37
Newport Pl. WC2—1F 37
Newport Rd. SW13—4C 46
Newport St. SE11—5B 38
Newquay Rd. SE6—2D 85
New Quebec St. W1—5B 22
New River Wlk. N1—3E 11
New Rd. E1—4D 27
New Rochford St. NW5—2B 8
New Row. WC2—1A 38
New Spring Gdns. Wlk. SE11
—1A 52
New Sq. WC2—5C 24
Newstead Rd. SE12—5B 72
Newstead Way. SW19—4A 76
New St. EC2—4A 26
New St. Hill. Brom—5D 87
New St. Sq. EC4—5C 24
Newton Gro. W4—5A 32
Newton Rd. E15—2F 15
Newton Rd. NW2—1E 5
Newton Rd. SW2—1D 51
Newton St. WC2—5A 24
Newton's Yd. SW18—3C 62
Newtown St. SW11—4D 51
(in two parts)
New Union Clo. E14—4E 43
New Union St. EC2—4F 25
New Wharf Rd. N1—1A 24
New Zealand Way. W12—1D 33
Nicholas La. EC4—1A 40
Nicholas Rd. E1—3E 27
Nichollsfield Wlk. N7—2B 10

Nicholl St. E2—5C 12
Nicholson St. SE1—2D 39
Nichol's Sq. E2—1B 26
Nicoll Rd. NW10—5A 4
Nicosia Rd. SW18—5A 64
Niederwald Rd. SE26—4A 84
Nigel Playfair Av. W6—1D 47
Nigel Rd. E7—2E 17
Nigel Rd. SE15—1C 68
Nigeria Rd. SE7—3F 59
Nightingale Gro. SE13—3F 71
Nightingale La.—5B 64
   SW4 1-25
   SW12 remainder
Nightingale Rd. NW10—1B 18
Nightingale Sq. SW12—5C 64
Nightingale Wlk. SW4—4D 65
Nile Rd. E13—1E 31
Nile St. N1—2F 25
Nile Ter. SE15—1B 54
Nimegan Way. SE22—3A 68
Nimrod Rd. SW16—5D 79
Nine Elms La. SW8—3E 51
Niton St. SW6—3F 47
Noble St. EC2—5E 25
Noel Rd. N1—1D 25
Noel St. W1—5E 23
Nolan Way. E5—1C 12
Norbiton Rd. E14—5B 28
Norbroke St. W12—1B 32
Norburn St. W10—4A 20
Norcott Gdns. SE22—5C 68
Norcroft Gdns. SE22—5C 68
Norfolk Cres. W2—5A 22
Norfolk Ho. Rd. SW16—3F 79
Norfolk Pl. W2—5F 21
Norfolk Rd. NW8—5F 7
Norfolk Rd. NW10—4A 4
Norfolk Row. SE11—5B 38
Norfolk Sq. W2—5F 21
Norfolk St. E7—2C 16
Norfolk Ter. W6—1A 48
Norgrove St. SW12—5C 64
Norland Pl. W11—2A 34
Norland Rd. W11—2F 33
Norland Sq. W11—2A 34
Norley Vale. SW15—1C 74
Normanby Clo. SW15—3B 62
Normanby Rd. NW10—1B 4
Normand M. W14—2A 48
Normand Rd. W14—2B 48
Normandy Rd. SW9—4C 52
Normandy Ter. E16—5D 31
Norman Gro. E3—1A 28
Normanhurst Rd. SW2—2B 80
Norman Rd. SE10—3D 57
Norman's Bldgs. EC1—2E 25
Norman St. EC1—2E 25
Norman Ter. NW6—2B 6
Normanton Av. SW19—2C 76

Normanton St. SE23—2F 83
Normington Clo. SW16—5C 80
Norris St. SW1—1F 37
Norroy Rd. SW15—2F 61
Norstead Pl. SW15—2C 74
Northampton Gro. N1—2F 11
Northampton Pk. N1—3E 11
Northampton Rd. EC1—3C 24
Northampton Sq. EC1—2D 25
Northampton St. N1—4E 11
N. Audley St. W1—1C 36
North Bank. NW8—2A 22
Northbourne Rd. SW4—3F 65
Northbrook Rd. SE13—3A 72
Northburgh St. EC1—3D 25
Northchurch. SE17—1F 53
Northchurch Rd. N1—4F 11
(in two parts)
Northchurch Ter. N1—4A 12
North Circular Rd. NW10—2A 4
Northcote M. SW11—2A 64
Northcote Rd. NW10—4A 4
Northcote Rd. SW11—3A 64
North Ct. W1—4E 23
North Cres. WC1—4F 23
North Crofts. SE23—1D 83
N. Cross Rd. SE22—3B 68
Northdown St. N1—1B 24
North Dri. SW16—4E 79
N. East Pier. E1—2D 41
N. End Cres. W14—5B 34
N. End Rd. —5A 34   SW6
W14 1-311 & 2-234
Northern Rd. E13—1D 31
N. Eyot Gdns. W6—1B 46
Northey St. E14—1A 42
Northfields. SW18—2C 62
N. Flockton St. SE16—3C 40
N. Gower St. NW1—2E 23
North St. E8—5D 13
Northington St. WC1—3B 24
Northlands St. SE5—5E 53
N. Lodge Clo. SW15—3F 61
North M. WC1—3B 24
Northolme Rd. N5—1E 11
Northover. Brom—3B 86
N. Park Av. NW10 & NW2—2D 5
North Pas. SW18—2C 62
N. Pole Rd. W10—4E 19
Northport St. N1—5F 11
North Rd. N7—3A 10
North Rd. SW19—5D 77
North Row. W1—1B 36
North Several. SE3—5F 57
Northstead Rd. SW2—2C 80
North St. E13—1D 31
North St. SW4—1E 65
North St. Pas. E13—1D 31
N. Tenter St. E1—5B 26

North Ter. SW3—4A 36
Northumberland All. EC3
—5A 26
Northumberland Av. WC2
—2A 38
Northumberland Pl. W2—5C 20
Northumberland St. WC2
—3C 38
Northumbria St. E14—5C 28
N. Verbena Gdns. W6—1C 46
North View. NW10—1B 4
N. View Cres. NW10—1B 4
North Vs. NW1—3F 9
Northway Rd. SE5—1E 67
N. West Pier. E1—2D 41
Northwest Pl. N1—1C 24
N. Wharf Rd. W2—4F 21
Northwick Clo. NW8—3F 21
Northwick Ter. NW8—3F 21
Northwood Rd. SE23—1B 84
Northwood Way. SE19—5F 81
N. Woolwich Rd. E16—2D 45
(in two parts)
N. Worple Way. SW14—1A 60
Norton Folgate. E1—4A 26
Norway Ga. SE16—4A 42
Norway Pl. E14—5B 28
Norway St. SE10—2D 57
Norwich Rd. E7—2C 16
Norwich St. EC4—5C 24
Norwood High St. SE27—3D 81
Norwood Pk. Rd. SE27—5E 81
Norwood Rd.—1D 81 SE27
SE24 1-339 & 2-150
Notley St. SE5—3F 53
Notting Barn Rd. W10—3F 19
Nottingham Av. E16—4E 31
Nottingham Ct. WC2—5A 24
Nottingham Pl. W1—4C 22
Nottingham Rd. SW17—1B 78
Nottingham St. W1—4C 22
Notting Hill Ga. W11—2C 34
Novello St. SW6—4C 48
Nowell Rd. SW13—2C 46
Noyna Rd. SW17—3B 78
Nuding Clo. SE13—1C 70
Nugent Ter. NW8—1E 21
Nunhead Cres. SE15—1D 69
Nunhead Grn. SE15—1D 69
Nunhead Gro. SE15—1E 69
Nunhead La. SE15—1D 69
Nursery Clo. SW15—2F 61
Nursery La. E7—3C 16
Nursery La. W10—4E 19
Nursery Rd. E9—3E 13
Nursery Rd. SW9—2B 66
Nutbourne St. W10—2A 20
Nutbrook St. SE15—1C 68
Nutcroft Rd. SE15—3D 55

Nutfield Rd. E15—1E 15
Nutfield Rd. SE22—2B 68
Nutford Pl. W1—5B 22
Nuthurst Av. SW2—2B 80
Nutley Ter. NW3—3E 7
Nutmeg La. E14—5F 29
Nuttall St. N1—1A 26
Nutt St. SE15—3B 54
Nutwell St. SW17—5A 78
Nynehead St. SE14—3A 56
Nyon Gro. SE6—2B 84

Oakbank Gro. SE24—2E 67
Oakbrook Clo. Brom—4D 87
Oakbury Rd. SW6—5D 49
Oak Cottage Clo. SE6—1B 86
Oak Cres. E16—4A 30
Oakcroft Rd. SE13—5F 57
Oakdale Rd. E7—4D 17
Oakdale Rd. SE15—1E 69
Oakdale Rd. SW16—5A 80
Oak Dene. SE15—4D 55
Oakden St. SE11—5C 38
Oake Ct. SW15—3A 62
Oakey La. SE1—4C 38
Oakfield Gdns. SE19—5B 82
(in two parts)
Oakfield Rd. SW19—3F 75
Oakfield St. SW10—2C 49
Oakford Rd. NW5—1E 9
Oak Gro. NW2—1A 6
Oakham Clo. SE6—2B 84
Oakhill Av. NW3—1D 7
Oak Hill Pk. NW3—1D 7
Oak Hill Pk. M. NW3—1E 7
Oakhill Pl. SW15—3C 62
Oakhill Rd. SW15—3B 62
Oak Hill Way. NW3—1E 7
Oakhurst Gro. SE22—2C 68
Oakington Rd. W9—3C 20
Oaklands Est. SW4—4E 65
Oaklands Gro. W12—2C 32
Oaklands Pl. SW4—2E 65
Oaklands Rd. NW2—1F 5
Oak La. E14—1B 42
Oakley Cres. EC1—1D 25
Oakley Gdns. SW3—2A 50
Oakley Pl. SE1—1B 54
Oakley Rd. N1—4F 11
Oakley Sq. NW1—1E 23
Oakley St. SW3—2A 50
Oakley Wlk. W6—2F 47
Oakmead Rd. SW12—1D 79
Oak Pk. Gdns. SW19—1F 75
Oak Pl. SW18—3D 63
Oakridge Rd. Brom—4A 86
Oaks Av. SE19—5A 82
Oaksford Av. SE26—3D 83

Oakshade Rd. Brom—4F 85
Oakshaw Rd. SW18—5D 63
Oak Tree Gdns. Brom—5D 87
Oak Tree Rd. NW8—2A 22
Oakview Rd. SE6—5D 85
Oak Village. NW5—1C 8
Oak Way. W3—2A 32
Oakwood Ct. W14—4B 34
Oakwood Dri. SE19—5F 81
Oakwood La. W14—4B 34
Oakworth Rd. W10—4F 19
Oat La. EC2—5E 25
Oban Rd. E13—2E 31
Oban St. E14—5F 29
Oberstein Rd. SW11—2F 63
Oborne Clo. SE24—3D 67
Observatory Gdns. W8—3C 34
Occupation Rd. SE17—1E 53
Ocean Est. E1—4A 28
(in two parts)
Ocean St. E1—4F 27
Ocean Wharf Development. E14
—3C 42
Ockendon Rd. N1—3F 11
Ockley Rd. SW16—4A 80
Octagon Arc. EC2—4A 26
Octavia St. SW11—4A 50
Octavius St. SE8—3C 56
Odessa Rd. E7—1B 16
Odessa Rd. NW10—1C 18
Odessa St. SE16—3B 42
Odger St. SW11—5B 50
Odhams Wlk. W1—5A 24
Offa's Mead. E9—1B 14
Offerton Rd. SW4—1E 65
Offley Rd. SW9—3C 52
Offord Rd. N1—4B 10
Offord St. N1—4B 10
Oglander Rd. SE15—1B 68
Ogle St. W1—4E 23
Ohio Rd. E13—3B 30
Oil Mill La. W6—1C 46
Okeburn Rd. SW17—5C 78
Okehampton Rd. NW10—5E 5
Olaf St. W11—1F 33
Oldacre M. SW12—5D 65
Old Bailey. EC4—5D 25
Old Barrack Yd. SW1—3C 36
Old Barrowfield. E15—5A 16
Old Bethnal Grn. Rd. E2—2C 26
Old Bond St. W1—1E 37
Old Brewer's Yd. WC2—5A 24
Old Brewery M. NW3—1F 7
Old Broad St. EC2—5F 25
Old Bromley Rd. Brom—5F 85
Old Brompton Rd.—1D 49
SW7 1-125 & 2-146
SW5 remainder
Old Burlington St. W1—1E 37

Oldbury Pl. W1—4C 22
Old Castle St. E1—5B 26
Old Cavendish St. W1—5D 23
Old Chelsea M. SW3—2F 49
Old Chu. Rd. E1—5F 27
Old Chu. St. SW3—1F 49
Old Compton St. W1—1F 37
Old Ct. Pl. W8—3D 35
Old Devonshire Rd. SW12
—5D 65
Old Dover Rd. SE3—3C 58
Oldfield Gro. SE16—5F 41
Oldfield Rd. NW10—4B 4
Oldfield Rd. SW19—5A 76
Oldfield Rd. W3—3B 32
Old Ford Rd.—1E 27
E2 1-211 & 2-232
E3 remainder
Old Forge M. W12—3D 33
Old Gloucester St. WC1—4A 24
Old Ho. Clo. SW19—5A 76
Old Jamaica Rd. SE16—4C 40
Old James St. SE15—1D 69
Old Jewry. EC2—5F 25
Old Kent Rd. SE1—5A 40
Old Mnr. Yd. SW5—5D 35
Old Marylebone Rd. NW1
—4A 22
Old Montague St. E1—4C 26
Old Nichol St. E2—3B 26
Old Oak Common La.—4A 18
W3 51-189 & 82-240
NW10 remainder
Old Oak La. NW10—2A 18
Old Oak Rd. W3—1B 32
Old Orchard, The. NW3—1B 8
Old Pal. Yd. SW1—4A 38
Old Paradise St. SE11—5B 38
Old Pk. Av. SW12—4C 64
Old Pk. La. W1—2D 37
Old Pye St. SW1—4F 37
Old Quebec St. W1—5B 22
Old Queen St. SW1—3F 37
Oldridge Rd. SW12—5C 64
Old Rd. SE13—2A 72
Old Seacoal La. EC4—5D 25
Old S. Lambeth Rd. SW8—3A 52
Old Sq. WC2—5C 24
Oldstead Rd. Brom—4F 85
Old St. E13—1E 31
Old St. EC1—3E 25
Old Town. SW4—1E 65
Old Woolwich Rd. SE10—2F 57
Old York Rd. SW18—3D 63
O'Leary Sq. E1—4E 27
Oley Pl. E1—4F 27
Olga St. E3—1A 28
Oliphant St. W10—2F 19
Oliver Goldsmith Est. SE15
—4C 54

Olive Rd. E13—2E 31
Olive Rd. NW2—1E 5
Olivers Yd. EC1—3F 25
Olivette St. SW15—2F 61
Ollerton Grn. E3—5B 14
Ollgar Clo. W12—2B 32
Olliffe St. E14—4E 43
Olmar St. SE1—2C 54
Olney Rd. SE17—2D 53
Olympia M. W2—1D 35
Olympia Way. W14—4A 34
Oman Av. NW2—1D 5
O'Meara St. SE1—2E 39
Omega St. SE14—4C 56
Ommaney Rd. SE14—4F 55
Ondine Rd. SE15—2B 68
Onega Ga. SE16—4A 42
One Tree Clo. SE23—4E 69
Ongar Rd. SW6—2C 48
Onslow Gdns. SW7—1F 49
Onslow M. E. SW7—5F 35
Onslow M. W. SW7—5F 35
Onslow Sq. SW7—5F 35
Onslow St. EC1—3C 24
Ontario St. SE1—4D 39
Opal Clo. E16—5F 31
Opal St. SE11—1D 53
Openview. SW18—1E 77
Ophir Ter. SE15—4C 54
Oppidans M. NW3—4B 8
Oppidans Rd. NW3—4B 8
Orange Ct. E1—2C 40
Orange Pl. SE16—4E 41
Orange St. WC2—1F 37
Orbain Rd. SW6—3A 48
Orbel St. SW11—4A 50
Orb St. SE17—5F 39
Orchard Clo. SE23—4E 69
Orchard Clo. W10—4B 20
Orchard Dri. SE3—5F 57
Orchard Hill. SE13—5D 57
Orchard M. N1—4F 11
Orchard Pl. E14—1A 44
Orchard Rd. SE3—5A 58
Orchardson St. NW8—3F 21
Orchard St. W1—5C 22
Orchard, The. SE3—5F 57
Orchid St. W12—1C 32
Orde Hall St. WC1—4B 24
Ordell Rd. E3—1B 28
Ordnance Cres. SE10—3A 44
Ordnance Hill. NW8—5F 7
Ordnance M. NW8—1F 21
Ordnance Rd. E16—4B 30
Orestes M. NW6—2C 6
Oriel Ct. NW3—1E 7
Oriel Rd. E9—3F 13
Oriental Rd. E16—2F 45
Orient St. SE11—5D 39

Orkney St. SW11—5C 50
Orlando Rd. SW4—1E 65
Orleston M. N7—3C 10
Orleston Rd. N7—3C 10
Orlop St. SE10—1A 58
Ormanton Rd. SE26—4C 82
Orme Ct. W2—1D 35
Orme La. W2—1D 35
Ormeley Rd. SW12—1D 79
Orme Sq. W2—1D 35
Ormiston Gro. W12—2D 33
Ormiston Rd. SE10—1C 58
Ormond Clo. WC1—4A 24
Ormonde Ga. SW3—1B 50
Ormonde Pl. SW1—5C 36
Ormonde Ter. NW8—5B 8
Ormond M. WC1—3A 24
Ormond Yd. SW1—2E 37
Ormsby St. E2—1B 26
Ormside St. SE15—2E 55
Ornan Rd. NW3—2A 8
Oronsay Wlk. N1—4E 11
Orpheus St. SE5—4F 53
Orsett St. SE11—1B 52
Orsett Ter. W2—5E 21
Orsman Rd. N1—5A 12
Orton St. E1—2C 40
Orville Rd. SW11—5F 49
Orwell Rd. E13—1E 31
Osberton Rd. SE12—3C 72
Osbert St. SW1—5F 37
Osborn Clo. E8—5C 12
Osborne Rd. E7—2D 17
Osborne Rd. E9—3B 14
Osborne Rd. NW2—3D 5
Osborn La. SE23—5A 70
Osborn St. E1—4B 26
Osborn Ter. SE3—2B 72
Oscar St. SE8—4C 56
Oseney Cres. NW5—2E 9
O'Shea Gro. E3—5B 14
Osiers Rd. SW18—2C 62
Osier St. E1—3E 27
Oslac Rd. SE6—5D 85
Osman Rd. W6—4E 33
Osmund St. W12—4D 18
Osnaburgh St. NW1—3D 23
Osnaburgh Ter. NW1—3D 23
Osprey St. SE16—5F 41
Ospringe Rd. NW5—1E 9
Ossington Bldgs. W1—4C 22
Ossington Clo. W2—1C 34
Ossington St. W2—1D 35
Ossory Rd. SE1—2C 54
Ossulston St. NW1—1F 23
Ostade Rd. SW2—5B 66
Osten M. SW7—4D 35
Osterley Rd. N16—1A 12
Oswald's Mead. E9—1A 14

Osward Rd. SW17—2B 78
Oswin St. SE11—5D 39
Oswyth Rd. SE5—5A 54
Otford Cres. SE4—4B 70
Othello Clo. SE11—1D 53
Otis St. E3—2E 29
Otley Rd. E16—5E 31
Otterburn St. SW17—5B 78
Otterden St. SE6—4C 84
Otto Clo. SE26—3D 83
Otto St. SE17—2D 53
(in two parts)
Ousley Rd. SW12—1B 78
Outer Circ. NW1—1A 22
Outgate Rd. NW10—4B 4
Outram Pl. N1—5A 10
Oval Pl. SW8—3B 52
Oval Rd. NW1—5D 9
Oval, The. E2—1D 27
Oval Way. SE11—1B 52
Overbrae. Beck—5C 84
Overbury St. E5—1F 13
Overcliff Rd. SE13—1C 70
Overdown Rd. SE6—4C 84
Overhill Rd. SE22—5C 68
Overstone Rd. W6—5E 33
Overton Rd. SW9—5C 52
Ovex Clo. E14—3E 43
Ovington Gdns. SW3—4A 36
Ovington Sq. SW3—4A 36
Ovington St. SW3—5A 36
Owen's Row. EC1—2D 25
Owen St. EC1—1D 25
Owens Way. SE23—5A 70
Owgan Clo. SE5—3F 53
Oxberry Av. SW6—5A 48
Oxendon St. SW1—1F 37
Oxenford St. SE15—1B 68
Oxestall's Rd. SE8—1A 56
Oxford Av. NW10—2E 19
Oxford Cir. Av. W1—5E 23
Oxford Gdns. W10—5F 19
Oxford Ga. W6—5F 33
Oxford Rd. E15—3F 15
(in two parts)
Oxford Rd. NW6—1C 20
Oxford Rd. SE19—5F 81
Oxford Rd. SW16—2A 62
Oxford Sq. W2—5A 22
Oxford St. W1—5C 22
Oxonian St. SE22—2B 68
Ozolins Way. E16—5C 30

Pacific Rd. E16—5C 30
Packington Sq. N1—5E 11
Packington St. N1—5D 11
Padbury Ct. E2—2B 26
Paddenswick Rd. W6—4C 32

Paddington Grn. W2—4F 21
Paddington St. W1—4C 22
Paddock Clo. SE3—1C 72
Paddock Clo. SE26—4F 83
Padfield Rd. SE5—1E 67
Pagden St. SW8—4D 51
Page Pl. E1—5D 27
Page St. SW1—5F 37
Page's Wlk. SE1—5A 40
Pages Yd. W4—2A 46
Paget St. EC1—2D 25
Pagnell St. SE14—3B 56
Pagoda Gdns. SE3—5F 57
Pakenham Clo. SW12—1C 78
Pakenham St. WC1—3B 24
Palace Av. W8—3D 35
Palace Ct. NW3—2D 7
Palace Ct. W2—1D 35
Palace Gdns. M. W8—2D 35
Palace Gdns. Ter. W8—2C 34
Palace Ga. W8—3E 35
Palace Grn. W8—2D 35
Palace M. SW6—3B 48
Palace Pl. SW1—4E 37
Palace Rd. SW2—1B 80
Palace St. SW1—4E 37
Palace View. SE12—2C 86
Palatine Av. N16—1A 12
Palatine Rd. N16—1A 12
Palermo Rd. NW10—1C 18
Palfrey Pl. SW8—3B 52
Palgrave Rd. W12—4B 32
Palissy St. E2—2B 26
(in two parts)
Palliser Rd. W14—1A 48
Pall Mall. SW1—2E 37
Pall Mall E. SW1—2F 37
Palmer Pl. N7—2C 10
Palmer Rd. E13—3D 31
Palmer's Rd. E2—1F 27
Palmerston Rd. E7—3D 17
Palmerston Rd. NW6—4B 6
(in two parts)
Palmerston Way. SW8—3E 51
Palmer St. SW1—4F 37
Pamber St. W10—5F 19
Pamela Wlk. E8—5C 12
Pancras La. EC4—5E 25
Pancras Rd. NW1—1F 23
Pandora Rd. NW6—3C 6
Pangbourne Av. W10—4E 19
Panmure Clo. N5—1D 11
Panmure Rd. SE26—3D 83
Pansy Gdns. W12—1C 32
Panton St. SW1—1F 37
Papillons Wlk. SE3—1C 72
Papworth Gdns. N7—2B 10
Papworth Way. SW2—5C 66
Parade M. SE27—2D 81

Parade, The. SW11—3B 50
Paradise Pas. N7—2C 10
Paradise Rd. SW4—5A 52
Paradise Row. E2—2D 27
Paradise St. SE16—3D 41
Paradise Wlk. SW3—2B 50
Paragon All. SE1—4A 40
Paragon M. SE1—5F 39
Paragon Pl. SE3—5B 58
Paragon Rd. E9—3E 13
Paragon Row. SE17—5F 39
Paragon, The. SE3—5C 58
Parbury Rd. SE23—4A 70
Pardoner St. SE1—4F 39
(in two parts)
Pardon St. EC1—3D 25
Parfett St. E1—4C 26
Parfrey St. W6—2E 47
Paris Garden. SE1—2D 39
Park App. SE16—4D 41
Park Av. E15—3A 16
Park Av. NW10—2D 5
(Dudden Hill)
Park Clo. E9—5E 13
Park Clo. SW1—3B 36
Park Clo. W14—4B 34
Park Ct. SE26—5D 83
Park Cres. W1—3D 23
Park Cres. M. E. W1—3D 23
Park Cres. M. W. W1—3D 23
Parkcroft Rd. SE12—5B 72
Park End. NW3—1A 8
Parker M. WC2—5A 24
Parke Rd. SW13—4C 46
Parker Rd. SW13—4C 46
Parker St. WC2—5A 24
Parkfield Av. SW14—2A 60
Parkfield Rd. NW10—4D 5
Parkfield Rd. SE14—4B 56
Parkfields. SW15—2E 61
Parkfield St. N1—1C 24
Park Ga. SE3—1B 72
Parkgate Rd. SW11—3A 50
Park Gro. E15—5C 16
Park Hall Rd. SE21—3F 81
Parkham St. SW11—4A 50
Park Hill. SE23—1D 83
Park Hill. SW4—3F 65
Park Hill Ct. SW17—3B 78
Parkhill Rd. NW3—2B 8
Parkhill Wlk. NW3—2B 8
Parkholme Rd. E8—3C 12
Parkhouse St. SE5—3F 53
Parkhurst Rd. N7—1A 10
Parkland Gdns. SW19—1F 75
Parklands Rd. SW16—5D 79
Park La. E15—5F 15
Park La. W1—1B 36
Parkmead. SW15—4D 61

Park M. SE24—5E 67
Park Pde. NW10—1B 18
Park Pl. SW1—2E 37
Park Pl. Gdns. W2—4E 21
Park Pl. Vs. W2—4E 21
Park Rise. SE23—1A 84
Park Rise Rd. SE23—1A 84
Park Rd. E6—5E 17
Park Rd. E15—5C 16
Park Rd.—2A 22
  NW1 1-71 & 2-98
  NW8 remainder
Park Rd. NW10—5A 4
Park Row. SE10—1F 57
Parkside. SW15—2B 62
Parkside. SW19—4F 75
Parkside Av. SW19—5F 75
Parkside Gdns. SW19—4F 75
Park Sq. E. NW1—3D 23
Park Sq. W. NW1—3D 23
Parkstead Rd. SW15—3D 61
Parkstone Rd. SE15—5C 54
Park St. SE1—2E 39
Park St. W1—1C 36
Park, The. SE23—1E 83
Parkthorne Rd. SW12—5F 65
Park Towers. W2—1E 35
Park View Est. E2—1F 27
Park View Rd. NW10—1B 4
Park Village E. NW1—1D 23
Park Village W. NW1—1D 23
Parkville Rd. SW6—3B 48
Park Vista. SE10—2F 57
Park Wlk. SW10—2E 49
Parkway. NW1—5D 9
Park W. Pl. W2—5A 22
Parkwood Rd. SW19—5B 76
Parliament Hill. NW3—1A 8
Parliament Sq. SW1—3A 38
Parliament St. SW1—3A 38
Parluke Clo. SE7—1F 59
Parma Cres. SW11—2B 64
Parmiter St. E2—1D 27
Parnell Rd. E3—5B 14
Parnham St. E14—5A 28
Parr Rd. E6—5F 17
Parr St. N1—1F 25
Parry St. SW8—2A 52
Parsifal Rd. NW6—2C 6
Parsonage St. E14—5E 43
Parson's Grn. SW6—5C 48
Parson's Grn. La. SW6—4C 48
Parson's Rd. E13—1E 31
Parthenia Rd. SW6—4C 48
Partridge Clo. E16—4F 31
Parvin St. SW8—4F 51
Pascal St. SW8—3F 51
Pascoe Rd. SE13—3F 71

Pasley Clo. SE17—1E 53
Passfield Dri. E14—4D 29
Passmore St. SW1—1C 50
Paston Cres. SE12—5D 73
Pastor St. SE11—5D 39
Pasture Rd. SE6—1B 86
Patcham Ter. SW8—4D 51
Paternoster Row. EC4—5E 25
Paternoster Sq. EC4—5D 25
Pater St. W8—4C 34
Pathfield Rd. SW16—5F 79
Patience Rd. SW11—5A 50
Patio Clo. SW4—4F 65
Patmore Est. SW8—4E 51
Patmore St. SW8—4E 51
Patmos Rd. SW9—3D 53
Paton Clo. E3—2C 28
Patrick Connolly Gdns. E3
  —2D 29
Patrick Pas. SW11—5A 50
Patrick Rd. E13—2E 31
Patriot Sq. E2—1E 27
Patrol Pl. SE6—4D 71
Patshull Pl. NW5—3E 9
Patshull Rd. NW5—3E 9
Pattenden Rd. SE6—1B 84
Patten Rd. SW18—5A 64
Patterdale Rd. SE15—3E 55
Paul Clo. E15—4A 16
Paulet Rd. SE5—5D 53
Paul St. E15—5A 16
Paul St. EC2—3F 25
Paul's Wlk. EC4—1E 39
Paultons Sq. SW3—2F 49
Paultons St. SW3—2F 49
Paveley Dri. SW11—3A 50
Paveley St. NW8—2A 22
Pavement, The. SW4—2E 65
Pavilion Rd. SW1—4B 36
Pavilion St. SW1—4B 36
Pawsey Clo. E13—5D 17
Paxton Pl. SE27—4A 82
Paxton Rd. W4—2A 46
Paynell Ct. SE3—1A 72
Payne Rd. E3—1D 29
Payne St. SE8—3B 56
Paynes Wlk. W6—2A 48
Peabody Av. SW1—1D 51
Peabody Bldgs. EC1—3E 25
Peabody Clo. SE10—4D 57
Peabody Est. SE24—5D 67
Peabody Est. W6—1E 47
Peabody Hill. SE21—1D 81
Peabody Sq. SE1—3D 39
Peabody Yd. N1—5E 11
Peach Rd. W10—2F 19
Peachum Rd. SE3—2B 58
Peacock St. SE17—5D 39
Peak Hill. SE26—4E 83

Peak Hill Av. SE26—4E 83
Peak Hill Gdns. SE26—4E 83
Peak, The. SE26—3E 83
Pearcefield Av. SE23—1E 83
Peardon St. SW8—5D 51
Pearfield Rd. SE23—3A 84
Pearl St. E1—2D 41
Pearman St. SE1—4C 38
Pear Pl. SE1—3C 38
Pearscroft Ct. SW6—4D 49
Pearscroft Rd. SW6—4D 49
Pearson's Av. SE14—4C 56
Pearson St. E2—1B 26
Pear Tree Ct. EC1—3C 24
Peartree La. E1—1E 41
Pear Tree St. EC1—3E 25
Peary Pl. E2—2E 27
Peckarmans Wood. SE26
—3C 82
Peckett Sq. N5—1E 11
Peckford Clo. SW9—5C 52
Peckford Pl. SW9—5C 52
Peckham Gro. SE15—3A 54
Peckham High St. SE15—4C 54
Peckham Hill St. SE15—3C 54
Peckham Pk. Rd. SE15—3C 54
Peckham Rd.—4A 54
  SE5 1-93 & 2-84
  SE15 remainder
Peckham Rye—1C 68
  SE15 1-261 & 2-132
  SE22 remainder
Peckwater St. NW5—2E 9
Pedlars Wlk. N7—2B 10
Pedley St. E1—3B 26
Pedworth Gdns. SE16—5E 41
Peek Cres. SW19—5F 75
Peel Gro. E2—1E 27
Peel Precinct. NW6—1C 20
Peel Rd. NW6—2B 20
Peel St. W8—2C 34
Peerless St. EC1—2F 25
Pegasus Pl. SE11—2C 52
Pegley Gdns. SE12—2C 86
Pekin St. E14—5C 28
Pelham Clo. SE5—1A 68
Pelham Cres. SW7—5A 36
Pelham Pl. SW7—5A 36
Pelham St. SW7—5F 35
Pelican Est. SE15—4B 54
Pelican Pas. E1—3E 27
Pelican Wlk. SW9—2D 67
Pelier St. SE17—2E 53
Pelinore Rd. SE6—2A 86
Pellant Rd. SW6—3A 48
Pellatt Rd. SE22—3B 68
Pellerin Rd. N16—2A 12
Pelling St. E14—5C 28

Pelly Rd. E13—5C 16
Pelter St. E2—2B 26
Pelton Rd. SE10—1A 58
Pember Rd. NW10—2F 19
Pemberton Pl. E9—4E 13
Pemberton Row. EC4—5C 24
Pembridge Cres. W11—1C 34
Pembridge Gdns. W2—1C 34
Pembridge M. W11—1C 34
Pembridge Pl. W2—1C 34
Pembridge Rd. W11—1C 34
Pembridge Sq. W2—1C 34
Pembridge Vs. W11—1C 34
Pembroke Clo. SW1—3C 36
Pembroke Gdns. W8—5B 34
Pembroke Gdns. Clo. W8—4C 34
Pembroke M. W8—4C 34
Pembroke Pl. W8—4C 34
Pembroke Rd. W8—5C 34
Pembroke Sq. W8—4C 34
Pembroke St. N1—4A 10
Pembroke Vs. W8—4C 34
Pembroke Wlk. W8—5C 34
Pembury Pl. E5—2D 13
Pembury Rd. E5—2D 13
Pernell Clo. E1—3E 27
Penally Pl. N1—5F 11
Penang St. E1—2D 41
Penarth St. SE15—2E 55
Penberth Rd. SE6—2E 85
Pencombe M. W11—1B 34
Pencraig Way. SE15—2D 55
Penda's Mead. E9—1A 14
Pendennis Rd. SW16—4A 80
Penderry Rise. SE6—2F 85
Penderyn Way. N7—1F 9
Pendle Ho. SE26—3C 82
Pendle Rd. SW16—5D 79
Pendragon Rd. Brom—3B 86
Pendrell Rd. SE4—5A 56
Penerley Rd. SE6—1D 85
Penfold Pl. NW1—4A 22
Penfold St.—3F 21
  NW1 1-11 & 2-28
  NW8 remainder
Penford Gdns. SE9—1F 73
Penford St. SE5—5D 53
Penge Rd. E13—5E 17
Penhall Rd. SE7—5F 45
Pennack Rd. SE15—2B 54
Pennant M. W8—5D 35
Pennard Rd. W12—3E 33
Penner Clo. SW19—2A 76
Pennethorne Clo. E9—5E 13
Pennethorne Rd. SE15—3D 55
Pennington Clo. SE27—4F 81
Pennington St. E1—1D 41
Penn Rd. N7—2A 10
Penn St. N1—5F 11

Pennyfields. E14—1C 42
Pennymoor Wlk. W9—2B 20
Penpoll Rd. E8—3D 13
Penrith Clo. SW15—3A 62
Penrith Pl. SE27—2D 81
Penrose Gro. SE17—1E 53
Penrose St. SE17—1E 53
Penryn St. NW1—1F 23
Penry St. SE1—5A 40
Pensbury Pl. SW8—5E 51
Pensbury St. SW8—5E 51
Penshurst Rd. E9—4F 13
Pentland Gdns. SW18—4E 63
Pentland St. SW18—4E 63
Pentlow St. SW15—1E 61
Pentney Rd. SW12—1E 79
Penton Gro. N1—1C 24
Penton Pl. SE17—1D 53
Penton Rise. WC1—2B 24
Penton St. N1—1C 24
Pentonville Rd. N1—1B 24
Pentridge St. SE15—3B 54
Penwith Rd. SW18—2D 77
Penwortham Rd. SW16—5D 79
Penywern Rd. SW5—1C 48
Penzance Pl. W11—2A 34
Penzance St. W11—2A 34
Peony Gdns. W12—1C 32
Peploe Rd. NW6—1F 19
Pepper St. SE1—3E 39
Pepys Rd. SE14—4F 55
Pepys St. EC3—1A 40
Perceval Av. NW3—2A 8
Perch St. E8—1B 12
Percival St. EC1—3D 25
Percy Cir. WC1—2B 24
Percy Rd. E16—4A 30
Percy Rd. NW6—2C 20
Percy Rd. W12—3C 32
Percy St. W1—4F 23
Percy Yd. WC1—2B 24
Peregrine Ct. SW16—4B 80
Perham Rd. W14—1A 48
Perifield. SE21—1E 81
Periton Rd. SE9—2F 73
Perkin's Rents. SW1—4F 37
Perks Clo. SE3—1A 72
Perran Rd. SW2—1D 81
Perren St. NW5—3D 9
Perrers Rd. W6—5D 33
Perrins Ct. NW3—1E 7
Perrin's La. NW3—1E 7
Perrin's Wlk. NW3—1E 7
Perry Hill. SE6—3B 84
Perrymead St. SW6—4D 49
Perryn Rd. SE16—4D 41
Perry Rise. SE23—3A 84
Perry's Pl. W1—5F 23
Perry Vale. SE23—2E 83

Persant Rd. SE6—2A 86
Perseverance Pl. SW9—3C 52
Perth Rd. E13—1D 31
Peter Av. NW10—4D 5
Peterboat Clo. SE10—5A 44
Peterborough Ct. EC4—5C 24
Peterborough M. SW6—5C 48
Peterborough Rd. SW6—5C 48
Peterborough Vs. SW6—4D 49
Petergate. SW11—2E 63
Peterley Business Centre. E2
—1D 27
Petersfield Rise. SW15—1D 75
Petersham La. SW7—4E 35
Petersham M. SW7—4E 35
Petersham Pl. SW7—4E 35
Peters Hill. EC4—1E 39
Peter's La. EC1—4D 25
Peter's Path. EC6—2B 26
Peterstow Clo. SW19—2A 76
Peter St. W1—1F 37
Petherton Rd. N5—2E 11
Petley Rd. W6—2F 47
Peto Pl. NW1—3D 23
Peto St. N. E16—5B 30
Peto St. S. E16—1B 44
Petrie Clo. NW2—3A 6
Petticoat La. E1—4A 26
Petticoat Sq. E1—5B 26
Pettiward Clo. SW15—2E 61
Petty France. SW1—4E 37
Petworth St. SW11—4A 50
Petyt Pl. SW3—2A 50
Petyward. SW3—5A 36
Pevensey Rd. E7—1B 16
Pevensey Rd. SW17—4F 77
Peyton Pl. SE10—3E 57
Phelp St. SE17—2F 53
Phene St. SW3—2A 50
Philbeach Gdns. SW5—1C 48
Philchurch Pl. E1—5C 26
Philippa Gdns. SE9—3F 73
Philip St. E13—3C 30
Philip Wlk. SE15—1C 68
Phillimore Wlk. NW10—5E 5
Phillimore Gdns. W8—3C 34
Phillimore Gdns. Clo. W8
—4C 34
Phillimore Pl. W8—3C 34
Phillimore Wlk. W8—4C 34
Phillipp St. N1—5A 12
Philpot La. EC3—1A 40
Philpot Sq. SW6—1D 63
Philpot St. E1—5D 27
(in two parts)
Phipp's M. SW1—5D 37
Phipp St. EC2—3A 26
Phoebeth Rd. SE4—3C 70
Phoenix Clo. E8—5B 12

Phoenix Pl. WC1—3B 24
Phoenix Rd. NW1—2F 23
Phoenix St. WC2—5F 23
Physic Pl. SW3—2B 50
Piccadilly. W1—2D 37
Piccadilly Cir. W1—1F 37
Pickard St. EC1—2D 25
Pickering M. W2—5D 21
Pickering St. N1—5D 11
Pickets St. SW12—5D 65
Pickwick Rd. SE21—5F 67
Pickwick St. SE1—3E 39
Pickworth Clo. SW8—3A 52
Picton Pl. W1—5C 22
Picton St. SE5—3F 53
Piermont Rd. SE22—3D 69
Pier St. E14—5E 43
Pier Ter. SW18—2D 63
Pigott St. E14—5C 28
Pike Clo. Brom—5D 87
Pilgrimage St. SE1—3F 39
Pilgrim Hill. SE27—4E 81
Pilgrim's La. NW3—1F 7
Pilgrim's Pl. NW3—1F 7
Pilgrim St. EC4—5D 25
Pilkington Rd. SE15—5D 55
Pilsdon Clo. SW19—1F 75
Pimlico Rd. SW1—1C 50
Pimlico Wlk. N1—2A 26
Pinchin St. E1—1C 40
Pindar St. EC2—4A 26
Pindock M. W9—3D 21
Pine Av. E15—2F 15
Pine Dene. SE15—4D 55
Pinefield Clo. E14—1C 42
Pine Gro. SW19—5B 76
Pine Rd. NW2—1E 5
Pine St. EC1—3C 24
Pinfold Rd. SW16—4A 80
Pinkerton Pl. SW16—4F 79
Pinnell Rd. SE9—2F 73
Pinto Way. SE3—2D 73
Pioneer Way. W12—5D 19
Piper Clo. N7—2B 10
Pirbright Rd. SW18—1B 76
Pirie St. E16—2D 45
Pitchford St. E15—4F 15
Pitfield Est. N1—2A 26
Pitfield St. N1—2A 26
Pitfold Clo. SE12—4D 73
Pitfold Rd. SE12—4C 72
Pitman St. SE5—3E 53
Pitsea Pl. E1—5F 27
Pitsea St. E1—5F 27
Pitt Cres. SW19—4D 77
Pitt's Head M. W1—2C 37
Pitt St. SE15—4B 54
Pitt St. W8—3C 34
Pixley St. E14—5B 28

Plaistow Gro. E15—5B 16
Plaistow Pk. Rd. E13—1D 31
Plaistow Rd. E15—5B 16
Plane St. SE26—3D 83
Plane Tree Wlk. SE19—5A 82
Plantain Pl. SE1—3F 39
Plantation. The. SE3—5C 58
Plashet Gro. E6—5E 17
Plashet Rd. E13—5C 16
Plassy Rd. SE6—5D 71
Plato Rd. SW2—2A 66
Platt's La. NW3—1C 6
Platt St. NW1—1F 23
Platt, The. SW15—1F 61
(in two parts)
Playfair St. W6—1E 47
Playfield Cres. SE22—3B 68
Playgreen Way. SE6—3C 84
Playhouse Yd. EC4—5D 25
Pleasance Rd. SW15—3D 61
Pleasance, The. SW15—2D 61
Pleasant Pl. N1—4D 11
Pleasant Row. NW1—5D 9
Plender St. NW1—5E 9
Pleshey Rd. N7—1F 9
Plevna St. E14—4E 43
Pleydell Av. W6—5B 32
Plimsoll Clo. E14—5D 29
Plough Ct. EC3—1F 39
Plough La. SE22—4B 68
Plough La.—5D 77
SW19 2-56 SW17 remainder
Ploughmans Clo. NW1—5F 9
Plough Pl. EC4—5C 24
Plough Rd. SW11—1F 63
Plough Ter. SW11—2F 63
Plough Way. SE16—5F 41
Plough Yd. EC2—3A 26
Plover Way. SE16—4A 42
Plumber's Row. E1—5C 26
Plumbridge St. SE10—4E 57
Plummer Rd. SW4—5F 65
Plumtree Ct. EC4—5D 25
Plymouth Rd. E16—4C 30
Plymouth Wharf. E14—5F 43
Plympton Av. NW6—4B 6
Plympton Pl. NW8—3A 22
Plympton Rd. NW6—4B 6
Plympton St. NW8—3A 22
Pocock St. SE1—3D 39
Podmore Rd. SW18—2C 63
Poets' Corner. SW1—4A 38
Poet's Rd. N5—2F 11
Point Clo. SE10—4E 57
Point Hill. SE10—4E 57
Point Pleasant. SW18—2C 62
Poland St. W1—5E 23
Polebrook Rd. SE3—1E 73

Polecroft La. SE6—2B 84
Pollard Clo. E16—1C 44
Pollard Clo. N7—1B 10
Pollard Row. E2—2C 26
Pollard St. E2—2C 26
Pollen St. W1—5E 23
Pollitt Dri. NW8—3F 21
Polsted Rd. SE6—5B 70
Polworth Rd. SW16—5A 80
Polygon Rd. NW1—1F 23
Polygon, The. SW4—2E 65
Pomell Way. E1—5B 26
Pomeroy St. SE14—3E 55
Pomfret Rd. SE5—1E 67
Pond Clo. SE3—5B 58
Pond Cotts. SE21—1A 82
Ponder St. N7—4B 10
Pondfield Ho. SE27—5E 81
Pond Mead. SE21—4F 67
Pond Pl. SW3—5A 36
Pond Rd. E15—1A 30
Pond Rd. NW3—2A 8
Pond Rd. SE3—5B 58
Ponler St. E1—5D 27
Ponsard Rd. NW10—2D 19
Ponsford St. E9—3E 13
Ponsonby Pl. SW1—1F 51
Ponsonby Rd. SW15—5D 61
Ponsonby Ter. SW1—1F 51
Pontefract Rd. Brom—5B 86
Ponton Rd. SW8—3F 51
Pont St. SW1—4B 36
Pont St. M. SW1—4B 36
Pontypool Pl. SE1—3D 39
Pool Clo. Beck—5C 84
Poole Rd. E9—3F 13
Pooles La. SW10—3E 49
Poole St. N1—5F 11
Poolmans St. SE16—3F 41
Poonah St. E1—5E 27
Pope Clo. SW19—5F 77
Pope's Head All. EC3—5F 25
Pope's Rd. SW9—1C 66
Pppe St. SE1—3A 40
Popham Rd. N1—5E 11
Poplar Bath St. E14—1D 43
Poplar Business Pk. E14
—1E 43
Poplar Ct. SW19—5C 76
Poplar Gro. W6—3E 33
Poplar High St. E14—1D 43
Poplar Pl. W2—1D 35
Poplar Rd. SE24—2E 67
Poplars Av. NW2—3E 5
Poplar Wlk. SE24—2E 67
Poppins Ct. EC4—5D 25
Porchester Clo. SE5—2F 67
Porchester Gdns. W2—1D 35
Porchester Gdns. M. W2—5D 21
Porchester M. W2—5D 21

Porchester Pl. W2—5A 22
Porchester Rd. W2—5D 21
Porchester Sq. W2—5D 21
Porchester Ter. W2—1E 35
Porchester Ter. N. W2—5D 21
Porden Rd. SW2—2B 66
Porlock Ho. SE26—3C 82
Porlock Rd. W10—3F 19
Porlock St. SE1—3F 39
Portal Clo. SE27—3C 80
Portbury Clo. SE15—4C 54
Port Cres. E13—3D 31
Portelet Rd. E1—2F 27
Porten Rd. W14—4A 34
Porter St. W1—4B 22
Porters Wlk. E1—1D 41
Porteus Rd. W2—4E 21
Portgate Clo. W9—3B 20
Porthcawe Rd. SE26—4A 84
Portia Way. E3—3B 28
Portinscale Rd. SW15—3A 62
Portland Gro. SW8—4B 52
Portland M. W1—5E 23
Portland Pl. W1—4D 23
Portland Rd. W11—1A 34
Portland Rd. Brom—4E 87
Portland Sq. E1—2D 41
Portland St. SE17—1F 53
Portman Clo. W1—5C 22
Portman M. S. W1—5C 22
Portman Pl. E2—2E 27
Portman Sq. W1—5C 22
Portman St. W1—5C 22
Portnall Rd. W9—2B 20
Portobello M. W11—1C 34
Portobello Rd.—4A 20
W11 1-275 & 2-262
W10 remainder
Portpool La. EC1—4C 24
Portree St. E14—5F 29
Portsea Pl. W2—5A 22
Portslade Rd. SW8—5E 51
Portsmouth Rd. SW15—5D 61
Portsmouth St. WC2—5B 24
Portsoken St. E1—1B 40
Portswood Pl. SW15—5B 60
Portugal St. WC2—5B 24
Portway. E15—5B 16
Portway Gdns. SE18—3F 50
Post Office App. E7—2D 17
Post Office Way. SW8
—2F 51
Potier St. SE1—4F 39
Potterne Clo. SW19—5F 61
Potters' Fields. SE1—2A 40
Potter's La. SW16—5F 79
Pottery La. W11—2A 34
Pottery St. SE16—3D 41
Pott St. E2—2D 27
Poulner Way. SE15—3B 54

Poulton Clo. E8—3D 13
Poultry. EC2—5F 25
Pound La. NW10—3C 4
Pound Pk. Rd. SE7—5F 45
Pountney Rd. SW11—1C 64
Powell Rd. E5—1D 13
Powell's Wlk. W4—2A 46
Powerscroft Rd. E5—1E 13
Powis Gdns. W11—5B 20
Powis M. W11—5B 20
Powis Pl. WC1—3A 24
Powis Rd. E3—2D 29
Powis Sq. W11—5B 20
Powis Ter. W11—5B 20
Powlett Pl. NW1—4D 9
Pownall Rd. E8—5C 12
Powster Rd. Brom—5C 86
Poynders Gdns. SW4—5E 65
Poynders Rd. SW4—4E 65
Poyntz Rd. SW11—5B 50
Poyser St. E2—1D 27
Praed M. W2—5F 21
Praed St. W2—5F 21
Pragel St. E13—1E 31
Pragnell Rd. SE12—2D 87
Prague Pl. SW2—3A 66
Prairie St. SW8—5D 51
Pratt M. NW1—5E 9
Pratt St. NW1—5E 9
Pratt Wlk. SE11—5B 38
Prebend Gdns.—5B 32
W4 1-37 & 2-40
W6 remainder
Prebend St. N1—5E 11
Prendergast Rd. SE3—1A 72
Prentis Rd. SW16—4F 79
Prentiss Ct. SE7—5F 45
Prescot St. E1—1B 40
Prescott Pl. SW4—2F 65
Presidents Dri. E1—2D 41
Prestbury Rd. E7—4E 17
Prested Rd. SW11—2A 64
Preston Clo. SE1—5A 40
Preston Gdns. NW10—3A 4
Preston Pl. NW2—3C 4
Preston Rd. SE19—5D 81
Preston's Rd. E14—1E 43
Prestwood St. N1—1E 25
Pretoria Rd. E16—3B 30
Pictoria Rd. SW16—5D 79
Price Clo. SW17—3R 78
Price's St. SE1—2D 39
Price's Yd. N1—5B 10
Prideaux Pl. WC1—2B 24
Prideaux Rd. SW9—1A 66
Priestfield Rd. SE23—3A 84
Priests Bri.—1A 60
SW15 2-20
SW14 remainder
Prima Rd. SW9—3C 52

Primrose Clo. SE6—5E 85
Primrose Gdns. NW3—3A 8
Primrose Hill. EC4—5C 24
Primrose Hill Rd. NW3—4B 8
Primrose St. EC2—4A 26
Primula St. W12—5C 18
Prince Albert Rd.—1A 22
  NW1 1-23
  NW8 remainder
Prince Arthur M. NW3—1E 7
Prince Arthur Rd. NW3—2E 7
Prince Charles Rd. SE3—5B 58
Prince Consort Rd. SW7—4F 35
Princedale Rd. W11—2A 34
Prince Edward Rd. E9—3B 14
Prince George Rd. N16—1A 12
Prince Henry Rd. SE7—3F 59
Princelet St. E1—4B 26
Prince of Orange La. SE10
  —3E 57
Prince of Wales Dri. SW11 &
  SW8—4B 50
Prince of Wales Rd. E16—5E 31
Prince of Wales Rd. NW5—3C 8
Prince of Wales Rd. SE3—4B 58
Prince of Wales Ter. W4—5A 32
Prince of Wales Ter. W8—3D 35
Prince Regent La.—2D 31
  E13 1-279 & 2-250
  E16 remainder
Prince's Gdns. SW7—4F 35
Prince's Ga. SW7—3F 35
  (in three parts)
Prince's Ga. Ct. SW7—3F 35
Prince's Ga. M. SW7—4F 35
Princes Pl. W11—2A 34
Prince's Rise. SE13—5E 57
Princess Ct. SE16—4B 42
Princess May Rd. N16—1A 12
Princess M. NW3—2F 7
Prince's Sq. W2—1D 35
Princess Rd. NW1—5C 8
Princess Rd. NW6—1C 20
Princess St. SE1—4D 39
Prince's St. EC2—5F 25
Princes St. W1—5D 23
Prince St. SE8—2B 56
Princes Way. SW19—5F 61
Princethorpe Rd. SE26—4F 83
Princeton St. WC1—4B 24
Pringle Gdns. SW16—4E 79
  (in two parts)
Printer St. EC4—5C 24
Printing Ho. Yd. E2—2A 26
Priolo Rd. SE7—1E 59
Prior Bolton St. N1—3D 11
Prioress Rd. SE27—3D 81

Prioress St. SE1—4A 40
Prior St. SE10—3E 57
Priory Av. W4—5A 32
Priory Ct. SW8—4F 51
Priory Gdns. SW13—1B 60
Priory Gdns. SW4—5A 32
Priory Grn. Est. N1—1B 24
Priory Gro. SW8—4A 52
Priory La. SW15—4A 60
Priory M. SW8—4F 51
Priory Pk. SE3—1B 72
Priory Pk. Rd. NW6—5B 6
Priory Rd. E6—5F 17
Priory Rd. NW6—5D 7
Priory St. E3—2D 29
Priory Ter. NW6—5D 7
Priory, The. SE3—2C 72
Priory Wlk. SW10—1E 49
Pritchard's Rd. E2—1C 26
Priter Rd. SE16—4C 40
Priter Way. SE16—4C 40
Probert Rd. SW2—3C 66
Probyn Rd. SW2—2D 81
Procter St. WC1—4B 24
Promenade App. Rd. W4—3A 46
Promenade, The. W4—4A 46
Prospect Clo. SE26—4D 83
Prospect Cotts. SW18—2C 62
Prospect Pl. E1—2E 41
  (in two parts)
Prospect Pl. NW3—1E 7
Prospect St. SE16—4D 41
Protheroe Rd. SW6—3B 48
Prout Gro. NW10—1A 4
Provence St. N1—1E 25
Providence Ct. W1—1C 36
Providence Pl. N1—5D 11
Provost Est. N1—2F 25
Provost Rd. NW3—4B 8
Provost St. N1—2F 25
Prowse Pl. NW1—4E 9
Prusom St. E1—2D 41
Pudding La. EC3—1F 39
Pudding Mill La. E15—5D 15
Puddle Dock. EC4—1D 39
Pulborough Rd. SW18—5B 62
Pullman Gdns. SW15—4E 61
Pulross Rd. SW9—1B 66
Pulteney Clo. E3—5B 14
Pulteney Ter. N1—5B 10
Pulton Pl. SW6—3C 48
Puma Ct. E1—4B 26
Pump Ct. EC4—5C 24
Pumping Sta. Rd. W4—3A 46
Punderson's Gdns. E2—2D 27
Purbrook St. SE1—4A 40
Purcell Cres. SW6—3A 48
Purcell M. NW10—4A 4
Purcell St. N1—1A 26

Purchese St. NW1—1F 23
Purdy St. E3—3D 29
Purley Pl. N1—4D 11
Purneys Rd. SE9—2F 73
Purser's Cross Rd. SW6—4B 48
Purves Rd. NW10—1D 19
Putney Bri. SW15 & SW6
  —1A 62
Putney Bri. App. SW6—1A 62
Putney Bri. Rd.—2A 62
  SW18 1-73 & 2-114
  SW15 remainder
Putney Comn. SW15—1E 61
Putney Exchange Shopping
  Centre. SW15—2F 61
Putney Heath. SW15—4D 61
Putney Heath La. SW15—4F 61
Putney High St. SW15—2A 62
Putney Hill. SW15—4F 61
Putney Pk. Av. SW15—2C 60
Putney Pk. La. SW15—2D 61
Pymers Mead. SE21—1E 81
Pym Ho. SW9—5C 52
Pyrland Rd. N5—2F 11
Pyrmont Gro. SE27—3D 81
Pytchley Rd. SE22—1A 68

Quadrangle, The. SW10—4E 49
Quadrant Gro. NW5—2B 8
Quaggy Wlk. SE3—2C 72
Quaker St. E1—3B 26
Quarley Way. SE15—3B 54
Quarrendon St. SW6—5C 48
Quarry Rd. SW18—4E 63
Quarterdeck, The. E14—3C 42
Quarter Mile La. E10 & E15
  —1D 15
Quayside Ho. E14—2C 42
Quebec M. W1—5B 22
Quebec Way. SE16—3F 41
Queen Anne M. W1—4D 23
Queen Anne Rd. E9—3F 13
Queen Anne's Gdns. W4—4A 32
Queen Anne's Ga. SW1—3F 37
Queen Anne's Gro. W4—4A 32
Queen Anne St. W1—4D 23
Queen Caroline St. W6—1E 47
Queen Elizabeth Ho. SW12
  —5C 64
Queen Elizabeth St. SE1—3B 40
Queen Elizabeth Wlk. SW13
  —4D 47
Queenhithe. EC4—1E 39
Queen Margaret's Gro. N1
  —2A 12
Queen Mary Rd. SE19—5D 81
Queen of Denmark Ct. SE16
  —4B 42

Queensberry M. W. SW7—5F 35
Queensberry Pl. SW7—5F 35
Queensberry Way. SW7—5F 35
Queensborough M. W2—1E 35
Queensborough Ter. W2—1D 35
Queensbridge Rd.—3B 12
  E2 1-173 & 2-120
  E8 remainder
Queensbury St. N1—4E 11
Queen's Cir. SW8—3D 51
Queen's Club Gdns. W14—2A 48
Queens Ct. SE23—2E 83
Queen's Cres. NW5—3C 8
Queenscroft Rd. SE9—4F 73
Queensdale Cres. W11—2F 33
Queensdale Pl. W11—2A 34
Queensdale Rd. W11—2A 34
Queensdale Wlk. W11—2A 34
Queensdown Rd. E5—1D 13
Queen's Elm Sq. SW3—1F 49
Queen's Gdns. SW1—3E 37
Queen's Gdns. W2—1E 35
Queen's Ga. SW7—4E 35
Queen's Ga. Gdns. SW7—4E 35
Queen's Ga. Gdns. SW15—2D 61
Queen's Ga. M. SW7—4E 35
Queensgate Pl. NW6—4C 6
Queen's Ga. Pl. SW7—4E 35
Queen's Ga. Pl. M. SW7—4E 35
Queen's Ga. Ter. SW7—4E 35
Queen's Gro. NW8—5F 7
Queen's Head St. N1—5D 11
Queensland Pl. N7—1C 10
Queensland Rd. N7—1C 10
Queensmead NW8—5F 7
Queensmere Clo. SW19—2F 75
Queensmere Rd. SW19—2F 75
Queen's M. W2—1D 35
Queensmill Rd. SW6—3F 47
Queens Sq. WC1—3A 24
Queens Ride. SW13 & SW15
  —1C 60
Queens Rd. E13—5D 17
Queen's Rd.—4D 55
  SE15 1-289 & 2-222
  SE14 remainder
Queens Rd. SW19—5C 76
Queens Rd. W. E13—1C 30
Queen's Row. SE17—2F 53
Queens Ter. E1—3E 27
Queen's Ter. E13—5D 17
Queen's Ter. NW8—1F 21
Queensthorpe Rd. SE26—4F 83
Queenstown Rd. SW8—1D 65
Queen St. EC4—1E 39
Queen St. W1—2D 37
Queen St. Pl. EC4—1E 39
Queensville Rd. SW12—5F 65
Queen's Wlk. SW1—2E 37

Queensway. W2—5D 21
Queenswood Ct. SE27—4F 81
Queenswood Rd. SE23—3F 83
Queen Victoria St. EC4—1D 39
Quemerford Rd. N7—2B 10
Quentin Pl. SE13—1A 72
Quentin Rd. SE13—1A 72
Quernmore Rd. Brom—5C 86
Querrin St. SW6—5E 49
Quex M. NW6—5C 6
Quex Rd. NW6—5C 6
Quick Pl. N1—5D 11
Quick Rd. W4—1A 46
Quick St. N1—1D 25
Quickswood. NW3—4A 8
Quill La. SW15—2F 61
Quilp St. SE1—3E 39
Quilter St. E2—2C 26
Quinton St. SW18—2E 77
Quixley St. E14—1F 43
Quorn Rd. SE22—2A 68

Rabbit Row. W8—2C 34
Raby St. E14—5A 28
Racton Rd. SW6—2C 48
Radbourne Clo. E5—1F 13
Radbourne Rd. SW12—5E 65
Radcliffe Av. NW10—1C 18
Radcliffe Sq. SW15—4F 61
Radcot St. SE11—1C 52
Raddington Rd. W10—4A 20
Radford Rd. SE13—4E 71
Radipole Rd. SW6—4B 48
Radland Rd. E16—5B 30
Radlet Av. SE26—2D 83
Radlett Clo. E7—3B 16
Radlett Pl. NW8—5A 8
Radley Ct. SE16—3F 41
Radley M. W8—4D 35
Radnor M. W2—5F 21
Radnor Pl. W2—5A 22
Radnor Rd. NW6—5A 6
Radnor Rd. SE15—3C 54
Radnor St. EC1—2E 25
Radnor Ter. W14—5B 34
Radnor Wlk. SW3—1A 50
Radstock St. SW11—3A 50
Raeburn St. SW2—2A 66
Raglan Ct. SE12—3C 72
Raglan St. NW5—3D 9
Railey M. NW2—2E 5
Railton Rd. SE24—2C 66
Railway App. SE1—2F 39
Railway Av. SE16—3E 41
Railway Gro. SE14—3B 56
Railway M. NW10—5A 20
Railway Rise. SE22—2A 68
Railway Side. SW13—1B 60

Railway St. N1—1A 24
Railway Ter. SE13—3D 71
Rainbow Av. E14—1D 57
Rainbow St. SE5—3A 54
Raine St. E1—2D 41
Rainham Clo. SW11—4A 64
Rainham Rd. NW10—2E 19
Rainhill Way. E3—2D 29
Rainsborough Av. SE8—5A 42
Rainton Rd. SE7—1C 58
Rainville Rd. W6—2E 47
Raleana Rd. E14—2E 43
Raleigh Gdns. SW2—4B 66
Raleigh St. N1—5D 11
Ralston St. SW3—1B 50
Ramac Way. SE7—1D 59
Rambler Clo. SW16—4E 79
Ramilles Clo. SW2—4A 66
Ramillies Pl. W1—5E 23
Ramillies St. W1—5E 23
Rampart St. E1—5D 27
Rampayne St. SW1—1F 51
Ram Pl. E9—3E 13
Ramsay Rd. E7—1A 16
Ramsdale Rd. SW17—5C 78
Ramsden Rd. SW12—4C 64
Ramsey St. E2—3C 26
Ramsey Wlk. N1—3F 11
Ramsgate St. E8—3B 12
Ram St. SW18—3D 63
Randall Clo. SW11—4A 50
Randall Pl. SE10—3E 57
Randall Rd. SE11—5B 38
Randall Row. SE11—5B 38
Randell's Rd. N1—5A 10
Randisbourne Gdns. SE6—3D 85
Randlesdown Rd. SE6—4C 84
Randolph App. E16—5E 31
Randolph Av. W9—2D 21
Randolph Cres. W9—3E 21
Randolph Gdns. NW6—1D 21
Randolph M. W9—3E 21
Randolph Rd. W9—3E 21
Randolph St. NW1—4E 9
Ranelagh Av. SW6—1B 62
Ranelagh Av. SW13—5C 46
Ranelagh Bri. W2—4D 21
Ranelagh Gdns. SW6—1A 62
Ranelagh Gdns. W6—4B 32
Ranelagh Gro. SW1—1C 50
Ranelagh Rd. E11—1A 16
Ranelagh Rd. E15—1A 30
Ranelagh Rd. NW10—1B 18
Ranelagh Rd. SW1—1E 51
Rangefield Rd. Brom—5A 86
Rangers Sq. SE10—4F 57
Ranmere St. SW12—1D 79
Rannoch Rd. W6—2E 47
Ransom Rd. SE7—1E 59

Ransom Wlk. SE7—5E 45
Ranston St. NW1—4A 22
Ranulf Rd. NW2—1B 6
Ranwell Clo. E3—5B 14
Raphael St. SW7—3B 36
Rashleigh St. SW8—1D 65
Rastell Av. SW2—1F 79
Ratcliffe Cross St. E1—5F 27
Ratcliffe La. E14—5A 28
Ratcliffe Orchard. E1—1F 41
Ratcliff Gro. EC1—2E 25
Ratcliff Rd. E7—2E 17
Rathbone Pl. W1—5F 23
Rathbone St. E16—5B 30
Rathbone St. W1—4E 23
Rathfern Rd. SE6—1B 84
Rathgar Rd. SW9—1D 67
Rathmell Dri. SW4—4F 65
Rathmore Rd. SE7—1D 59
Rattray Rd. SW2—2C 66
Raul Rd. SE15—5C 54
Raveley St. NW5—1E 9
Ravenet St. SW11—4D 51
Ravenfield Rd. SW17—3B 78
Ravenhill Rd. E13—1E 31
Ravenna Rd. SW15—3F 61
Raven Row. E1—4D 27
Ravensbourne Pk. SE6—5C 70
Ravensbourne Pk. Cres. SE6
—5B 70
Ravensbourne Pl. SE13—5D 57
Ravensbourne Rd. SE6—5B 70
Ravensbury Rd. SW18—2D 77
Ravensbury Ter. SW18—1D 77
Ravenscar Rd. Brom—4A 86
Ravenscourt Av. W6—5C 32
Ravenscourt Gdns. W6—5C 32
Ravenscourt Pk. W6—5C 32
Ravenscourt Pl. W6—5D 33
Ravenscourt Rd. W6—5D 33
Ravenscourt Sq. W6—4C 32
Ravenscroft Clo. E16—4C 30
Ravenscroft Rd. E16—4C 30
Ravenscroft St. E2—1B 26
Ravensdon St. SE11—1C 52
Ravenshaw St. NW6—2B 6
Ravenslea Rd. SW12—5B 64
Ravensmede Way. W4—5B 32
Ravens M. SE12—3C 72
Ravenstone St. SW12—1C 78
Ravens Way. SE12—3C 72
Ravenswood Rd. SW12—5D 65
Ravensworth Rd. NW10
—2D 19
Ravent Rd. SE11—5B 38
Ravey St. EC2—3A 26
Rawchester Clo. SW18—1B 76
Rawlings St. SW3—5B 36
Rawson St. SW11—4C 50

Rawstone Wlk. E13—1C 30
Rawstorne Pl. EC1—2D 25
Rawstorne St. EC1—2D 25
Rayford Av. SE12—5B 72
Raymond Bldgs. WC1—4B 24
Raymond Clo. SE26—5E 83
Raymond Rd. E13—5E 17
Raymond Rd. SW19—5A 76
Raymouth Rd. SE16—5D 41
Rayners Rd. SW15—3A 62
Raynham Rd. W6—5D 33
Raynor Pl. N1—4E 11
Ray St. EC1—3C 24
Reachview Clo. NW1—4E 9
Reade Wlk. NW10—4A 4
Reading La. E8—3D 13
Reapers Clo. NW1—5F 9
Reardon Path. E1—2D 41
Reardon St. E1—2D 41
Reaston St. SE14—3F 55
Rebecca Ter. SE16—4E 41
Reckitt Rd. W4—1A 46
Record St. SE15—2E 55
Recovery St. SW17—5A 78
Recreation Rd. SE26—4F 83
Rector St. N1—5E 11
Rectory Field Cres. SE7—3E 59
Rectory Gdns. SW4—1E 65
Rectory Gro. SW4—1E 65
Rectory La. SW17—5C 78
Rectory Orchard. SW19—4A 76
Rectory Rd. N16—1C 12
Rectory Rd. SW13—5C 46
Rectory Sq. E1—4F 27
Reculver Rd. SE16—1F 55
Red Anchor Clo. SW3—2F 49
Redan Pl. W2—5D 21
Redan St. W14—4F 33
Redan Ter. SE5—5D 53
Redberry Gro. SE26—3E 83
Redbridge Gdns. SE5—3A 54
Redburn St. SW3—2B 50
Redcar St. SE5—3F 53
Redcastle Clo. E1—1E 41
Redchurch St. E2—3B 26
Redcliffe Gdns. SW10—1D 49
Redcliffe M. SW10—1D 49
Redcliffe Pl. SW10—2E 49
Redcliffe Rd. SW10—2E 49
Redcliffe Sq. SW10—1D 49
Redcliffe St. SW10—2D 49
Redclyffe Rd. E6—5E 17
Redcross Way. SE1—3E 39
Reddins Rd. SE15—3C 54
Rede Pl. W2—5C 20
Redesdale St. SW3—2B 50
Redfern Rd. NW10—4A 4
Redfern Rd. SE6—5E 71
Redfield La. SW5—5C 34

Redgate Ter. SW15—4F 61
Redgrave Rd. SW15—1F 61
Redhill Ct. SW2—2C 80
Redhill St. NW1—1D 23
Redington Gdns. NW3—1D 7
Redington Rd. NW3—1D 7
Redlands Way. SW2—5B 66
Redlaw Way. SE16—1C 54
Red Lion Ct. EC4—5C 24
Red Lion Sq. WC1—4B 24
Red Lion St. WC1—4B 24
Red Lion Way. SE17—2E 53
Redman's Rd. E1—4E 27
Redmead La. E1—2C 40
Redmore Rd. W6—5D 33
Red Path. E9—3B 14
Red Pl. W1—1C 36
Red Post Hill—2F 67
  SE21 1-9 & 2-12
  SE24 remainder
Redriffe Rd. E13—5B 16
Redriff Rd. SE16—4F 41
Redruth Rd. E9—5E 13
Redstart Clo. SE14—3A 56
Redvers St. N1—2A 26
Redwald Rd. E5—1F 13
Redwood Clo. SE16—2A 42
Redwoods. SW15—1C 74
Reece M. SW7—5F 35
Reed Clo. E16—4C 30
Reed Clo. SE12—3C 72
Reedham St. SE15—1C 68
Reedholm Vs. N16—1F 11
Reed's Pl. NW1—4E 9
Reedworth St. SE11—5C 38
Rees St. N1—5E 11
Reeves M. W1—1C 36
Reform St. SW11—5B 50
Regal Clo. E1—4C 26
Regal La. NW1—5C 8
Regan Way. N1—1A 26
Regency Pl. SW7—5F 37
Regency St. SW1—5F 37
Regent Pl. W1—1E 37
Regent Rd. SE24—3D 67
Regent's Bri. Gdns. SW8—3A 52
Regents M. NW8—1E 21
Regent's Pk. Gdns. M. NW1
—5C 8
Regent's Pk. Rd. NW1—5B 8
Regent's Pk. Ter. NW1—5D 9
Regent's Pl. SE3—5C 58
Regent Sq. E3—2D 29
Regent Sq. WC1—2A 24
Regent's Row. E8—5C 12
Regent St. NW10—2F 19
Regent St.—
  SW1 1-37 & 2-36
  W1 remainder

Reginald Rd. E7—3C 16
Reginald Rd. SE8—3C 56
Reginald Sq. SE8—3C 56
Regis Rd. NW5—2D 9
Reigate Rd. Brom—3B 86
Relay Rd. W12—2E 33
Relf Rd. SE15—1C 68
Relton M. SW7—4A 36
Rembrandt Clo. E14—4E 43
Rembrandt Rd. SE13—2A 72
Remington St. N1—1D 25
Remnant St. WC2—5B 24
Rempstone M. N1—1F 25
Remus Rd. E3—4C 14
Rendlesham Rd. E5—1C 12
Renforth St. SE16—3E 41
Renfrew Rd. SE11—5D 39
Renmuir St. SW17—5B 78
Rennell St. SE13—1E 71
Rennie Est. SE16—5D 41
Rennie St. SE1—2D 39
Rephidim St. SE1—4A 40
Replingham Rd. SW18—1B 76
Reporton Rd. SW6—3A 48
Repton St. E14—5A 28
Reservoir Rd. SE4—5A 56
Restell Clo. SE3—2A 58
Reston Pl. SW7—3E 35
Retford St. N1—1A 26
Retreat Pl. E9—3E 13
Retreat, The. SW14—1A 60
Reveley Sq. SE16—3A 42
Revelon Rd. SE4—1A 70
Revelstoke Rd. SW18—2B 76
Reverdy Rd. SE1—5C 40
Rewell St. SW6—3E 49
Rex Pl. W1—1C 36
Reynold's Pl. SE3—3D 59
Reynolds Rd. SE15—2E 69
Rheidol M. N1—1E 25
Rheidol Ter. N1—5E 11
Rhoda St. E2—3B 26
Rhodes St. N7—2B 10
Rhodeswell Rd. E14—5B 28
Rhondda Gro. E3—2A 28
Rhyl St. NW5—3C 8
Ribblesdale Rd. SW16—5D 79
Ricardo St. E14—5D 29
Ricards Rd. SW19—5B 76
Richardson Clo. E8—5B 12
Richardson Rd. E15—1A 30
Richard's Pl. SW3—5A 36
Richard St. E1—5D 27
(in two parts)
Richbell Pl. WC1—4B 24
Richborne Ter. SW8—3B 52
Richborough Rd. NW2—1A 6
Richford Rd. E15—5B 16

Richford St. W6—3E 33
Rich La. SW5—1D 49
Richmond Av. N1—5B 10
Richmond Av. NW10—3E 5
Richmond Bldgs. W1—5F 23
Richmond Cres. N1—5C 10
Richmond Gro. N1—4D 11
Richmond M. W1—5F 23
Richmond Rd. E7—2D 17
Richmond Rd. E8—4B 12
Richmond St. E13—1C 30
Richmond Ter. SW1—3A 38
Richmond Ter. M. SW1—3A 38
Richmond Way—3F 33
  W12 1-15 & 2-52
  W14 remainder
Richmount Gdns. SE3—1C 72
Rich St. E14—1B 42
Rickard Clo. SW2—1C 80
Rickett St. SW6—2C 48
Rickman St. E1—3E 27
Riddons Rd. SE12—3A 87
Ridgebrook Rd. SE3—1F 73
Ridgdale St. E3—1D 29
Ridgeway. SE19—5A 82
Ridgeway Dri. Brom—5D 87
Ridgewell Clo. N1—5E 11
Ridgmount Gdns. WC1—4F 23
Ridgmount Pl. WC1—4F 23
Ridgmount Rd. SW18—3D 63
Ridgmount St. WC1—4F 23
Ridgway. SW19—5A 76
Ridgway Pl. SW19—5A 76
Ridgway Rd. SW9—1D 67
Ridgwell Rd. E16—4E 31
Riding Ho. St. W1—4E 23
Ridley Rd. E7—1E 17
Ridley Rd. E8—2B 12
Ridley Rd. NW10—1C 18
Ridley Several. SE3—5C 58
Riffel Rd. NW2—2E 5
Rifle Ct. SE11—2C 52
Rifle St. E14—4D 29
Rigault Rd. SW6—5A 48
Rigden St. E14—5D 29
Rigeley Rd. NW10—2C 18
Rigge Pl. SW4—2F 65
Riggindale Rd. SW16—5F 79
Riley Rd. SE1—4B 40
Riley St. SW10—3F 49
Rinaldo Rd. SW12—5D 65
Ringcroft St. N7—2C 10
Ringford Rd. SW18—3B 62
Ringmer Av. SW6—4A 48
Ringmore Rise. SE23—5D 69
Ringstead Rd. SE6—5D 71
Ring, The. W2—2A 36
Ringwood Gdns. SW15—1C 74

Ripley Rd. E16—5E 31
Ripplevale Gro. N1—4B 10
Risborough St. SE1—3D 39
Risdon St. SE16—3E 41
Riseholme St. E9—3B 14
Riseldine Rd. SE23—4A 70
Risinghill St. N1—1C 24
Rita Rd. SW8—2A 52
Ritchie St. N1—1C 24
Ritherdon Rd. SW17—2C 78
Ritson Rd. E8—3C 12
Rivaz Pl. E9—3E 13
River Barge Clo. E14—3E 43
Rivercourt Rd. W6—5D 33
Riverdale. SE13—1E 71
River Ho. SE26—3D 83
Rivermead Ct. SW6—1B 62
River Pk. Trading Est. E14
  —4C 42
River Pl. N1—4E 11
Riverside. SE7—4E 45
Riverside Business Centre. SW18
  —1D 77
Riverside Ct. SW8—2F 51
Riverside Gdns. W6—1E 47
Riverside Rd. E15—1E 29
Riverside Rd. SW17—4D 77
Riverside Wlk. SE1—2B 38
  (Lambeth)
Riverside Wlk. SE1—2D 39
  (Southwark)
Riverside Wlk. SE10—4A 44
River St. EC1—2C 24
River Ter. W6—1E 47
Riverton Clo. W9—2B 20
Riverview Gdns. SW13—2D 47
Riverview Pk. SE6—2C 84
River Way. SE10—4B 44
Rivington Bldgs. EC2—2A 26
Rivington Ct. NW10—5C 4
Rivington Pl. EC2—2A 26
Rivington St. EC2—2A 26
Rivington Wlk. E8—5C 12
Roach St. E3—4C 14
Roan St. SE10—3D 57
Robert Adam St. W1—5C 22
Roberta St. E2—2C 26
Robert Clo. W9—3E 21
Robert Dashwood Way. SE17
  —5E 39
Robert Keen Clo. SE15—4C 54
Robert Lowe Clo. SE14—3F 55
Roberts M. SW1—4C 36
Robertson Rd. E15—5E 15
Robertson St. SW8—1D 65
Roberts Pl. EC1—3C 24
Robert St. NW1—2D 23
Robert St. WC2—1A 38

Robeson St. E3—4B 28
Robin Ct. SE16—5C 40
Robin Hood La. E14—1E 43
Robin Hood La. SW15—4A 74
Robin Hood Rd. SW19—5C 74
Robin Hood Way. Rich & SW20
—3A 74
Robins Ct. SE12—3E 87
Robinson Rd. E2—1F 27
Robinson St. SW19—5A 78
Robinson St. SW3—2B 50
Robsart St. SW9—5C 52
Robson Av. NW10—5C 4
Robson Rd. SE27—3E 81
Rochdale Way. SE8—3C 56
Rochelle Clo. SW11—2F 63
Rochelle St. E2—2B 26
(in two parts)
Rochester Av. E13—5E 17
Rochester Clo. SE3—1E 73
Rochester M. NW1—4E 9
Rochester Pl. NW1—3E 9
(in two parts)
Rochester Rd. NW1—3E 9
Rochester Row. SW1—5E 37
Rochester Sq. NW1—4E 9
Rochester St. SW1—5F 37
Rochester Ter. NW1—3E 9
Rochester Way.—4D 59
    SE3 1-325 & 2-364
    SE9 remainder
Rochford Clo. E6—1F 31
Rochford Wlk. E8—4C 12
Rockbourne Rd. SE23—1F 83
Rockell's Pl. SE22—4D 69
Rockhall Rd. NW2—1F 5
Rockhampton Clo. SE27—4C 80
Rockhampton Rd. SE27—4C 80
Rock Hill. SE26—4B 82
Rockingham Clo. SW15—2B 60
Rockingham St. SE1—4E 39
Rockland Rd. SW15—2A 62
Rockley Rd. W14—3F 33
Rocks La. SW13—1C 60
Rockwells Gdns. SE19—5A 82
Rockwood Pl. W12—3E 33
Rocliffe St. N1—1D 25
Rocombe Cres. SE23—5E 69
Rocque La. SE3—1B 72
Rodenhurst Rd. SW4—4E 65
Roderick Rd. NW3—1B 8
Roding M. E1—2C 40
Roding Rd. E5—1F 13
Rodmarton St. W1—4B 22
Rodmere St. SE10—1A 58
Rodmill La. SW2—5A 66
Rodney Pl. SE17—5E 39
Rodney Rd. SE17—5F 39

Rodney St. N1—1B 24
Rodsley St. SE1—2C 54
Rodway Rd. SW15—5C 60
Rodwell Rd. SE22—4B 68
Roedean Cres. SW15—4A 60
Roehampton Clo. SW15—2C 60
Roehampton Ga. SW15—4A 60
Roehampton High St. SW15
—5C 60
Roehampton La. SW15—2C 60
Roehampton Vale. SW15
—3B 74
Roffey St. E14—3E 43
Rogers Rd. E16—5B 30
Rogers Rd. SW17—4F 77
Roger St. WC1—3B 24
Rojack Rd. SE23—1F 83
Rokeby Rd. SE4—5B 56
Rokeby St. E15—5A 16
Roland Gdns. SW7—1E 49
Roland M. E1—4F 27
Roland Way. SE17—1F 53
Roland Way. SW7—1E 49
Rollins St. SE15—2E 55
Rollit St. N7—2C 10
Rolls Bldgs. EC4—5C 24
Rollscourt Av. SE24—3E 67
Rolls Rd. SE1—1B 54
Rolt St. SE8—2A 56
Roman Rise. SE19—5F 81
Roman Rd.—2E 27
    E2 1-229 & 2-256
    E3 remainder
Roman Rd. W4—5B 32
Roman Way. N7—3B 10
Roman Way. SE15—3E 55
Roma Read Clo. SW15—5D 61
Romberg Rd. SW17—3C 78
Romborough Gdns. SE13
—3E 71
Romborough Way. SE13—3B 71
Romero Clo. SW9—1B 66
Romero Sq. SE3—2E 73
Romeyn Rd. SW16—3B 80
Romford Rd.—3A 16
    E15 1-191 & 2-166a
    E7 193-607 & 168-544
    E12 remainder
Romilly St. W1—1F 37
Romilly Ct. SW6—5B 48
Rommany Rd. SE27—4F 81
Romney Clo. SE14—3E 55
Romney Rd. SE10—2F 57
Romney St. SW1—4A 38
Romola Rd. SE24—1D 81
Ronald Av. E15—2A 30
Ronalds Rd. N5—2C 10
Ronald St. E1—5E 27

Rona Rd. NW3—1C 8
Rondu Rd. NW2—2A 6
Ronver Rd. SE12—1B 86
Rood La. EC3—1A 40
Rookery Rd. SW4—2E 65
Rooke Way. SE10—1B 58
Rookstone Rd. SW17—5B 78
Ropemaker Rd. SE16—4A 42
Ropemakers' Fields. E14
—1B 42
Ropemaker St. EC2—4F 25
Roper La. SE1—3A 40
Ropers Wlk. SW2—5C 66
Ropery St. E3—3B 28
Rope St. SE16—5A 42
Rope Wlk. Gdns. E1—5C 26
Ropley St. E2—1C 26
Rosa Alba M. N5—1E 11
Rosaline Rd. SW6—3A 48
Rosamond St. SE26—3D 83
Rosary Gdns. SW7—5E 35
Rosaville Rd. SW6—3B 48
Roscoe St. EC1—3E 25
Rose All. SE1—2E 39
Rose & Crown Yd. SW1—2E 37
Rosebank Gdns. E3—1B 28
Rosebank Wlk. NW1—4F 9
Roseberry Pl. E8—3B 12
Roseberry St. SE16—5D 41
Rosebery Av. EC1—3C 24
Rosebery Rd. SW2—4A 66
Rosebury Rd. SW6—5D 49
Rosedale Ct. N5—1D 11
Rosedale Rd. E7—2E 17
Rosedale Rd. SE21—1E 81
Rosedene Av. SW16—3B 80
Rosedew Rd. W6—2F 47
Rosefield Gdns. E14—1C 42
Rosehart M. SW18—5C 20
Rosehill Rd. SW18—4E 63
Roseleigh Av. N5—1D 11
Rosemary Rd. SE15—3B 54
Rosemary Rd. SW17—3E 77
Rosemary St. N1—5F 11
Rosemont Rd. NW3—3E 7
Rosemoor St. SW3—5B 36
Rosenau Cres. SW11—4B 50
Rosenau Rd. SW11—4A 50
Rosendale Rd.—5E 67
    SE21 1-245 & 2-248
    SE24 remainder
Roseneath Rd. SW11—4C 64
Rosenthal Rd. SE6—4D 71
Rosenthorpe Rd. SE15—3F 69
Roserton St. E14—3E 43
Rose St. WC2—1A 38
Rosethorn Clo. SW12—5F 65
Rosetta Clo. SW8—3A 52

Roseveare Rd. SE12—4E 87
Rose Way. SE12—3C 72
Roseway. SE21—4F 67
Rosewood Gdns. SE13—5E 57
Rosewood Sq. W12—5C 18
Rosher Clo. E15—4F 15
Rosina St. E9—3F 13
Roskell Rd. SW15—1F 61
Roslin Way. Brom—5C 86
Rosmead Rd. W11—1A 34
Rosoman Pl. EC1—3C 24
Rosoman St. EC1—2C 24
Rossdale Rd. SW15—2E 61
Rossedale Way. NW1—4E 9
Rosse M. SE3—4D 59
Rossiter Rd. SW12—1D 79
Rosslyn Av. SW13—1A 60
Rosslyn Hill. NW3—1F 7
Rosslyn M. NW3—1F 7
Rosslyn Pk. M. NW3—2F 7
Rossmore Rd. NW1—3A 22
Rostella Rd. SW17—4F 77
Rostrevor M. SW6—4B 48
Rostrevor Rd. SW6—4B 48
Rostrevor Rd. SW19—5C 76
Rotary St. SE1—4D 39
Rothbury Rd. E9—4B 14
Rotherfield St. N1—4E 11
Rotherhithe New Rd. SE16
—1D 55
Rotherhithe Old Rd. SE16
—5F 41
Rotherhithe St. SE16—3E 41
Rotherhithe Tunnel. SE16
—3E 41
Rotherwood Rd. SW15—1F 61
Rothsay Rd. E7—4E 17
Rothsay St. SE1—4A 40
Rothschild St. SE27—4D 81
Rothwell St. NW1—5B 8
Rotterdam Dri. E14—4E 43
Rouel Rd. SE16—4C 40
Roundacre. SW19—2F 75
Roundhay Clo. SE23—2F 83
Round Hill. SE26—3E 83
Roundtable Rd. Brom—3B 86
Roundwood Rd. NW10—3B 4
Rounton Rd. E3—3C 28
Roupell Rd. SW2—1B 80
Roupell St. SE1—2C 38
Rousden St. NW1—4E 9
Rouse Gdns. SE21—4A 82
Routh Rd. SW18—5A 64
Rovel Rd. SE16—5C 40
Rowallan Rd. SW6—3A 48
Rowan Rd. W6—5F 33
Rowan Wlk. W10—3A 20
Rowberry Clo. SW6—3E 47

Rowcross St. SE1—1B 54
Rowditch La. SW11—5C 50
Rowdon Av. NW10—4D 5
Rowe La. E9—2E 13
Rowena Cres. SW11—5A 50
Rowfant Rd. SW17—1C 78
Rowhill Rd. E5—1D 13
Rowington Clo. W2—4D 21
Rowland Ct. E16—3B 30
Rowland Gro. SE26—3D 83
Rowland Hill St. NW3—2A 8
Rowley Way. NW8—5D 7
Rowse Clo. E15—5E 15
Rowstock Gdns. N7—2F 9
Roxburgh Rd. SE27—5D 81
Roxby Pl. SW6—2C 48
Roxley Rd. SE13—4D 71
Roxwell Rd. W12—3C 32
Royal Albert Dock Spine Rd. E16
—1F 45
Royal Av. SW3—1B 50
Royal Cir. SE27—3C 80
Royal College St. NW1—4E 9
Royal Ct. SE16—4B 42
Royal Cres. W11—2F 33
Royal Cres. M. W11—2F 33
Royal Hill. SE10—3E 57
Royal Hospital Rd. SW3—2B 50
Royal Mint St. E1—1B 40
Royal Mint St. E1—1B 40
Royal Naval Pl. SE14—3B 56
Royal Oak Pl. SE22—4D 69
Royal Oak Rd. E8—3D 13
Royal Opera Arc. SW1—2F 37
Royal Pde. SE3—5B 58
Royal Pde. SW6—3A 48
Royal Pl. SE10—3E 57
Royal Rd. E16—5E 31
Royal Rd. SE17—2D 53
Royal St. SE1—4B 38
Royal Victoria Patriotic
Building. SW18—4F 63
Royal Victor Pl. E3—1F 27
Roycroft Clo. SW2—1C 80
Roy Sq. E14—1B 42
Royston Ct. SE24—4E 67
Royston St. E2—1E 27
Rozel Rd. SW4—1E 65
(in two parts)
Rubens St. SE6—2B 84
Ruby St. SE15—2D 55
Ruby Triangle. SE15—2D 55
Ruckholt Rd. E10—1D 15
Rucklidge Av. NW10—1B 18
Rudall Cres. NW3—1F 7
Rudloe Rd. SW12—5E 65
Rudolf Rd. E13—1B 30
Rudolph Rd. NW6—1C 20

Rufford St. N1—5A 10
Rufus St. N1—2A 26
Rugby Rd. W4—3A 32
Rugby St. WC1—3B 24
Rugg St. E14—1C 42
Ruislip St. SW17—4B 78
Rumbold Rd. SW6—3D 49
Rum Clo. E1—1E 41
Rumsey Rd. SW9—1B 66
Runcorn Pl. W11—1C 74
Runnymede Ct. SW15—1C 74
Rupack St. SE16—3E 41
Rupert Ct. W1—1F 37
Rupert Gdns. SW9—5D 53
Rupert Rd. NW6—1B 20
Rupert Rd. W4—4A 32
Rupert St. W1—1F 37
Ruscoe Rd. E16—5B 30
Rusham Rd. SW12—4B 64
Rushcroft Rd. SW2—2C 66
Rushey Grn. SE6—5D 71
Rushey Mead. SE4—3C 70
Rushford Rd. SE4—4B 70
Rush Hill Rd. SW11—1C 64
Rushmead. E2—2D 27
Rushmore Rd. E5—1E 13
Rusholme Gro. SE19—5A 82
Rusholme Rd. SW15—4F 61
Rushton St. N1—1F 25
Ruskin St. SE1—3D 39
Ruskin Pk. Ho. SE5—1F 67
Ruskin Wlk. SE24—3E 67
Russell Clo. SE7—3E 59
Russell Gdns. W14—4A 34
Russell Gdns. M. W14—4A 34
Russell Gro. SW9—3C 52
Russell Pl. NW3—2A 8
Russell Pl. SE16—4A 42
Russell Rd. E16—5C 30
Russell Rd. W14—4A 34
Russell's Footpath. SW16
—5A 80
Russell Sq. WC1—4A 24
Russell St. WC2—1A 38
Russet Cres. N7—2B 10
Russett Way. SE13—5D 57
Russia Dock Rd. SE16—2A 42
Russia La. E2—1E 27
Russia Row. EC2—5E 25
Russia Wlk. SE16—3A 42
Ruston M. W11—5A 20
Ruston St. E3—5B 14
Rust Sq. SE5—3F 53
Rutford Rd. SW16—5A 80
Ruth Ct. E3—1A 28
Rutherford St. SW1—5F 37
Ruthin Rd. SE3—2C 58
Ruthven St. E9—5F 13

Rutland Gdns. SW7—3A 36
Rutland Gdns. M. SW7—3A 36
Rutland Ga. SW7—3A 36
Rutland Gro. W6—1D 47
Rutland M. NW8—5D 7
Rutland Pk. NW2—2E 5
Rutland Pk. SE6—2B 84
Rutland Pl. EC1—4D 25
Rutland Rd. E7—4F 17
Rutland Rd. E9—5F 13
Rutland St. SW7—4A 36
Rutland Wlk. SE6—2B 84
Rutley Clo. SE17—2D 53
Rutt's Ter. SE14—4F 55
Ruvigny Gdns. SW15—1F 61
Ryan Clo. SE3—2E 73
Rycott Path. SE22—5C 68
Ryculf Sq. SE3—5B 58
Rydal Gdns. SW15—5A 74
Rydal Rd. SW16—4F 79
Ryder Clo. Brom—5D 87
Ryders Ter. NW8—1E 21
Ryder St. SW1—2E 37
Ryder Yd. SW1—2E 37
Ryde Vale Rd. SW12—2E 79
Rydon St. N1—5E 11
Rydston Clo. N7—4A 10
Ryecotes Mead. SE21—1A 82
Ryecroft Rd. SE13—3E 71
Ryecroft Rd. SW16—5C 80
Ryecroft St. SW6—4D 49
Ryedale. SE22—4D 69
Ryefield Path. SW15—1C 74
Rye Hill Pk. SE15—2E 69
Ryelands Cres. SE12—4E 73
Rye La. SE15—5C 54
Rye Pas. SE15—1C 68
Rye Rd. SE15—2F 69
Rye Wlk. SW15—3F 61
Ryfold Rd. SW19—3C 76
Ryland Rd. NW5—3D 9
Rylett Cres. W12—4B 32
Rylett Rd. W12—3B 32
Rylston Rd. SW6—2B 48
Rymer St. SE24—4D 67
Rysbrack St. SW3—4B 36

Sabbarton St. E16—5B 30
Sabella Ct. E3—1B 28
Sabine Rd. SW11—1B 64
Sable St. N1—4D 11
Sackville St. W1—1E 37
Sackville Way. SE22—1C 82
Saffron Hill. EC1—4C 24
Saffron St. EC1—4C 24
Sage St. E1—1E 41
Saigasso Clo. E16—5F 31

Sail St. SE11—5B 38
Sainfoin Rd. SW17—2C 78
Sainsbury Rd. SE19—5A 82
St Agnes Clo. E9—5E 13
St Agnes Pl. SE11—2D 53
St Aidan's Rd. SE22—4D 69
St Alban's Gro. W8—4D 35
St Alban's M. W2—4F 21
St Alban's Pl. N1—5D 11
St Albans Rd. NW10—5A 4
St Alban's St. SW1—1F 37
St Alban's Ter. W6—2A 48
St Alfege Pas. SE10—2E 57
St Alfege Rd. SE7—2F 59
St Alphage Garden. EC2—4E 25
St Alphonsus Rd. SW4—2E 65
St Amunds Clo. SE6—4C 84
St Andrew's Ct. SW18—2E 77
St Andrew's Hill. EC4—5D 25
St Andrew's M. SE3—3C 58
St Andrew's Pl. NW1—3D 23
St Andrew's Rd. E13—2D 31
St Andrew's Rd. NW10—3D 5
St Andrew's Rd. W3—1A 32
St Andrew's Rd. W14—2A 48
St Andrew's Sq. W11—5A 20
St Andrew St. EC4—4C 24
St Anne's Ct. W1—5F 23
St Anne's Pas. E14—5B 28
St Anne's Row. E14—5B 28
St Anne St. E14—5B 28
St Ann's Cres. SW18—4E 63
St Ann's Gdns. NW5—3C 8
St Ann's Hill. SW18—4D 63
St Ann's La. SW1—4F 37
St Ann's Pk. Rd. SW18—4E 63
St Ann's Pas. SW13—1A 60
St Ann's Rd. SW13—5B 46
St Ann's Rd. W11—1F 33
St Ann's St. SW1—4F 37
St Ann's Ter. NW8—1F 21
St Ann's Vs. W11—2F 33
St Anselm's Pl. W1—1D 37
St Anthony's Clo. E1—2C 40
St Anthony's Clo. SW17—2A 78
St Antony's Rd. E7—4D 17
St Asaph Rd. SE4—1F 69
St Aubyn's Av. SW19—5B 76
St Augustine's Rd. NW1—4F 9
St Austell Rd. SE13—5E 57
St Barnabas Clo. SE22—1C 50
St Barnabas Ter. E9—2F 13
St Barnabas Vs. SW8—4A 52
St Bartholomew's Clo. SE26
—4E 83
St Benedict's Clo. SW17—5C 78
St Benet's Clo. SW17—2A 78
St Benet's Pl. EC3—1A 40

St Bernard's Clo. SE27—4F 81
St Bernard's Rd. E6—5F 17
St Botolph Row. EC3—5B 26
St Botolph St. EC3—5B 26
St Bride St. EC4—5D 25
St Catherine's Clo. SW17
—2A 78
St Catherine's Dri. SE14—5F 55
St Catherines M. SW3—5B 36
St Chad's Pl. WC1—2B 24
St Chad's St. WC1—2A 24
St Charles Pl. W10—4A 20
St Charles Sq. W10—4A 20
St Christopher's Pl. W1—5C 22
St Clair Rd. E13—1D 31
St Clare St. EC3—5B 26
St Clements Ct. N7—3B 10
St Clement's Heights. SE26
—3C 82
St Clement's La. WC2—5B 24
St Clement St. N7—4C 10
St Cloud Rd. SE27—4E 81
St Crispin Clo. NW3—1A 8
St Cross St. EC1—4C 24
St Cuthbert's Rd. NW2—3B 6
St Cuthbert's Wlk. NW6—3B 6
St Cyprian's St. SW17—4B 78
St Denis Rd. SE27—4F 81
St Dionis Rd. SW6—5B 48
St Donatt's Rd. SE14—4B 56
St Dunstan's Ct. EC4—5C 24
St Dunstan's Hill. EC3—1A 40
St Dunstan's La. EC3—1A 40
St Dunstan's Rd. E7—3E 17
St Dunstan's Rd. W6—1F 47
St Edmund's Clo. NW8—5B 8
St Edmund's Clo. SW17—2A 78
St Edmund's Ter. NW8—5A 8
St Elmo Rd. W12—3B 32
St Elmos Rd. SE16—3A 42
St Ervan's Rd. W10—4B 20
St Faith's Rd. SE21—1D 81
St Fillans Rd. SE6—1E 85
St Francis Rd. SE22—2A 68
St Gabriel's Rd. NW2—2F 5
St George's Av. E7—4D 17
St George's Av. N7—1F 9
St George's Bldgs. SE11—3E 39
St George's Cir. SE1—4D 39
St George's Dri. SW1—5D 37
St George's Fields. W2—5A 22
St George's Gro. SW17—3F 77
St George's M. NW1—4B 8
St George's Rd. E7—4D 17
St George's Rd. SE1—4D 39
St George's Sq. E7—4D 17
St Georges Sq. E14—1A 42
St Georges Sq. SE8—5B 42

St George's Sq. SW1—1F 51
St George's Sq. M. SW1—1F 51
St George's Ter. NW1—4B 8
St George St. W1—1D 37
St George's Way. SE15—2A 54
St Gerard's Clo. SW4—3E 65
St German's Pl. SE3—4C 58
St German's Rd. SE23—1A 84
St Giles Cir. W1, WC1 & WC2
—5F 23
St Giles High St. WC2—5F 23
St Giles Rd. SE5—3A 54
St Gothard Rd. SE27—4F 81
St Helena Rd. SE16—5F 41
St Helena St. WC1—2C 24
St Helen's Gdns. W10—5F 19
St Helen's Pl. EC3—5A 26
St Hilda's Clo. NW6—5F 5
St Hilda's Clo. SW17—2A 78
St Hilda's Rd. SW13—2D 47
St Hughe's Clo. SW17—2A 78
St James' Ct. SW1—4E 37
St James Ga. NW1—4F 9
St James Gro. SW11—5B 50
St James M. E14—4E 43
St James' Rd. E15—2B 16
St James's. SE14—4A 56
St James's Av. E2—1E 27
St James's Clo. SW17—2B 78
St James's Cres. SW9—1C 66
St James's Dri. SW17—1B 78
St James's Gdns. W11—2A 34
St James's Mkt. SW1—1F 37
St James's Pl. SW1—2E 37
St James's Rd.—4C 40
SE16 1-167 & 2-144
SE1 remainder
St James's Row. EC1—3D 25
St James's Sq. SW1—2E 37
St James's St. SW1—2E 37
St James's Ter. M. NW8—5B 8
St James St. W6—1E 47
St John's Av. NW10—5B 4
St John's Av. SW15—3F 61
St John's Chu. Rd. E9—2E 13
St John's Clo. SW6—3C 48
St Johns Ct. N5—1D 11
St John's Cres. SW9—1C 66
St John's Dri. SW18—1D 77
St John's Est. N1—1F 25
St Johns Gro. SW13—5B 46
St John's Hill. SW11—2F 63
St John's Hill Gro. SW11—2F 63
St John's La. EC1—3D 25
St John's M. W11—5C 20
St John's Pk. SE3—3B 58

St Johns Pathway. SE23—1E 83
St John's Pl. EC1—3D 25
St John's Rd. E16—5C 30
St John's Rd. SW11—2A 64
St John's Sq. EC1—3D 25
St John's Ter. E7—3D 17
St John's Ter. W10—3F 19
St John St. EC1—2D 25
St John's Vale. SE8—5C 56
St John's Wood High St. NW8
—1A 22
St John's Wood Pk. NW8—5F 7
St John's Wood Rd. NW8—3F 21
St John's Wood Ter. NW8
—1A 22
St Joseph's Clo. W10—4A 20
St Joseph's St. SW8—4D 51
St Joseph's Vale. SE3—1F 71
St Jude's Rd. E2—1D 27
St Jude St. N16—2A 12
St Julian's Clo. SW16—4C 80
St Julian's Farm Rd. SE27
—4C 80
St Julian's Rd. NW6—5C 6
St Katharine's Precinct. NW1
—1D 23
St Katharine's Way. E1—2B 40
St Kitts Ter. SE19—5A 82
St Laurence's Clo. NW6—5F 5
St Lawrence St. E14—2E 43
St Lawrence Ter. W10—4A 20
St Lawrence Way. SW9—5C 52
St Leonard's Rd. E14—4D 29
(in two parts)
St Leonard's Sq. NW5—3C 8
St Leonard's St. E3—2D 29
St Leonard's Ter. SW3—1B 50
St Leonard St. NW5—3C 8
St Loo Av. SW3—2A 50
St Louis Rd. SE27—4F 81
St Luke's Av. SW4—2F 65
St Luke's Clo. EC1—3E 25
St Luke's Est. EC1—2F 25
St Luke's M. W11—5B 20
St Luke's Rd. W11—4B 20
St Luke's Sq. E16—5B 30
St Luke's St. SW3—1A 50
St Luke's Yd. W9—1E 20
St Margaret's Ct. SE1—2F 39
St Margaret's Cres. SW15
—3D 61
St Margaret's Pas. SE13
—1A 72
St Margaret's Rd. NW10—2E 19
St Margaret's Rd. SE4—2B 70
St Margaret's Sq. SE4—2B 70
St Margaret St. SW1—3A 38
St Mark's Clo. SE10—3E 57

St Mark's Clo. W11—5A 20
St Mark's Cres. NW1—5C 8
St Mark's Ga. E9—4B 14
St Mark's Gro. SW10—2D 49
St Mark's Industrial Est. E16
—2F 45
St Mark's Pl. SW19—5B 76
St Mark's Pl. W11—5A 20
St Mark's Rise. E8—2B 12
St Mark's Rd.—4F 19
W11 1-53a & 2-22
W10 remainder
St Mark's Sq. NW1—5C 8
St Mark St. E1—5B 26
St Martin's Av. E6—1F 31
St Martin's Clo. NW1—5E 9
St Martin's Ct. WC2—1A 38
St Martin's Est. SW2—1C 80
St Martin's La. WC2—1A 38
St Martin's le Grand. EC1
—5E 25
St Martin's Pl. WC2—1A 38
St Martin's Rd. SW9—5B 52
St Martin's St. WC2—1F 37
St Martin's Way. SW17—3E 77
St Mary Abbot's Pl. W8—4B 34
St Mary Abbot's Ter. W14
—4B 34
St Mary at Hill. EC3—1A 40
St Mary Axe. EC3—5A 26
St Marychurch St. SE16—3E 41
St Mary Graces Ct. EC3—1B 40
St Mary's Ct. SE7—3F 59
St Mary's Gdns. SE11—5C 38
St Mary's Gro. N1—3D 11
St Mary's Gro. SW13—1D 61
St Mary's Mans. W2—4F 21
St Mary's M. NW6—4D 7
St Mary's Path. N1—5D 11
St Mary's Rd. E13—1D 31
St Mary's Rd. NW10—5A 4
St Mary's Rd. SE15—4E 55
St Mary's Rd. SW19—5A 76
St Mary's Sq. W2—4F 21
St Mary's Ter. W2—4F 21
St Mary's Wlk. SE11—5C 38
St Matthew's Rd. SW2—3B 66
St Matthew's Row. E2—3C 26
St Matthew St. SW1—4F 37
St Maur Rd. SW6—4B 48
St Michael's All. EC3—5F 25
St Michael's Clo. E16—4F 31
St Michael's Gdns. W10—4A 20
St Michael's Rd. NW2—1E 5
St Michael's Rd. SW9—5B 52
St Michael's St. W2—5F 21
St Mildred's Ct. EC2—5F 25
St Mildred's Rd. SE12—5B 72

St Nicholas Glebe. SW17
—5C 78
St Nicholas St. SE8—4B 56
St Norbert Grn. SE4—2A 70
St Norbert Rd. SE4—3F 69
St Olaf's Rd. SW6—3A 48
St Olave's Ct. EC2—5F 25
St Olave's Gdns. SE11—5C 38
St Oswald's Pl. SE11—1B 52
St Pancras Way. NW1—4E 9
St Paul's Av. NW2—3E 5
St Paul's Av. SE16—2F 41
St Paul's Chyd. EC4—5D 25
St Paul's Clo. SE7—1F 59
St Pauls Courtyard. SE8—3C 56
St Paul's Cres. NW1—4F 9
St Paul's Dri. E15—2F 15
St Paul's M. NW1—4F 9
St Paul's Pl. N1—3F 11
St Paul's Rd. N1—3D 11
St Pauls Ter. SE17—2D 53
St Paul St. N1—5E 11
(in two parts)
St Paul's Way. E3—4B 28
St Peter's Av. E2—1C 26
St Petersburgh M. W2—1D 35
St Petersburgh Pl. W2—1D 35
St Peter's Clo. E2—1C 26
St Peter's Clo. SW17—2A 78
St Peter's Gdns. SE27—3C 80
St Peter's Gro. W6—5C 32
St Peter's Rd. W6—1C 46
St Peter's Sq. E2—1C 26
St Peter's Sq. W6—1C 46
St Peter's St. N1—5D 11
St Peter's Ter. SW6—3B 48
St Peter's Vs. W6—5C 32
St Peter's Way. N1—4A 12
St Philip Sq. SW8—5D 51
St Philip's Rd. E8—3C 12
St Philip St. SW8—5D 51
St Philip's Way. N1—5E 11
St Quintin Av. W10—4E 19
St Quintin Gdns. W10—4E 19
St Quintin Rd. E13—2D 31
St Rule St. SW8—5E 51
St Saviour's Est. SE1—4B 40
(in two parts)
St Saviour's Rd. SW2—3B 66
Saints Dri. E7—2F 17
St Silas Pl. NW5—3C 8
St Simon's Av. SW15—3E 61
St Stephen's Av. W12—3D 33
St Stephen's Clo. NW8—5A 8
St Stephen's Cres. SW2
St Stephen's Gdns. SW15
—3B 62

St Stephen's Gdns. W2—5C 20
(in two parts)
St Stephen's Gro. SE13—1E 71
St Stephen's M. W2—4C 20
St Stephen's Rd. E3—5A 14
St Stephen's Rd. E6—4E 17
St Stephen's Ter. SW8—3B 52
St Swithin's La. EC4—1F 39
St Swithun's Rd. SE13—4F 71
St Thomas' Gdns. NW5—3C 8
St Thomas Rd. E16—5C 30
St Thomas's Pl. E9—4E 13
St Thomas's Rd. NW10—5A 4
St Thomas's Sq. E9—4E 13
St Thomas St. SE1—2F 39
St Thomas's Way. SW6—3B 48
St Vincent Clo. SE27—5D 81
St Vincent St. W1—4C 22
Salamanca Pl. SE1—5B 38
Salamanca St. SE1 & SE11
—5B 38
Salcombe Rd. N16—2A 12
Salcott Rd. SW11—3A 64
Salehurst Rd. SE4—4B 70
Salem Rd. W2—1D 35
Sale Pl. W2—5A 22
Sale St. E2—3C 26
Salford Rd. SW2—1F 79
Salisbury Clo. SE17—5F 39
Salisbury Ct. EC4—5D 25
Salisbury M. SW6—3B 48
Salisbury Pl. W1—4B 22
Salisbury Rd. E7—3C 16
Salisbury Rd. E12—2F 17
Salisbury Rd. E17—4D 17
Salisbury Sq. EC4—5C 24
Salisbury St. NW8—3A 22
Salisbury Ter. SE15—1E 69
Salmen Rd. E13—1B 30
Salmon La. E14—5A 28
Salmon St. E14—5B 28
Salomons Rd. E13—4E 31
Saltcoats Rd. W4—3A 32
Salter Rd. SE16—2F 41
Salters Hill. SE19—5F 81
Salters Rd. W10—3F 19
Salter St. E14—1C 42
Salter St. NW10—2C 18
Saltoun Rd. SW2—2C 66
Saltram Cres. W9—2B 20
Saltwell St. E14—1C 42
Saltwood Gro. SE17—1F 53
Salusbury Rd. NW6—5A 6
Salvador. SW17—5A 78
Salvin Rd. SW15—1F 61
Salway Pl. E15—3F 15
Salway Rd. E15—3F 15
Sam Bartram Clo. SE7—1E 59

Sambruck M. SE6—1D 85
Samels Ct. W6—1C 46
Samford St. NW8—3A 22
Sampson St. E1—2C 40
Samson St. E13—1E 31
Samuda Est. E14—4E 43
Samuel Clo. E8—5B 12
Samuel Johnson Clo. SW16
—4B 80
Samuel Jones Industrial Est. SE5
—4A 54
Sancroft St. SE11—1B 52
Sanctuary St. SE1—3E 39
Sandall Rd. NW5—3E 9
Sandal St. E15—5A 16
Sandalwood Clo. E1—3A 28
Sandbourne Rd. SE4—5A 56
Sandell St. SE1—3C 38
Sanderson Clo. NW5—1D 9
Sanderstead Clo. SW12—5E 65
Sandgate La. SW18—1A 78
Sandgate St. SE15—2D 55
Sandhurst Rd. SE6—1F 85
Sandilands Rd. SW6—4D 49
Sandison St. SE15—1C 68
Sandland St. WC1—4B 24
Sandmere Rd. SW4—2A 66
Sandpit Rd. Brom—5A 86
Sandringham Rd. E7—2E 17
Sandringham Rd. E8—2B 12
Sandringham Rd. NW2—3D 5
Sandringham Rd. Brom—5C 86
Sandrock Rd. SE13—1C 70
Sand's End La. SW6—4D 49
Sandstone Rd. SE12—2D 87
Sandtoft Rd. SE7—2D 59
Sandwell Cres. NW6—3C 6
Sandwich St. WC1—2A 24
Sandys Row. E1—4A 26
Sanford St. SE14—2A 56
Sanford Wlk. SE14—2A 56
Sangley Rd. SE6—5D 71
Sangora Rd. SW11—2F 63
Sansom St. SE5—4F 53
Sans Wlk. EC1—3C 24
Santley St. SW4—2B 66
Santos Rd. SW18—3C 62
Sapcote Trading Est. NW10
—3B 4
Sapphire Rd. SE8—5A 42
Saracen St. E14—5C 28
Sarah St. N1—2A 26
Saratoga Rd. E5—1E 13
Sardinia St. WC2—5B 24
Sark Wlk. E16—5D 31
Sarre Rd. NW2—2B 6
Sarsfeld Rd. SW12—1B 78
Sartor Rd. SE15—2F 69

Satanita Clo. E16—5F 31
Satchwell Rd. E2—2C 26
Saunders Ness Rd. E14—1E 57
Saunders St. SE11—5B 38
Savage Gdns. EC3—1A 40
Savernake Rd. NW3—1B 8
Savile Row. W1—1E 37
Savona St. SW8—3E 51
Savoy Clo. E15—5A 16
Savoy Ct. WC2—1B 38
Savoy Hill. WC2—1B 38
Savoy Pl. WC2—1A 38
Savoy St. WC2—1B 38
Sawkins Clo. SW19—2A 76
Sawley Rd. W12—2C 32
Sawyer St. SE1—3E 39
Saxby Rd. SW2—5A 66
Saxon Rd. E3—1B 28
Saxton Clo. SE13—1F 71
Sayes Ct. SE8—1B 56
Sayes Ct. St. SE8—2B 56
Scala St. W1—4E 23
Scampston M. W10—5F 19
Scandrett St. E1—2D 41
Scarborough St. E1—5B 26
Scarlet Rd. SE6—3A 86
Scarlette Mnr. Way. SW2
—5C 66
Scarsbrook Rd. SE3—1F 73
Scarsdale Pl. W8—4D 35
Scarsdale Vs. W8—4C 34
Scarth Rd. SW13—1B 60
Scawen Rd. SE8—1A 56
Scawfell St. E2—1B 26
Sceau Gdns. SE5—4A 54
Sceptre Rd. E2—2E 27
Schofield Wlk. SE3—3D 59
Scholars St. SW12—1E 79
School App. E2—2A 26
School Ho. La. E1—1F 41
School La. SE23—2D 83
Schooner Clo. SE16—3F 41
Schubert Rd. SW15—3B 62
Sclater St. E1—3B 26
Scoble Pl. N16—1B 12
Scoles Cres. SW2—1C 80
Scoresby St. SE1—2D 39
Scotland Pl. SW1—2A 38
Scotsdale Rd. SE12—3D 73
Scotswood St. EC1—3C 24
Scott Ellis Gdns. NW8—2F 21
Scott Lidgett Cres. SE16—3C 40
Scotts Rd. W12—3D 33
Scott St. E1—3D 27
Scoulding Rd. E16—5C 30
Scout App. NW10—1A 4
Scout La. SW4—1E 65

Scovell Rd. SE1—3E 39
Scriven St. E8—5B 12
Scrooby St. SE6—4D 71
Scrubs La. NW10—2C 18
Scrutton Clo. SW12—5F 65
Scrutton St. EC2—3A 26
Scutari Rd. SE22—3E 69
Scylla Rd. SE15—1D 69
   (in two parts)
Seabright St. E2—2D 27
Seacoal La. EC4—5D 25
Seaford St. WC1—2A 24
Seaforth Cres. N5—2E 11
Seager Pl. E3—4B 28
Seagrave Rd. SW6—2C 48
Seal St. E8—1B 12
Searles Clo. SW11—3A 50
Searles Rd. SE1—5F 39
Sears St. SE5—3F 53
Seaton Clo. E13—3C 30
Seaton Clo. SE11—1C 52
Seaton Clo. SW15—1D 75
Sebastian St. EC1—2D 25
Sebbon St. N1—4D 11
Sebert Rd. E7—2D 17
Sebright Pas. E2—1C 26
Secker St. SE1—2C 38
Second Av. E13—2C 30
Second Av. SW14—1A 60
Second Av. W3—2B 32
Second Av. W10—3A 20
Sedan Way. SE17—1A 54
Sedding St. SW1—5C 36
Seddon St. WC1—2B 24
Sedgebrook Rd. SE3—1F 73
Sedgeford Rd. W12—2B 32
Sedgehill Rd. SE6—4C 84
Sedgeway. SE6—1B 86
Sedgmoor Pl. SE5—3A 54
Sedgwick St. E9—2F 13
Sedleigh Rd. SW18—4B 62
Sedlescombe Rd. SW6—2C 48
Sedley Pl. W1—5D 23
Seeley Dri. SE21—4A 82
Seely Rd. SW17—5C 78
Seething La. EC3—1A 40
Sefton St. SW15—1E 61
Segal Clo. SE23—5A 70
Sekforde St. EC1—3D 25
Selbie Av. NW10—2B 4
Selborne Rd. SE5—5F 53
Selby Rd. E13—4D 31
Selby St. E1—3C 26
Selden Rd. SE15—5E 55
Selkirk Rd. SW17—4A 78
Sellincourt Rd. SW17—5A 78
Sellon M. SE11—5B 38
Sellons Av. NW10—5B 4

Selsdon Rd. E13—5E 17
Selsdon Rd. SE27—3C 80
Selsea Pl. N16—2A 12
Selsey St. E14—4C 28
Selwood Pl. SW7—1F 49
Selwood Ter. SW7—1F 49
Selworthy Rd. SE6—3B 84
Selwyn Rd. E3—1B 28
Selwyn Rd. E13—5D 17
Selwyn Rd. NW10—4A 4
Semley Ga. E9—3B 14
Semley Pl. SW1—5C 36
Senate St. SE15—5E 55
Senior St. W2—4D 21
Senlac Rd. SE12—1D 87
Senrab St. E1—5F 27
Serjeant's Inn. EC4—5C 24
Serle St. WC2—5B 24
Serpentine Rd. W2—2A 36
Setchell Rd. SE1—5B 40
Setchell Way. SE1—5B 40
Seth St. SE16—3E 41
Settle Rd. E13—1C 30
Settles St. E1—4C 26
Settrington Rd. SW6—5D 49
Seven Dials. WC2—5A 24
Sevenoaks Rd. SE4—4A 70
Severnake Clo. E14—5C 42
Severn Way. NW10—2B 4
Severus Rd. SW11—2A 64
Seville St. SW1—3B 36
Sevington St. W9—3D 21
Sewardstone Rd. E2—1E 27
Seward St. EC1—2E 25
Sewdley St. E5—1F 13
Sewell St. E13—2C 30
Sextant Av. E14—5F 43
Seymour Clo. EC1—3D 25
Seymour Gdns. SE4—1A 70
Seymour M. W1—5C 22
Seymour Pl. W1—4B 22
Seymour Rd. E6—1F 31
Seymour Rd. SW18—4B 62
Seymour Rd. SW19—3F 75
Seymour St.—5B 22
  W1 1-61 & 2-68
  W2 remainder
Seymour Wlk. SW10—2E 49
Seyssel St. E14—5E 43
Shackleton Clo. SE23—2D 83
Shackleton Rd. N16—1B 12
Shacklewell Grn. E8—1B 12
Shacklewell La. E8—2B 12
Shacklewell Rd. N16—1B 12
Shacklewell Row. E8—1B 12
Shacklewell St. E2—2B 26
Shad Thames. SE1—3B 40
Shadwell Pierhead. E1—1E 41
Shadwell Pl. E1—1E 41

Shaftesbury Av.—1F 37
W1 1-111 & 2-136
WC2 remainder
Shaftesbury Rd. E7—4E 17
Shaftesbury St. N1—1E 25
Shafto M. SW1—4B 36
Shafton Rd. E9—5F 13
Shafts Ct. EC3—5A 26
Shakespeare Rd. SE24—3D 67
Shakspeare Wlk. N16—1A 12
Shalcomb St. SW10—2E 49
Shalfleet Dri. W10—1F 33
Shamrock St. SW4—1F 65
Shandon Rd. SW4—4E 65
Shand St. SE1—3A 40
Shandy St. E1—4F 27
Shanklin Way. SE15—3B 54
Shannon Gro. SW9—2B 66
Shannon Pl. NW8—1A 22
Shap St. E2—1B 26
(in two parts)
Shardcroft Av. SE24—3D 67
Shardeloes Rd. SE14—5B 56
Shard's Sq. SE15—2C 54
Sharon Gdns. E9—5E 13
Sharpleshall St. NW1—4B 8
Sharratt St. SE15—2E 55
Sharsted St. SE17—1D 53
Shawbrooke Rd. SE9—3F 73
Shawbury Rd. SE22—3B 68
Shawfield St. SW3—1A 50
Shawford Ct. SW15—5C 60
Shaw Rd. Brom—3B 86
Shearling Way. N7—3A 10
Shearman Rd. SE3—2B 72
Sheba St. E1—3B 26
Sheenewood. SE26—4D 83
Sheen Gro. N1—5C 10
Sheepcote La. SW11—5B 50
Sheep La. E8—5D 13
Sheerwater Rd. E16—4F 31
Sheffield Sq. E3—2B 28
Sheffield St. WC2—5B 24
Sheffield Ter. W8—2C 34
Shelburne Rd. N7—1B 10
Shelbury Rd. SE22—3D 69
Sheldon Clo. SE12—3D 73
Sheldon Rd. NW2—1F 5
Sheldrake Pl. W8—3C 34
Shelgate Rd. SW11—3A 64
Shelley Way. SW19—5F 77
Shelliness Rd. E5—2D 13
Shell Rd. SE13—1D 71
Shellwood Rd. SW11—5B 50
Shelmerdine Clo. E3—4C 28
Shelton St. WC2—5A 24
(in two parts)
Shenfield St. N1—1A 26

Shenley Rd. SE5—4A 54
Shepherdess Pl. N1—2F 25
Shepherdess Wlk. N1—1E 25
Shepherd Mkt. W1—2D 37
Shepherd's Bush Centre. W12
—3F 33
Shepherd's Bush Grn. W12
—3E 33
Shepherd's Bush Mkt. W12
—3E 33
Shepherd's Bush Pl. W12
—3F 33
Shepherd's Bush Rd. W6—5E 33
Shepherd's La. E9—3F 13
Shepherds Pl. W1—1C 36
Shepherd St. W1—2D 37
Shepherd's Wlk. NW3—2F 7
Sheppard St. E16—3B 30
Shepperton Rd. N1—5F 11
Sheppey Wlk. N1—3E 11
Sheraton St. W1—5F 23
Sherborne La. EC4—1F 39
Sherborne St. N1—5F 11
Sherbrooke Rd. SW6—3A 48
Sherfield Gdns. SW15—4B 60
Sheridan Pl. SW13—1B 60
Sheridan St. E1—5D 27
Sheringham Rd. N7—3C 10
Sherington Rd. SE7—2D 59
Sherlock M. W1—4C 22
Sherrard Rd.—3E 17
E7 1-195 & 2-210
E12 remainder
Sherrick Grn. Rd. NW10—2D 5
Sherriff Rd. NW6—3C 6
Sherwin Rd. SE14—4F 55
Sherwood Clo. SW15—1D 61
Sherwood Gdns. E14—5C 42
Sherwood St. W1—1E 37
Shetland Rd. E3—1B 28
Shillingford St. N1—4D 11
Shinfield St. W12—5E 19
Shinford Path. SE23—3F 83
Ship & Mermaid Row. SE1
—3F 39
Shipka Rd. SW12—1D 79
Shipman Rd. E16—5D 31
Shipman Rd. SE23—2F 83
Ship St. SE8—4C 56
Ship Tavern Pas. EC3—1A 40
Shipton Pl. NW5—3C 8
Shipton St. E2—2B 26
Shipwright Rd. SE16—3A 42
Shirburn Clo. SE23—5E 69
Shirbutt St. E14—1D 43
Shirebrook Rd. SE3—1F 73
Shirland M. W9—2B 20
Shirland Rd. W9—2B 20

Shirley Gro. SW11—1C 64
Shirley Ho. Dri. SE7—3E 59
Shirley Rd. E15—4A 16
Shirley St. E16—5B 30
Shirlock Rd. NW3—1B 8
Shoe La. EC4—5C 24
Shooters Hill Rd.—4F 57
SE3 1-311 & 2-238
SE18 remainder
Shoot up Hill. NW2—2A 6
Shoreditch High St. E1—3A 26
Shoreham Clo. SW18—3D 63
Shore Pl. E9—4E 13
Shore Rd. E9—4E 13
Shorncliffe Rd. SE1—1B 54
Shorndean St. SE6—1E 85
Shorrold's Rd. SW6—3B 48
Shorter St. E1—1B 40
Shortlands. W6—5F 33
Short Rd. E15—5F 15
Short Rd. W4—2A 46
Shorts Gdns. WC2—5A 24
Short St. SE1—3C 38
Short Wall. E15—2E 29
Shotfield Av. SW14—2A 60
Shottendane Rd. SW6—4C 48
Shoulder of Mutton All. E14
—1A 42
Shouldham St. W1—4A 22
Shrewsbury Rd. E7—2F 17
Shrewsbury Rd. SE20—5C 20
Shroffold Rd. Brom—4A 86
Shropshire Pl. WC1—3E 23
Shroton St. NW1—4A 22
Shrubbery Rd. SW16—4A 80
Shrubland Rd. E8—5C 12
Shuna Wlk. N1—3F 11
Shurland Gdns. SE15—3B 54
Shuttle St. E1—3C 26
Shuttleworth Rd. SW11—5A 50
Sibella Rd. SW4—5F 51
Sibthorpe Rd. SE12—5D 73
Sickert Ct. N1—4E 11
Sidbury St. SW6—4A 48
Sidcup Rd.—4E 73
SE12 1-59 & 2-188
SE9 remainder
Siddons La. NW1—3B 22
Siddons Rd. SE23—2A 84
Sidford Pl. SE1—4C 38
Sidmouth Rd. NW2—4E 5
Sidmouth Rd. SE15—4B 54
Sidmouth St. WC1—2B 24
Sidney Est. E1—4E 27
(in two parts)
Sidney Gro. EC1—1D 25
Sidney Rd. SW9—5B 52
Sidney Sq. E1—4E 27

Sidney St. E1—4E 27
Sidworth St. E8—4D 13
Siebert Rd. SE3—2C 58
Siemens Rd. SE18—4F 45
Sigdon Rd. E8—2C 12
Silbury Ho. SE26—3C 82
Silbury St. N1—2F 25
Silchester Rd. W10—5F 19
Silesia Bldgs. E8—4D 13
Silex St. SE1—3D 39
Silk Clo. SE12—3C 72
Silk Mills Path. SE13—5E 57
Silk St. EC2—4E 25
Silver Clo. SE14—3A 56
Silverdale. SE26—4E 83
Silvermere Rd. SE6—5D 71
Silver Pl. W1—1E 37
Silver Rd. W12—1F 33
Silverthorne Rd. SW8—5D 51
Silverton Rd. W6—2F 47
Silvertown By-Pass. E16
—2F 45
Silvertown Way. E16—5B 30
Silver Wlk. SE16—2B 42
Silvester Rd. SE22—3B 68
Silvester St. SE1—3F 39
Silwood Est. SE16—5E 41
Silwood St. SE16—5E 41
Simla Clo. SE14—2A 56
Simms Rd. SE1—5C 40
Simnel Rd. SE12—5D 73
Simon Clo. W11—1B 34
Simons Wlk. E15—2F 15
Simpson's Rd. E14—1D 43
Simpson St. SW11—5A 50
Simrose Ct. SW18—3C 62
Sims Wlk. SE3—2B 72
Sinclair Gdns. W14—3F 33
Sinclair Rd. W14—3F 33
Singer St. EC2—2F 25
Sir Alexander Clo. W3—2B 32
Sir Alexander Rd. W3—2B 32
Sirdar Rd. W11—1F 33
Sispara Gdns. SW18—4B 62
Sister Mabel's Way. SE15
—3C 54
Sisters Av. SW11—1B 64
Sistova Rd. SW12—1D 79
Sisulu Pl. SW9—1C 66
Siward Rd. SW17—3E 77
Sixth Av. W10—2A 20
Skardu Rd. NW2—2A 6
Skeena Hill. SW18—5A 62
Skelbrook St. SW18—2E 77
Skelgill Rd. SW15—2B 62
Skelley Rd. E15—4B 16
Skelton Clo. E8—3B 12
Skelton Rd. E7—3C 16

Skelwith Rd. W6—2E 47
Sketchley Gdns. SE16—1F 55
Skiers St. E15—5A 16
Skiffington Clo. SW2—1C 80
Skinner Ct. E2—1D 27
Skinners La. EC4—1E 39
Skinner's Row. SE10—4D 57
Skinner St. EC1—3C 24
Skipton St. SE1—4D 39
Skipworth Rd. E9—5E 13
Skomer Wlk. N1—3E 11
Skylines. E14—3D 43
Sladebrook Rd. SE3—1F 73
Sladen Pl. E5—1D 13
Slade Wlk. SE17—2E 53
Slagrove Pl. SE13—3C 70
Slaidburn St. SW10—2E 49
Slaithwaite Rd. SE13—2E 71
Slaney Pl. N7—2C 10
Sleaford St. SW8—3E 51
Slievemore Clo. SW4—1F 65
Slingsby Pl. WC2—1A 38
Slippers Pl. SE16—4D 41
Sloane Av. SW3—5A 36
Sloane Ct. E. SW3—1C 50
Sloane Ct. W. SW3—1C 50
Sloane Gdns. SW1—5C 36
Sloane Sq. SW1—5B 36
Sloane St. SW1—4B 36
Sloane Ter. SW1—5C 36
Sly St. E1—5D 27
Smallbrook M. W2—5F 21
Smallwood Rd. SW17—4F 77
Smart's Pl. WC2—5A 24
Smart St. E2—2F 27
Smeaton Rd. SW18—5C 62
Smeaton St. E1—2D 41
Smedley St.—5F 51
SW8 1-3
SW4 remainder
Smeed Rd. E3—4C 14
Smith Clo. SE16—2F 41
Smithfield St. EC1—4D 25
Smithies Ct. E15—2E 15
Smith Sq. SW1—4A 38
Smith St. SW3—1B 50
Smiths Yd. SW18—2E 77
Smith Ter. SW3—1B 50
Smithwood Clo. SW19—1A 76
Smithy St. E1—4E 27
Smugglers Way. SW18—2D 63
Smyrk's Rd. SE17—1A 54
Smyrna Rd. NW6—4C 6
Smythe St. E14—1D 43
Snarsgate St. W10—4E 19
Sneyd Rd. NW2—2E 5
Snowbury Rd. SW6—5D 49
Snowden St. EC2—3A 26

Snow Hill. EC1—4D 25
Snow Hill Ct. EC1—5D 25
Snowsfields. SE1—3F 39
Soames St. SE15—1B 68
Soho Sq. W1—5F 23
Soho St. W1—5F 23
Solebay St. E1—3A 28
Solent Rd. NW6—2C 6
Soley M. WC1—2C 24
Solna Av. SW15—3E 61
Solomon's Pas. SE15—2D 69
Solon New Rd. SW4—2A 66
Solon New Rd. Est. SW4—2A 66
Solon Rd. SW2—2A 66
Solway Rd. SE22—2C 68
Somali Rd. NW2—2B 6
Somerford Est. N16—1B 12
Somerford Gro. N16—1B 12
Somerford St. E1—3D 27
Somerford Way. SE16—3A 42
Somerleyton Rd. SW9—2C 66
Somers Clo. NW1—1F 23
Somers Cres. W2—5A 22
Somerset Est. SW11—4A 50
Somerset Gdns. SE13—5D 57
Somerset Rd. SW19—3F 75
Somerset Sq. W14—3A 34
Somers M. W2—5A 22
Somers Pl. SW2—5B 66
Somers Rd. SW2—4B 66
Somerton Rd. SE15—2D 69
Somertrees Av. SE12—2D 87
Sondes St. SE17—2F 53
Sonia Gdns. NW10—1B 4
Sophia Clo. N7—3B 10
Sophia Rd. E16—5D 31
Sorrell Clo. SE14—3A 56
Sorrell Clo. SW9—5C 52
Sotheron Rd. SW6—3D 49
Soudan Rd. SW11—4B 50
Souldern Rd. W14—4F 33
S. Africa Rd. W12—2D 33
Southall Pl. SE1—3F 39
Southampton Bldgs. WC2
—4C 24
Southampton Pl. WC1—4A 24
Southampton Rd. NW5—2B 8
Southampton Row. WC1
—4A 24
Southampton St. WC2—1A 38
Southampton Way. SE5—3F 53
Southam St. W10—3A 20
S. Audley St. W1—1C 36
S. Black Lion La. W6—1C 46
S. Bolton Gdns. SW5—1E 49
Southborough Rd. E9—5F 13
Southbourne Gdns. SE12
—3D 73

Southbrook M. SE12—4B 72
Southbrook Rd. SE12—4B 72
S. Carriage Dri. SW7 & SW1
—3F 35
Southcombe St. W14—5A 34
Southcote Rd. N19—1E 9
South Cres. WC1—4F 23
Southcroft Rd. SW17—5C 78
S. Croxted Rd. SE21—3F 81
Southdean Gdns. SW19—2B 76
S. Eaton Pl. SW1—5C 36
S. Edwardes Sq. W8—4C 34
South End. W8—4D 35
S. End Clo. NW3—1A 8
S. End Grn. NW3—1A 8
Southend La.—4B 84
SE6 1-299 & 2-298
SE26 remainder
S. End Rd. NW3—1A 8
Southend Rd. Beck—5D 85
S. End Row. W8—4D 35
Southern Clo. E8—5C 12
Southerngate Way. SE14—3A 56
Southern Gro. E3—2B 28
Southern Rd. E13—1D 31
Southern Row. W10—3A 20
Southern St. N1—1B 24
Southerton Rd. W6—5E 33
S. Esk Rd. E7—3E 17
Southey Rd. SW9—4C 52
Southfield Rd. W4—4A 32
Southfields Pas. SW18—4C 62
Southfields Rd. SW18—4C 62
Southgate Gro. N1—4F 11
Southgate Rd. N1—5F 11
S. Hill Pk. NW3—1A 8
Southill St. E14—5D 29
S. Lambeth Pl. SW8—2A 52
S. Lambeth Rd. SW8—2A 52
Southmead Rd. SW19—1A 76
S. Molton La. W1—1D 37
S. Molton Rd. E16—5C 30
S. Molton St. W1—5D 23
Southmoor Way. E9—3B 14
S. Oak Rd. SW16—4B 80
Southolm St. SW11—4D 51
Southover. Brom—5C 86
South Pde. SW3—1F 49
South Pde. W4—5A 32
S. Park Cres. SE6—1B 86
S. Park M. SW6—1D 63
South Pl. EC2—4F 25
South Pl. M. EC2—4F 25
S. Quay Plaza. E14—3D 43
South Rd. SE23—2F 83
South Row. SE3—5B 58
S. Sea St. SE16—4B 42
South Side. W6—4B 32

Southside Comn.—5F 75
South Sq. WC1—4C 24
South St. W1—2C 36
S. Tenter St. E1—1B 40
South Ter. SW7—5A 36
Southvale Rd. SE3—5A 58
Southview Av. NW10—2B 4
Southview Rd. Brom—4F 85
South Vs. NW1—3F 9
Southville. SW8—4F 51
Southwark Bri. SE1 & EC4
—1E 39
Southwark Bri. Rd. SE1—3E 39
Southwark Gro. SE1—2E 39
Southwark Pk. Rd. SE16—5B 40
Southwark St. SE1—2D 39
Southwater Clo. E14—5B 28
Southwell Gdns. SW7—4E 35
Southwell Rd. SE5—1E 67
S. W. India Dock Entrance. E14
—3E 43
S. Wharf Rd. W2—5F 21
Southwick M. W2—5A 22
Southwick Pl. W2—5A 22
Southwick St. W2—5A 22
S. Worple Av. SW14—1A 60
S. Worple Way. SW14—1A 60
Sovereign M. E2—1B 26
Spa Ct. SW16—4B 80
Spafield St. EC1—3C 24
Spalding Rd. SW17—5D 79
Spanby Rd. E3—3C 28
Spanish Pl. W1—5C 22
Spanish Rd. SW18—3E 63
Spa Rd. SE16—4B 40
Sparrick's Row. SE1—3F 39
Sparta St. SE10—4E 57
Spear M. SW5—5C 34
Speedwell St. SE8—3C 56
Speldhurst Rd. E9—4F 13
Spellbrook Wlk. N1—5E 11
Spelman St. E1—4C 26
Spencer M. W6—2A 48
Spencer Pk. SW18—3D 63
Spencer Pl. EC1—2D 25
Spencer Rd. E6—5F 17
Spencer Rd. SW18—3D 63
Spencer St. EC1—2D 25
Spencer Wlk. SW15—2F 61
Spenser Gro. N16—1A 12
(in two parts)
Spenser Rd. SE24—3D 67
Spenser St. SW1—4E 37
Spert St. E14—1A 42
Spey St. E14—4E 29
Spezia Rd. NW10—1C 18
Spicer Clo. SW9—5D 53
Spindrift Av. E14—5C 42
Spinney Gdns. SE19—5B 82
Spinney, The. SW16—3E 79

Spirit Quay. E1—2C 40
Spital Sq. E1—4A 26
Spital St. E1—4C 26
Spital Yd. E1—4A 26
Spode Wlk. NW6—2D 7
Sportsbank St. SE6—5E 71
Sprimont Pl. SW3—5B 36
Springall St. SE15—3D 55
Springbank Rd. SE13—4F 71
Springbank Wlk. NW1—4F 9
Spring Ct. NW6—3B 6
Springdale Rd. N16—1F 11
Springfield Gro. SE7—2E 59
Springfield La. NW6—5D 7
Springfield Rise. SE26—3D 83
Springfield Rd. E15—2A 30
Springfield Rd. NW8—5E 7
Springfield Rd. SE26—5D 83
Springfield Rd. SW19—5B 76
Springfield Wlk. NW6—5D 7
Spring Gdns. N5—2E 11
Spring Gdns. SW1—2F 37
Spring Hill. SE26—4E 83
Springhill Clo. SE5—1F 67
Spring M. W1—4B 22
Spring Path. NW3—2F 7
Spring Pl. NW5—2D 9
Springrice Rd. SE13—4F 71
Spring St. W2—5F 21
Spring Vale Ter. W14—4F 33
Springwell Av. NW10—5B 4
Springwell Clo. SW16
—4B 80
Springwell Rd. SW16—4C 80
Sprowston M. E7—3C 16
Sprowston Rd. E7—2C 16
Sprules Rd. SE4—5A 56
Spurgeon St. SE1—4F 39
Spurling Rd. SE22—2B 68
Spur Rd. SW1—3E 37
Spurstowe Rd. E8—2D 13
Spurstowe Ter. E8—3D 13
Square Rigger Row. SW11
—1E 63
Square, The. W6—1E 47
Squarey St. SW17—3E 77
Squires Ct. SW19—4C 76
Squirrels, The. SE13—1F 71
Squirries St. E2—2C 26
Stable M. SE27—5E 81
Stables Way. SE11—1C 52
Stable Way. W10—5E 19
Stable Yd. SW9—5B 52
Stable Yd. Rd. SW1—3E 37
Stacey St. WC2—5C 23
Stacy Path. SE5—3A 54
Stadium St. SW10—3E 49
Stafford Clo. NW6—2C 20
Stafford Pl. SW1—4E 37

Stafford Rd. E3—1B 28
Stafford Rd. E7—3F 17
Stafford Rd. NW6—2C 20
Staffordshire St. SE15—4C 54
Stafford St. W1—2E 37
Stafford Ter. W8—3C 34
Staff St. EC1—2F 25
Stag La. SW15—3B 74
Stag Pl. SW1—4E 37
Stainer St. SE1—2F 39
Staining La. EC2—5E 25
Stainsbury St. E2—1E 27
Stainsby Pl. E14—5C 28
Stainsby Rd. E14—5C 28
Stainton Rd. SE6—4F 71
Stalbridge St. NW1—4A 22
Stalham St. SE16—4D 41
Stamford Brook Av. W6—4B 32
Stamford Brook Rd. W6—4B 32
Stamford Rd. N1—4A 12
Stamford St. SE1—2C 38
Stamp Pl. E2—1B 26
Stanborough Pas. E8—3B 12
Stanbridge Rd. SW15—1E 61
Stanbury Rd. SE15—5D 55
(in two parts)
Standen Rd. SW18—5B 62
Standish Rd. W6—5C 32
Stane Pas. SW16—5A 80
Stane Way. SE18—3F 59
Stanfield Rd. E3—1A 28
Stanford Ct. SW6—4D 49
Stanford Pl. SE17—5A 40
Stanford Rd. W8—4D 35
Stanford St. SW1—5F 37
Stanhope Clo. SE16—3F 41
Stanhope Gdns. SW7—5E 35
Stanhope Ga. W1—2C 36
Stanhope M. E. SW7—5E 35
Stanhope M. S. SW7—5E 35
Stanhope M. W. SW7—5E 35
Stanhope Pde. NW1—2E 23
Stanhope Pl. W2—1B 36
Stanhope Row. W1—2D 37
Stanhope St. NW1—2E 23
(in two parts)
Stanhope Ter. W2—1F 35
Stanier Rd. W14—1B 48
Stanlake M. W12—2E 33
Stanlake Rd. W12—2E 33
Stanlake Vs. W12—2E 33
Stanley Clo. SW8—2B 52
Stanley Cres. W11—1B 34
Stanley Gdns. NW2—2E 5
Stanley Gdns. W3—3A 32
Stanley Gdns. W11—1B 34
Stanley Gro. SW8—5C 50
Stanley Pas. NW1—1A 24

Stanley Rd. E15—5F 15
Stanley St. SE8—3B 56
Stanmer St. SW11—5A 50
Stanmore Pl. NW1—5D 9
Stanmore St. N1—5B 10
Stannard Rd. E8—3C 12
Stannary St. SE11—2C 52
Stansfeld Rd. E16 & E6—4F 31
Stansfield Rd. SW9—1B 66
Stanstead Gro. SE6—1B 84
Stanstead Rd.—1F 83
    SE23 1-319 & 2-302
    SE6 remainder
Stanswood Gdns. SE5—3A 54
Stanthorpe Clo. SW16—5A 80
Stanthorpe Rd. SW16—5A 80
Stanton Rd. SE26—4B 84
Stanton Rd. SW13—5B 46
Stanton St. SE15—4C 54
Stanton Way. SE26—4B 84
Stanway Ct. N1—1A 26
Stanway St. N1—1A 26
Stanwick Rd. W14—5B 34
Stanworth St. SE1—4B 40
Staplefield Clo. SW2—1A 80
Stapleford Clo. SW19—5A 62
Staplehurst Rd. SE13—3A 72
Staple Inn Bldgs. WC1—4C 24
Staples Clo. SE16—2A 42
Staple St. SE1—3F 39
Stapleton Rd. SW17—3C 78
Starboard Way. E14—4C 42
Starcross St. NW1—2E 23
Starfield Rd. W12—3C 32
Starkleigh Way. SE16—1D 55
Star La. E16—3A 30
Star Rd. W14—2B 48
Star St. E16—4B 30
Star St. W2—5A 22
Star Yd. WC2—5C 24
Statham Gro. N16—1F 11
Station App. E7—1D 17
Station App. NW10—2B 18
Station App. SE3—1D 73
Station App. SE26—4E 83
Station App. SW6—1A 64
Station App. SW16—5F 79
Station Av. SW9—1D 67
Station Cres. SE3—1C 58
Stationer's Hall Ct. EC4—5D 25
Station Pde. NW2—3E 5
Station Rise. SE27—2D 81
Station Rd. E7—1C 16
Station Rd. NW10—1B 18
Station Rd. SE20—5E 83
Station Rd. SW13—5B 46
Station Sq. SE26—4B 84
Station St. E15—4F 15

Station Ter. NW10—1F 19
Station Ter. SE5—4E 53
Station Way. SE15—5C 54
Staunton St. SE8—2B 56
Staveley Clo. E9—2E 13
Staveley Clo. N7—1A 10
Staveley Clo. SE15—4E 55
Staverton Rd. NW2—4E 5
Stave Yd. Rd. SE16—2A 42
Stavordale Rd. N5—1D 11
Stayners Rd. E1—3F 27
Stead St. SE17—5F 39
Stean St. E8—5B 12
Stebondale St. E14—5E 43
Steedman St. SE17—5E 39
Steele Rd. E11—1A 16
Steele's M. N. NW3—3B 8
Steele's M. S. NW3—3B 8
Steele's Rd. NW3—3B 8
Steel's La. E1—5E 27
Steen Way. SE22—3A 68
Steep Hill. SW16—3F 79
Steeple Clo. SW6—5A 48
Steeple Clo. SW19—5A 76
Steerforth St. SW18—2E 77
Steers Way. SE16—3A 42
Stella Rd. SW17—5B 78
Stephan Clo. E8—5C 12
Stephendale Rd. SW6—5D 49
Stephen M. W1—4F 23
Stephenson St. E16—3A 30
Stephenson St. NW10—2A 18
Stephenson Way. NW1—3E 23
Stephen's Rd. E15—5A 16
Stephen St. W1—4F 23
Stepney Causeway. E1—5F 27
Stepney Grn. E1—4F 27
Stepney High St. E1—4F 27
Stepney Way. E1—4D 27
Sterling St. SW7—4A 36
Sterndale Rd. W14—4F 33
Sterne St. W12—3F 33
Sternhall La. SE15—1C 68
Sternhold Av. SW2—2F 79
Sterry St. SE1—3F 39
Steugers La. SE23—1A 84
Steve Biko La. SE6—4C 84
Stevenage Rd. SW6—4F 47
Stevens Av. E9—3E 13
Stevens St. SE1—4A 40
Steventon Rd. W12—1B 32
Steward St. E1—4A 26
Stewart Rd. E15—1F 15
Stewart's Gro. SW3—1F 49
Stewart's Rd. SW8—3E 51
Stewart St. E14—3E 43
Stew La. EC4—1E 39
Stillingfleet Rd. SW13—2C 46

Stillington St. SW1—5E 37
Stillness Rd. SE23—4A 70
Stirling Rd. E13—1D 31
Stirling Rd. SW9—5A 52
Stockfield St. SW16—3B 80
Stockholm Rd. SE16—1E 55
Stockhurst Clo. SW15—5F 47
Stock Orchard Cres. N7—2B 10
Stock Orchard St. N7—2B 10
Stocks Pl. E14—1B 42
Stock St. E13—1C 30
Stockwell Av. SW9—1B 66
Stockwell Gdns. SW9—4B 52
Stockwell Gdns. Est. SW9
—5B 52
Stockwell Grn. SW9—5B 52
Stockwell La. SW9—5B 52
Stockwell M. SW9—5B 52
Stockwell Pk. Cres. SW9
—5B 52
Stockwell Pk. Rd. SW9—4B 52
Stockwell Pk. Wlk. SW9—1C 66
Stockwell Rd. SW9—5B 52
Stockwell St. SE10—2E 57
Stockwell Ter. SW9—4B 52
Stofield Gdns. SE9—3F 87
Stoford Clo. SW19—1A 76
Stokenchurch St. SW6—4D 49
Stoke Newington Rd. N16
—2B 12
Stoke Pl. NW10—2B 18
Stokesley St. W12—5B 18
Stoms Path. SE6—5C 84
Stondon Pk. SE23—4A 70
Stondon Wlk. E6—1F 31
Stonebridge Comn. E8—4B 12
Stonecutter St. EC4—5D 25
Stonefield St. N1—5C 10
Stonefield Way. SE7—3F 59
Stoneleigh Pl. W11—1F 33
Stoneleigh St. W11—1F 33
Stonell's Rd. SW11—4B 64
Stones End St. SE1—3E 39
Stoneyard La. E14—1D 43
Stoneycroft Clo. SE12—5B 72
Stoney La. E1—5A 26
Stoney St. SE1—2F 39
Stonhouse St. SW4—2F 65
Stonor Rd. W14—5B 34
Stopford Rd. E13—5C 16
Stopford Rd. SE17—1D 53
Storers Quay. E14—5F 43
Store St. E15—2F 15
Store St. WC1—4F 23
Storey's Ga. SW1—3F 37
Stories M. SE5—5A 54
Stories Rd. SE5—1A 68

Stork Rd. E7—3C 16
Stork's Rd. SE16—4C 40
Stormont Rd. SW11—1C 64
Story St. N1—4B 10
Stothard Pl. EC2—4A 26
Stothard St. E1—3E 27
Stoughton Clo. SE11—5B 38
Stoughton Clo. SW15—1C 74
Stourcliffe St. W1—5B 22
Stourhead Clo. SW19—5F 61
Stour Rd. E3—4C 14
Stowage. SE8—2D 57
Stowe Rd. W12—3D 33
Stracey Rd. E7—1C 16
Stradbroke Rd. N5—1E 11
Stradella Rd. SE24—4E 67
Strafford St. E14—3C 42
Strahan Rd. E3—2A 28
Straightsmouth. SE10—3E 57
Straker's Rd. SE15—2D 69
Strand. WC2—1A 38
Strand La. WC2—1B 38
Strangways Ter. W14—4B 34
Stranraer Way. N1—4B 10
Stratford Av. W8—4C 34
Stratford Gro. SW15—2F 61
Stratford Mkt. E15—5F 15
Stratford Pl. W1—5D 23
Stratford Rd. E13—5B 16
Stratford Rd. W8—4C 34
Stratford Shopping Centre. E15
—4F 15
Stratford Vs. NW1—4F 9
Strathan Clo. SW18—4B 62
Strathaven Rd. SE12—4D 73
Strathblaine Rd. SW11—2F 63
Strathdale. SW16—5B 80
Strathdon Dri. SW17—3F 77
Strathearn Pl. W2—5A 22
Strathearn Rd. SW19—5C 76
Stratheden Rd. SE3—3C 58
Strathleven Rd. SW2—3A 66
Strathmore Gdns. W8—2C 34
Strathmore Rd. SW19—3C 76
Strathnairn St. SE1—5C 40
Strathray Gdns. NW3—3A 8
Strath Ter. SW11—2A 64
Strathville Rd. SW18—2C 76
Strattondale St. E14—4E 43
Stratton St. W1—2D 37
Streatham Clo. SW16—2A 80
Streatham Comn. N. SW16
—5A 80
Streatham Comn. S. SW16
—5A 80
Streatham High Rd. SW16
—4A 80
Streatham Hill. SW2—2A 80

Streatham Pl. SW2—5A 66
Streatham St. WC1—5A 24
Streathbourne Rd. SW17
—3C 78
Streatley Pl. NW3—1E 7
Streatley Rd. NW6—4B 6
Streetfield M. SE3—1C 72
Streimer Rd. E15—1E 29
Strelley Way. W3—1A 32
Strickland Row. SW18—5F 63
Strickland St. SE8—4C 56
Stride Rd. E13—1B 30
Strode Rd. E7—1C 16
Strode Rd. NW10—3C 4
Strode Rd. SW6—3A 48
Strone Rd.—3E 17
E7 1-209 & 2-216
E12 remainder
Stronsa Rd. W12—3B 32
Stroud Cres. SW15—3C 74
Stroudley Wlk. E3—2D 29
Stroud Rd. SW19—3C 76
Strouts Pl. E2—2B 26
Strutton Ground. SW1—4F 37
Strype St. E1—4B 26
Stuart Rd. NW6—2C 20
Stuart Rd. SE15—2E 69
Stuart Rd. SW19—3C 76
Stucley Pl. NW1—4D 9
Studdridge St. SW6—5C 48
Studd St. N1—5D 11
Studholme Ct. NW3—1C 6
Studholme St. SE15—3D 55
Studland Rd. SE26—5F 83
Studland Rd. W6—5D 33
Studley Clo. E5—2A 14
Studley Est. SW4—4A 52
Studley Rd. E7—3D 17
Studley Rd. SW4—4A 52
Stukeley Rd. E7—4D 17
Stukeley St. WC2—5A 24
Sturdy Rd. SE15—5D 55
Sturgeon Rd. SE17—1E 53
Sturge St. SE1—3E 39
Sturmer Way. N7—2B 10
Sturry St. E14—5D 29
Sturt St. N1—1E 25
Stutfield St. E1—5C 26
Styles Gdns. SW9—1D 67
Sudbourne Rd. SW2—3A 66
Sudbrooke Rd. SW12—4B 64
Sudbury Cres. Brom—5C 86
Sudeley St. N1—1D 25
Sudlow Rd. SW18—3C 62
Sudrey St. SE1—3E 39
Sufferance Wharf Development.
E14—3C 42
Suffolk La. EC4—1F 39

Suffolk Pl. SW1—2F 37
Suffolk Rd. E13—2C 30
Suffolk Rd. NW10—4A 4
Suffolk Rd. SW13—3B 46
Suffolk St. E7—1C 16
Suffolk St. SW1—1F 37
Sugar Ho. La. E15—1E 29
Sugar Loaf Wlk. E2—2E 27
Sugden Rd. SW11—1C 64
Sugden St. SE5—2F 53
Sulgrave Rd. W6—4E 33
Sulina Rd. SW2—5A 66
Sulivan Ct. SW6—5C 48
Sulivan Rd. SW6—1C 62
Sullivan Av. F16—4F 31
Sullivan Clo. SW11—1A 64
Sullivan Rd. SE11—5D 39
Sultan St. SE5—3E 53
Sumatra Rd. NW6—2C 6
Sumburgh Rd. SW12—4C 64
Summercourt Rd. E1—5E 27
Summerfield Av. NW6—1A 20
Summerfield St. SE12—5B 72
Summerley St. SW18—2D 77
Summers St. EC1—3C 24
Summerstown. SW17—4E 77
Summit Clo. NW2—2A 6
Sumner Av. SE15—4B 54
Sumner Est. SE15—3B 54
Sumner Pl. SW7—5F 35
Sumner Pl. M. SW7—5F 35
Sumner Rd. SE15—2B 54
Sumner St. SE1—2D 39
Sumpter Clo. NW3—3E 7
Sunbury La. SW11—4F 49
Suncroft Pl. SE26—3E 83
Sunderland Rd. SE23—1F 83
Sunderland Ter. W2—5D 21
Sundew Av. W12—1C 32
Sundorne Rd. SE7—1E 59
Sundra Wlk. E1—3F 27
Sunfields Pl. SE3—3D 59
Sun La. SE3—3D 59
Sunningdale Av. W3—1A 32
Sunninghill Rd. SE13—5D 57
Sunnydale Rd. SE12—3D 73
Sunnydene St. SE26—4A 84
Sunnyhill Rd. SW16—4A 80
Sunnymead Rd. SW15—3D 61
Sunnyside. SW19—5A 76
Sunray Av. SE24—2F 67
Sun Rd. W14—1B 48
Sunset Rd. SE5—2E 67
Sun St. EC2—4F 25
Sunwell Clo. SE15—4D 55
Surrendale Pl. W9—3C 20
Surrey Canal Rd. SE15 & SE14
—2E 55

Surrey Gro. SE17—1A 54
Surrey La. SW11—4A 50
Surrey La. Est. SW11—4A 50
Surrey M. SE27—4A 82
Surrey Mt. SE23—1D 83
Surrey Quays Retail Centre. SE16
—4F 41
Surrey Quays Rd. SE16—4E 41
Surrey Rd. SE15—3F 69
Surrey Row. SE1—3D 39
Surrey Sq. SE17—1A 54
Surrey St. E13—2D 31
Surrey St. WC2—1B 38
Surrey Ter. SE17—1A 54
Surrey Water Rd. SE16—2F 41
Surr St. N7—2A 10
Susannah St. E14—5D 29
Susan Rd. SE3—5D 59
Sussex Gdns. W2—5F 21
Sussex M. W. W2—1F 35
Sussex Pl. NW1—3B 22
Sussex Pl. W2—5F 21
Sussex Pl. W6—1E 47
Sussex Sq. W2—1F 35
Sussex St. E13—2D 31
Sussex St. SW1—1D 51
Sussex Wlk. SW2—2D 67
Sutherland Av. W9—3C 20
Sutherland Gdns. SW14—1A 60
Sutherland Gro. SW18—4A 62
Sutherland Pl. W2—5C 20
Sutherland Rd. E3—1B 28
Sutherland Rd. W4—2A 46
Sutherland Row. SW1—1D 51
Sutherland Sq. SE17—1E 53
Sutherland St. SW1—1D 51
Sutherland Wlk. SE17—1E 53
Sutlej Rd. SE7—3E 59
Sutterton St. N7—3B 10
Sutton Ct. Rd. E13—2E 31
Sutton Est. W10—4E 19
Sutton Est., The. SW3—1A 50
Sutton Est., The. N1—4D 11
Sutton Pl. E9—2E 13
Sutton Rd. E13—3B 30
Sutton Row. W1—5F 23
Sutton Sq. E9—2E 13
Sutton St. E1—1E 41
Sutton's Way. EC1—3E 25
Sutton Way. W10—3E 19
Swaby Rd. SW18—1E 77
Swaffield Rd. SW18—5D 63
Swainson Rd. W3—3B 32
Swallands Rd. SE6—4D 85
(in two parts)
Swallow Clo. SE14—4F 55
Swallow Ct. SE12—5C 72
Swallowfield Rd. SE7—1D 59

Swallow Pl. W1—5D 23
Swallow St. W1—1E 37
Swanage Rd. SW18—4E 63
Swandon Way. SW18—2D 63
Swanfield St. E2—2B 26
Swan La. EC4—1F 39
Swan Mead. SE1—4A 40
Swan M. SW9—4B 52
Swan Pl. SW13—5B 46
Swan Rd. SE16—3E 41
Swan Rd. SE18—4F 45
Swanscombe Rd. W4—1A 46
Swanscombe Rd. W11—2F 33
Swan St. SE1—4E 39
Swanton Gdns. SW19—1F 75
Swan Wlk. SW3—2B 50
Swanwick Clo. SW15—5B 60
Swan Yd. N1—3D 11
Swaton Rd. E3—3C 28
Swedenborg Gdns. E1—1D 41
Sweden Ga. SE16—4A 42
Swedish Quays Development.
SE16—4A 42
Sweeney Cres. SE1—3B 40
Swete St. E13—1C 30
Sweyn Pl. SE3—5C 58
Swiftsden Way. Brom—5A 86
Swift St. SW6—4B 48
Swinbrook Rd. W10—4A 20
Swinburne Rd. SW15—2C 60
Swindon St. W12—2E 33
Swinford Gdns. SW9—1D 67
Swinnerton St. E9—2A 14
Swinton Pl. WC1—2B 24
Swinton St. WC1—2B 24
Swiss Ter. NW6—4F 7
Sycamore Clo. E16—4A 30
Sycamore Gdns. W6—4D 33
Sycamore Gro. SE6—4E 71
Sycamore St. EC1—3E 25
Sycamore Wlk. W10—3A 20
Sydcote. SE21—1E 81
Sydenham Av. SE26—5D 83
Sydenham Cotts. SE12—2E 87
Sydenham Hill.—4B 82
  SE26 1-135 & 2-48
  SE23 remainder
Sydenham Pk. SE26—3E 83
Sydenham Pk. Rd. SE26—3E 83
Sydenham Pl. SE27—3D 81
Sydenham Rise. SE23—2D 83
Sydenham Rd. SE26—4E 83
Sydmons Ct. SE23—5E 69
Sydner M. N16—1B 12
Sydner Rd. N16—1B 12
Sydney Clo. SW3—5F 35
Sydney M. SW3—5F 35
Sydney Pl. SW7—5F 35

Sydney St. SW3—1A 50
Sylvan Gro. SE15—2D 55
Sylvan Rd. E7—3C 16
Sylvester Path. E8—3D 13
Sylvester Rd. E8—3D 13
Symes M. NW1—1E 23
Symons St. SW3—5B 36

Tabard Garden Est. SE1—4F 39
Tabard St. SE1—3F 39
Tabernacle Av. E13—3C 30
Tabernacle St. EC2—3F 25
Tableer Av. SW4—3F 65
Tabley Rd. N7—1A 10
Tabor Rd. W6—4D 33
Tachbrook Est. SW1—1F 51
Tachbrook M. SW1—5E 37
Tachbrook St. SW1—5E 37
Tack M. SE4—1C 70
Tadema Rd. SW10—3E 49
Tadmor St. W12—2F 33
Taeping St. E14—5D 43
Taft Way. E3—2D 29
Talacre Rd. NW5—3C 8
Talbot Pl. SE3—5A 58
 (in two parts)
Talbot Rd. E7—1C 16
Talbot Rd.—5B 20
 W2 1-97 & 2-102
 W11 remainder
 (in two parts)
Talbot Sq. W2—5F 21
Talbot Wlk. NW10—3A 4
Talbot Yd. SE1—2F 39
Talcott Path. SW2—1C 80
Talfourd Pl. SE15—4B 54
Talfourd Rd. SE15—4B 54
Talgarth Rd.—1F 47
 W14 1-155
 W6 remainder
Talisman Sq. SE26—4C 82
Tallis Gro. SE7—2D 59
Tallis St. EC4—1C 38
Talmage Clo. SE23—5E 69
Talma Rd. SW2—2C 66
Talwin St. E3—2D 29
Tamarind Yd. E1—2C 40
Tamarisk Sq. W12—1B 32
Tamworth St. SW6—2C 48
Tanfield Av. NW2—1A 4
Tangley Gro. SW15—4B 60
Tankerton St. WC1—2A 24
Tanner's Hill. SE8—4B 56
Tanner St. SE1—3A 40
Tannsfeld Rd. SE26—5F 83
Tansley Clo. N7—2F 9
Tantallon Rd. SW12—1C 78

Tant Av. E16—5B 30
Tanza Rd. NW3—1B 8
Taplow St. N1—1E 25
Tappesfield Rd. SE15—1E 69
Tapp St. E1—3D 27
Tarbert Rd. SE22—3A 68
Tarbert Wlk. E1—1E 41
Tarleton Gdns. SE23—2D 83
Tarling Rd. E16—5B 30
Tarling St. E1—5E 27
Tarling St. Est. E1—5E 27
Tarn St. SE1—4E 39
Tarrington Clo. SW16—3F 79
Tarry La. SE8—5A 42
Tarver Rd. SE17—1D 53
Tarves Way. SE10—3D 57
Tasker Rd. NW3—2B 8
Tasman Rd. SW4—1A 66
Tasman Wlk. E16—5F 31
Tasso Rd. W6—2A 48
Tatnell Rd. SE23—4A 70
Tatum St. SE17—5F 39
Taunton M. NW1—3B 22
Taunton Pl. NW1—3B 22
Taunton Rd. SE12—3A 72
Taverners Clo. W11—2A 34
Taverner Sq. N5—1E 11
Tavern La. SW9—5C 52
Tavistock Clo. N16—2A 12
Tavistock Cres. W11—4B 20
Tavistock Ho. WC1—3F 23
Tavistock M. W11—5B 20
Tavistock Pl. WC1—3A 24
Tavistock Rd. E7—1B 16
Tavistock Rd. E15—3B 16
Tavistock Rd. NW10—1B 18
Tavistock Rd. W11—5B 20
Tavistock Sq. WC1—3F 23
Tavistock St. WC2—1A 38
Tavistock Tower. SE16—4A 42
Taviton St. WC1—3F 23
Tawny Way. SE16—5F 41
Taybridge Rd. SW11—1C 64
Tayburn Clo. E14—5E 29
Taylor Ct. E15—2E 15
Taylors Grn. W3—5A 18
Taylors La. NW10—4A 4
Taylor's La. SE26—4D 83
Taymount Rise. SE23—2E 83
Tayport Clo. N1—4B 10
Teak Clo. SE16—2A 42
Teal Clo. E16—4F 31
Teale St. E2—1C 26
Teasel Way. E15—2A 30
Tedworth Sq. SW3—1B 50
Teesdale Clo. E2—1D 27
Teesdale St. E2—1D 27
Tee, The. W3—5A 18

Teignmouth Clo. SW4—2F 65
Teignmouth Rd. NW2—2F 5
Telegraph Rd. SW15—5D 61
Telegraph St. EC2—5F 25
Teleman Sq. SE3—2D 73
Telephone Pl. SW6—2B 48
Telferscot Rd. SW12—1F 79
Telford Av. SW2—1F 79
Telford Rd. W10—4A 20
Telfords Yd. E1—1C 40
Telford Way. W3—4A 18
Tell Gro. SE22—2B 68
Tellson Av. SE18—4F 59
Temeraire St. SE16—3E 41
Temperley Rd. SW12—5C 64
Templar Ho. NW2—3B 6
Templars Ho. E15—2D 15
Templar Sq. S0—5D 53
Temple Av. EC4—1C 38
Templecombe Rd. E9—5E 13
Temple La. EC4—5C 24
Temple Mill La. E15—1D 15
Temple Mills Rd. E15—1C 14
Temple Pl. WC2—1B 38
Temple Rd. NW2—1E 5
Temple St. E2—1D 27
Templeton Clo. N16—2A 12
Templeton Pl. SW5—5C 34
Tenbury Clo. E7—2F 17
Tenbury Ct. SW2—1F 79
Tench St. E1—2D 41
Tenda Rd. SE16—5D 41
Tenham Av. SW2—2F 79
Tenison Ct. W1—1E 37
Tenison Way. SE1—2C 38
Tenniel Clo. W2—1E 35
Tennis St. SE1—3F 39
Tennyson Clo. SW19—5E 77
Tennyson Rd. E15—4A 16
Tennyson Rd. NW6—5B 6
Tennyson St. SW8—5D 51
Tenterden St. W1—5D 23
Tenter Ground. E1—4B 26
Tent St. E1—3D 27
Terborch Way. SE22—3A 68
Terminus Pl. SW1—4D 37
Terrace Gdns. SW13—5B 46
Terrace Rd. E9—4F 13
Terrace Rd. E13—5C 16
Terrace, The. NW6—5C 6
Terrace, The. SW1—3A 38
Terrace, The. SW13—5A 46
Terrapin Rd. SW17—3D 79
Terretts Pl. N1—4D 11
Terrick St. W12—5D 19
Tessa Sanderson Pl. SW8
—1D 65

Testerton Wlk. W11—1F 33
Tetbury Pl. N1—5D 11
Tetcott Rd. SW10—3E 49
Tetterby Way. SE16—1C 54
Teversham La. SW8—4A 52
Teviot St. E14—4E 29
Tewkesbury Av. SE23—5D 69
Thackeray Rd. E6—1F 31
Thackeray Rd. SW8—5D 51
Thackeray St. W8—4D 35
Thakeham Clo. SE26—5D 83
Thalia Clo. SE10—2F 57
Thame Rd. SE16—3F 41
Thames Av. SW10—4E 49
Thameside Industrial Est. E16
—3F 45
Thames Pl. E14—1B 42
Thames Quay. E14—3D 43
Thames Rd. E16—2F 45
Thames Rd. Industrial Est. E16
—2F 45
Thames St. SE10—2D 57
Thanet St. WC1—2A 24
Thavies Inn. EC1—5C 24
Thaxton Rd. W14—2B 48
Thayer St. W1—5C 22
Theatre St. SW11—1B 64
Theberton St. N1—5C 10
Theed St. SE1—2C 38
Thelma Gdns. SE3—4F 59
Theobald's Rd. WC1—4B 24
Theodore Ct. SE13—4F 71
Theodore Rd. SE13—4F 71
Therapia Rd. SE22—4E 69
Theresa Rd. W6—5C 32
Thermopylae Ga. E14—5D 43
Thessaly Rd. SW8—3E 51
Third Av. E13—2C 30
Third Av. W3—2B 32
Third Av. W10—2A 20
Thirleby Rd. SW1—4E 37
Thirlmere Rd. SW16—4F 79
Thirsk Rd. SW11—1C 64
Thistle Gro. SW10—1E 49
Thomas Baines Rd. SW11
—1F 63
Thomas Doyle St. SE1—4D 39
Thomas La. SE6—5C 70
Thomas More St. E1—2C 40
Thomas Rd. E14—5B 28
Thompson Rd. SE22—4B 68
Thompson's Av. SE5—3E 53
Thorburn Sq. SE1—5C 40
Thoresby St. N1—2E 25
Thornbury Rd. SW2—4A 66
Thorncliffe Rd. SW2—4A 66
Thorncombe Rd. SE22—3A 68
Thorncroft St. SW8—3A 52

Thorndean St. SW18—2E 77
Thorndike Rd. SW10—3E 49
Thorne Clo. E11—1A 16
Thorne Clo. E16—5C 30
Thorne Pas. SW13—5A 46
Thorne Rd. SW8—3A 52
Thorne St. SW13—1A 60
Thorney Cres. SW11—3F 49
Thorney St. SW1—5A 38
Thornfield Rd. W12—3D 33
Thornford Rd. SE13—3E 71
Thorngate Rd. W9—3C 20
Thorngrove Rd. E13—5D 17
Thornham Gro. E15—2F 15
Thornham St. SE10—2D 57
Thornhaugh M. WC1—3F 23
Thornhaugh St. WC1—3F 23
Thornhill Cres. N1—4B 10
Thornhill Gro. N1—4B 10
Thornhill Rd. N1—4C 10
Thornhill Sq. N1—4B 10
Thornlaw Rd. SE27—4C 80
Thornley Pl. SE10—1A 58
Thornsbeach Rd. SE6—1E 85
Thornsett Rd. SW18—1D 77
Thornton Av. SW2—1F 79
Thornton Av. W4—5A 32
Thornton Gdns. SW12—1F 79
Thornton Pl. W1—4B 22
Thornton Rd. SW12—5F 65
Thornton Rd. Brom—5C 86
Thornton St. SW9—5C 52
Thorntree Rd. SE7—1F 59
Thornville St. SE8—4C 56
Thornwood Rd. SE13—3A 72
Thorogood Gdns. E15—2A 16
Thorparch Rd. SW8—4F 51
Thorpebank Rd. W12—2C 32
Thorpe Clo. W10—5A 20
Thorpe Rd. E7—1B 16
Thorpewood Av. SE26—2D 83
Thorsden Way. SE19—5A 82
Thoydon Rd. E3—1A 28
Thrale Rd. SW16—5D 79
Thrale St. SE1—2E 39
Thrasher Clo. E8—5B 12
Thrawl St. E1—4B 26
Threadneedle St. EC2—5F 25
Three Colts La. E2—3D 27
Three Colt St. E14—5B 28
Three Kings Yd. W1—1D 37
Three Mill La. E3—2E 29
Three Oak La. SE1—3B 40
Threshers Pl. W11—1A 34
Thriffwood. SE26—3F 83
Thrisk Rd. SW11—1C 64
Throckmorten Rd. E16—5D 31
Throgmorton Av. EC2—5F 25

Throgmorton St. EC2—5F 25
Thrush St. SE17—1E 53
Thruxton Way. SE15—3B 54
Thurbarn Rd. SE6—5D 85
Thurland Rd. SE16—4C 40
Thurlby Rd. SE27—4C 80
Thurleigh Av. SW12—4C 64
Thurleigh Rd. SW12—4B 64
Thurlestone Rd. SE27—4C 80
Thurloe Clo. SW7—5A 36
Thurloe Pl. SW7—5F 35
Thurloe Sq. SW7—5A 36
Thurloe St. SW7—5F 35
Thurlow Hill. SE21—1E 81
Thurlow Pk. Rd. SE21—2D 81
Thurlow Rd. NW3—2F 7
Thurlow St. SE17—1F 53
Thurlow Ter. NW5—2C 8
Thurlow Wlk. SE17—1A 54
Thursley Gdns. SW19—2F 75
Thurso St. SW17—4F 77
Thurston Rd. SE13—5D 57
Thurtle Rd. E2—1B 26
Tibbenham Wlk. E13—1B 30
Tibberton Sq. N1—4E 11
Tibbet's Clo. SW19—1F 75
Tibbet's Corner. SW19—1F 75
Tibbet's Ride. SW15—5F 61
Tiber Gdns. N1—5A 10
Ticehurst Rd. SE23—2A 84
Tidal Basin Rd. E16—1B 44
Tideswell Rd. SW15—2E 61
Tideway Wlk. SW8—2E 51
Tidey St. E3—4C 28
Tidworth Rd. E3—3C 28
Tierney Rd. SW2—1A 80
Tiger Way. E5—1D 13
Tilbrook Rd. SE3—1E 73
Tilbury Clo. SE15—3B 54
Tildesley Rd. SW15—4E 61
Tilehurst Rd. SW18—1F 77
Tile Yd. E14—5B 28
Tileyard Rd. N7—4A 10
Tilford Gdns. SW19—1F 75
Tilia Rd. E5—1D 13
Tiller Rd. E14—4C 42
Tillett Sq. SE16—3A 42
Tillet Way. E2—2C 26
Tillman St. E1—5D 27
Tilloch St. N1—4B 10
Tillotson St. E1—4F 27
Tilney Ct. EC1—3E 25
Tilney Gdns. N1—3F 11
Tilney St. W1—2C 36
Tilson Gdns. SW2—5A 66
Tilton St. SW6—2A 48
Timberland Rd. E1—5D 27
Timber Mill Way. SW4—1F 65

Timber Pond Rd. SE16—2F 41
Timber St. EC1—3E 25
Timothy Clo. SW4—3E 65
Timothy Rd. E3—4B 28
Timsbury Wlk. SW15—1C 74
Tindal St. SW9—4D 53
Tinsley Rd. E1—4E 27
Tintagel Cres. SE22—2B 68
Tintern Clo. SW15—3A 62
Tintern St. SW4—2A 66
Tinto Rd. E16—3C 30
Tinworth St. SE11—1A 52
Tipthorpe Rd. SW11—1C 64
Titchborne Row. W2—5A 22
Titchfield Rd. NW8—1B 22
Titchwell Rd. SW18—1F 77
Tite St. SW3—2B 50
Titmuss St. W12—3D 33
Tiverton Rd. NW10—5F 5
Tiverton St. SE1—4E 39
Tivoli Rd. SE27—5E 81
Tobacco Dock. E1—1D 41
Tobago St. E14—3C 42
Tobin Clo. NW3—4A 8
Toby La. E1—3A 28
Tokenhouse Yd. EC2—5F 25
Toland Sq. SW15—3C 60
Tollbridge Clo. W10—3B 20
Tollet St. E1—3F 27
Tollgate Dri. SE21—2A 82
Tollgate Gdns. NW6—1D 21
Tollgate Rd.—4E 31
 E16 1-153 & 2-130
 E6 remainder
Tollington Rd. N7—1B 10
Tolmers Sq. NW1—3E 23
Tolpuddle St. N1—1C 24
Tolsford Rd. E5—2D 13
Tomlin's Gro. E3—2C 28
Tomlinson Clo. E2—2B 26
Tomlins Ter. E14—5A 28
Tompion St. EC1—2D 25
Tom Smith Clo. SE10—2A 58
Tonbridge St. WC1—2A 24
Tonsley Hill. SW18—3D 63
Tonsley Pl. SW18—3D 63
Tonsley Rd. SW18—3D 63
Tonsley St. SW18—3D 63
Took's Ct. EC4—5C 24
Tooley St. SE1—2A 40
Tooting Bec Gdns. SW16—4F 79
 (in two parts)
Tooting Bec Rd. SW17 & SW16
 —3C 78
Tooting B'way. SW17—5B 78
Tooting Gro. SW17—5A 78
Tooting High St. SW17—5A 78
Topham St. EC1—3C 24

Topley St. SE9—2E 73
Topsham Rd. SW17—3B 78
Torbay Rd. NW6—4B 6
Torbay St. NW1—4D 9
Torcross Dri. SE23—2E 83
Tor Gdns. W8—3C 34
Toronto Rd. E11—1F 15
Torquay St. W2—4D 21
Torrens Rd. E15—3B 16
Torrens Rd. SW2—3B 66
Torrens Sq. E15—3B 16
Torrens St. EC1—1D 25
Torriano Av. NW5—2F 9
Torriano Cotts. NW5—2E 9
Torriano M. NW5—2E 9
Torridge Gdns. SE15—2E 69
Torridon Rd.—5F 71
 SE13 1 & 3
 SE6 remainder
Torrington Pl. E1—2C 40
Torrington Pl. WC1—4F 23
Torrington St. WC1—3F 23
Torwood Rd. SW15—3C 60
Tothill St. SW1—3F 37
Tottenham Ct. Rd. W1—3E 23
Tottenham M. W1—4E 23
Tottenham Rd. N1—3A 12
Tottenham St. W1—4E 23
Totterdown St. SW17—4B 78
Totty St. E3—1A 28
Toulmin St. SE1—3E 39
Toulon St. SE5—3E 53
Tournay Rd. SW6—3B 48
Toussaint Wlk. SE16—4C 40
Towcester Rd. E3—3E 29
Tower Bri. SE1 & E1—2B 40
Tower Bri. Wharf E1—2C 40
Tower Bri. App. E1—1B 40
Tower Bri. Rd. SE1—4A 40
Tower Clo. NW3—2F 7
Tower Hamlets Rd. E7—1B 16
Tower Hill. EC3—1B 40
Tower Rd. NW10—4C 4
Tower Royal. EC4—1F 39
Tower St. WC2—5A 24
Town Hall Rd. SW11—1B 64
Townley Ct. E15—3B 16
Townley Rd. SE22—3A 68
Townley St. SE17—1F 53
 (in two parts)
Townmead Rd. SW6—1D 63
Townsend Rd. SE17—5A 40
Townshend Est. NW8—1A 22
Townshend Rd. NW8—5A 8
Towpath, The. SW6—4E 49
Towton Rd. SE27—2E 81
Toynbee St. E1—4B 26
Tracey Av. NW2—2E 5

Tradescant Rd. SW8—3A 52
Trafalgar Av. SE15—1B 54
Trafalgar Clo. SE16—5A 42
Trafalgar Gdns. E1—4F 27
Trafalgar Gro. SE10—2F 57
Trafalgar Gro. SE10—2F 57
Trafalgar Sq. WC2 & SW1
 —2F 37
Trafalgar St. SE17—1F 53
Trafford Clo. E15—2D 15
Tramway Av. E15—4F 15
Tranley M. NW3—1A 8
Tranmere Rd. SW18—2E 77
Tranquil Pas. SE3—5B 58
Tranquil Vale. SE3—5A 58
Transay Wlk. N1—3F 11
Transept St. NW1—4A 22
Transwell St. SE1—3C 38
Tranton Rd. SE16—4C 40
Treadgold St. W11—1F 33
Treadway St. E2—1D 27
Treaty St. N1—5B 10
Trebeck St. W1—2D 37
Trebovir Rd. SW5—1C 48
Treby St. E3—3B 28
Trecastle Way. N7—1F 9
Tredegar M. E3—2B 28
Tredegar Rd. E3—1B 28
Tredegar Sq. E3—2B 28
Tredegar Ter. E3—2B 28
Trederwen Rd. E8—5C 12
Tredown Rd. SE26—5E 83
Tredwell Rd. SE27—4D 81
Treen Av. SW13—1B 60
Tree Rd. E16—5E 31
Treewall Gdns. Brom—4D 87
Trefil Wlk. N7—1A 10
Trefoil Rd. SW18—3E 63
Tregarvon Rd. SW11—2C 64
Trego Rd. E9—4C 14
Tregothnan Rd. SW9—1A 66
Tregunter Rd. SW10—2E 49
Treherne Ct. SW9—4D 53
Treherne Ct. SW17—4C 78
Trehurst St. E5—2A 14
Trelawney Est. E9—3E 13
Trelawn Rd. SW2—3C 66
Trellis Sq. E3—2B 28
Tremadoc Rd. SW4—2F 65
Tremaine Clo. SE4—5C 56
Trenchard St. SE10—1F 57
Trenchold St. SW8—2A 52
Trenmar Gdns. NW10—2D 19
Trentham St. SW18—1C 76
Trent Rd. SW2—3B 66
Treport St. SW18—5D 63
Tresco Rd. SE15—2D 69
Tresham Cres. NW8—3A 22

Tresham Wlk. E9—2E 13
Tressell Clo. N1—4D 11
Tressillian Cres. SE4—1C 70
Tressillian Rd. SE4—2B 70
Trevanion Rd. W14—1A 48
Trevelyan Gdns. NW10—5E 5
Trevelyan Rd. E15—1B 16
Trevelyan Rd. SW17—5A 78
Treveris St. SE1—2D 39
Treverton St. W10—3F 19
Treville St. SW15—5D 61
Treviso Rd. SE23—2F 83
Trevithick St. SE8—2C 56
Trevor Pl. SW7—3A 36
Trevor Sq. SW7—3B 36
Trevor St. SW7—3A 36
Trewint St. SW18—2E 77
Trewsbury Rd. SE26—5F 83
Triangle Ct. E16—4F 31
Triangle Pl. SW4—2F 65
Triangle Rd. E8—5D 13
Triangle, The. E8—5D 13
Trident St. SE16—5F 41
Trigon Rd. SW8—3B 52
Trilby Rd. SE23—2F 83
Trinidad St. E14—1B 42
Trinity Business Centre. SE16
　　　　　　　—3B 42
Trinity Church Pas. SW13
　　　　　　　—2D 47
Trinity Chu. Rd. SW13—2D 47
Trinity Chu. Sq. SE1—4E 39
Trinity Clo. NW3—1F 7
Trinity Clo. SE13—2F 71
Trinity Clo. N1—5A 12
Trinity Ct. W2—5E 21
Trinity Cres. SW17—2B 78
Trinity Gdns. E16—4B 30
Trinity Gdns. SW9—2B 66
Trinity Gro. SE10—4E 57
Trinity M. W10—5F 19
Trinity Pl. EC3—1B 40
Trinity Rise. SW2—1C 80
Trinity Rd.—2E 63
　　SW17 1-259 & 4-226
　　SW18 remainder
Trinity Rd. SW19—5C 76
Trinity Sq. EC3—1B 40
Trinity St. E16—4B 30
Trinity St. SE1—3E 39
Trinity Wlk. NW3—3E 7
Trinity Way. W3—1A 32
Trinity Wharf Business Centre.
　　　　　　SE16—3B 42
Trio Pl. SE1—3E 39
Tristan Sq. SE3—1A 72
Tristram Rd. Brom—4B 86
Triton Sq. NW1—3E 23

Tritton Rd. SE21—3F 81
Troon St. E1—5A 28
Trossachs Rd. SE22—3A 68
Trothy Rd. SE1—5C 40
Trott St. SW11—4A 50
Troughton Rd. SE7—1D 59
Troutbeck Rd. SE14—4A 56
Trouville Rd. SW4—4E 65
Trowbridge Rd. E9—3B 14
Troy Town. SE15—1C 68
Truman's Rd. N16—2A 12
Trumpington Rd. E7—1B 16
Trump St. EC2—5E 25
Trundle's Rd. SE8—1F 55
Trundley's Ter. SE8—5F 41
Truro St. NW5—3C 9
Truslove Rd. SE27—5C 80
Trussley Rd. W6—4E 33
Trust Wlk. SE21—1D 81
Tryon St. SW3—1B 50
Tubbs Rd. NW10—1B 18
Tuckton Wlk. SW15—5B 60
Tudor Clo. NW3—2A 8
Tudor Gdns. SW13—1A 60
Tudor Gro. E9—4E 13
Tudor Rd. E6—5E 17
Tudor Rd. E9—5D 13
Tudor Rd. EC4—1C 38
Tudway Rd. SE3—1D 73
Tufnell Pk. Rd.—1E 9
　　N7 1-217 & 2-210
　　N19 remainder
Tufton St. SW1—4A 38
Tugela St. SE6—2B 84
Tulse Hill. SW2—4C 66
Tulse Hill Est. SW2—4C 66
Tulse Ho. SW2—4C 66
Tulsemere Rd. SE27—2E 81
Tunis Rd. W12—2E 33
Tunley Grn. E14—4B 28
Tunley Rd. NW10—5A 4
Tunley Rd. SW17—2C 78
Tunmarsh La. E13—2E 31
Tunnel App. E14—1A 42
Tunnel App. SE10—3A 44
Tunnel Av. SE10—3F 43
　　(in two parts)
Tunnel Rd. SE16—3E 41
Tunstall Rd. SW9—2B 66
Tunworth Cres. SW15—4B 60
Turenne Clo. SW18—2E 63
Turin St. E2—2C 26
Turk's Head Yd. EC1—4D 25
Turks Row. SW3—1B 50
Turley Clo. E15—5A 16
Turnberry Quay. E14—4D 43
Turnchapel M. SW4—1D 65
Turner's All. EC3—1A 40

Turner's Rd. E3—4B 28
Turner St. E1—4D 27
Turner St. E16—5B 30
Turneville Rd. W14—2B 48
Turney Rd. SE21—5E 67
Turnham Grn. Ter. W4—5A 32
Turnham Grn. Ter. M. W4
　　　　　　　—5A 32
Turnham Rd. SE4—3A 70
Turnmill St. EC1—4D 25
Turnpike Clo. SE8—3B 56
Turnpin La. SE10—2E 57
Turnstone Clo. E13—2C 30
Turpentine La. SW1—1D 51
Turquand St. SE17—5E 39
Turret Gro. SW4—1E 65
Turville St. E2—3B 26
Tuskar St. SE10—2A 58
Tustin Est. SE15—2E 55
Tweedale Ct. E15—2E 15
Tweedmouth Rd. E13—1D 31
Twelvetrees Cres. E3—3E 29
Twilley St. SW18—5D 63
Twine Ct. E1—1E 41
Twisden Rd. NW5—1D 9
Twyford Pl. WC2—5B 24
Twyford St. N1—5B 10
Tyas Rd. E16—3B 30
Tyburn Way. W1—1B 36
Tyers Ga. SE1—3A 40
Tyers St. SE11—1B 52
Tyers Ter. SE11—1B 52
Tyler Clo. E2—1B 26
Tyler St. SE10—1A 58
Tilney Av. SE19—5B 82
Tilney Rd. E7—1E 17
Tyndale La. N1—4D 11
Tyndale Ter. N1—4D 11
Tyneham Clo. SW11—1C 64
Tyneham Rd. SW11—5C 50
Tynemouth St. SW6—5E 49
Tyne St. E1—5B 26
Tynwald Ho. SE26—3C 82
Type Sq. E2—1F 27
Tyrawley Rd. SW6—4D 49
Tyrrell Rd. SE22—2C 68
Tyrwhitt Rd. SE4—1C 70
Tysoe St. EC1—2C 24
Tyson Gdns. SE23—5E 69
Tyson Rd. SE23—5E 69
Tyssen Pas. E8—3B 12
Tyssen St. E8—3B 12

Uamvar St. E14—4D 29
Udall St. SW1—5E 37
Uffington Rd. NW10—5C 4
Uffington Rd. SE27—4C 80

184

Ufford St. SE1—3C 38
Ufton Gro. N1—4F 11
Ufton Rd. N1—4A 12
Ujima Ct. SW16—4A 80
Ullin St. E14—4E 29
Ullswater Rd. SE27—2D 81
Ullswater Rd. SW13—3C 46
Ulster Pl. NW1—3D 23
Ulundi Rd. SE3—2A 58
Ulva Rd. SW15—3F 61
Ulverscroft Rd. SE22—3C 68
Ulverstone Rd. SE27—2D 81
Ulysses Rd. NW6—2B 6
Umberston St. E1—5C 26
Umbria St. SW15—4C 60
Undercliff Rd. SE13—1C 70
Underhill Rd. SE22—3C 68
Underhill St. NW1—5D 9
Undershaft. EC3—5A 26
Undershaw Rd. Brom—3B 86
Underwood Rd. E1—3C 26
Underwood Row. N1—2E 25
Underwood St. N1—2E 25
Undine Rd. E14—5D 43
Undine St. SW17—5B 78
Unicorn Pas. SE1—2A 40
Union Cotts. E15—4A 16
Union Dri. E1—3A 28
Union Gro. SW8—5F 51
Union Rd.—5F 51
   SW4 1-93 & 2-102
   SW8 remainder
Union Sq. N1—5E 11
Union St. E15—5E 15
Union St. SE1—2D 39
Union Wlk. E2—2A 26
Union Yd. W1—5D 23
Unity Way. SE18—4F 45
University St. WC1—3E 23
Unwin Clo. SE15—2C 54
Unwin Rd. SW7—4F 35
Upbrook M. W2—5E 21
Upcerne Rd. SW10—3E 49
Upgrove Mnr. Way. SW2—5C 66
Upham Pk. Rd. W4—5A 32
Upland Rd. E13—3C 30
Upland Rd. SE22—5C 68
Upnor Way. SE17—1A 54
Up. Addison Gdns. W14—3A 34
Up. Belgrave St. SW1—4C 36
Up. Berkeley St. W1—5B 22
Up. Brockley Rd. SE4—5B 56
Up. Brook St. W1—1C 36
Up. Cheyne Row. SW3—2A 50
Up. Grosvenor St. W1—1C 36
Up. Ground. SE1—2C 38
Up. Harley St. NW1—3C 22

Up. James St. W1—1E 37
Up. John St. W1—1E 37
Up. Mall. W6—1C 46
Up. Marsh. SE1—4A 38
Up. Montagu St. W1—4B 22
Up. North St. E14—4C 28
Up. Park Rd. NW3—2B 8
Up. Phillimore Gdns. W8—3C 34
Up. Richmond Rd. SW15—2B 60
Upper Rd. E13—2C 30
Up. Saint Martin's La. WC2
   —1A 38
Upper St. N1—1D 25
Up. Tachbrook St. SW1—5E 37
Up. Thames St. EC4—1D 39
Upperton Rd. E. E13—2E 31
Upperton Rd. W. E13—2E 31
Up. Tooting Pk. SW17—2B 78
Up. Tooting Rd. SW17—4B 78
Up. Tulse Hill. SW2—5B 66
Up. Wimpole St. W1—4C 22
Up. Woburn Pl. WC1—2F 23
Upstall St. SE5—4D 53
Upton Av. E7—4C 16
Upton La. E7—4C 16
Upton Pk. Rd. E7—4D 17
Upwood Rd. SE12—4C 72
Urlwin St. SE5—2E 53
Urlwin Wlk. SW9—4C 52
Urmston Dri. SW19—1A 76
Ursula St. SW11—4A 50
Urswick Rd. E9—2E 13
Usborne M. SW8—3B 52
Usher Rd. E3—1B 28
   (in two parts)
Usk Rd. SW11—2E 63
Usk St. E2—2F 27
Uverdale Rd. SW10—3E 49
Uxbridge Rd. W12—2C 32
Uxbridge St. W8—2C 34

Vale Clo. W9—2E 21
Vale Cres. SW15—4A 74
Vale End. SE22—2B 68
Valentia Pl. SW9—2C 66
Valentine Ct. SE23—2F 83
Valentine Pl. SE1—3D 39
Valentine Rd. E9—3F 13
Valentine Row. SE1—3D 39
Valerian Way. E15—2A 30
Vale Rd. E7—3D 17
Vale Royal. N7—4A 10
Vale St. SE27—3F 81
Valeswood Rd. Brom—5B 86
Vale, The. SW3—2F 49
Vale, The. W3—2B 32
Valetta Gro. E13—1C 30

Valetta Rd. W3—3A 32
Valette St. E9—3E 13
Vallance Rd.—3C 26
   E1 1-121 & 2-168
   E2 remainder
Valleyfield Rd. SW16—5B 80
Valley Gro. SE7—1E 59
Valley Rd. SW16—5B 80
Valliere Rd. NW10—2C 18
Valmar Rd. SE5—4E 53
Valmar Trading Est. SE5—4E 53
Valnay St. SW17—5B 78
Valonia Gdns. SW18—4B 62
Vanbrugh Clo. E16—4F 31
Vanbrugh Fields. SE3—3B 58
Vanbrugh Hill—1B 58
   SE3 1-31 & 2-44
   SE10 remainder
Vanbrugh Pk. SE3—3B 58
Vanbrugh Pk. Rd. SE3—3B 58
Vanbrugh Pk. Rd. W. SE3
   —3B 58
Vanbrugh Ter. SE3—4B 58
Vancouver Rd. SE23—2A 84
Vanderbilt Rd. SW18—1E 77
Vandome Clo. E16—5D 31
Vandon Pas. SW1—4E 37
Vandon St. SW1—4E 37
Vandyke Clo. SW15—4F 61
Vandy St. EC2—3A 26
Vane Clo. NW3—1F 7
Vane St. SW1—5E 37
Van Gogh Ct. E14—4F 43
Vanguard St. SE8—4C 56
Vanoc Gdns. Brom—4C 86
Vansittart Rd. E7—1B 16
Vansittart St. SE14—2A 56
Vanston Pl. SW6—3C 48
Vant Rd. SW17—5B 78
Varcoe Rd. SE16—1D 55
Vardens Rd. SW11—2F 63
Varden St. E1—5D 27
Varley Rd. E16—5D 31
Varna Rd. SW6—3A 48
Varndell St. NW1—2E 23
Vassall Rd. SW9—3C 52
Vauban Est. SE16—4B 40
Vauban St. SE16—4B 40
Vaughan Av. W6—5B 32
Vaughan Rd. E15—3B 16
Vaughan Rd. SE5—5E 53
Vaughan Way. E1—2C 40
Vaughan Williams Clo. SE8
   —3C 56
Vauxhall Bri. SW1 & SE1
   —1A 52
Vauxhall Bri. Rd. SW1—5E 37
Vauxhall Cross. SE1—1A 52

Vauxhall Gro. SW8—2B 52
Vauxhall St. SE11—1B 52
Vauxhall Wlk. SE11—1B 52
Vawdrey Clo. E1—3E 27
Veda Rd. SE13—2C 70
Velde Way. SE22—3A 68
Venables St. NW8—3F 21
Vencourt Pl. W6—5C 32
Venetian Rd. SE5—5E 53
Venner Rd. SE26—5E 83
Venn St. SW4—2E 65
Ventnor Rd. SE14—3F 55
Venue St. E14—4E 29
Vera Lynn Clo. E7—1C 16
Vera Rd. SW6—4A 48
Verbena Gdns. W6—1C 46
Verdant La. SE6—5A 72
Verdun Rd. SW13—2C 46
Vereker Rd. W14—1A 48
Vere St. W1—5D 23
Verity Clo. W11—1A 34
Ver Meer Ct. E14—4F 43
Vermont Rd. SW18—4D 63
Verney Rd. SE16—1D 55
Verney Way. SE16—1D 55
Vernon Pl. WC1—4A 24
Vernon Rise. WC1—2B 24
Vernon Rd. E3—1B 28
Vernon Rd. E15—4A 16
Vernon Sq. WC1—2B 24
Vernon St. W14—5A 34
Vernon Yd. W11—1B 34
Verona Rd. E7—4C 16
Veronica Rd. SW17—2D 79
Verran Rd. SW12—5D 65
Verulam St. WC1—4C 24
Vesey Path. E14—5D 29
Vespan Rd. W12—3C 32
Vesta Rd. SE4—5A 56
Vestris Rd. SE23—2F 83
Vestry M. SE5—4A 54
Vestry Rd. SE5—4A 54
Vestry St. N1—2F 25
Vevey St. SE6—2B 84
Viaduct Bldgs. EC1—4C 24
Viaduct Pl. E2—2D 27
Viaduct St. E2—2D 27
Vian St. SE13—1D 71
Vibart Gdns. SW2—5B 66
Vicarage Av. SE3—3C 58
Vicarage Ct. W8—3D 35
Vicarage Cres. SW11—4F 49
Vicarage Gdns. W8—2C 34
Vicarage Ga. W8—2D 35
Vicarage Gro. SE5—4F 53
Vicarage La. E15—4A 16
Vicarage Rd. E15—4B 16
Vicarage Wlk. SW11—4F 49

Vicar's Clo. E9—5E 13
Vicars Clo. E15—5C 16
Vicar's Hill. SE13—2D 71
Vicars Oak Rd. SE19—5A 82
Vicar's Rd. NW5—2C 8
Viceroy Rd. SW8—4A 52
Victoria Av. E6—5F 17
Victoria Av. EC2—4A 26
Victoria Ct. SE26—5E 83
Victoria Cres. SE19—5A 82
Victoria Dock Rd. E16—5A 30
Victoria Dri. SW19—5F 61
Victoria Embkmt. SW1, WC2 &
EC4—3A 38
Victoria Gdns. W11—2C 34
Victoria Gro. W8—4E 35
Victoria Gro. M. W2—1C 34
Victoria Industrial Est., The.
NW10—3A 18
Victoria M. NW6—5C 6
Victoria M. SW4—2D 65
Victoria Pk. Rd. E9—5E 13
Victoria Pk. Sq. E2—2E 27
Victoria Rise. SW4—1D 65
Victoria Rd. E11—1A 16
Victoria Rd. E13—1C 30
Victoria Rd. NW6—1B 20
Victoria Rd. NW10—3A 18
Victoria Rd. W8—4E 35
Victoria Sq. SW1—4D 37
Victoria St. E15—4A 16
Victoria St. SW1—4C 37
Victoria Way. SE7—1D 59
Victor Rd. NW10—2D 19
Victory Pl. SE17—5F 39
Victory Sq. SE5—2F 53
Victory Wlk. SE8—4C 56
Victory Way. SE16—3A 42
Viewfield Rd. SW18—4B 62
Vigilant Clo. SE26—4C 82
Vigo St. W1—1E 37
Viking St. SW6—2C 48
Village, The. SE7—2F 59
Village Way. NW10—1A 4
Village Way. SE21—4F 67
Villa Rd. SW9—1C 66
Villa St. SE17—1F 53
Villa Wlk. SE17—1F 53
Villiers Rd. NW2—3C 4
Villiers St. WC2—2A 38
Vincent Clo. SE16—3A 42
Vincent Sq. SW1—5F 37
Vincent St. E16—4B 30
Vincent St. SW1—5F 37
Vincent Ter. N1—1D 25
Vince St. EC1—2F 25
Vine Ct. E1—4C 26
Vinegar St. E1—2D 41

Vine Hill. EC1—3C 24
Vine La. SE1—2A 40
Vineries, The. SE6—1C 84
Vine Rd. E15—4B 16
Vine Rd. SW13—1B 60
Vine St. EC3—1B 40
  (in two parts)
Vine St. W1—1E 37
Vine St. Bri. EC1—3C 24
Vineyard Clo. SE6—1C 84
Vineyard Hill Rd. SW19—4C 76
Vineyard Wlk. EC1—3C 24
Viney Rd. SE13—1D 71
Vining St. SW9—2C 66
Vintners Pl. EC4—1E 39
Viola Sq. W12—1B 32
Violet Hill. NW8—1E 21
Violet Rd. E3—3D 29
Violet St. E2—3D 27
Virgil Pl. W1—4B 22
Virgil St. SE1—4B 38
Virginia Rd. E2—2B 26
Virginia St. E1—1C 40
Virginia Wlk. SW2—4B 66
Viscount St. EC1—3E 25
Vista, The. SE9—4F 73
Vivian Rd. E3—1A 28
Vivian Sq. SE15—1D 69
Voltaire Rd. SW4—1F 65
Voss St. E2—2C 26
Vulcan Rd. SE4—5B 56
Vulcan Ter. SE4—5B 56
Vulcan Way. N7—3B 10
Vyner St. E2—5D 13

Wadding St. SE17—5F 39
Waddington Rd. E15—2F 15
Waddington St. E15—3F 15
Wade Rd. E16—5E 31
Wadeson St. E2—1D 27
Wade's Pl. E14—1D 43
Wadham Gdns. NW3—4A 8
Wadham Rd. SW15—2A 62
Wadhurst Rd. SW8—4E 51
Wager St. E3—3B 28
Waghorn Rd. E13—5E 17
Waghorn St. SE15—1C 68
Wagner St. SE15—3E 55
Wainford Clo. SW19—1F 75
Waite Davies Rd. SE12—5B 72
Waite St. SE15—2B 54
Wakefield M. WC1—2A 24
Wakefield St. E6—5F 17
Wakefield St. WC1—2A 24
Wakeham St. N1—3F 11
Wakehurst Rd. SW11—3A 64
Wakeling St. E14—5A 28
Wakelin Rd. E15—1A 30
Wakeman Rd. NW10—2E 19

Wakley St. EC1—2D 25
Walberswick St. SW8—3A 52
Walbrook. EC4—1F 39
Walburgh St. E1—5D 27
Walcorde Av. SE17—5E 39
Walcot Sq. SE11—5C 38
Walcott St. SW1—5E 37
Waldeck Gro. SE27—3D 81
Waldemar Av. SW6—4A 48
Waldemar Rd. SW19—5C 76
Waldenshaw Rd. SE23—1E 83
Walden St. E1—5D 27
Waldo Clo. SW4—3E 65
Waldo Rd. NW10—2C 18
Waldram Cres. SE23—1E 83
Waldram Pk. Rd. SE23—1F 83
Waldram Pl. SE23—1E 83
Waldron M. SW3—2F 49
Waldron Rd. SW18—3E 77
Walerand Rd. SE13—5E 57
Waley St. E1—4A 28
Walford Rd. N16—1A 12
Walham Gro. SW6—3C 48
Walham Yd. SW6—3C 48
Walkerscroft Mead. SE21
—1E 81
Walkers Pl. SW15—2A 62
Walkford Way. SE15—3B 54
Wallace Rd. N1—3E 11
Wallbutton Rd. SE4—5A 56
Waller Rd. SE14—4F 55
Wallflower St. W12—1B 32
Wallgrave Rd. SW5—5D 35
Wallingford Av. W10—5F 19
Wallis Clo. SW11—1F 63
Wallis Rd. E9—3B 14
Wall St. N1—3F 11
Wallwood St. E14—4B 28
Walmer Rd. W11—1A 34
Walmer St. W1—4B 22
Walm La. NW2—3E 5
Walney Wlk. N1—3E 11
Walnut Clo. SE8—2B 56
Walnut Gdns. E15—2A 16
Walnut Tree Clo. SW13—4B 46
Walnut Tree Cotts. SW19
—5A 76
Walnut Tree Rd. SE10—1A 58
(in two parts)
Walnut Tree Wlk. SE11—5C 38
Walpole Rd. E6—4E 17
Walpole Rd. SE14—3B 56
Walpole Rd. SW19—5F 77
Walpole St. SW3—1B 50
Walsham Rd. SE14—5F 55
Walter St. E2—2F 27
Walters Way. SE23—4F 69
Walter Ter. E1—5F 27

Walterton Rd. W9—3B 20
Walton Clo. SW8—3A 52
Walton Pl. SW3—4B 36
Walton Rd. E13—1E 31
Walton St. SW3—5A 36
Walworth Pl. SE17—1E 53
Walworth Rd. SE 39
SE17 2-96
SE17 remainder
Wanborough Dri. SW15—1D 75
Wandle Rd. SW17—2A 78
Wandle Way. SW18—1D 77
Wandon Rd. SW6—3D 49
Wandsworth Bri. SW6 & SW18
—1D 63
Wandsworth Bri. Rd. SW6
—4D 49
Wandsworth Comn. N. Side.
SW18—3F 63
Wandsworth Comn. W. Side.
SW18—3E 63
Wandsworth High St. SW18
—3C 62
Wandsworth Plain. SW18
—3D 63
Wandsworth Rd. SW8—1D 65
Wanless Rd. SE24—1E 67
Wanley Rd. SE5—2F 67
Wanlip Rd. E13—3D 31
Wansbeck Rd. E9—4B 14
Wansdown Pl. SW6—3D 49
Wansey St. SE17—5E 39
Wantage Rd. SE12—3B 72
Wapping Dock St. E1—2D 41
Wapping High St. E1—2C 40
Wapping La. E1—1D 41
Wapping Wall. E1—2E 41
Warbeck Rd. W12—3D 33
Warburton Rd. E8—5D 13
Wardale Clo. SE16—4D 41
Wardalls Clo. SE14—3E 55
Warden Rd. NW5—3C 8
Wardens Gro. SE1—2E 39
Wardle St. E9—2F 13
Wardley St. SW18—5D 63
Wardo Av. SW6—4A 48
Wardour St. W1—5E 23
Ward Rd. E15—5F 15
Warfield Rd. NW10—2F 19
Wardham St. SE5—3D 53
(in two parts)
Waring St. SE27—4E 81
Warley St. E2—2F 27
Warlock Rd. W9—3B 20
Warlters Clo. N7—1A 10
Warlters Rd. N7—1A 10
Warmington Rd. SE24—4E 67
Warndon St. SE16—5F 41

Warneford St. E9—5D 13
Warner Clo. E15—2A 16
Warner Pl. E2—1C 26
Warner Rd. SE5—4E 53
Warner St. EC1—3C 24
Warple Way. W3—3A 32
Warren Clo. SE21—5E 67
Warrender Rd. N19—1E 9
Warren Gdns. E15—2F 15
Warren M. W1—3E 23
Warren St. W1—3E 23
Warren Wlk. SE7—2E 59
Warriner Gdns. SW11—4B 50
Warrington Cres. W9—3E 21
Warrington Gdns. W9—3E 21
Warton Rd. E15—4E 15
Warwick Av.—3D 21
    W2 1-5a & 2-16
    W9 remainder
Warwick Ct. WC1—4B 24
Warwick Cres. W2—4E 21
Warwick Dri. SW15—1D 61
Warwick Est. W2—4D 21
Warwick Gdns. W14—5B 34
Warwick Ho. St. SW1—2F 37
Warwick La. EC4—5D 25
Warwick Pl. W9—4E 21
Warwick Pl. N. SW1—5E 37
Warwick Rd. E15—3B 16
Warwick Rd.—5B 34
    SW5 1-133 & 2-76
    W14 remainder
Warwick Row. SW1—4E 37
Warwickshire Path. SE8—3B 56
Warwick Sq. EC4—5D 25
Warwick Sq. SW1—1E 51
Warwick Sq. M. SW1—5E 37
Warwick St. W1—1E 37
Warwick Way. SW1—1D 51
Warwick Yd. EC1—3E 25
Washington Rd. E6—4E 17
Washington Rd. SW13—3C 46
Wastdale Rd. SE23—1F 83
Waterbank Rd. SE6—4E 85
Waterden Rd. E15—2C 14
Waterer Ho. SE6—4E 85
Waterfall Cotts. SW19—5F 77
Waterfall Rd. SW19—5F 77
Waterfall Ter. SW17—5A 78
Waterford Rd. SW6—3D 49
Watergate. EC4—1D 39
Watergate St. SE8—2C 56
Watergate Wlk. WC2—2A 38
Waterhouse Clo. E16—4F 31
Waterhouse Clo. NW3—2F 7
Waterhouse Clo. W6—5F 33
Water La. E15—3A 16
Water La. NW1—4D 9

Waterloo Bri. WC2 & SE1
—1B 38
Waterloo Clo. E9—2E 13
Waterloo Gdns. E2—1E 27
Waterloo Pas. NW6—4B 6
Waterloo Pl. SW1—2F 37
Waterloo Rd. E6—4E 17
Waterloo Rd. E7—2B 16
Waterloo Rd. SE1—3C 38
Waterloo Ter. N1—4D 11
Waterman St. SW15—1F 61
Watermans Wlk. SE16—4A 42
Waterman Way. E1—2D 41
Watermead Rd. SE6—4E 85
Waterside Clo. SE16—3C 40
Waterside Pl. NW1—5C 8
Waterside Point. SW11—3A 50
Waterside Way. SW17—4E 77
Waterson St. E2—2B 26
Waters Rd. SE6—3A 86
Waterworks Rd. SW2—4B 66
Watford Clo. SW11—4A 50
Watford Rd. E16—4C 30
Watkinson Rd. N7—3B 10
Watling Gdns. NW2—3A 6
Watling St. EC4—5E 25
Watlington Gro. SE26—5A 84
Watney Mkt. E1—5D 27
Watney St. E1—5D 27
Watson Clo. N16—2F 11
Watson's M. W1—4A 22
Watson's St. SE8—3C 54
Watson St. E13—1D 31
Watts Gro. E3—4D 29
Watts St. E1—2D 41
Wat Tyler Rd. SE10—5E 57
Wavel M. NW6—4D 7
Wavel Pl. SE26—5B 82
Waveney Av. SE15—2D 69
Waveney Clo. E1—2C 40
Waverley Ct. SE26—5E 83
Waverley Pl. NW8—1F 21
Waverton Rd. SW18—5E 63
Waverton St. W1—2D 37
Wavertree Rd. SW2—1B 80
Waxwell Ter. SE1—3B 38
Wayford St. SW11—5A 50
Wayland Av. E8—2C 12
Waylett Pl. SE27—3D 81
Waynflete Sq. W10—1F 33
Waynflete St. SW18—2E 77
Weardale Rd. SE13—2E 71
Wear Pl. E2—2D 27
Wearside Rd. SE13—2D 71
Weatherley Clo. E3—4B 28
Weaver's La. SE1—2A 40
Weavers Ter. SW6—2C 48
Weaver St. E1—3C 26

Weavers Way. NW1—5F 9
Weaver Wlk. SE27—4E 81
Webber Row. SE1—3D 39
Webber St. SE1—3C 38
Webb Gdns. E13—3C 30
Webb Pl. NW10—2B 18
Webb Rd. SE3—2B 58
Webb's Rd. SW11—3B 64
Webb St. SE1—4A 40
Webster Rd. SE16—4C 40
Wedderburn Rd. NW3—2F 7
Wedgwood M. W1—5F 23
Wedlake St. W10—3A 20
Weech Rd. NW6—1C 6
Weedington Rd. NW5—2C 8
Weekley Sq. SW11—1F 63
Weigall Rd. SE12—3C 72
Weighhouse St. W1—5C 22
Weimar St. SW15—1A 62
Weir Rd. SW12—5E 65
Weir Rd. SW19—3D 77
Weir's Pas. NW1—2F 23
Weiss Rd. SW15—1F 61
Welbeck Av. Brom—4C 86
Welbeck Rd. E6—2F 31
Welbeck St. W1—4C 22
Welbeck Way. W1—5D 23
Welby St. SE5—4D 53
Welfare Rd. E15—4A 16
Welford Pl. SW19—4A 76
Welham Rd.—5C 78
  SW16 1-289 & 2-334
  SW17 remainder
Welland M. E1—2C 40
Welland St. SE10—2E 57
Well Clo. SW16—4B 80
Wellclose Sq. E1—1C 40
Wellclose St. E1—1C 40
Well Ct. EC4—5E 25
Wellers Ct. NW1—1A 24
Weller St. SE1—3E 39
Wellesley Av. W6—4D 33
Wellesley Rd. NW5—2C 8
Wellesley St. E1—4F 27
Wellesley Ter. N1—2E 25
Wellfield Rd. SW16—4A 80
Wellfit St. SE24—1D 67
Wellington Bldgs. SW1—1C 50
Wellington Clo. SE14—4F 55
Wellington Clo. W11—5C 20
Wellington Est. E2—1E 27
Wellington Gdns. SE7—1E 59
Wellington M. SE22—2C 68
Wellington Pl. NW8—2F 21
Wellington Rd. E7—1B 16
Wellington Rd. NW8—1F 21
Wellington Rd. NW10—2F 19
Wellington Rd. SW19—2C 76

Wellington Row. E2—2B 26
Wellington Sq. SW3—1B 50
Wellington St. WC2—1B 38
Wellington Ter. E1—2D 41
Wellington Ter. W2—1D 35
Wellington Way. E3—2C 28
Wellmeadow Rd.—4A 72
  SE13 1-85 & 2-52
  SE6 remainder
Wells Ho. Rd. NW10—4A 18
Wells M. W1—5E 23
Wells Pk. Rd. SE26—3C 82
Wells Rise. NW8—5B 8
Wells Rd. W12—3E 33
Wells Sq. WC1—2B 24
Wells St. W1—4E 23
Well St. E9—4E 13
Well St. E15—3A 16
Wells Way. SE5—2F 53
Wells Way. SW7—4F 35
Wells Yd. N7—2C 10
Well Wlk. NW3—1F 7
Welsford St. SE1—5C 40
Welsh Clo. E13—2C 30
Welshpool St. E8—5C 12
Weltje Rd. W6—5C 32
Welwyn St. E2—2E 27
Wemyss Rd. SE3—5B 58
Wendell Rd. W12—3B 32
Wendon St. E3—5B 14
Wendover. SE17—1A 54
  (in two parts)
Wendover Rd. NW10—1B 18
Wendover Rd. SE9—1F 73
Wenlock Rd. N1—1E 25
Wenlock St. N1—1E 25
Wennington Rd. E3—1F 27
Wentland Clo. SE6—2F 85
Wentland Rd. SE6—2F 85
Wentworth Cres. SE15—3C 54
Wentworth M. E3—3A 28
  (in two parts)
Wentworth Rd. E12—1F 17
Wentworth St. E1—4B 26
Werrington St. NW1—1E 23
Werter Rd. SW15—2A 62
Wesleyan Pl. NW5—1D 9
Wesley Clo. SE17—5D 39
Wesley Sq. W11—5A 20
Wesley St. W1—4C 22
Wessex St. E2—2E 27
W. Arbour St. E1—5F 27
Westbere Rd. NW2—1A 6
Westbourne Cres. W2—1F 35
Westbourne Dri. SE23—2F 83
Westbourne Gdns. W2—5D 21
Westbourne Gro.—1B 34

W2 1-133 & 2-112
W11 remainder
Westbourne Gro. M. W11
—5C 20
Westbourne Gro. Ter. W2
—5D 21
Westbourne Pk. Pas. W2—4C 20
Westbourne Pk. Rd.—5B 20
W2 1-139 & 2-150
W11 remainder
Westbourne Pk. Vs. W2—4C 20
Westbourne Rd. N7—3B 10
Westbourne Rd. SE26—5F 83
Westbourne St. W2—1F 35
Westbourne Ter. W2—5E 21
Westbourne Ter. M. W2—5E 21
Westbourne Ter. Rd. W2—4E 21
Westbridge Rd. SW11—4F 49
Westbrook Rd. SE3—4D 59
Westbury Rd. E7—3D 17
Westbury St. SW8—5E 51
Westbury Ter. E7—3D 17
W. Carriage Dri. W2—1A 36
W. Central St. WC1—5A 24
W. Centre Av. NW10—2D 19
Westcombe Hill. SE3—3C 58
Westcombe Pk. Rd. SE3—2A 58
Westcote Rd. SW16—5E 79
West Cotts. NW6—2C 6
Westcott Rd. SE17—2D 53
Westcroft Clo. NW2—1A 6
Westcroft Sq. W6—5C 32
Westcroft Way. NW2—1A 6
W. Cromwell Rd.—1B 48
SW5 1-87 & 2-94 W14 remainder
W. Cross Route.—1F 33
Westdean Av. SE12—1D 87
Westdean Clo. SW18—4D 63
Westdown Rd. E15—1E 15
Westdown Rd. SE6—5C 70
West Dri. SW16—4E 79
W. Ella Rd. NW10—4A 4
W. End La. NW6—2C 6
Westerdale Rd. SE10—1C 58
Westerley Cres. SE26—5B 84
Western Av. W3—5A 18
Western La. SW12—5C 64
Western Pl. SE16—3E 41
Western Rd. E13—1E 31
Western Rd. SW9—1C 66
W. Ferry Rd. E14—2C 42
Westfields. SW13—1B 60
Westfields Av. SW13—1A 60
Westfield St. SE18—4F 45
W. Garden Pl. W2—5A 22
West Gdns. E1—1D 41
West Gdns. SW19—5A 78

Westgate St. E8—5D 13
Westgate Ter. SW10—2D 49
West Gro. SE10—4E 57
Westgrove La. SE10—4E 57
W. Halkin St. SW1—4C 36
W. Ham La. E15—4A 16
W. Hampstead M. NW6—3D 7
W. Harding St. EC4—5C 24
West Hill—5F 61
SW18 1-61 & 2-70
SW15 remainder
W. Hill Rd. SW18—4B 62
Westhorne Av.—5C 72
SE12 1-421 & 2-320
SE9 remainder
Westhorpe Rd. SW15—1E 61
W. House Clo. SW19—1A 76
W. India Dock Pier Development.
E14—3C 42
W. India Dock Rd. E14—1C 42
Westland Pl. N1—2F 25
Westlands Ter. SW12—4E 65
West La. SE16—3D 41
Westleigh Av. SW15—3D 61
Westmead. SW15—4B 61
Westminster Bri. SW1 & SE1
—3A 38
Westminster Bri. Rd. SE1
—4C 38
Westminster Industrial Est.
SE18—4F 45
Westmoor St. SE7—4F 45
Westmoreland Pl. SW1—1D 51
Westmoreland Rd. SE17—2F 53
Westmoreland Rd. SW13
—4B 46
Westmoreland St. W1—4C 22
Westmoreland Ter. SW1—1D 51
Weston Rise. WC1—2B 24
Weston St. SE1—3A 40
Westover Rd. SW18—5E 63
Westow Hill. SE19—5A 82
West Pier. E1—2D 41
West Pl. SW19—5E 75
Westport Rd. E13—3D 31
Westport St. E1—5F 27
W. Poultry Av. EC1—4D 25
W. Quarters. W12—5C 18
West Quay. SW10—4E 49
West Rd. E15—5B 16
West Rd. SW3—2B 50
West Rd. SW4—3F 65
Westrow. SW15—4E 61
West Row. W10—3A 20
W. Side Comn. SW19—5E 75
W. Smithfield. EC1—4D 25
West Sq. SE11—4D 39
West St. E2—1D 27

West St. WC2—5F 23
W. Tenter St. E1—1B 40
W. View Clo. NW10—2B 4
Westville Rd. W12—3C 32
W. Warwick Pl. SW1—5E 37
Westway. W12, W10, W9 & W2
—1B 32
Westwick Gdns. W14—3F 33
Westwood Gdns. SW13—1B 60
Westwood Hill. SE26—5C 82
Westwood Pk. SE23—5D 69
Westwood Rd. E16—2D 45
Westwood Rd. SW13—1B 60
Wetherby Gdns. SW5—5E 35
Wetherby M. SW5—1D 49
Wetherby Pl. SW7—5E 35
Wetherell Rd. E9—5F 13
Wexford Rd. SW12—5B 64
Weybourne St. SW18—2E 77
Weydown Clo. SW19—1A 76
Weyhill Rd. E1—5C 26
Weyman Rd. SE3—4E 59
Weymouth M. W1—4D 23
Weymouth St. W1—4C 22
Weymouth Ter. E2—1B 26
(in two parts)
Whalebone La. E15—4A 16
Wharfdale Rd. N1—1A 24
Wharfedale St. SW10—1D 49
Wharf Pl. E2—5D 13
Wharf Rd. E15—5F 15
Wharf Rd. N1—1E 25
Wharfside Rd. E16—5A 30
Wharf St. E16—4A 30
Wharton Clo. NW10—3A 4
Wharton Cotts. WC1—2B 24
Wharton St. WC1—2B 24
Whateley Rd. SE22—3B 68
Whatman Rd. SE23—5F 69
Wheatlands Rd. SW17—3C 78
Wheatley St. W1—4C 22
Wheatsheaf La. SW6—3E 47
Wheatsheaf La. SW8—3A 52
Wheatsheaf Ter. SW6—3B 48
Wheelwright St. N7—4B 10
Wheler St. E1—3B 26
Whellock Rd. W4—4A 32
Whetstone Pk. WC2—5B 24
Whetstone Rd. SE3—5E 59
Whidborne Clo. SE8—5C 56
Whidborne St. WC1—2A 24
Whinfell Clo. SW16—5F 79
Whiskin St. EC1—2D 25
Whistlers Av. SW11—3F 49
Whistler St. N5—2D 11
Whistler Wlk. SW3—3F 49
Whiston Rd. E2—5B 12
Whitbread Rd. SE4—2A 70

Whitburn Rd. SE13—2E 71
Whitby Ct. N7—1A 10
Whitby St. E1—3B 26
Whitcher Clo. SE14—2A 56
Whitcher Pl. NW1—3E 9
Whitchurch Rd. W11—1F 33
Whitcomb St. WC2—1F 37
Whiteadder Way. E14—5D 43
Whitear Wlk. E15—3F 15
Whitebeam Clo. SW9—3B 52
White Bear Pl. NW3—1F 7
Whitechapel High St. E1—5B 26
Whitechapel Rd. E1—4C 26
White Chu. La. E1—5C 26
White City Clo. W12—1E 33
White City Est. W12—1D 33
White City Rd. W12—1D 33
White Conduit St. N1—1C 24
Whitecross Pl. EC2—4F 25
Whitecross St. EC1 & EC2
—3E 25
Whitefield Clo. SW18—4A 62
Whitefoot La. Brom—4E 85
Whitefoot Ter. Brom—3B 86
Whitefriars St. EC4—5C 24
Whitehall. SW1—2A 38
Whitehall Ct. SW1—2A 38
Whitehall Pl. E7—2C 16
Whitehall Pl. SW1—2A 38
White Hart La. NW10—3B 4
White Hart La. SW13—1A 60
White Hart St. SE11—1C 52
White Hart Yd. SE1—2F 39
Whitehaven St. NW8—3A 22
Whitehead Clo. SW18—5E 63
Whitehead's Gro. SW3—5A 36
White Horse La. E1—4F 27
Whitehorse M. SE1—4C 38
White Horse Rd. E1—5A 28
(in two parts)
White Horse St. W1—2D 37
White Horse Yd. EC2—5F 25
White Kennett St. E1—5B 26
Whitelegg Rd. E13—1B 30
Whiteley Rd. SE19—5F 81
Whiteley's Cotts. W14—5B 34
White Lion Hill. EC4—1D 39
White Lion St. N1—1C 24
White Post La. E9—3C 14
Whitepost La. SE13—1C 70
White Post St. SE15—3E 55
White Rd. E15—4A 16
White's Grounds. SE1—3A 40
White's Row. E1—4B 26
White's Sq. SW4—2F 65
White Swan M. W4—2A 46
Whitethorn St. E3—4C 28
Whitfield Rd. E6—4E 17

Whitfield Rd. SE3—4F 57
Whitfield St. W1—3E 23
Whitgift St. SE11—5B 38
Whitlock Dri. SW19—5A 62
Whitman Rd. E3—3A 28
Whitmore Gdns. NW10—1E 19
Whitmore Rd. N1—5A 12
Whitnell Way. SW15—3E 61
Whittaker Rd. E6—5E 31
Whittaker St. SW1—5C 36
Whittaker Way. SE1—5C 40
Whitta Rd. E12—1F 17
Whittell Gdns. SE26—3E 83
Whittingstall Rd. SW6—4B 48
Whittington Av. EC3—5A 26
Whittlesey St. SE1—2C 38
Whitton Wlk. E3—2C 28
Whitwell Rd. E13—2C 30
Whitworth St. SE10—1A 58
Whorlton Rd. SE15—1D 69
Whyteville Rd. E7—3D 17
Wickersley Rd. SW11—5C 50
Wickers Oake. SE19—4B 82
Wicker St. E1—5D 27
Wickford St. E1—3E 27
Wickham Gdns. SE4—1B 70
Wickham M. SE4—5B 56
Wickham Rd. SE4—1B 70
Wickham St. SE11—1B 52
Wick La. E3—5C 14
(in two parts)
Wicklow St. WC1—2B 24
Wick Rd. E9—3F 13
Wicks Clo. SE9—4F 87
Wick Sq. E9—3B 14
Wickwood St. SE5—5D 53
Widdenham Rd. N7—1B 10
Widdin St. E15—4A 16
Widegate St. E1—4A 26
Widley Rd. W9—2C 20
Wigmore Pl. W1—5D 23
Wigmore St. W1—5C 22
Wigston Rd. E13—3D 31
Wigton Pl. SE11—1C 52
Wilberforce Way. SW19—5F 75
Wilbraham Pl. SW1—5B 36
Wilby M. W11—2B 34
Wilcox Clo. SW8—3A 52
Wilcox Pl. SW1—4E 37
Wilcox Rd. SW8—3A 52
Wild Ct. WC2—5B 24
Wildcroft Mnr. SW15—5E 61
Wildcroft Rd. SW15—5E 61
Wilde Clo. E8—5C 12
Wilde Pl. SW18—5F 63
Wildfell Rd. SE6—5D 71
Wild Goose Dri. SE14—4E 55
Wild's Rents. SE1—4A 40

Wild St. WC2—5A 24
Wildwood Clo. SE12—5B 72
Wilfred Owen Clo. SW19—5E 77
Wilfred St. SW1—4E 37
Wilkes St. E1—4B 26
(in two parts)
Wilkie Way. SE22—1C 82
Wilkinson Ct. SW17—4F 77
Wilkinson Rd. E16—5E 31
Wilkinson St. SW8—3B 52
Wilkin St. NW5—3D 9
Wilkin St. M. NW5—3D 9
Wilks Pl. N1—1A 26
Willan Wall. E16—1B 44
Willard St. SW8—1D 65
Will Crooks Gdns. SE9—2F 73
Willesden La.—3E 5
NW6 1-221 & 2-218
NW2 remainder
Willes Rd. NW5—3D 9
Willet Way. SE16—1D 55
William Bonney Est. SW4
—2F 65
William Ellis Way. SE16—4C 40
William IV St. WC2—1A 38
William Gdns. SW15—3D 61
William Gunn Ho. NW3—2A 8
William Guy Gdns. E3—2D 29
William Margrie Clo. SE15
—5C 54
William M. SW1—3B 36
William Morley Clo. E6—5F 17
William Rd. NW1—2E 23
William's Bldgs. E2—3E 27
Williamson Clo. SE10—1B 58
Williamson St. N7—1A 10
William St. SW1—3B 36
Willingham Clo. NW5—2E 9
Willingham Ter. NW5—2E 9
Willington Rd. SW9—1A 66
Willis Rd. E15—1B 30
Willis St. E14—5D 29
Willoughby Rd. NW3—1F 7
Willoughby Way. SE7—5D 45
Willow Av. SW13—5B 46
Willow Bank. SW6—1A 62
Willow Bri. Rd. N1—3E 11
Willowbrook Rd. SE15—2B 54
Willow Gro. E13—1C 30
Willow Lodge. SW6—4F 47
Willow Pl. SW1—5E 37
Willow Rd. NW3—1F 7
Willow St. EC2—3A 26
Willow Tree Clo. SW18—1D 77
Willow Vale. W12—2C 32
Willow Wlk. SE1—5A 40
Willow Way. SE26—3E 83
Willow Way. W11—1F 33

Wilman Gro. E8—4C 12
Wilmer Gdns. N1—5A 12
(in two parts)
Wilmer Lea Clo. E15—4F 15
Wilmington Sq. WC1—2C 24
Wilmington St. WC1—2C 24
Wilmot Clo. SE15—3C 54
Wilmot Pl. NW1—4E 9
Wilmot St. E2—3D 27
Wilna Rd. SW18—5E 63
Wilsham St. W11—2A 34
Wilshaw St. SE14—4C 56
Wilson Gro. SE16—3D 41
Wilson Rd. E6—2F 31
Wilson Rd. SE5—4A 54
Wilson's Pl. E14—5B 28
Wilson's Rd. W6—1F 47
Wilson St. EC2—4F 25
Wilton Av. W4—1A 46
Wilton Cres. SW1—3C 36
Wilton M. SW1—4C 36
Wilton Pl. SW1—3C 36
Wilton Rd. SW1—5E 37
Wilton Row. SW1—3C 36
Wilton Sq. N1—5F 11
Wilton St. SW1—4D 37
Wilton Ter. SW1—4C 36
Wilton Way. E8—3C 12
Wiltshire Clo. SW3—5B 36
Wiltshire Rd. SW9—1C 66
Wiltshire Row. N1—5F 11
Wimbart Rd. SW2—5B 66
Wimbledon Hill Rd. SW19
—5A 76
Wimbledon Pk. Rd.—2A 76
SW18 1-257 & 2-218
SW19 remainder
Wimbledon Pk. Side. SW19
—2F 75
Wimbledon Rd. SW17—4E 77
Wimbledon Stadium Business
Centre. SW17—3D 77
Wimbolt St. E2—2C 26
Wimborne Clo. SE12—3B 72
Wimborne Ct. SW12—3E 79
Wimbourne St. N1—1F 25
Wimpole M. W1—4D 23
Wimpole St. W1—4D 23
Winans Wlk. SW9—5C 52
Wincanton Rd. SW18—5B 62
Winchcomb Gdns. SE9—1F 73
Winchelsea Clo. SW15—3F 61
Winchelsea Rd. E7—1C 16
Winchendon Rd. SW6—4B 48
Winchester Av. NW6—5A 6
Winchester Clo. SE17—5D 39
Winchester Pl. E8—2B 12
Winchester Rd. NW3—4F 7

Winchester Sq. SE1—2F 39
Winchester St. SW1—1D 51.
Winchester Wlk. SE1—2F 39
Winchfield Rd. SE26—5A 84
Wincott St. SE11—5C 38
Windermere Av. NW6—5A 6
Windermere Rd. SW15—4A 74
Winders Rd. SW11—5A 50
Windfield Clo. SE26—4F 83
Windlass Pl. SE8—5A 42
Windlesham Gro. SW19—1F 75
Windley Clo. SE23—2E 83
Windmill Ct. NW2—3A 6
Windmill Dri. SW4—3D 65
Windmill La. E15—3F 15
Windmill M. W4—5A 32
Windmill Pas. W4—5A 32
Windmill Rd. SW18—4D 63
Windmill Rd. SW19—4D 75
Windmill Rd. W4—5A 32
Windmill Row. SE11—1C 52
Windmill St. W1—4F 23
(in two parts)
Windmill Wlk. SE1—2C 38
Windrose Clo. SE16—3F 41
Windrush Clo. SW11—2F 63
Windrush La. SE23—3F 83
Windsor Clo. SE27—4E 81
Windsor Ct. SW11—5F 49
Windsor Gdns. W9—4C 20
Windsor Gro. SE27—4E 81
Windsor Pl. SW1—5E 37
Windsor Rd. E7—2D 17
Windsor Rd. NW2—3D 5
Windsor St. N1—5D 11
Windsor Ter. N1—2E 25
Windsor Wlk. SE5—5F 53
Windsor Way. W14—5A 34
Windspoint Dri. SE15—2D 55
Windy Ridge Clo. SW19—5F 75
Wine Clo. E1—1E 41
Wine Office Ct. EC4—5C 24
Winforton St. SE10—4E 57
Winfred Gro. SW11—2B 64
Winfrith Rd. SW18—1E 77
Wingate Rd. W6—4D 33
Wingfield Rd. E15—1A 16
Wingfield St. SE15—1C 68
Wingford Rd. SW2—4A 66
Wingmore Rd. SE24—1E 67
Wingrave Rd. W6—2E 47
Wingrove Rd. SE6—2A 86
Winkfield Rd. E13—1D 31
Winkley St. E2—1D 27
Winkley's Wharf Development.
E14—5C 42
Winlaton Rd. Brom—4F 85
Winnett St. W1—1F 37

Winn Rd. SE12—1C 86
Winsford Rd. SE6—3B 84
Winsham Gro. SW11—3C 64
Winslade Rd. SW2—3A 66
Winslade Way. SE6—5D 71
Winsland M. W2—5F 21
Winsland St. W2—5F 21
Winsley St. W1—5E 23
Winslow Rd. W6—2E 47
Winstanley Est. SW11—1F 63
Winstanley Rd. SW11—1F 63
Winston Rd. N16—1F 11
Winterbourne Rd. SE6—1B 84
Winterbrook Rd. SE24—4E 67
Winterfold Clo. SW19—2A 76
Winterstoke Rd. SE6—1B 84
Winterton Pl. SW10—2E 49
Winterwell Rd. SW2—3A 66
Winthorpe Rd. SW15—2A 62
Winthrop St. E1—4D 27
Winton Way. SW16—5C 80
Wirrall Ho. SE26—3C 82
Wise Rd. E15—5F 15
Wiseton Rd. SW17—1A 78
Wishart Rd. SE3—5F 59
Wisley Rd. SW11—3C 64
Wisteria Rd. SE13—2F 71
Witan St. E2—2D 27
Witherfield Way. SE16—1D 55
Witherington Rd. N5—2C 10
Withers Pl. EC1—3E 25
Withycombe Rd. SW19—5F 61
Witney Path. SE23—3F 83
Wittersham Rd. Brom—5B 86
Wivenhoe Clo. SE15—1D 69
Wiverton Rd. SE26—5E 83
Wix's La. SW4—1D 65
Woburn Pl. WC1—3A 24
Woburn Sq. WC1—3F 23
Woburn Wlk. WC1—2F 23
Woking Clo. SW15—2B 60
Wolfe Cres. SE7—1F 59
Wolfe Cres. SE16—3F 41
Wolfe Gdns. E15—3B 16
Wolfington Rd. SE27—4D 81
Wolfram Clo. SE13—3A 72
Wolftencroft Clo. SW11—1A 64
Wollaston Clo. SE1—5E 39
Wolseley Av. SW19—2C 76
Wolseley Rd. E7—4D 17
Wolseley St. SE1—3C 40
Wolsey M. NW5—3E 9
Wolsey Rd. N1—2F 11
Wolsey St. E1—4E 27
Wolverley St. E2—2D 27
Wolverton. SE17—1A 54
Wolverton Gdns. W6—5F 33
Wontner Rd. SW17—2B 78

Woodbank Rd. Brom—3B 86
Woodbastwick Rd. SE26—5F 83
Woodbine Ter. E9—3E 13
Woodborough Rd. SW15
　　　　　—2D 61
Woodbourne Av. SW16—3F 79
Woodbridge St. EC1—3D 25
Woodbury Ho. SE26—3C 82
Woodbury St. SW17—5A 78
Woodchester Sq. W2—4D 21
Wood Clo. E2—3C 26
Woodcombe Cres. SE23—1E 83
Woodcote Pl. SE27—5D 81
Woodend. SE19—5E 81
Wooder Gdns. E7—1C 16
Woodfall St. SW3—1B 50
Woodfarrs. SE5—2F 67
Woodfield Av. SW16—3F 79
Woodfield Gdns. W9—4C 20
Woodfield Gro. SW16—3F 79
Woodfield La. SW16—3F 79
Woodfield Pl. W9—3B 20
Woodfield Rd. W9—4B 20
Woodford Rd. E7—1D 17
Woodger Rd. W12—3E 33
Woodgrange Rd. E7—2D 17
Woodhall Av. SE21—3B 82
Woodhall Dri. SE21—3B 82
Woodham Rd. SE6—3E 85
Woodin St. E14—4D 29
Woodison St. E3—3A 28
Woodland Clo. SE19—5A 82
Woodland Cres. SE10—2A 58
Woodland Gro. SE10—1A 58
Woodland Hill. SE19—5A 82
Woodland Rd. SE19—5A 82
Woodlands Ct. SE22—5D 69
Woodlands Pk. Rd. SE10
　　　　　—2A 58
Woodlands Rd. SW13—1B 60
Woodlands St. SE13—5F 71
Woodlands, The. SE13—5F 71
Woodland St. E8—3B 12
Woodlands Way. SW15—3B 62
Woodland Wlk. NW3—2A 8
Woodland Wlk. SE10—1A 58
Woodland Wlk. Brom—4A 86
(in two parts)
Wood La. W12—5E 19
Woodlawn Clo. SW15—3B 62
(Wandsworth)
Woodlawn Rd. SW6—3F 47
Woodleigh Gdns. SW16—3A 80
Woodman's M. W12—4D 19
Woodmere Clo. SW11—1C 64
Woodnook Rd. SW16—5D 79
Woodpecker Rd. SE14—2A 56

Woodquest Av. SE24—3E 67
Woodrush Clo. SE14—3A 56
Woodseer St. E1—4B 26
Woodsford Sq. W14—3A 34
Woodside. SW19—5B 76
Woodside Rd. E13—3E 31
Woods M. W1—1C 36
Woodspring Rd. SW19—2A 76
Woods Rd. SE15—4D 55
Woodstock Ct. SE12—4C 72
Woodstock Gro. W12—3F 33
Woodstock Rd. E7—4E 17
Woodstock Rd. W4—4A 32
Woodstock St. E16—5B 30
Woodstock St. W1—5D 23
Woodstock Ter. E14—1D 43
Wood St. E16—1D 45
Wood St. EC2—5E 25
Wood St. W4—1A 46
Woodsyre. SE26—4B 82
Woodthorpe Rd. SW15—2D 61
Wood Vale. SE23—1D 83
Wood Vale Est. SE23—4E 69
Woodvale Wlk. SE27—5E 81
Woodville Clo. SE12—3C 72
Woodville Rd. N16—2A 12
Woodville Rd. NW6—1B 20
Woodwarde Rd. SE22—4A 68
Woodwell St. SW18—3E 63
Wood Wharf Business Pk. E14
　　　　　—2E 43
Woodyard Clo. NW5—2C 8
Woodyard La. SE21—5A 68
Woodyates Rd. SE12—4C 72
Woolacombe Rd. SE3—5E 59
Wooler St. SE17—1F 53
Woolmore St. E14—1E 43
Woolneigh St. SW6—1D 63
Woolstaplers Way. SE16
　　　　　—5C 42
Woolstone Rd. SE23—2A 84
Woolwich Rd.—1B 58
　SE10 1-265 & 2-160
　SE7 remainder
Wooster Gdns. E14—5F 29
Wootton St. SE1—2C 38
Worcester M. NW6—3D 7
Worcester Pl. EC4—1E 39
Worcester Rd. SW19—5B 76
Wordsworth Rd. N16—1A 12
Worfield St. SW11—3A 50
Worgan St. SE11—1B 52
Worland Rd. E15—4A 16
World's End Pas. SW10—3F 49
Worlidge St. W6—1E 47
Worlingham Rd. SE22—2B 68
Wormholt Rd. W12—1C 32

Wormwood St. EC2—5A 26
Wornington Rd. W10—3A 20
Woronzow St. NW8—5F 7
Worship St. EC2—3F 25
Worslade Rd. SW17—4F 77
Worsley Bri. Rd. Beck—5C 84
Worsley Bri. Rd. SE26 & Beck
　　　　　—4B 84
Worsley Rd. E11—1A 16
Worsopp Dri. SW4—3E 65
Worthing Clo. E15—5A 16
Wortley Rd. E6—4F 17
Wotton Rd. SE8—2B 56
Wouldham Rd. E16—5B 30
Wren Av. NW2—2E 5
Wren Clo. E16—5B 30
Wren Rd. SE5—4F 53
Wren St. WC1—3B 24
Wrentham Av. NW10—1F 19
Wrenthorpe Rd. Brom—4A 86
Wrexham Rd. E3—1C 28
Wricklemarsh Rd. SE3—4E 59
Wrigglesworth St. SE14—3F 55
Wright Rd. N1—3A 12
Wrights Clo. SE13—2F 71
Wright's Grn. SW4—2F 65
Wright's La. W8—4D 35
Wright's Rd. E3—1B 28
Wrotham Rd. NW1—4E 9
Wrottesley Rd. NW10—1C 18
Wroughton Rd. SW11—4B 64
Wroxton Rd. SE15—5E 55
Wulfstan St. W12—4B 18
Wyatt Pk. Rd. SW2—2B 80
Wyatt Rd. E7—3C 16
Wybert St. NW1—3E 23
Wycherley Clo. SE3—3B 58
Wychwood Way. SE19—5F 81
Wycliffe Rd. SW11—5C 50
Wyclif St. EC1—2D 25
Wydeville Mnr. Rd. SE12
　　　　　—4D 87
Wye St. SW11—5F 49
Wyfold Rd. SW6—3A 48
Wyke Rd. E3—4C 14
Wyleu St. SE23—5A 70
Wyllen Clo. E1—3E 27
Wymering Rd. W9—2C 20
Wymond St. SW15—1E 61
Wynan Rd. E14—1D 57
Wyndcliffe Rd. SE7—2D 59
Wyndham Est. SE5—3E 53
Wyndham M. W1—4B 22
Wyndham Pl. W1—4B 22
Wyndham Rd. E6—4F 17
Wyndham St. SE5—3E 53
Wyndham St. W1—4B 22
Wyndham Yd. W1—4B 22

Wyneham Rd. SE24—3F 67
Wynell Rd. SE23—3F 83
Wynford Rd. N1—1B 24
Wynne Rd. SW9—5C 52
Wynnstay Gdns. W8—4C 34
Wynter St. SW11—2E 63
Wynyard Ter. SE11—1B 52
Wynyatt St. EC1—2D 25
Wythburn Pl. W1—5B 22
Wyvil Rd. SW8—2A 52
Wyvis St. E14—4D 29

Yabsley St. E14—2E 43
Yalding Rd. SE16—4C 40
Yardley St. WC1—2C 24
Yarmouth Pl. W1—2D 37
Yarnfield Sq. SE15—4C 54
Yately St. SE18—4F 45
Yeate St. N1—4F 11
Yeats Clo. SE13—5F 57
Yeldham Rd. W6—1F 47
Yelverton Rd. SW11—5F 49
Yeoman Clo. SE27—3D 81

Yeoman's Row. SW3—4A 36
Yeoman St. SE8—5A 42
Yeo St. E3—4D 29
Yewfield Rd. NW10—3B 4
Yew Gro. NW2—1F 5
Yew Tree Rd. W12—1B 32
Yoke Clo. N7—3A 10
York Bri. NW1—3C 22
York Bldgs. WC2—1A 38
York Ga. NW1—3C 22
York Gro. SE15—4E 55
York Hill. SE27—3D 81
York Ho. Pl. W8—3D 35
York M. NW5—2D 9
York Pl. SW11—1F 63
York Rise. NW5—1D 9
York Rd. E7—3C 16
York Rd. SE1—3B 38
York Rd. SW11—2E 63
York Rd. SW19—5E 77
Yorkshire Grey Pl. NW3—1E 7
Yorkshire Pl. E14—5A 28
Yorkshire Rd. E14—5A 28
York Sq. E14—5A 28

York St. W1—4B 22
York Ter. E. NW1—3C 22
York Ter. W. NW1—3C 22
Yorkton St. E2—1C 26
York Way—3F 9
    N1 1-7 & 2-178
    N7 remainder
York Way Ct. N1—5A 10
Young Ct. NW6—4A 6
Young Rd. E16—5E 31
Young St. W8—3D 35
Yukon Rd. SW12—5D 65
Yuletide Clo. NW10—4A 4

Zampa Rd. SE16—1E 55
Zander Ct. E2—2C 26
Zangwill Rd. SE3—4F 59
Zealand Rd. E3—1A 28
Zennor Rd. SW12—1E 79
Zenoria St. SE22—2B 68
Zetland St. E14—4E 29
Zimbabwe Rd. SW9—5A 52
Zoar St. SE1—2E 39